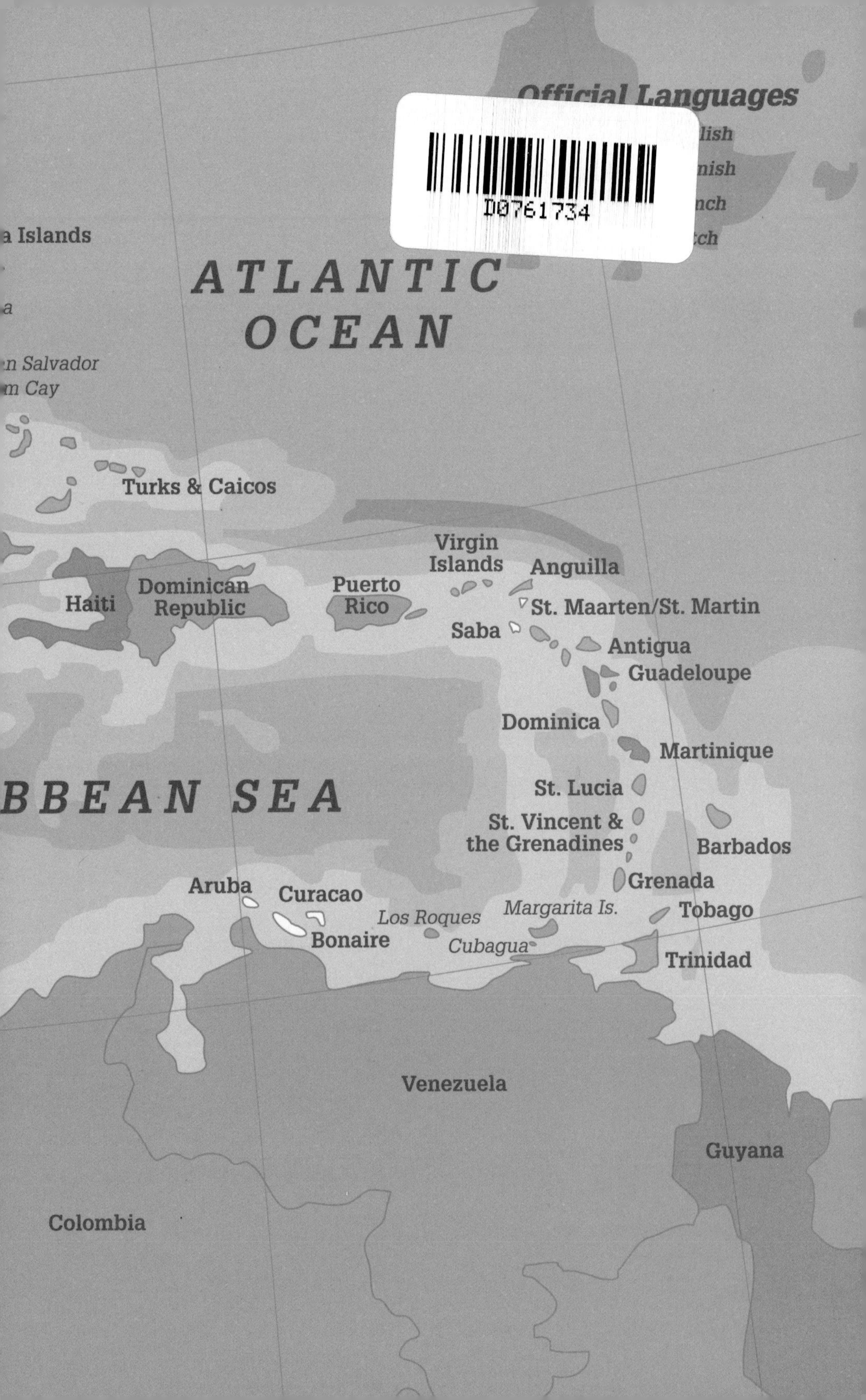

Official Languages

...lish
...nish
...nch
...tch

a Islands

...a

n Salvador
m Cay

ATLANTIC OCEAN

Turks & Caicos

Haiti

Dominican
Republic

Puerto
Rico

Virgin
Islands

Anguilla

St. Maarten/St. Martin

Saba

Antigua

Guadeloupe

Dominica

Martinique

BBEAN SEA

St. Lucia

St. Vincent &
the Grenadines

Barbados

Grenada

Aruba

Curacao

Los Roques

Margarita Is.

Tobago

Bonaire

Cubagua

Trinidad

Venezuela

Guyana

Colombia

REEF
CREATURE
Identification

FLORIDA CARIBBEAN BAHAMAS

PAUL HUMANN
NED DELOACH

NEW WORLD PUBLICATIONS, INC.

Jacksonville, Florida USA

Printed by
Star Standard Industries Pte Ltd
Singapore

Acknowledgments

This book was the result of considerable encouragement, help, and advice from many friends and acquaintances. It became a much larger undertaking and involved many more people than ever expected. We wish to express our sincere gratitude to everyone involved. Naturally, the names of a few who played especially significant roles come to mind.

Copy editor, friend and confidante, Patricia Reilly-Collins, spent untold hours making sure the text was phrased in comprehensible English. Mary DeLoach, Nancy DeLoach and Fred McConnaughey also gave valuable assistance in the editing process.

Wonderful friends, John and Marion Bacon gave generously of their time, assistance, and boat, helping us photograph and collect marine invertebrates of Florida. Professional marine life photographers Mike Bacon, Marjorie Bank, Doug Perrine and Fred McConnaughey assisted by providing their knowledge of abundance, distribution, habitat and behavior of many species. Helping collect photographed specimens for scientific examination: Mike Bacon; Captains Graeme Teague, Louis Usie and Clay Weismen of the Aggressor Fleet; Phil Bush, Asst. Scientific Officer, and Michael Grundy, Marine Parks Officer, Cayman Islands Natural Resources Laboratory; Nick DeLoach.

PHOTO CREDITS

Mike Bacon, 137b, 185b 203b, 207m, 261b, 263t, 267t, 277b, 283t, 285m, 327tm&b, 331t, 359t&m; *Marjorie Bank,* 77b, 83b, 145m, 235b, 241t, 273t, 287b, 289b, 317t; *Dave Behrens,* 183b; *Cathy Church,* 203b; *Helmut Debelius,* 171m, 227m; *Ned DeLoach,* 79b, 119b, 185m, 179t, 181m, 209m, 213m, 215m, 230bl, 231m, 232m&b, 233t, 237m, 238mr, 239ml, 344m&b, 345b ; *Denise Feingold,* 347t; *Josh Feingold,* 173t, 243b, 251b; *Joe Froelich,* 147b; *Steven Frink,* 349m; *Dr. John Forsythe,* 340m, 349t; *David Hall,* 124m, 191b, 321b, 367b; *Jeff Hamann,* 287c, 289t&m, 297m&b, 299b, 301t, 303m&b, 307tm&b, 313t&m, 315m&b, 317b, 318m, 319tm&b, 323tm&b, 325t; *Dr. Roger Hanlon,* 347m&b, 339m&b; *Dr. Linda Harrison,* 265b; *Robert Lipe,* 263b, 267m, 269m, 271b, 273m&b, 277m&b, 279t&b; *Barry Lipman,* 119m, 230br, 231b, 299m, 325m; *Larry Lipsky,* 275b; *Ken Marks,* 4,197m, 205m, 267b, 389m; *Fred McConnaughey,* 195t,219t; *John Miller,* 361t, 365b, 369b, 381b, 399m; *Geri Murphy,* 399t; *Doug Perrine,* 231t, 299t, 341t&b, 375t; *Lee Peterson,* 189t, 275t, 385b; *Steve Powell,* 179m, 183t, 309m; *John Rhodes,* 169t; *Eric Riesch,* 219m, 237b, 295t, 305m; *Jeff Rotman,* 375m; *Dee Scarr,* 233mr; *Dr. Gus Schwartz,* 87t; *David Snyder,* 209b, 213b, 229t, 389t; *Bill Spencer,* 243; *Stephen Spotte,* 173m&b, 175t, 181t; *Sipke Stapert,* 195b, 229b; *Walter Stearns,* 147m, 359b, 369t; *Suzi Swygert,* 207b; *Graeme Teague,* 139m, 305t, 369m, 373b; *Louis Usie,* 139t,175m, 321t; *Bryan Willy,* 341m, 361b; *Lawson Wood,* 285B; all other pictures were taken by the author, *Paul Humann.*

CREDITS

Photography Editor: Eric Riesch
Art Direction: Michael O'Connell
Illustrations: Joe Gies
ISBN 1-878348-30-2
First Printing 2002, Second Printing 2003.
First Edition: Copyright, ©1992; Second Edition Copyright, ©2002 by Paul Humann
Published and Distributed by New World Publications, Inc., 1861 Cornell Road, Jacksonville, FL 32207, Phone (904) 737-6558

Scientific Acknowledgments

Special tribute must be given to the numerous scientists who gave freely of their time, advice and knowledge. Without this most generous assistance, the book could have never been published. Every attempt was made to keep this text and the identifications as accurate as possible; however, I'm sure a few errors crept in, and they are my sole responsibility.

The invaluable assistance of Dr. Walter Goldberg, of Florida International University, deserves special mention. He undertook the Herculean task of principal scientific adviser, and coordinator for this project.

Following are the scientists who assisted with identifications and other information. Their specialty and institution are also listed. Those taking the time and effort to make laboratory examinations of photographed and collected specimens are specially noted with an asterisk.

Mike Bacon, North Palm Beach, FL– Gastropods
David W. Behrens – Opisthobranchs
Dr. Anita Brinckmann Voss – Hydromedusa
Dr. Louise Bush, Gray Museum, Marine Biological Laboratory, Woods Hole, MA – General Assistance
Phil Bush, Natural Resources Laboratory, Georgetown, Cayman Islands – General Assistance
*Dr. Dale Calder, Royal Ontario Museum, Toronto, Canada – Hydroids
Dr. Kerry Clark, Florida Institute of Technology, Melbourne, FL – Opisthobranchs
Dr. Charles E. Cutress, University of Puerto Rico, Mayaguez, PR – Anemones, Zoanthids, Corallimorphs
Dr. Kristian Fauchald, National Museum of Natural History, Smithsonian Institute, Washington, DC – Segmented Worms
Dr. Daphnie Fautin, Snow Museum, University Of Kansas, Lawrence, KS – Anemones, Zoanthids, Corallimorphs
Dr. Josh Feingold, Rosenstiel School of Marine Sciences, Miami University, FL – General Assistance
John W. Forsythe, National Resource Center for Cephalopods – Cephalopods
Dr. Lisa-Ann Gershwin, University of California at Berkeley – Jellyfishes
Dr. D.I. Gibson, British Museum of Natural History, London, England – General Assistance
Dr. Ivan Goodbody, The University of the West Indies, Kingston, Jamaica – Tunicates
Dr. Ken Grange, Department of Scientific Research, Wellington, New Zealand – Mollusks
Dr. Robert H. Gore, BIO-ECON, Inc., Naples, FL – Crustaceans
Jeff Hamann, El Cajon, CA – Opisthobranchs
Dr. Roger T. Hanlon, Woods Hole Oceanographic Institution, Woods Hole, MA – Cephalopods
Dr. Gordon L. Hendler, Natural History Museum of L.A., Los Angeles, CA – Echinoderms
John Jackson, Odyssey Publications, San Diego, CA – Gastropods
Dr. Ronald Larson, Oregon – Jellyfishes, Comb Jellies
Dr. Larry Madin, Woods Hole Oceanographic Institution, Woods Hole, MA – Hydromedusa
Dr. Raymond B. Manning, National Museum Of Natural History, Smithsonian Institution, Washington, DC – Mantis Shrimps
Dr. Richard Mariscal, Florida State University, Tallahassee, FL – Anemones, Zoanthids, Corallimorphs
Dr. George I. Matsumoto, Monterey Bay Aquarium Research Institute, Pacific Grove, CA – Comb Jellies
*Dr. Patsy A. McLaughlin, Shannon Point Marine Center, Western Washington University, Anacortes, WA – Hermit Crabs
Dr. Charles G. Messing, NOVA University Oceanographic Center, Dania, FL – Echinoderms, General Reference
Dr. Claudia Mills, Friday Harbor Laboratories, University of Washington – Hydromedusa
Dr. Francoise Monniot, Museum National d'Histoire Naturelle, Paris, France – Tunicates
Dr. Hazel A. Oxenford, Bellairs Research Institute, Holetown, St. James, Barbados, W.I. – General Assistance
*Dr. David L. Pawson, National Museum of Natural History, Smithsonian Institution, Washington, DC – Echinoderms
*Thomas H. Perkins, Florida Marine Research Institute, St. Petersburg, FL – Segmented Worms
Dr. Marian H. Pettibone, National Museum Of Natural History, Smithsonian Institution, Washington, DC – Scale Worms
Dr. Stephen Prudhoe, British Museum of Natural History, London, England – Flatworms
Dr. Phil Pugh, Institute of Oceanographic Sciences, Surrey, England – Siphonophores
*Dr. Shirley Pomponi, Harbor Branch Oceanographic Institute, Ft. Pierce, FL – Sponges
Dr. Clyde Roper, National Museum of Natural History, Smithsonian Institution, Washington, DC – Cephalopods
Dr. Shalia Van Sickle, Ft. Lewis State College, Durango, CO – Phonetics
Dr. Robert Van Syoc, California Academy of Sciences, San Francisco, CA – Barnacles
Dr. Nancy Voss, Rosenstiel School Of Marine Sciences, University of Miami, FL – Cephalopods
*Dr. Mary K. Wicksten, Texas A & M University, College Station, TX - Crustaceans
Dr. Gary Williams, California Academy of Science, San Francisco, CA – Sea Pens
*Dr. Judith E. Winston, Virginia Museum of Natural History, Martinsville, VA – Bryzoans
Dr. Russel L. Zimmer, University of Southern California – Phoronids

About the Authors

Paul Humann & Ned DeLoach

Paul Humann took his first underwater photograph in 1964, What began as a hobby turned into a full-time enterprise seven years later when he left his established law practice in Wichita, Kansas, to become captain/owner of the diving cruiser Cayman Diver, the Caribbean's first successful live aboard. For the next eight years he spent thousands of hours underwater documenting the rich biological diversity of coral reefs in the Caribbean.

Paul soon discovered that many of his passengers shared his interest in the reefs' natural history. Evening hours always found a group gathered in the ship's salon sharing diving experiences and attempting to identify the many fish and invertebrates sighted during the day. To satisfy his growing curiosity and as a service to guests, Paul began to seriously study marine biology. As his knowledge grew he organized his underwater slides into a series of identification presentations called "Sea Talks". These enjoyable evening programs teaching identification of both fish and invertebrates quickly became a featured part of every trip.

In 1979 he sold the Cayman Diver to travel, photograph and write full time. His photographs and articles have appeared in nearly every major diving and wildlife publication as well as 14 marine life books. Today Paul spends much of his time leading diving tours and presenting his ever-popular "Sea Talks" for live-aboard cruisers throughout the world. He continues to study marine biology, write, photograph, and collaborate with scientists on methods to visually identify marine life species in their natural habitat.

After finishing a degree in education in 1967, Ned DeLoach moved from his childhood home in West Texas to Florida so that he would be able to do what he loves best – dive. In 1971 he completed his first diving guide to the state, *Diving Guide to Underwater Florida*, which was released in its 10th edition in 2001. Throughout the 1970s and 1980s Ned was active in the Florida's cave diving community as a photographer, filmmaker and editor of educational materials.

A mutual friend, who had vacationed on the *Cayman Diver*, introduced Paul to Ned in the mid-80s. Two years later the pair was reunited as co-editors of *Ocean Realm* magazine. It was during this period that the idea of a marine life identification series designed for divers was born. Ned and wife Anna live in Jacksonville, Florida.

Authors' Note

Life began in the sea. Today, warm tropical waters still provide the quintessential environment for life on Earth. Here tiny coral polyps have proliferated, forming limestone structures that offer habitat for a biological diversity of exotic and colorful species that can only be rivaled by the world's great rain forests.

When a diver swims over a coral garden, the abundance of life is staggering. First to attract the eye are the many dazzling fishes that move by with endless energy; but, when the sunlit crest is left behind and the reef's craggy surface is explored, a new realm is discovered: this is the domain of the marine invertebrate, where many of the Earth's most beautiful and bizarre creatures make their home.

Reef Creature Identification is a comprehensive, pictorial guide for the visual identification of marine invertebrates that live in, on, and around the reefs of Florida, the Caribbean and Bahamas. It is a companion text to *Reef Fish Identification,* published in its 1st edition in 1989, and the second of a three-volume reference set that includes *Reef Coral Identification.*

Too often in the past, the underwater naturalist's enthusiasm was tempered by his inability to identify the strange creatures encountered on the reef. This frustrating situation stemmed from the fact that scientific identifications, the majority completed well before the advent of Scuba, relied on laboratory examinations of preserved specimens. Such studies found it impractical to take into account visual clues such as colors and patterns exhibited by creatures in the wild.

As divers are becoming more conscious of the reef's natural history, marine biologists are also spending more research time underwater. Both groups understand the importance of bridging the gap between laboratory taxonomy and visual identification. *Reef Creature Identification* represents a cooperative collaboration between the scientific community and author/photographer Paul Humann. Over thirty biologists, specialists in their fields, contributed information, advice and lab time to this project. This process, requiring numerous photographic/collection dives, careful packaging and shipping of specimens, lab examinations and documentation has, for the first time, made it possible to identify many invertebrates by visual characteristics alone.

Underwater identification plays a significant role in the protection of our coral reef systems by functioning as a catalyst for environmental awareness. When we learn to recognize a new species, we immediately begin to familiarize ourselves with the creature's patterns of behavior and, when we begin to understand the nature of an animal, concern for its welfare always follows.

Contents

The Need For Taxonomic Research 10
Overview 11
How To Use This Book 11
Name 12
Size 12
Depth 12
Visual ID 12
Abundance & Distribution 12
Habitat & Behavior 13
Effect on Diver 13
Reaction to Diver 13
Similar Species 13
Note 13

Ten Identification Groups
Common & Proper Phylum Names

1. Sponges – Porifera   14-61

Typical Shapes of Sponges

2. Cnidarians – Cnidaria   62-125

Hydroid   Hydromedusa   Siphonophores

True Jellyfish   Box Jellies

6

Sea Anemones

Zoanthids

Corallimorphs

Tube-Dwelling
Anemones

3. Comb Jellies – Ctenophora 126-133

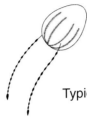

Typical Shapes of Comb Jellies

4. Flatworms – Platyhelminthes 134-139
Ribbon Worms – Rhynchocoela

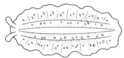

Flatworms

Ribbon Worms

5. Segmented Worms – Annelida 140-163

Fire Worms

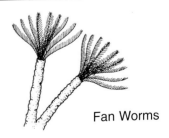

Fan Worms

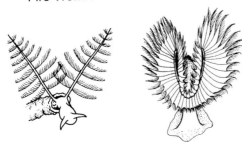

Calcareous Tube Worms

Spaghetti Worms

7

6. Crustaceans – Arthropoda 164-243

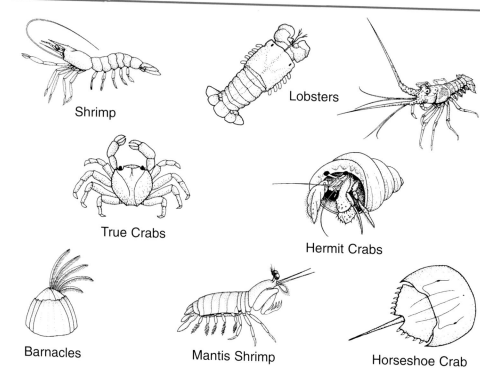

Shrimp

Lobsters

True Crabs

Hermit Crabs

Barnacles

Mantis Shrimp

Horseshoe Crab

7. Bryozoans – Ectoprocta 244-255

TYpical Shapes of Bryozoan Colonies

8. Mollusks – Mollusca 256-349

Snails

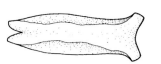

Head-Shield Slugs

Sea Hares

Side-Gill Slugs

Sea Slugs

Nudibranchs

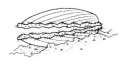
Bivalves

Chitons

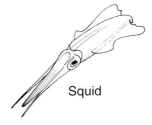
Squid

Octopuses

9. Echinoderms – Echinodermata   350-399

Feather Stars

Sea Stars

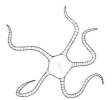
Brittle Stars

Basket Stars

Sea Urchins

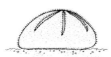
Heart Urchins

Sand Dollars

Sea Cucumbers

10. Tunicates – Chordata   400-420

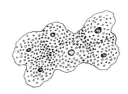

Pelagic
Tunicates

TYpical Shapes of Tunicate Colonies

The Need for Taxonomic Research

Biological scientists that specialize in identifying, describing and classifying plants and animals according to their natural relationships, are called taxonomists. Unfortunately; due to limited funding there are few researchers working in this critical field today. In fact, for many taxonomists, including many world authorities, the classification of animals is more of a hobby than a salaried profession. For example, Dr. Dennis Opresko, the recognized authority on black corals, works as an atomic energy researcher at Oak Ridge. Although his interest in the classification of corals began in graduate school, he can only devote weekends and his yearly vacation time to taxonomic research.

Finding taxonomists to help with the identification process has been one of the most pressing problems in compiling material for the *Reef Set*. For instance, to acquire information concerning flatworms for the *Reef Creature Identification* text we had to rely on the good graces of a retired scientist from the British Museum of Natural History – No one currently working in the United States had the necessary knowledge. To answer our many question about tunicates, we found it necessary to ship collected specimens to the Museum of Natural History in Paris.

Since writing the first volumes of the *Reef Set,* just over a decade ago, the situation has deteriorated at an accelerated rate. For example, Dr. Charles Cutress, the acknowledged authority on Caribbean sea anemones and their allies, who provided extensive assistance with identifications for the 1st edition of *Reef Creature Identification* passed away. In the ten ensuing years no university or museum has established a position to continue his work. Because of this void, 14 anemone species included in the 2nd edition appear without scientific identifications. This lack of expertise continues with Caribbean nudibranchs and their allies. Eleven of these beautiful and fascinating creatures – all-time favorites with underwater naturalists – are regrettably presented without scientific identification.

To further bedevil the plight of marine taxonomy, many countries have recently implemented rigorous permitting procedures for the collection of marine specimens. Although at first, these requirements seem a good idea they have thrown up ludicrous roadblocks to taxonomic researchers. For example, you can collect most marine creatures (except those on the endangered species list) and put them in your aquarium where they will probably die, but you cannot send the specimen to the Smithsonian for research without a special permit. Recently while diving in South America, I discovered what I believed to be an undescribed seabass. It was perfectly legal for me to catch and eat the fish, but if I took it back to the States for laboratory classification I was committing a crime. On a recent collecting trip with several well-known marine biologists from established institutions, the group had to fill out reams of nonsensical forms before finally being granted a permit to take a limited number of marine specimens. With authorization in hand, we arrived on site only to find local officials demanding additional paper work including a list (genus and species) of all the animals we intended to collect. Our argument – that it was impossible to provide a list of undescribed species – fell on deaf ears. To our dismay, it took almost two days – 25 percent of the valuable collecting time of six researchers – before we were allowed to continue with our work.

Biological research and strategies for establishing sound marine life management practices are grounded in taxonomy. In a 1992 paper Nancy Knowlton, et al, documented evidence that Boulder Star Coral, *Montastarea annularis,* commonly used as an indicator of reef health, is probably four closely related but separate species with different growth rates and reactions to environmental changes. If her findings are correct, it means that the conclusions drawn from years of ecological and environmental research in Florida, the Bahamas and Caribbean may be invalid

If we expect to properly manage our natural resources it is imperative that we stop leapfrogging the classification of organisms: the foundation of biological knowledge. Those of us interested in natural science and the preservation of marine wildlife should encourage our educational and governmental institutions to provide the funding and positions necessary for proper taxonomical research.

our educational and governmental institutions to provide the funding and positions necessary for proper taxonomical research.

Overview

Over one million species of animals have been described in the Animal Kingdom. Of these, approximately seven percent are single-celled animals. The rest are multicellular animals that fall into two general groups: the vertebrates — animals with backbones, and the invertebrates — animals without backbones. Vertebrates make up only four or five percent of the multicellular species total but, in the sea, they include some rather important animals such as fishes, dolphins, whales, seals and, of course, sport divers. The remaining and overwhelming majority (about 88 percent) are invertebrates. In the sea they include many commonly known groups such as sponges, jellyfishes, corals, shrimp, crabs, snails, octopuses, sea stars and sea urchins. This book deals with the identification of marine invertebrates that live on or near the reefs of Florida, the Caribbean and Bahamas. Those included are the species most likely to be encountered by divers, with the exception of the invertebrates commonly called corals, which are identified in a separate volume.

How To Use This Book

The hundreds of marine invertebrates that inhabit reefs and their adjacent habitats are divided into eleven major scientific classification groups called phyla. The members of each phylum are presented together in one of ten Identification Groups. This format varies only in ID Group 4, Flatworms and Ribbonworms, where two small phyla are included together. The ID Groups/Phyla appear in the order of general anatomical complexity, from the simplest — sponges, to the most complex — tunicates. A brief explanation of the predominant anatomical features that distinguish each phylum is given in the ID Groups' introduction. It is important to note that although animals within a phylum share basic anatomical similarities, some appear distinctly different from their relatives within these broad scientific classifications.

The animals in a phylum are classified further into class, order, family, genus and species. In some cases, even these classifications are subdivided further. Similar appearing invertebrates commonly recognized by the public as a group, such as jellyfish, crabs, sea stars, etc., usually fall completely within one of the lower classifications. These **Commonly Recognized Groups** are important reference keys for using this text. Each of the 50 groups are summarized in their corresponding ID Group/Phyla introduction. They are also listed with a visual reference diagram under their associated phylum in the content pages; in the master index on the inside front and back covers; at the top of the left page where their members are described in the text; and in bold type next to the identification photograph. It is important, as a first step in invertebrate identification, to become familiar with these groups and their locations within the text.

Names

Information about each species begins with the animal's common name (that used by the general public). In the past, using common names for identification was impractical because several species were known by more than one name. For example, the Giant Anemone is often improperly known as the Pink Tipped Anemone. The common names used in this text are based on previously published names, and the standardized common names published by The American Fisheries Society. Many species included have never had a common name published. In these instances, a name was selected that describes a distinctive feature that can be used for visual identification. In this book, common species names are capitalized to help set them apart, although this practice is not considered grammatically correct.

Below the common name, in italics, is the two-part scientific name. The first word (always capitalized) is the genus. The genus name is given to a group of animals with very similar physiological characteristics. The second word (never capitalized) is the species. A species includes only animals that are sexually compatible and produce fertile offspring. Occasionally "sp." appears in the place of a species name. This means the species is not known; "spp." means there are two or more undescribed species. Continuing below genus and species, in descending order, is a list of classification categories to which the genus and species belong. This scientific nomenclature, rooted in Latin (L.) and Greek (Gr.), is used by scientists throughout the world.

Size

The size range of the species that divers are most likely to observe. This is followed by a maximum species' size when appropriate. Occasionally, the length of tentacles, spines, etc. is also given if this information is useful in making a visual identification.

Depth

The average depth range at which divers are most likely to sight a species, although species are occasionally found outside this range. Depths below the recommended safe diving limit of 130 feet are not given even if the species regularly inhabits these waters. Species that live exclusively below 130 feet are not included in this book.

Visual ID

Colors, markings and anatomical differences that distinguish the species from similar appearing species. In most cases, these features are readily apparent to divers, but occasionally they are quite subtle. The features listed first are considered the most distinctive visual characteristics of the species.

Abundance & Distribution

Abundance refers to a diver's likelihood of observing a species in its normal habitat and depth range on any given dive. This is not always indicative of the actual population. Definitions are as follows:

Abundant – At least several sightings can be expected on nearly every dive.
Common – Sightings are frequent, but not necessarily to be expected on every dive.
Occasional – Sightings are not unusual, but are not to be expected on a regular basis.
Uncommon – Sightings are unusual.
Rare – Sightings are exceptional.

Distribution describes where the species may be found geographically within the range of the map on the opposite page. The Turks and Caicos Islands, an extension of the Bahama Islands' chain, are also included. Described species may also be found in areas such as Bermuda, Brazil, etc., but no attempt has been made to include this specific information, although additional data has occasionally been included. In many cases the extent of a species' geographical range is not yet known; consequently, species may occasionally be found in areas not listed. If sightings are made that do not correspond with the geographic information provided, the publisher is interested in obtaining details for updating future editions.

Habitat & Behavior

Habitat is the type of underwater terrain or associated organism where a particular species is likely to be found. Only habitats frequented by divers, such as natural and artificial reefs, adjacent areas of sand and rubble, sea grass beds and walls are emphasized.

Behavior is the animal's normal activities that can be observed by a diver and help in identification.

Effect On Divers

If a species is known to have a negative effect on divers, it is listed. The agent of the injury, how it might occur, symptoms, and recommended treatment are included where appropriate.

Reaction To Divers

Relates to the species' normal reaction to divers, if any, and describes tactics a diver can use to make a closer observation.

Similar Species

Occasionally there are similar appearing species that are not pictured. Usually they are invertebrates that are rarely observed by divers. Characteristics and information are given that distinguish them from the species pictured.

Note

Additional information that may help in the visual identification process such as: recent changes in classification, other common names also used for the same species, or details relating to the method used to identify the photographed specimen.

Queen Conch eyes.

IDENTIFICATION GROUP 1

Phylum Porifera

(Por-IF-er-uh / L. hole-bearing)

Sponges

Sponges are the simplest of the multicellular animals. The individual cells display a considerable degree of independence, and form no true tissue layers or organs. Depending upon a cell's location within the sponge, they do, however, perform somewhat specialized functions. A sponge's surface is perforated with numerous small holes called **incurrent pores** or ostia. Water is drawn into the sponge through these pores and pumped through the interior by the beating of whip-like extensions on the cells called flagella. As water passes through the sponge, food and oxygen are filtered out. The water exits into the body's interior cavity and out the animal's one or more large **excurrent openings** or oscula.

Sponges come in many sizes, colors and shapes. Some are quite small, less than half an inch across, while the Giant Barrel Sponge may attain a height of over six feet. Their colors range from drab grays and browns to bright reds, oranges, yellows, greens, and violets. The shape of what can be considered a typical sponge resembles a vase. However, growth patterns vary tremendously. Those with one large body opening form bowls, barrels and tubes. Sponges with multiple body openings may form irregular masses, or shapes like ropes, candles, branching horns or, in the case of encrusting sponges, take the shapes of what they overgrow.

Although sponges come in many forms, they can usually be recognized as a group by their excurrent openings that are generally large and distinct. Another key is their lack of any evident movement. Nearly all animals react with an obvious protective movement when approached or touched, but sponges show no reaction when disturbed. Sponges may occasionally be confused with tunicates (Identification Group 10), which often have similar-appearing body openings and grow in comparable patterns, shapes and colors. Tunicates, however, are highly evolved animals, having a nervous system and relatively complex muscles that can rapidly close their body openings.

While sponges are easy to recognize as a group, many individual species are difficult to identify. This is because the same species may grow in different shapes and patterns, which is the consequence of several factors, including age, location, depth and water movement. Color is often another poor clue to identification. Variations of color within the same species may result from the water chemistry, depth, light conditions and the presence of algae living in symbiosis with the sponge. For these reasons, correct identification of many species can only be made in the laboratory, by microscopic examination of the tissue or the shape of tiny structural elements called spicules. Fortunately, a number of the more common sponges found on reefs grow in relatively consistent patterns, shapes and colors, making visual identification possible.

For the convenience of visual reference this Identification Group is arranged by shape rather than scientific classification. The order of these shape/categories is: tubes, vases and barrels, balls, irregular masses, ropes, encrusting, boring, and finally, the calcareous sponges.

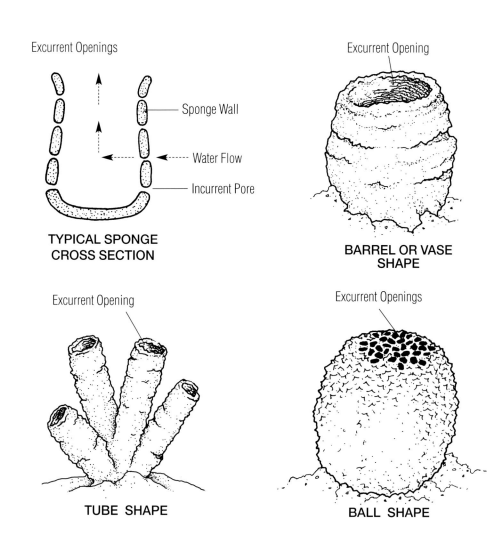

Excurrent Openings

Sponge Wall

Water Flow

Incurrent Pore

TYPICAL SPONGE CROSS SECTION

Excurrent Opening

BARREL OR VASE SHAPE

Excurrent Opening

TUBE SHAPE

Excurrent Openings

BALL SHAPE

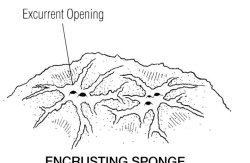

Excurrent Opening

ENCRUSTING SPONGE

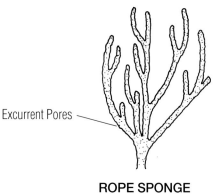

Excurrent Pores

ROPE SPONGE

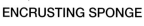

VISUAL ID: Cluster of numerous tubes extend and branch from a base mass. Profusion of small bumps on exterior gives these sponges a stippled texture. Interiors of openings are shades of yellow. Exterior color variable, including yellow, purple, orange and olive green.

ABUNDANCE & DISTRIBUTION: Abundant Caribbean; common Bahamas; occasional South Florida.

HABITAT & BEHAVIOR: Inhabit coral reefs, often grow on walls.

NOTE: Visual identifications confirmed by microscopic examination of small samples collected from pictured specimens.

Branching Tube Sponge
Purple variation.

Branching Tube Sponge
Orange variation.

BRANCHING
TUBE SPONGE

BRANCHING TUBE SPONGE
Pseudoceratina crassa

CLASS:
Sponges
Demospongiae

SIZE: 6 - 18 in.
DEPTH: 20 - 80 ft.

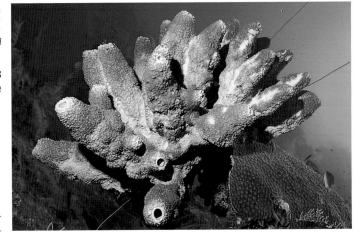

Branching Tube Sponge
Yellow variation.
Note the bright red
Erect Rope Sponge [pg.43].

Branching Tube Sponge
Olive variation.

VISUAL ID: Large, thick-walled tube with rough exterior and numerous small finger-like projections. Lip of tube opening is thin and protrudes from mass of sponge. Usually covered with a variety of algal growth and sediment. Color variable due to encrusting organisms, but sponge itself is dark gray to black. Grows as a solitary tube.

ABUNDANCE & DISTRIBUTION: Occasional Caribbean, Bahamas; rare Florida.

HABITAT & BEHAVIOR: Inhabit drop-off areas. Usually hang from walls, under ledges or in other protected areas.

NOTE: Visual identification confirmed by microscopic examination of small sample collected from pictured specimen.

VISUAL ID: Tubes are long, slender, thin, and soft-walled. Exterior, shades of lavender [opposite], shades of gray [below] or brown [below right]. Tubes' interiors often cream colored, but may be lighter shade of exterior color. Grow as solitary specimens or in clusters.

ABUNDANCE & DISTRIBUTION: Common Caribbean; occasional Bahamas.

HABITAT & BEHAVIOR: Inhabit deeper reefs, often grow on walls.

Stove-pipe Sponge
Gray variation.

ROUGH TUBE SPONGE
Oceanapia bartschi

CLASS:
Sponges
Demospongiae

SIZE: 1 ½ - 4 ft.
DEPTH: 60 - 130 ft.

STOVE-PIPE SPONGE
Aplysina archeri

CLASS:
Sponges
Demospongiae

SIZE: 2 - 6 ft.
DEPTH: 50 - 100 ft.

Stove-pipe Sponge

Brown variation.

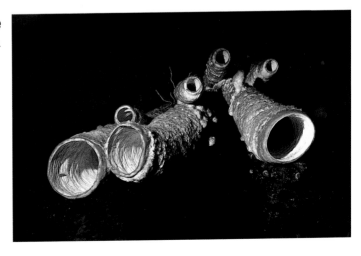

VISUAL ID: Tubes are yellow to orange, and soft-walled. Usually in clusters joined at the base. In shallow water, clusters tend to be shorter with antler-like growths extending from around the openings [opposite]. In deeper water, especially along walls, tubes tend to be longer and without antler-like growths [below]. In natural light, especially in deeper water, appear to be yellow-green. Retain yellow-green color even at great depth, probably the result of fluorescent pigments.

ABUNDANCE & DISTRIBUTION: Abundant Caribbean; common Bahamas; occasional Florida.

HABITAT & BEHAVIOR: Inhabit coral reefs, especially in open water areas and on walls. Gobies and cardinal fish often live inside the tubes.

NOTE: If squeezed, secrete a purple dye that will stain skin for several days.

Yellow Tube Sponge
Growth pattern.

VISUAL ID: Massive, thick-walled barrels or tubes. Deeply convoluted and pitted exteriors. Ridges dark green to yellowish green, valleys and pits yellow-green to yellow. Interior walls have yellow excurrent pores. Grow solitary or in small groups.

ABUNDANCE & DISTRIBUTION: Occasional Bahamas, Caribbean.

HABITAT & BEHAVIOR: Inhabit coral reefs and walls. May attach to solid substrate and grow upright like barrels, or attach to walls and extend outward as massive tubes. Often have sediment, algae and various organisms on surface.

YELLOW TUBE SPONGE
Aplysina fistularis
CLASS:
Sponges
Demospongiae

SIZE: 2 - 4 ft.
DEPTH: 15 - 100 ft.

Yellow Tube Sponge
Growth pattern.

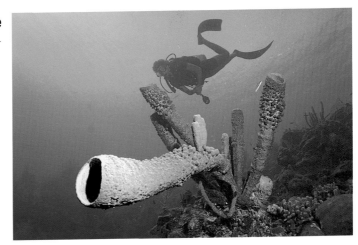

CONVOLUTED BARREL SPONGE
Aplysina lacunosa
CLASS:
Sponges
Demospongiae

SIZE: 1 - 3 ft.
DEPTH: 60 - 130 ft.

VISUAL ID: Soft-walled tubes are medium brown to tan to grayish brown with lighter interiors. Although the exterior can be somewhat lumpy or pitted, the surface texture tends to be quite smooth (compare with similar growth patterns of Brown Encrusting Octopus Sponge, *Ectyoplasia ferox* [pg. 37] distinguished by a felt-like surface texture). Grow in clusters joined at the base [opposite], but occasionally form shapes like moose antlers [below, right page], octopus arms [below right], or trumpets [below left].

ABUNDANCE & DISTRIBUTION: Common Bahamas, Caribbean; occasional Florida.

HABITAT & BEHAVIOR: Inhabit reefs and walls, especially in more protected areas such as in canyons, crevices and other large recesses. Golden Zoanthids *Parazoanthus swiftii*, [pg. 105 and opposite] or Maroon Sponge Zoanthids, *P. puertoricense*, [pg. 105] and below right page], may grow on the surface.

VISUAL ID: Cluster of smooth, small brown tubes grows from a common basal mass. Tube openings are often irregular and may appear pinched in.

ABUNDANCE & DISTRIBUTION: Occasional Florida, Bahamas, Caribbean.

HABITAT & BEHAVIOR: Inhabit reef tops. Often grow around the bases of coral heads.

NOTE: Visual identification confirmed by microscopic examination of small sample collected from pictured specimen.

BROWN TUBE SPONGE
Agelas conifera
CLASS:
Sponges
Demospongiae

SIZE: 1 - 3 ft.
DEPTH: 35 - 130 ft.

Brown Tube Sponge
Growth pattern.

BROWN CLUSTERED TUBE SPONGE
Agelas wiedenmyeri
CLASS:
Sponges
Demospongiae

SIZE: Tubes 1 - 3 in.
DEPTH: 15 - 75 ft.

VISUAL ID: Thin, stiff-walled tubes. Outer walls commonly have many irregular conical projections. Usually in clusters, ranging from a few to 20 or 30 tubes. Vary from lavender [opposite] to brownish gray [below] to greenish gray [below right] and occasionally light tan. When growing in areas of strong current and/or sedimentation, they form vases and fans [below right].

ABUNDANCE & DISTRIBUTION: Common South Florida, Bahamas, Caribbean.

HABITAT & BEHAVIOR: Inhabit shallow and mid-range coral reefs, walls, and rocky areas. Exterior surface frequently covered with Sponge Zoanthids, *Parazoanthus parasiticus*, [pg. 105], and often have associated Sponge Brittle Stars, *Ophiothrix suensonii*, [pg. 371].

Branching Vase Sponge
Brownish gray variation. Note sponge, zoanthids and Sponge Brittle Stars.

VISUAL ID: Pink to purple and fluoresces light blue, vase-like sponge. Exterior elaborately sculptured with numerous convoluted ridges and valleys. Grow solitary or in groups of two or three. On rare occasions, apparently when colony is dying, pale yellow to gold.

ABUNDANCE & DISTRIBUTION: Common to occasional Caribbean; occasional South Florida, Bahamas.

HABITAT & BEHAVIOR: Inhabit coral reefs, most commonly grow on walls. Often have associated Sponge Brittle Stars, *Ophiothrix suensonii*, [pg. 371].

BRANCHING VASE SPONGE
Callyspongia vaginalis
CLASS:
Sponges
Demospongiae

SIZE: 6 - 36 in
DEPTH: 6 - 65 ft.

Branching Vase Sponge
*Fan-shaped growth pattern,
greenish gray variation.*

AZURE VASE SPONGE
Callyspongia plicifera
CLASS:
Sponges
Demospongiae

SIZE: 6 - 18 in.
DEPTH: 20 - 75 ft.

VISUAL ID: Brilliant shades of red and orange. Vase- or cup-like with rough-textured exterior. Usually in a cluster of several joined individuals, but may be solitary. Appear dark burgundy at depth without artificial light.

ABUNDANCE & DISTRIBUTION: Occasional Florida Keys, Bahamas, Caribbean.

HABITAT & BEHAVIOR: Inhabit coral reefs, most commonly grow on walls. Attach to solid substrate, branches of Black Coral trees [pictured] and occasionally stalks of dead gorgonians. Often have associated Sponge Brittle Stars, *Ophiothrix suensonii*, [pg. 371].

VISUAL ID: Pink, lavender, blue, greenish gray or gray. Usually vase- or bowl-shaped. Edge of opening bordered with a nearly transparent membrane.

ABUNDANCE & DISTRIBUTION: Occasional South Florida, Bahamas, Caribbean.

HABITAT & BEHAVIOR: Inhabit coral reefs. Exterior surface frequently covered with Sponge Zoanthids, *Parazoanthus parasiticus*, [pg. 105]. Often have associated Sponge Brittle Stars, *Ophiothrix suensonii*, [pg. 371].

VISUAL ID: Brown to reddish brown. Stiff, usually bowl-shaped. Bowls often have an irregular or incomplete shape and may encrust small areas around base. Surface has sandpaper-like texture.

ABUNDANCE & DISTRIBUTION: Occasional South Florida, Bahamas, Caribbean.

HABITAT & BEHAVIOR: Inhabit coral reefs, often in rubble areas between reefs, or on walls.

STRAWBERRY VASE SPONGE
Mycale laxissima
CLASS:
Sponges
Demospongiae

SIZE: 3 - 12 in.
DEPTH: 35 - 130 ft.

PINK VASE SPONGE
Niphates digitalis
CLASS:
Sponges
Demospongiae

SIZE: 4 - 12 in.
DEPTH: 25 - 75 ft.

BROWN BOWL SPONGE
Cribrochalina vasculum
CLASS:
Sponges
Demospongiae

SIZE: 8 - 18 in.
DEPTH: 35 - 100 ft.

VISUAL ID: Large barrel-shape, diameter about half its height. Exterior has distinctive, raised, net-like texture and appears rubbery. Dark green, olive, yellow-green, yellow-brown or green-brown. Smooth interior walls are often a lighter yellowish color and pitted with numerous, round excurrent pores.

ABUNDANCE & DISTRIBUTION: Occasional Bahamas, Caribbean; rare Florida.

HABITAT & BEHAVIOR: Inhabit exposed areas of moderate to deep clear water reefs. Several species of fish and possibly turtles occasionally bite this sponge, leaving bright yellow pits.

VISUAL ID: Huge barrel-shape with rough, often jagged, stone-hard exterior. Shades of gray, brown, or red-brown. Generally solitary, but one or two smaller individuals occasionally grow around base.

ABUNDANCE & DISTRIBUTION: Common Bahamas, Caribbean; occasional Florida.

HABITAT & BEHAVIOR: Inhabit mid-range to deep coral reefs. Often abundant on steep slopes.

NOTE: The size of these sponges often tempts divers to climb inside. This practice is discouraged because the lip breaks easily, disrupting the pumping action of the sponge and allowing the entry of organisms that may cause the colony's death. A sponge large enough to hold a diver may be over 100 years old, as they grow only about one-half inch a year!

VISUAL ID: Squatty barrel-shape with thick, hard, leathery walls. Exterior often heavily pitted. Shades of brown and gray.

ABUNDANCE & DISTRIBUTION: Common Florida Keys, Bahamas, Caribbean.

HABITAT & BEHAVIOR: Inhabit coral reefs. Usually covered with sediment and algal growth. The pictured sponge is "smoking," which is a release of sperm cells, one way in which some species of sponges reproduce.

NOTE: Visual identification confirmed by microscopic examination of small sample collected from pictured specimen

NETTED BARREL SPONGE
Verongula gigantea
CLASS:
Sponges
Demospongiae

SIZE: 2 - 5 ft.
DEPTH: 35 - 130 ft.

GIANT BARREL SPONGE
Xestospongia muta
CLASS:
Sponges
Demospongiae

SIZE: 2 - 6 ft.
DEPTH: 50 - 130 ft.

LEATHERY BARREL SPONGE
Geodia neptuni
CLASS:
Sponges
Demospongiae

SIZE: 1 1/2 - 2 1/2 ft.
DEPTH: 40 - 100 ft.

VISUAL ID: Squatty barrel-shape with flattened top. Central depression has numerous excurrent openings. Hard, leathery, convoluted surface. Exterior shades of gray to dark brown, central depression dark brown to black.

ABUNDANCE & DISTRIBUTION: Common Florida, Bahamas, Caribbean.

HABITAT & BEHAVIOR: Found in a variety of habitats, including shallow patch reefs and areas of sedimentation. Surface often covered with sediment and algal growth. Frequently host a large number of symbiotic shrimp that live in its canals.

VISUAL ID: Ball- or cake-shaped, occasionally with lobes. One or more slight depressions with clusters of excurrent openings. Soft external surface covered with conical knobs. Black to gray overall, knobs are whitish with fine radiating lines.

ABUNDANCE & DISTRIBUTION: Common to occasional Florida, Bahamas, Caribbean. May be locally abundant.

HABITAT & BEHAVIOR: Inhabit shallow to mid-range coral reefs. Prefer brightly lit areas.

VISUAL ID: Single, black excurrent openings scattered over surface. Light gray or light brown with hexagonal design of low, white knobs, often with interconnecting lines. Shape varies, though most commonly encrusting lobes.

ABUNDANCE & DISTRIBUTION: Abundant to common Florida, Bahamas, Caribbean.

HABITAT & BEHAVIOR: Inhabit shallow to mid-range reefs, often grow near living coral.

NOTE: Common name derives from its foul odor when removed from the water.

LOGGERHEAD SPONGE
Spheciospongia vesparium
CLASS:
Sponges
Demospongiae

SIZE: 1 ½ - 5 ft.
DEPTH: 15 - 60 ft.

BLACK-BALL SPONGE
Ircinia strobilina
CLASS:
Sponges
Demospongiae

SIZE: 1 - 1 ½ ft.
DEPTH: 15 - 75 ft.

STINKER SPONGE
Ircinia felix
CLASS:
Sponges
Demospongiae

SIZE: 6 - 12 in.
DEPTH: 5 - 65 ft

VISUAL ID: Orange, ball-shaped sponge, pitted with excurrent openings.

ABUNDANCE & DISTRIBUTION: Common South Florida, Bahamas, Caribbean.

HABITAT & BEHAVIOR: Inhabit protected areas of coral reef, especially under ledges and in caves. Often covered with growths of algae and sediment.

NOTE: There are two similar appearing Orange Ball Sponges: *Cinachyra alloclada* is more common; *C. kuekenthali* is known primarily from deeper reefs. Because they are difficult to distinguish visually, microscopic examination of specimens is required for positive identification.

VISUAL ID: Dark reddish brown to black, soft, irregular mass. Smooth-textured surface with scattered excurrent openings that form volcano-like projections.

ABUNDANCE & DISTRIBUTION: Occasional Caribbean; rare Florida, Bahamas. Common in some locations.

HABITAT & BEHAVIOR: Inhabit reefs, especially small patch reefs in exposed areas. Maroon Sponge Zoanthids, *Parazoanthus puertoricense*, [pg. 105] may grow on the surface.

NOTE: Visual identification confirmed by microscopic examination of small sample collected from pictured specimen.

VISUAL ID: Brown to tan encrusting lobes with numerous pits and ridges over surface. Excurrent openings not grouped and often lighter in color with tints of yellow.

ABUNDANCE & DISTRIBUTION: Occasional Florida Keys, Bahamas, Caribbean.

HABITAT & BEHAVIOR: Inhabit coral reefs.

ORANGE BALL SPONGE
Cinachyra sp.
CLASS:
Sponges
Demospongiae

SIZE: 4 ½ - 6 ½ in.
DEPTH: 15 - 100 ft.

DARK VOLCANO SPONGE
Calyx podatypa
CLASS:
Sponges
Demospongiae

SIZE: 1 - 3 ft.
DEPTH: 30 - 90 ft.

PITTED SPONGE
Verongula rigida
CLASS:
Sponges
Demospongiae

SIZE: 6 - 14 in.
DEPTH: 20 - 80 ft.

VISUAL ID: Pink, lumpy mass, with numerous short, cone-like and knob-like projections. Red, vein-like canals radiate and meander from excurrent openings.

ABUNDANCE & DISTRIBUTION: Common South Florida; occasional to uncommon Bahamas, Caribbean.

HABITAT & BEHAVIOR: Found in a variety of habitats, including reefs.

NOTE: Visual identification confirmed by microscopic examination of small sample collected from pictured specimen.

VISUAL ID: Pinkish to lavender-gray, lumpy mass. Often form rope-like appearance by overgrowing gorgonians and using stalks as support.

ABUNDANCE & DISTRIBUTION: Common Florida, Bahamas, Caribbean.

HABITAT & BEHAVIOR: Found in a variety of habitats, including reefs.

NOTE: Identification made by microscopic examination of small sample collected from pictured specimen.

SIMILAR SPECIES: *Desmapsamma anchorata*, can only be distinguished by microscopic examination.

VISUAL ID: Orange to red, irregular mass with scattered excurrent openings that often form volcano-like projections.

ABUNDANCE & DISTRIBUTION: Common Florida, Bahamas, Caribbean.

HABITAT & BEHAVIOR: Inhabit bays, lagoons, turtle grass beds and rubble areas around shallow patch reefs.

EFFECT ON DIVERS: Contact with bare skin can result in a severe irritating reaction, including burning pain, numbness, swelling and rash that may last several days. Treat with vinegar, followed by a sprinkling of meat tenderizer; rinse and soothe with hydrocortisone ointment.

PINK LUMPY SPONGE
Monanchora unguifera
CLASS:
Sponges
Demospongiae

SIZE: 4 - 16 in.
DEPTH: 30 - 100 ft.

LUMPY OVERGROWING SPONGE
Holopsamma helwigi
CLASS:
Sponges
Demospongiae

SIZE: 4 - 16 in.
DEPTH: 15 - 75 ft.

FIRE SPONGE
Tedania ignis
CLASS:
Sponges
Demospongiae

SIZE: 4 - 12 in.
DEPTH: 1 - 35 ft.

VISUAL ID: Massive, dark brown, lumpy surface has a felt-like texture. Grows in a wide variety of irregular patterns. Large, uneven excurrent openings. Interior surface is covered with white specks that are actually tiny polychaete Sponge Worms, *Haplosyllis* sp. [pg. 145].

ABUNDANCE & DISTRIBUTION: Abundant to occasional Florida, Bahamas, Caribbean.

HABITAT & BEHAVIOR: Found in a variety of habitats, from shallow inshore reefs and adjacent areas of rubble to deep fore reefs. A number of animals live in association with this sponge, including Touch-Me-Not Fanworm, *Hydroides spongicola*, [pg. 159], Sponge Brittle Star, *Ophiothrix sensonii*, [pg. 371], Florida Tubeworm Snails, *Vernicularia knorii*, [pg. 287], Yellowline Goby, *Gobiosoma horsti*, and Shortstripe Goby, *G. chancei*.

EFFECT ON DIVERS: Contact with bare skin can result in a severe allergic reaction, including pain, numbness, swelling and rash that may last several days. Treat with vinegar, followed by a sprinkling of meat tenderizer; rinse and soothe with hydrocortisone ointment. Severe reactions may include difficulty in breathing, requiring oral antihistamine and medical attention. Interestingly, the species' Latin name, nolitangere, means "do-not-touch."

VISUAL ID: Shades of reddish brown to brown with numerous raised excurrent openings ringed with a lighter colored lip. Lumpy, with felt-like surface texture. Encrusts dead areas of reef [opposite], and overgrows gorgonian stalks, may extend long arms that resemble octopus tentacles [below] (compare similar growth patterns of Brown Tube Sponge, *Agelas conifera*, [pg. 23] distinguished by smooth surface texture).

ABUNDANCE & DISTRIBUTION: Common Caribbean, Bahamas; occasional Florida Keys.

HABITAT & BEHAVIOR: Inhabit reefs and adjacent areas. Often grow over coral rubble and dead areas of reef.

NOTE: Visual identification confirmed by microscopic examination of small sample collected from pictured specimens, opposite and below right. Encrusting variation also commonly known as "Brown Volcano Sponge."

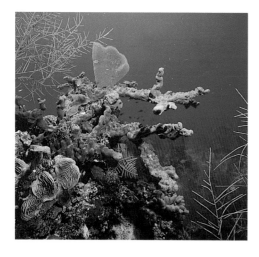

TOUCH-ME-NOT SPONGE
Neofibularia nolitangere
CLASS:
Sponges
Demospongiae

SIZE: 1 - 4 ft.
DEPTH: 10 - 130 ft.

BROWN ENCRUSTING OCTOPUS SPONGE
Ectyoplasia ferox
CLASS:
Sponges
Demospongiae

SIZE: 6 - 16 in.
DEPTH: 40 - 75 ft.

**Brown Encrusting
Octopus Sponge**
Growth pattern.

VISUAL ID: Shades of lavender, occasionally somewhat pinkish. Long and rope-like with porous, somewhat rough texture. Often in tangled masses.

ABUNDANCE & DISTRIBUTION: Scattered distribution, but can be locally common in South Florida, Bahamas, Caribbean.

HABITAT & BEHAVIOR: Inhabit reefs and frequently walls. Often hang from ledges and other outcroppings. Usually covered with Sponge Zoanthids, *Parazoanthus parasiticus*, [pg.105] and Sponge Brittle Stars, *Ophiothrix suensonii*, [pg. 371].

VISUAL ID: Excurrent openings form long rows [see below] (compare similar Scattered Pore Rope Sponge [next]). These openings have thin, protruding lips, often of lighter color. Surface texture is not porous (compare similar Erect Rope Sponge, *Amphimedon compressa*, [pg. 43]). Long, branching and rope-like; generally hang downward with last few inches curving upward. Color highly variable and not distinctive, and include among others red [right], purple [below right], lavender [below].

ABUNDANCE & DISTRIBUTION: Common Bahamas, Caribbean; occasional South Florida.

HABITAT & BEHAVIOR: Inhabit deep sloping reefs and walls.

Row Pore Rope Sponge
Lavender variation. Note rows of excurrent openings.

LAVENDER ROPE SPONGE
Niphates erecta
CLASS:
Sponges
Demospongiae

SIZE: 3 - 6 ft.
DEPTH: 40 - 100 ft.

ROW PORE ROPE SPONGE
Aplysina cauliformis
CLASS:
Sponges
Demospongiae

SIZE: 4 - 8 ft.
DEPTH: 40 - 130 ft.

Row Pore Rope Sponge
Purple variation.

VISUAL ID: Excurrent openings are scattered [see below] (compare similar Row Pore Rope Sponge [previous]). These openings have thin, protruding lips, often of lighter color. Surface texture is not porous (compare similar Erect Rope Sponge, *Amphimedon compressa*, [pg. 43]). Long, branching and rope-like; generally hang downward with last few inches curving upward. Color highly variable and not distinctive, and include among others tan [opposite], yellow-green [below right], brown and purple [below].

ABUNDANCE & DISTRIBUTION: Common Bahamas, Caribbean; occasional South Florida.

HABITAT & BEHAVIOR: Inhabit deep sloping reefs and walls.

NOTE: Visual identification confirmed by microscopic examination of small sample collected from pictured specimens below and below right.

Scattered Pore Rope Sponge

Brown and lavender variation. Note scattered excurrent openings. Red is Erect Rope Sponge [pg. 43], note porous texture.

VISUAL ID: Thin, rope-like, often in tangled masses. Shades of red to pink.

ABUNDANCE & DISTRIBUTION: Common South Florida, Bahamas, Caribbean.

HABITAT & BEHAVIOR: Inhabit coral reefs and frequently walls. Often covered with winding chains of Golden Zoanthids, *Parazoanthus swiftii*, [pg. 105 and opposite].

NOTE: Visual identification confirmed by microscopic examination of small sample collected from pictured specimens opposite and below right. Formerly classified in the genus *Thalysias*.

SCATTERED PORE ROPE SPONGE
Aplysina fulva

CLASS:
Sponges
Demospongiae

SIZE: 4 - 8 ft.
DEPTH: 10 - 130 ft.

Scattered Pore Rope Sponge
Yellow-green variation.

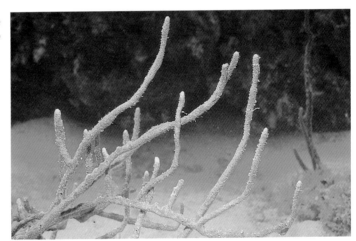

THIN ROPE SPONGE
Rhaphidophlus juniperinus

CLASS:
Sponges
Demospongiae

SIZE: 1 - 5 ft.
DEPTH: 20 - 100 ft.

VISUAL ID: Numerous finger-like branches mottled in shades of green. May grow erect ,in tangled masses or hang from outcroppings.

ABUNDANCE & DISTRIBUTION: Common South Florida, Bahamas, Caribbean.

HABITAT & BEHAVIOR: Inhabit coral reefs and walls. Frequently covered with winding chains of Golden Zoanthids, *Parazoanthus swiftii,* [pg. 105].

NOTE: If squeezed, secrete a black dye.

VISUAL ID: Rope-like, usually branched structure grows upward from substrate. Smooth, but surface is porous (compare with Row Pore Rope Sponge, *Aplysina cauliformis,* [pg. 39] and Scattered Pore Rope Sponge, *Aplysina fulva,* [pg. 40]). Usually brilliant red, but can be burgundy or maroon. Excurrent openings are scattered and do not have thin, light-colored lips.

ABUNDANCE & DISTRIBUTION: Common Florida, Bahamas, Caribbean.

HABITAT & BEHAVIOR: Inhabit coral reef tops, occasionally walls. On walls may closely resemble Row Pore Rope Sponge or Scattered Pore Rope Sponge, but their characteristic upward growth pattern remains distinctive [see pg. 38].

VISUAL ID: Red to orange, branched, rope-like structure grows upward from substrate. Surface texture is rough.

ABUNDANCE & DISTRIBUTION: Uncommon Caribbean, Bahamas; rare Florida.

HABITAT & BEHAVIOR: Inhabit coral reef tops, often near drop-offs.

NOTE: The similarity in appearance between three species, *Ptilocaulis gracilis, P. walpersi,* and *P. spiculifera* requires microscopic examination for positive identification.

GREEN FINGER SPONGE
Iotrochota birotulata
CLASS:
Sponges
Demospongiae

SIZE: 1 - 3 ft.
DEPTH: 15 - 60 ft.

ERECT ROPE SPONGE
Amphimedon compressa
CLASS:
Sponges
Demospongiae

SIZE: 2 - 3 ½ ft.
DEPTH: 35 - 70 ft.

RED-ORANGE BRANCHING SPONGES
Ptilocaulis sp.
CLASS:
Sponges
Demospongiae

SIZE: 8 - 15 in.
DEPTH: 40 - 80 ft.

VISUAL ID: White, lumpy encrusting sponge with scattered, large excurrent openings. Often has light shadings of gold or pink.
ABUNDANCE & DISTRIBUTION: Common South Florida.
HABITAT & BEHAVIOR: Encrust dead areas of reef and shipwrecks.
NOTE: Visual identification confirmed by microscopic examination of small sample collected from pictured specimen.

VISUAL ID: Smooth, encrusting mass is speckled pink and/or red.
ABUNDANCE & DISTRIBUTION: Occasional Florida, Bahamas, Caribbean.
HABITAT & BEHAVIOR: Inhabit reefs and walls. Prefer shaded, protected areas; encrust around undercut bases of coral heads, in recesses, and wall faces under ledge overhangs.
NOTE: Visual identification confirmed by microscopic examination of small sample collected from pictured specimen.

VISUAL ID: Bright red encrusting sponge with circular, raised, sieve-like areas of tightly packed, tiny incurrent pores that surround small, protruding excurrent openings. (Note different appearance of meandering, sieve-like areas of Orange Sieve Encrusting Sponge [next]).
ABUNDANCE & DISTRIBUTION: Occasional Caribbean.
HABITAT & BEHAVIOR: Inhabit reefs and walls. Prefer shaded, protected areas; encrust around undercut bases of coral heads, in recesses, and wall faces under ledge overhangs.
REACTION TO DIVERS: One of the few sponges that reacts to being touched; it slowly closes its openings and pores.
NOTE: Visual identification confirmed by microscopic examination of small sample collected from pictured specimen.

**WHITE LUMPY
ENCRUSTING SPONGE**
Ptilocaulis sp.
CLASS:
Sponges
Demospongiae

SIZE: 8 - 15 in.
DEPTH: 40 - 80 ft.

**PINK & RED
ENCRUSTING SPONGE**
Spirastrella coccinea
CLASS:
Sponges
Demospongiae

SIZE: 1 - 3 ft.
DEPTH: 30 - 100 ft.

**RED SIEVE
ENCRUSTING SPONGE**
Phorbas amaranthus
CLASS:
Sponges
Demospongiae

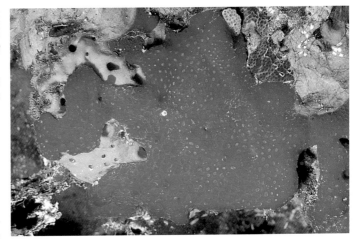

SIZE: 6 - 18 in.
DEPTH: 20 - 100 ft.

VISUAL ID: Red-orange encrusting sponge with raised, often meandering, sieve-like areas of tightly packed incurrent pores that surround large, protruding, excurrent openings. (Note different appearance of circular, sieve-like areas of Red Sieve Encrusting Sponge [previous]).

ABUNDANCE & DISTRIBUTION: Occasional Caribbean.

HABITAT & BEHAVIOR: Inhabit reefs and walls. Prefer shaded, protected areas; encrust around undercut bases of coral heads, in recesses, and wall faces under ledge overhangs.

NOTE: Identification of genus determined by microscopic examination of small sample collected from pictured specimen. Possibly an undescribed species.

VISUAL ID: Red-orange, thin, encrusting sponge. Several root-like canals radiate from the slightly raised excurrent openings. These canals often intertwine and connect with canals radiating from other excurrent openings. (Note, areas between canals do not have scattered white spots like Red Encrusting Sponge [next].)

ABUNDANCE & DISTRIBUTION: Common Caribbean; occasional South Florida, Bahamas.

HABITAT & BEHAVIOR: Inhabit coral reefs, prefer shaded areas. Often encrust under ledge overhangs, in recesses and caves.

NOTE: Visual identification confirmed by microscopic examination of small sample collected from pictured specimen.

VISUAL ID: Brilliant red, thin, encrusting sponge. Several root-like canals radiate from the slightly raised excurrent openings. These canals often intertwine and connect with canals radiating from other excurrent openings. Areas between canals have scattered white spots; occasionally this area appears pink.

ABUNDANCE & DISTRIBUTION: Common Caribbean; occasional South Florida, Bahamas.

HABITAT & BEHAVIOR: Encrust dead areas of reefs, especially around the bases of living coral heads.

NOTE: Visual identification confirmed by microscopic examination of small sample collected from pictured specimen.

**ORANGE SIEVE
ENCRUSTING SPONGE**
Diplastrella sp.
CLASS:
Sponges
Demospongiae

SIZE: 6 - 18 in.
DEPTH: 20 - 75 ft.

**RED-ORANGE
ENCRUSTING SPONGE**
Diplastrella megastellata
CLASS:
Sponges
Demospongiae

SIZE: 4 - 10 in.
DEPTH: 25 - 75 ft.

**RED
ENCRUSTING SPONGE**
Monanchora barbadensis
CLASS:
Sponges
Demospongiae

SIZE: 4 - 10 in.
DEPTH: 25 - 75 ft.

VISUAL ID: Peach-colored, thin, encrusting sponge. Several root-like canals radiate from the slightly raised excurrent openings. These canals often intertwine and connect with canals radiating from other excurrent openings. Numerous large incurrent pores distinguish this species.

ABUNDANCE & DISTRIBUTION: Common Caribbean; occasional South Florida, Bahamas.

HABITAT & BEHAVIOR: Encrust dead areas of reefs and walls, especially under ledges, in recesses and other protected areas.

NOTE: Identification of genus confirmed by microscopic examination of small sample collected from pictured specimen. Possibly an undescribed species.

VISUAL ID: This thin, encrusting sponge is distinguished by several canals that radiate in a star-shaped pattern from small groups of pitted excurrent openings. These "stars" are well separated. Unlike several similar appearing sponges, the canals are only occasionally branched, and do no intertwine or interconnect. See "NOTE" regarding color.

ABUNDANCE & DISTRIBUTION: Occasional Florida, Bahamas, Caribbean.

HABITAT & BEHAVIOR: Encrust dead areas of reefs and walls, especially under ledges, in recesses and other protected areas.

NOTE: Identification of genus confirmed by microscopic examination of small sample collected from pictured specimen [opposite]. Possibly an undescribed species that apparently comes in a variety of colors [below and below right].

**Star
Encrusting Sponge**
Color variation.

PEACH ENCRUSTING SPONGE
Clathria sp.

CLASS:
Sponges
Demospongiae

SIZE: 4 - 10 in.
DEPTH: 25 - 75 ft.

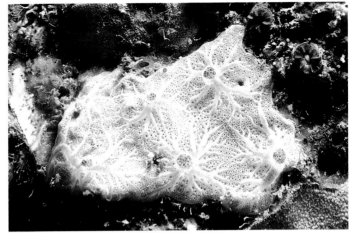

STAR ENCRUSTING SPONGE
Halisarca sp.

CLASS:
Sponges
Demospongiae

SIZE: 3 - 10 in.
DEPTH: 25 - 100 ft.

Star Encrusting Sponge
Color variation.

VISUAL ID: Orange encrusting sponge. Numerous vein-like canals radiate from protruding excurrent openings. These canals often intertwine and connect with canals radiating from other excurrent openings. Areas between canals often lighter color. Relatively large incurrent pores scattered over surface.

ABUNDANCE & DISTRIBUTION: Occasional Florida, Bahamas, Caribbean.

HABITAT & BEHAVIOR: Encrust dead areas of reefs and walls, especially under ledges, in recesses, caves and other protected areas.

NOTE: Visual identification confirmed by microscopic examination of small sample collected from pictured specimen.

VISUAL ID: Bright orange encrusting sponge with large, white to transparent, projecting excurrent openings. Encrust edges and under margins of coral plates and ledges. Modify growth of coral around excurrent openings, causing the margins of coral plates to have a scalloped pattern.

ABUNDANCE & DISTRIBUTION: Abundant to common Florida, Bahamas, Caribbean.

HABITAT & BEHAVIOR: Grow in association with a variety of living hard coral species, protecting the coral from bioerosion by boring sponges.

VISUAL ID: Orange, rough-textured, soft, encrusting sponge. Excurrent openings blend into texture of sponge (similar species, Orange Icing Sponge [previous], has protruding white to transparent excurrent openings).

ABUNDANCE & DISTRIBUTION: Common Florida, Bahamas, Caribbean.

HABITAT & BEHAVIOR: Found in a wide variety of habitats, from roots of mangroves to areas of reef rubble and living reefs. Encrust dead areas of substrate, often around edges of living coral.

SIMILAR SPECIES: Orange, thin encrusting sponge, *Ulosa hispida,* commonly grows on mangrove roots.

**ORANGE VEINED
ENCRUSTING SPONGE**
Rhaphidophlus venosus
CLASS:
Sponges
Demospongiae

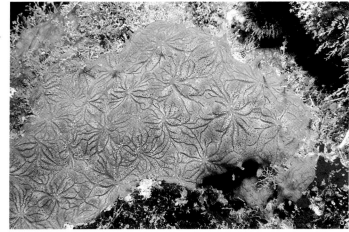

SIZE: 4 - 12 in.
DEPTH: 25 - 100 ft.

ORANGE ICING SPONGE
Mycale laevis
CLASS:
Sponges
Demospongiae

SIZE: 4 - 18 in.
DEPTH: 20 - 100 ft.

**ORANGE LUMPY
ENCRUSTING SPONGE**
Ulosa ruetzleri
CLASS:
Sponges
Demospongiae

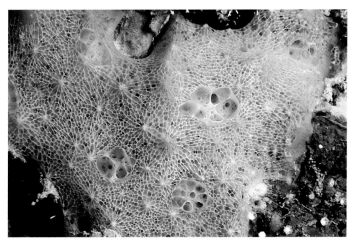

SIZE: 4 - 12 in.
DEPTH: 15 - 75 ft.

VISUAL ID: Massive, orange encrusting sponge. Convoluted surface, consisting of ridges and valleys, forms a maze-like pattern. Scattered excurrent openings raised slightly. Often has algal growth and sediment on surface.

ABUNDANCE & DISTRIBUTION: Occasional Caribbean, Bahamas. Can be common in some locations.

HABITAT & BEHAVIOR: Inhabit caves and undercuts on drop-off walls and other moderate to deep reef areas. Prefer protected locations with little current.

EFFECT ON DIVERS: Contact with bare skin can result in a severe irritating reaction, including burning pain, numbness, swelling and rash that may last several days. Treat with vinegar, followed by a sprinkling of meat tenderizer; rinse and soothe with hydrocortisone ointment.

NOTE: Identification made by microscopic examination of small sample collected from pictured specimen. Another sponge, *Didiscus oxeatus,* looks identical; positive identification requires microscopic examination of spicules.

VISUAL ID: Massive, thick, rubbery, orange sponge, with pitted and convoluted surface texture. Grow in a variety of irregular masses and patterns. Often form huge mounds and/or encrust large areas of reef. Occasionally extend from walls in large, flat, mat-like formations that sometimes resemble large ears.

ABUNDANCE & DISTRIBUTION: Common to occasional Florida, Bahamas, Caribbean. Can be abundant in some locations.

HABITAT & BEHAVIOR: Inhabit reefs and walls, prefer areas with some water movement. Often compound tunicates, hydroids and a variety of other organisms grow on their surface.

CONVOLUTED ORANGE SPONGE
Myrmekioderma styx
CLASS:
Sponges
Demospongiae

SIZE: ¹/₂ - 3 ft.
DEPTH: 40 - 130 ft.

ORANGE ELEPHANT EAR SPONGE
Agelas clathrodes
CLASS:
Sponges
Demospongiae

SIZE: 2 - 6 ft.
DEPTH: 35 - 130 ft.

Orange Elephant Ear Sponge
Growth patterns.

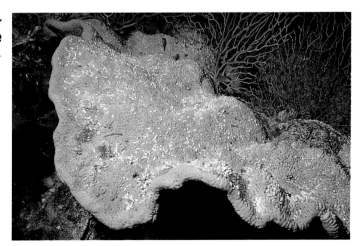

VISUAL ID: Brown encrusting sponge; appearance often resembles a flow of viscous material. Smooth surface with occasional excurrent openings.

ABUNDANCE & DISTRIBUTION: Common Florida, Bahamas, Caribbean.

HABITAT & BEHAVIOR: Inhabit reefs and walls. Often grow on faces of undercuts, walls of canyons, and in caves.

VISUAL ID: Tan to brown, irregular-shaped sponge that appears to encrust the substrate. May have irregular structures and excurrent openings protruding prominently. There is also a massive variation that grows on the substrate, see below.

ABUNDANCE & DISTRIBUTION: Common to uncommon Florida, Bahamas, Caribbean.

HABITAT & BEHAVIOR: Bore into solid substrate of deeper reefs by secreting minute amounts of acid. There appears to be little or no visible damage; however, the base rock of the reef may be riddled with tunnels and chambers.

VISUAL ID: Tan to brown, massive, lumpy, irregular sponge. Excurrent openings of lighter color protrude prominently.

HABITAT & BEHAVIOR: Inhabit shallow fringing and patch reefs, areas of coral rubble, and grass flats.

VISCOUS SPONGE
Plakortis angulospiculatus
CLASS:
Sponges
Demospongiae

SIZE: 3 - 12 in.
DEPTH: 30 - 100 ft.

**BROWN
VARIABLE SPONGE**
**Encrusting/
Boring Variation**
Anthosigmella varians
CLASS:
Sponges
Demospongiae

SIZE: 6 - 18 in.
DEPTH: 10 - 100 ft.

**Brown
Variable Sponge**
Massive variation.

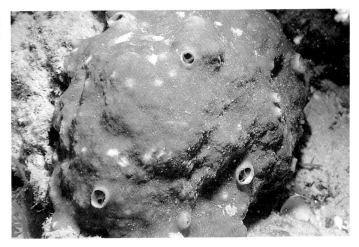

VISUAL ID: Tan to yellow-brown, irregular, massive sponge. Often forms hollow, antler-like structures above the substrate.
ABUNDANCE & DISTRIBUTION: Uncommon Caribbean; rare Bahamas.
HABITAT & BEHAVIOR: Variety of habitats, most often in dead areas of coral rubble and sand, between and around reefs.

VISUAL ID: Olive to dull brown, thin encrusting and boring sponge. Numerous tiny excurrent openings. Overgrows and bores into living coral heads.
ABUNDANCE & DISTRIBUTION: Common to occasional Caribbean; rare Florida, Bahamas.
HABITAT & BEHAVIOR: Inhabit coral reefs. Overgrow and bore into living coral, taking on the pattern of the underlying structure. Note small gray patch of remaining living coral in photograph.
NOTE: Identification confirmed by microscopic examination of small sample collected from pictured specimen. Another species, *C. aprica,* looks identical; positive identification requires microscopic examination.

VISUAL ID: Red to red-orange sponge that appears to encrust, but actually bores into coral heads. Numerous low wart-like spots on surface, with excurrent openings that protrude prominently.
ABUNDANCE & DISTRIBUTION: Occasional South Florida, Bahamas, Caribbean.
HABITAT & BEHAVIOR: Bore into coral heads by secreting minute amounts of acid. From the exterior there is usually no visible damage. However, the corals' interiors may be riddled with tunnels and chambers that may eventually cause their structures to disintegrate. Sponge Zoanthids, *Parazoanthus parasiticus,* [pg. 105] and Sponge Brittle Stars, *Ophiothrix suensonii,* [pg. 371] often live in association with this species.

ANTLER SPONGE
Sphleciospongia cuspidifera
CLASS:
Sponges
Demospongiae

SIZE: 6 - 24 in.
DEPTH: 10 - 100 ft.

CORAL ENCRUSTING SPONGE
Cliona langae
CLASS:
Sponges
Demospongiae

SIZE: 6 - 36 in.
DEPTH: 15 - 100 ft.

RED BORING SPONGE
Cliona delitrix
CLASS:
Sponges
Demospongiae

SIZE: 6 - 12 in.
DEPTH: 15 - 100 ft.

VISUAL ID: Sulfur- to lemon-yellow, occasionally white, deep boring sponge. Grow in a wide variety of patterns: appear as an encrusting sponge [right]; vase-like tubes extending from coral heads [below left]; finger-like branches extending from coral [below right]; tiny tubes extending from dead coral areas [below right page].

ABUNDANCE & DISTRIBUTION: Common Caribbean, Bahamas; occasional to rare Florida.

HABITAT & BEHAVIOR: Inhabit coral reefs and drop-off walls. Bore into coral by secreting minute amounts of acid. From the exterior there is usually little or no visible damage; however, these sponges bore large, fist-sized holes in coral heads.

NOTE: Pictured specimens below were identified visually. Visual identification of pictured specimens opposite and below right were confirmed by microscopic examination of small collected samples.

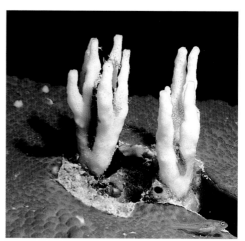

VISUAL ID: Small, white tube-like or vase-like structures. Occasionally have light pink, gold or green shading. May be solitary or grow in small clusters.

ABUNDANCE & DISTRIBUTION: Common Caribbean; rare Bahamas, Florida.

HABITAT & BEHAVIOR: Inhabit the ceilings of caves and deep-undercuts, especially along drop-off walls. Prefer areas protected from current and water motion.

**VARIABLE
BORING SPONGE**
*Siphonodictyon
coralliphagum*
CLASS:
Sponges
Demospongiae

SIZE: 2 - 4 in.
DEPTH: 30 - 130 ft.

**Variable
Boring Sponge**
Growth patterns.

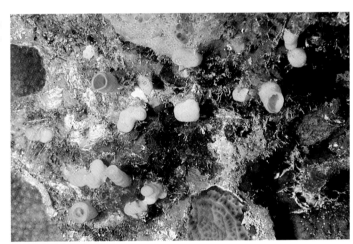

WHITE CRYPTIC SPONGE
Leucandra aspera
CLASS:
Calcareous Sponges
Calcarea

SIZE: 2 - 12 in.
DEPTH: 50 - 130 ft.

VISUAL ID: Bright yellow, small intertwined tubes. Soft and quite fragile.

ABUNDANCE & DISTRIBUTION: Occasional to rare Florida, Bahamas, Caribbean.

HABITAT & BEHAVIOR: Inhabit the ceilings of caves, deep-undercuts, and other dark protected recesses.

NOTE: Visual identification was confirmed by microscopic examination of small sample collected from pictured specimen.

VISUAL ID: White, small intertwined tubes. Skeletal network of calcareous spicules can be seen. Soft and quite fragile.

ABUNDANCE & DISTRIBUTION: Occasional to rare Florida, Bahamas, Caribbean.

HABITAT & BEHAVIOR: Inhabit the ceilings of caves, deep-undercuts, and other dark, protected recesses.

VISUAL ID: Tiny white ball with single excurrent opening and numerous needle-like spines protruding from surface. May have some algal growth and debris on spines.

ABUNDANCE & DISTRIBUTION: Common to rare Caribbean; rare Florida, Bahamas.

HABITAT & BEHAVIOR: Inhabit dark, protected areas of the reef, especially caves.

YELLOW CALCAREOUS SPONGE
Clathrina canariensis
CLASS:
Calcareous Sponges
Calcarea

SIZE: 2 - 4 in.
DEPTH: 25 - 75 ft.

WHITE CALCAREOUS SPONGE

CLASS:
Calcareous Sponges
Calcarea

SIZE: 2 - 4 in.
DEPTH: 25 - 75 ft.

SPINY BALL SPONGE
Leucetta barbata
CLASS:
Calcareous Sponges
Calcarea

SIZE: ¹/₂ - ³/₄ in.
DEPTH: 25 - 130 ft.

IDENTIFICATION GROUP 2
Phylum Cnidaria
(Nigh-DARE-ee-uh / L. a nettle)
Hydroids, Jellyfishes & Anemones

Most cnidarians are tiny individual animals that group together, by the thousands, to form colonies, such as, corals and hydroids. These colonies, that vary greatly in size and shape, attach to substrate or living organisms to form most of a coral reef's hard and soft structure. A few species, such as jellyfish and anemones, are not colonial and live as individuals in open water or attached to the substrate by hydrostatic pressure.

Animals in this phylum have a simple structure consisting of a cup-shaped body, a central, single opening that functions both as a **mouth** and **anus,** and a number of **tentacles** that encircle the mouth. When the animal is attached, it is called a **polyp;** if it is unattached and free-swimming, it is called a **medusa.** A unique characteristic shared by all cnidarians is numerous stinging capsules, called **nematocysts,** which is the origin of the phylum's Latin name. These minute capsules, located primarily on the tentacles, are used for both capturing prey and defense.

The stings of most cnidarians have no harmful effect on divers, but a few are quite toxic and should be avoided. In the event of a sting, never rub the affected area or wash with fresh water or soap. Both actions can cause additional nematocysts to discharge. Saturating the area with vinegar will immobilize unspent nematocysts; a sprinkling of meat tenderizer may help to alleviate the symptoms.

The phylum is divided into three classes that include hydroids, jellyfish, anemones and their relatives. Corals (fire, lace, soft, stony and black) and gorgonians are also classified in this phylum; however, they are identified in a separate volume.

HYDROIDS

CLASS: Hydrozoa (High-druh-ZO-uh / Gr. water animal)
ORDER: Hydroida (High-DROY-duh / Gr. water form)

Hydroids are usually colonial, and have a branched skeleton that generally grows in patterns resembling feathers or ferns. Individual polyps are attached to this structure. The arrangement of the **stalk, branches** and attached **polyps** is usually the key to visual identification. Most species are whitish or neutral shades, ranging from brown to gray or black and rarely display vibrant colors.

Most hydroids have a complex life cycle. The polyps in an adult colony are specialized for either feeding or reproduction. The reproductive polyps give rise to buds that form free-swimming medusae. This stage, often small in size and short-lived, is only occasionally observable by divers. When in these reproductive stages, called **hydromedusae,** they can be distinguished from similar-appearing "true" jellyfish by the margin of their **dome,** which turns inward, forming a "shelf" called a **velum. Radial canals** run from the **mouth** to the margin of the velum. The velum is absent in jellyfish. Varying numbers of **tentacles** with stinging nematocysts hang from the dome's margin. The hydromedusa is the dominant stage in a few species.

The stinging nematocysts of several hydroids are toxic enough to cause a painful burning sensation that may produce a visible rash, redness or even welts. Fire and lace corals are also members of this class, but classified in different orders.

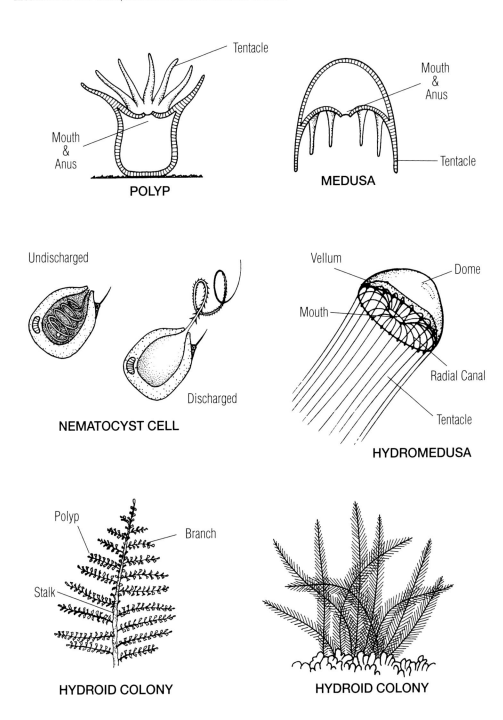

POLYP

MEDUSA

NEMATOCYST CELL

HYDROMEDUSA

HYDROID COLONY

HYDROID COLONY

SIPHONOPHORES

CLASS: Hydrozoa
ORDER: Siphonophora (Sigh-fawn-NOFF-or-uh / Gr. to have hollow tubes)

Siphonophores are a complex form of unattached hydroid colonies that float by means of a **gas-filled float.** Below the float hang numerous nematocyst-bearing **tentacles** that can be contracted close to the float, or relaxed to extend to great lengths. The best known example is the **Portuguese Man-Of-War,** which floats on the surface and moves by turning its float to the wind. These unique animals are capable of stinging a diver so severely that medical attention is required. Unlike the Portuguese Man-Of-War, most siphonophores float below the surface in open water, controlling their depth by regulating the gas content of the sack. They move about by pulsating modified medusae, called **swimming bells,** that are just below the gas float. Their sting is not a threat to divers, but can be felt for a short time.

TRUE JELLYFISHES

CLASS: Scyphozoa (Sky-fuh-ZO-uh / Gr. cup-shaped animal)

True jellyfish are translucent, unattached medusae that swim in open water. All have a **prominent dome** which varies in shape from a shallow saucer to a deep bell. Hanging from the margin of the dome are **nematocyst-bearing tentacles,** the number and length of which vary greatly from species to species. Occasionally the margin is scalloped, forming lobes called **lappets.** The mouth is at the end of a **feeding tube** that extends from the center of the dome's underside. In some species, **four frilly oral arms** hang to considerable length from the feeding tube. Both the feeding tube and oral arms carry stinging nematocysts. Many species are large, long-lived and quite colorful.

Jellyfish move through the water by pulsating contractions of the dome. Although only a few jellyfish are toxic, caution should be taken with all members of the class.

BOX JELLIES

CLASS: Scyphozoa
SUBCLASS: Cubomedusae (Cue-BO-muh-due-see / L. cube-shaped medusa)

Box jellies, also commonly called sea wasps, can be identified by their distinctive **cuboidal dome.** One or more nematocyst-bearing **tentacles** hang from each of the four corners of the open end of the cube. Additional tentacles are absent from the remaining margin. The sting of many box jellies can be severe, occasionally requiring medical attention. Many zoologists believe box jellies are only distantly related to scyphozoans and place them in their own class, the Cubozoa.

CLASS: Anthozoa (An-thuh-ZO-uh / L. flower-like animal)

The class Anthozoa contains many familiar marine invertebrates, including stony and soft corals, black corals and sea anemones. All have only the polyp stage in their life cycles. There are two major sub-classes: Octocorallia, **animals with eight tentacles,** which include sea fans, sea whips and soft corals (not included in this volume); and Hexacorallia, **animals with tentacles in multiples of six,** which include stony and black corals (also not included in this volume), sea anemones, zoanthids, corallimorphs and tube-dwelling anemones.

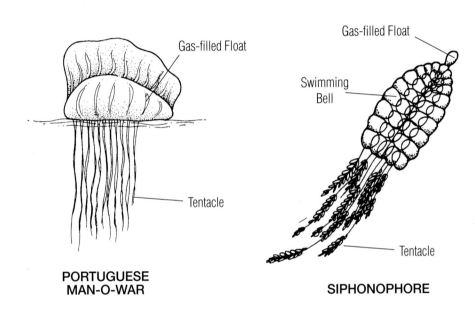

PORTUGUESE
MAN-O-WAR

SIPHONOPHORE

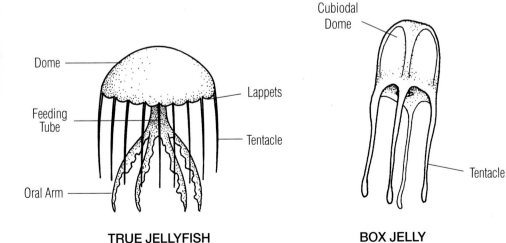

TRUE JELLYFISH

BOX JELLY

SEA ANEMONES

CLASS: Anthozoa
SUBCLASS: Hexacorallia (Hex-uh-core-AL-ee-uh / Gr. & L. six and coral animal)
ORDER: Actiniaria (Ack-TIN-ee-AIR-ee-uh / L. a ray)

Sea anemones are solitary polyps that attach to the bottom. They lack any hard skeletal parts and are generally quite large compared to the polyps of other cnidarians. Their bodies range from a few inches to over a foot across. The **tentacles,** which vary in length, shape, color and number, are often keys to identification. The pattern of tentacles often appears random, although some species exhibit distinct rings.

Stinging nematocysts on the tentacles rarely affect divers, but are toxic enough to paralyze small fish and invertebrates that stray into their reach. The immobilized prey is drawn by the tentacles into a **slit-like mouth** in the center of the **oral disc.** Living in association with many anemones are certain species of fish, shrimp and crab that are not affected by the nematocysts. Anemones rarely move, but can relocate in a slow, snail-like manner. They prefer secluded areas of the reef where they often lodge in crevices with only their tentacles exposed. If disturbed they can contract their tentacles for protection.

ZOANTHIDS

CLASS: Anthozoa, Subclass Hexacorallia
ORDER: Zoanthidea (Zo-an-THID-ee-uh / Gr. animal flower)

Zoanthids appear similar to anemones, but are considerably smaller, usually no larger than a half inch, and are generally colonial or live in close proximity to one another. The **oral disc** is without tentacles except for **two rings of tentacles** around the outer edge, which visually distinguish them from other anemone-like animals. Some species live in association with sponges, hydroids and other invertebrates.

CORALLIMORPHS

CLASS: Anthozoa, Subclass Hexacorallia
ORDER: Corallimorpharia (Core-AL-uh-more-FAIR-ee-uh / Gr. & L. coral-like)

Corallimorphs are easily confused with anemones. The best visual clue to the order's identity is the arrangement of the tentacles, which form two geometric patterns concurrently. **Tentacles radiate out** from the center of the **oral disc,** like spokes, and form **concentric circles** which progressively increase in diameter from the center. These patterns, however, are often obscure. The tentacles in most species are short and stubby, resembling nubs or warts. Generally, the oral disc is quite flat, and the **mouth protrudes** noticeably. They are occasionally called false corals because their polyps' structure is much like those of hard corals, except they secrete no calcareous skeleton. Corallimorphs may be solitary, but also live in close association, occasionally crowding together so closely that the individual polyps are difficult to distinguish from one another.

TUBE-DWELLING ANEMONES

CLASS: Anthozoa, Subclass Hexacorallia
ORDER: Ceriantharia (Sair-ee-an-THAIR-ee-uh / L. & Gr. wax flower)

These anemones live inside **tubes** buried in mud, sand or fine gravel. Their oral disc and crown of tentacles nearly always remain hidden during the day, only extending at night when the animals feed. They can be distinguished from other anemone-like animals by the arrangement of their tentacles. Several rings of long, **pointed outer tentacles** extend from the edge of the **oral disc**, and at the center is a **tuft of shorter tentacles** that often hide the mouth.

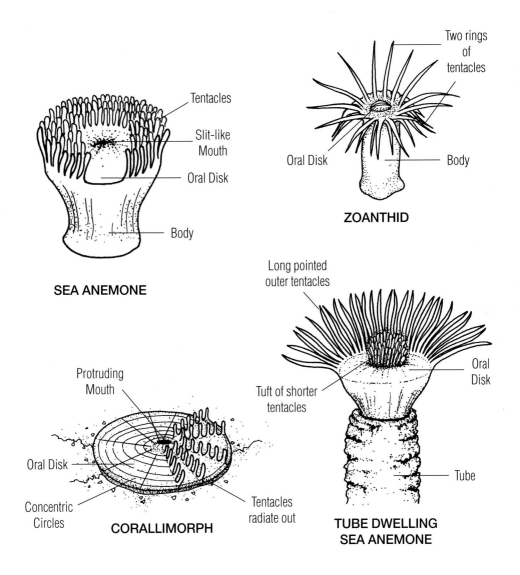

Tentacles

Slit-like Mouth

Oral Disk

Body

SEA ANEMONE

Two rings of tentacles

Oral Disk

Body

ZOANTHID

Protruding Mouth

Oral Disk

Concentric Circles

Tentacles radiate out

CORALLIMORPH

Long pointed outer tentacles

Oral Disk

Tuft of shorter tentacles

Tube

TUBE DWELLING SEA ANEMONE

VISUAL ID: Thin, tightly spaced, whitish branches extend alternately in a single plane from a brown central stalk. Tiny white polyps lining the branches are visible. Usually grow in clusters. Compare with similar Slender Feather Hydroid [next].

ABUNDANCE & DISTRIBUTION: Common to occasional Caribbean.

HABITAT & BEHAVIOR: Inhabit reef tops. Prefer clear water and some current.

EFFECT ON DIVERS: Toxic; sting bare skin.

VISUAL ID: Thin, tightly spaced branches extend alternately in a single plane from a dark central stalk. Compared to similar Feather Hydroid [previous], branches tend to be shorter, giving colony an overall thinner appearance. Usually grow in clusters.

ABUNDANCE & DISTRIBUTION: Common to occasional Southeast Florida, Bahamas, Caribbean.

HABITAT & BEHAVIOR: Inhabit reef tops. Prefer clear water and some current.

EFFECT ON DIVERS: Toxic; sting bare skin.

NOTE: Visual identification confirmed by microscopic examination of collected specimen matched with photograph.

VISUAL ID: Branches extend alternately on a single plane from stout, brownish central stalk. Obvious white polyps attached, alternately, to the top and bottom of branches. May grow solitary, but more commonly in clusters.

ABUNDANCE & DISTRIBUTION: Occasional Central to North Florida.

HABITAT & BEHAVIOR: Most commonly inhabit floats of pelagic Sargassum; also attach to hard bottom substrates.

EFFECT ON DIVERS: Slightly toxic; produce sting to sensitive skin.

FEATHER HYDROID
Gymnangium longicauda
ORDER:
Thecate Hydroids
Thecatae

SIZE: 3 1/2 - 5 1/2 in.,
12 in. max.
DEPTH: 25 - 100 ft.

SLENDER FEATHER HYDROID
Gymnangium speciosum
ORDER:
Thecate Hydroids
Thecatae

SIZE: 2 1/2 - 5 in.,
12 in. max.
DEPTH: 20 - 100 ft.

FEATHER PLUME HYDROID
Aglaophenia latecarinata
ORDER:
Thecate Hydroids
Thecatae

SIZE: 1 - 3 in.
DEPTH: 0 - 120 ft.

Hydroids

VISUAL ID: Branches extend alternately on a single plane from stout, brownish central stalk. Obvious white polyps attached, alternately, to the top and bottom of branches. Grow solitary or in small clusters.

ABUNDANCE & DISTRIBUTION: Common to occasional Florida, Bahamas, Caribbean.

HABITAT & BEHAVIOR: Inhabit all areas on reef, especially around recesses. Often on shipwrecks. Prefer areas with some water movement.

EFFECT ON DIVERS: Slightly toxic; produce sting to sensitive skin.

VISUAL ID: Branches extend alternately on a single plane from stout, brown central stalk. A single white, obvious polyp at tip of branches and stalk. Additional polyps grow along branches. Hair-like tentacles which extend from the polyp may be discernible. Usually grow in small clusters.

ABUNDANCE & DISTRIBUTION: Common to occasional Florida, Bahamas, Caribbean.

HABITAT & BEHAVIOR: Inhabit all areas on reef. Often found attached to dead gorgonians and hard corals, sponge colonies and shipwrecks. Prefer areas with current.

EFFECT ON DIVERS: Slightly toxic; produce sting to sensitive skin.

VISUAL ID: A few heavy branches on a stout central stalk support visible alternating polyps. Colony grows on a single plane. Generally grow in clumps, often partially covered with algae.

ABUNDANCE & DISTRIBUTION: Common to occasional Florida, Bahamas, Caribbean.

HABITAT & BEHAVIOR: Inhabit all areas of reef and, often, shipwrecks.

EFFECT ON DIVERS: Slightly toxic; may produce mild sting to sensitive skin.

BRANCHING HYDROID
Sertularella speciosa
ORDER:
Thecate Hydroids
Thecatae

SIZE: 3 - 5½ in.
DEPTH: 30 - 100 ft.

CHRISTMAS TREE HYDROID
Halocordyle disticha
ORDER:
Athecate Hydroids
Athecatae

SIZE: 1½ - 3½ in.
DEPTH: 10 - 60 ft.

ALGAE HYDROID
Thyroscyphus ramosus
ORDER:
Thecate Hydroids
Thecatae

SIZE: 2 - 5 in.
DEPTH: 5 - 130 ft.

Hydroids

VISUAL ID: Heavy, unbranched stalk supports visible alternating polyps. Generally grow in clusters, often partially covered with algae.

ABUNDANCE & DISTRIBUTION: Common to occasional Florida, Bahamas, Caribbean.

HABITAT & BEHAVIOR: Inhabit all areas of reef, especially dead gorgonians and hard corals. Often grow on shipwrecks.

EFFECT ON DIVERS: Slightly toxic; may produce mild sting to sensitive skin.

VISUAL ID: Robust, often curved, brown central stem supports short alternating white branches in a single plane; each branch ends with a terminal polyp. Grow in clumps.

ABUNDANCE & DISTRIBUTION: Common to occasional Florida, Bahamas, Caribbean; also north to North Carolina, Bermuda, and south to Brazil; circumtropical.

HABITAT & BEHAVIOR: Inhabit reefs and rock outcroppings.

REACTION TO DIVERS: Toxic; sting bare skin.

NOTE: Visual identification was confirmed by microscopic examination of collected specimen.

VISUAL ID: Heavy central stalk supports a few primary branches of similar size. Thin, tightly spaced, polyp-bearing secondary branches extend from stalk and primary branches. Tiny white polyps are barely visible. All branches are on same plane.

ABUNDANCE & DISTRIBUTION: Occasional Florida, Bahamas, Caribbean.

HABITAT & BEHAVIOR: Inhabit all areas on reef.

EFFECT ON DIVERS: Toxic; sting bare skin.

UNBRANCHED HYDROID
Cnidoscyphus marginatus
ORDER:
Thecate Hydroids
Thecatae

SIZE: 2¹/₂ - 3¹/₂ in.
DEPTH: 5 - 130 ft.

WHITE STINGER
Macrorhynchia philippia
ORDER:
Thecate Hydroids
Thecatae

SIZE: 1 - 4 in.,
max. 8 in.
DEPTH: 3 - 45 ft.

STINGING HYDROID
Macrorhynchia allmani
ORDER:
Thecate Hydroids
Thecatae

SIZE: 1¹/₂ - 3 in.
DEPTH: 30 - 100 ft.

VISUAL ID: Dark stalk with numerous primary branches and sub-branches, all lined with fine, tightly spaced, polyp-bearing secondary branches. Colonies usually grow in clusters.

ABUNDANCE & DISTRIBUTION: Occasional Southeast Florida, Bahamas, Caribbean.

HABITAT & BEHAVIOR: Inhabit all areas on and around reef.

EFFECT ON DIVERS: Toxic; sting bare skin.

NOTE: Visual identification confirmed by microscopic examination of collected specimen matched with photograph.

VISUAL ID: Long, thin central stalk lined with short, alternating, polyp-bearing side branches. Grow in clusters.

ABUNDANCE & DISTRIBUTION: Common to occasional Southeast Florida, Bahamas, Caribbean.

HABITAT & BEHAVIOR: Inhabit all areas on reef.

EFFECT ON DIVERS: Mildly toxic; sting sensitive bare skin.

NOTE: Visual identification confirmed by microscopic examination of collected specimen matched with photograph.

VISUAL ID: Bush-like colony of stout central stalks and numerous angular primary branches and sub-branches. Primary branches and sub-branches lined with fine, tightly spaced, polyp-bearing secondary branches. Colonies usually have Hydroid Zoanthids, *Parazoanthus tunicans,* [pg. 107] growing on their branches.

ABUNDANCE & DISTRIBUTION: Occasional to common Florida, Bahamas, Caribbean.

HABITAT & BEHAVIOR: Inhabit reef tops, outcroppings along walls and hard flat substrates, especially in areas with current. Grow with the plane of the colony perpendicular to the current.

EFFECT ON DIVERS: Toxic; sting bare skin.

NOTE: Visual identification confirmed by microscopic examination of collected specimen matched with photograph.

STINGING BUSH HYDROID
Macrorhynchia robusta
ORDER:
Thecate Hydroids
Thecatae

SIZE: 4 - 8 in.,
12 in. max.
DEPTH: 20 - 100 ft.

THREAD HYDROID
Halopteris carinata
ORDER:
Thecate Hydroids
Thecatae

SIZE: 2 - 4 in.,
6 in. max.
DEPTH: 20 - 100 ft.

FEATHER BUSH HYDROID
Dentitheca dendritica
ORDER:
Thecate Hydroids
Thecatae

SIZE: 8 - 12 in.
DEPTH: 30 - 130 ft.

VISUAL ID: Reddish to purple stalk is heavily branched and lined with thin, short, polyp-bearing, whitish branches, all on a single plane.

ABUNDANCE & DISTRIBUTION: Uncommon South Florida, Bahamas and Caribbean.

HABITAT & BEHAVIOR: Attach to rocky outcroppings in areas of surge or current. Prefer clear water.

EFFECT ON DIVERS: Slightly toxic; may produce mild sting to sensitive skin.

VISUAL ID: Large, white, solitary polyp with long, thin, translucent tentacles. Attach to tips of gorgonian branches, especially sea plumes, *Pseudopterogorgia* sp. Outstretched tentacles often curl at tip.

ABUNDANCE & DISTRIBUTION: Occasional to rare Caribbean, Bahamas.

HABITAT & BEHAVIOR: Inhabit reefs where sea plumes and other gorgonians grow. Several may grow from the same sea plume, but never more than one per branch tip. Outstretched tentacles curl if disturbed.

EFFECT ON DIVERS: Toxic; sting bare skin.

NOTE: Visual identification confirmed by microscopic examination of collected specimen matched with photograph.

VISUAL ID: Large, pinkish, solitary polyp with long, thin, translucent tentacles. Attach to sponges. Outstretched tentacles do not tend to curl at tips as similar species, Solitary Gorgonian Hydroid [previous].

ABUNDANCE & DISTRIBUTION: Occasional Florida, Bahamas, Caribbean.

HABITAT & BEHAVIOR: Inhabit reefs where sponges grow. Attach to a wide variety of sponge species, usually in clusters of several individuals. Outstretched tentacles curl if disturbed.

EFFECT ON DIVERS: Toxic; sting bare skin.

SEAFAN HYDROID
Solanderia gracilis
ORDER:
Athecate Hydroids
Athecate

SIZE: 6 - 18 in.
DEPTH: 15 - 80 ft.

SOLITARY GORGONIAN HYDROID
Ralpharia gorgoniae
ORDER:
Athecate Hydroids
Athecate

SIZE: ¹/₂ - 1 in.
DEPTH: 15 - 65 ft.

SOLITARY SPONGE HYDROID
Zyzzyzus warreni
ORDER:
Athecate Hydroids
Athecate

SIZE: ¹/₂ - 1 in.
DEPTH: 20 - 100 ft.

VISUAL ID: Transparent hemispherical dome. Distinctive club-shaped organ at the base of each tentacle where it attaches to margin of bell. Few radial canals are visible on velum.

ABUNDANCE & DISTRIBUTION: Occasional Florida, Bahamas, Caribbean.

HABITAT & BEHAVIOR: Float near surface of open water, often in large aggregations.

EFFECT ON DIVERS: Slightly toxic; may produce mild sting to sensitive skin.

NOTE: The hydromedusae stage is the dominant life phase of this species.

VISUAL ID: Translucent hemispherical dome of thick jelly, with numerous long tentacles attached to margin of bell. Numerous radial canals are visible on velum.

ABUNDANCE & DISTRIBUTION: Occasional to uncommon Florida, Bahamas, Caribbean.

HABITAT & BEHAVIOR: Float near surface of open water.

EFFECT ON DIVERS: Slightly toxic; may produce mild sting to sensitive skin.

NOTE: The hydromedusae stage is the dominant life phase of this species.

VISUAL ID: Small, transparent cone-shaped dome trailing two long tentacles. Brown mass below dome is an extended mouth surrounded by gonads.

ABUNDANCE & DISTRIBUTION: Uncommon Florida, Bahamas, Caribbean; also circumtropical.

HABITAT & BEHAVIOR: Considered pelagic; occasionally float over or near reefs. This species trails two long tentacles to capture prey: primarily other medusae, especially jellyfishes.

REACTION TO DIVERS: Slightly toxic, may produce mild sting.

NOTE: The hydromedusae stage is the dominant life phase of this species.

CLUB HYDROMEDUSA
Orchistoma pileus
ORDER:
Hydromedusae
Leptothecatae
FAMILY:
Orchistomatidae

SIZE: 1 in.
DEPTH: 0 - 15 feet.

JELLY HYDROMEDUSA
Aequorea aequorea
ORDER:
Hydromedusae
Leptothecatae
FAMILY:
Aequoreidae

SIZE: 1½ - 4 in.
DEPTH: 0 - 20 ft.

TWO-TENTACLE HYDROMEDUSA
Stomotoca pterophylla
ORDER:
Hydromedusae
Anthomedusae
FAMILY:
Pandeidae

SIZE: Dome ¾ - 2 in.
DEPTH: Near surface

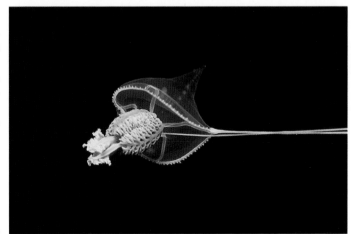

VISUAL ID: Pink to purple, translucent, gas-filled float with numerous long, thin, retractable tentacles.

ABUNDANCE & DISTRIBUTION: Occasional Florida, Bahamas, Caribbean.

HABITAT & BEHAVIOR: Float on surface, propelled by wind. Large individuals are often accompanied by a school of small, banded Man-of-War Fish, *Nomeus gronovii.*

EFFECT ON DIVERS: Highly toxic; contact with tentacles will produce intense sting causing redness, welting and blistering. Numerous stings may require medical attention. Beware, tentacles often extend far behind or below float. If washed ashore, they remain toxic for some time.

VISUAL ID: Small, bubble-like float above stem bears numerous, highly contractile tentacles. When contracted [pictured], colony is only one or two inches in length. Relaxed tentacles may reach 30 feet. Transparent to translucent. Do not have swimming bells below float.

ABUNDANCE & DISTRIBUTION: Occasional Caribbean.

HABITAT & BEHAVIOR: Float in open water. Control depth by amount of carbon monoxide gas secreted into float.

EFFECT ON DIVERS: Toxic; contact with tentacles will produce an intense, but short-lived, sting. May cause minor redness and welts.

NOTE: There are two species, *R. filiformis* which is greenish, and *R. eysenhardti* which is pale pink. In young individuals [pictured], this coloration is not always obvious.

VISUAL ID: Below a tiny gas float is a series of paired swimming bells that range from less than one to several inches in length. Below the bells is a rigid structure (siphosome) that appears to be constructed of angular brackets. Numerous tentacles may extend below, often in a spiral pattern that can reach 12 inches in length. Transparent to translucent.

ABUNDANCE & DISTRIBUTION: Occasional South Florida, Bahamas, Caribbean.

HABITAT & BEHAVIOR: Float in open water. When feeding they extend (relax) their tentacles in a wide spiral pattern by rotating in the water.

EFFECT ON DIVERS: Toxic; contact with tentacles will produce an intense, but short-lived, sting. May cause minor redness and welts.

NOTE: Species identification can be confirmed by noting the dot-like attachments to the tentacles, called tentilla. When relaxed, two long, lateral projecting parts are visible. In the pictured specimen, they are apparent only from the fourth tentilla down.

PORTUGUESE MAN-OF-WAR
Physalia physalis
ORDER:
Siphonophores
Siphonophora
SUBORDER:
Cystonectae

SIZE: Float 2 - 6 in.
Tentacles 10 - 30 ft.
DEPTH: Float on surface.

FLOATING SIPHONOPHORE
Rhizophysa spp.
ORDER:
Siphonophores
Siphonophora
SUBORDER:
Cystonectae

SIZE: See ID
DEPTH: 0 - 130 ft.

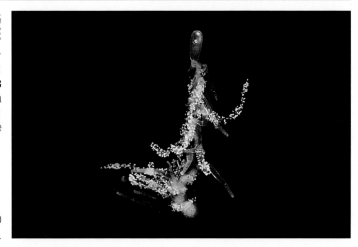

PAIRED-BELL SIPHONOPHORE
Agalma okeni
ORDER:
Siphonophores
Siphonophora
SUBORDER:
Physonectae
FAMILY:
Agalmidae

SIZE: See ID
DEPTH: 0 - 130 ft.

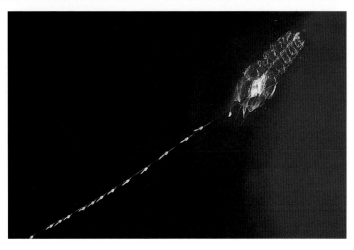

VISUAL ID: Beneath a tiny gas float numerous swimming bells,s ranging from less than one to several inches in length, stick out in all directions. Beneath, attached to a stem, are numerous dot-like appendages, called palpons, that contain a red pigment. Also attached to the stem are numerous tentacles which, when relaxed, can reach several inches in length. Transparent to translucent.

ABUNDANCE & DISTRIBUTION: Occasional South Florida, Bahamas, Caribbean.

HABITAT & BEHAVIOR: Float in open water. Extend (relax) long tentacles to ensnare prey.

EFFECT ON DIVERS: Toxic; contact with tentacles will produce an intense, but short-lived, sting. May cause minor redness and welt.

NOTE: Species identification confirmed by being the only member of the family found within safe scuba diving depths.

VISUAL ID: Surface of dome has nematocyst-bearing warts. Eight highly contractile marginal tentacles and four long, frilly oral arms. Translucent, often pinkish with pink warts and tentacles, occasionally purple, yellow or brown. Luminescent at night.

ABUNDANCE & DISTRIBUTION: Occasional circumtropical.

HABITAT & BEHAVIOR: Inhabit surface oceanic waters, occasionally float over reefs.

EFFECT ON DIVERS: Toxic; contact with bare skin can produce an intense sting. May cause redness and welts.

VISUAL ID: Blue to blue-green with white spots. Thick dome, finely grained surface. Oral arms have long, club-like appendages and filaments hanging from them. No marginal tentacles.

ABUNDANCE & DISTRIBUTION: Occasional Caribbean.

HABITAT & BEHAVIOR: Inhabit surface waters, often in harbors and bays, occasionally over reefs.

EFFECT ON DIVERS: Mildly toxic; contact with bare skin can produce sting. May cause redness and welts.

RED-SPOTTED SIPHONOPHORE
Forskalia edwardsi

ORDER:
Siphonophores
Siphonophora
SUBORDER:
Physonectae
FAMILY:
Forskaliidae

SIZE: See ID
DEPTH: 0 - 130 ft.

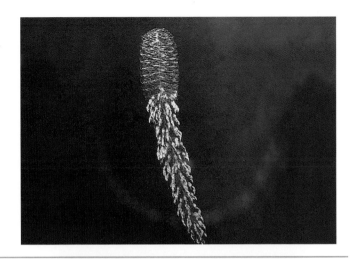

WARTY JELLYFISH
Pelagia noctiluca

CLASS:
Jellyfishes
Scyphozoa

SIZE: ³/₄ - 1¹/₄ in.,
4 in. max.
DEPTH: 0 - 10 ft.

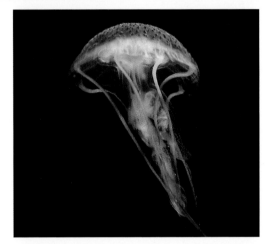

BLUE-TINTED JELLYFISH
Phyllorhiza punctata

CLASS:
Jellyfishes
Scyphozoa

SIZE: 6 - 8 in.,
20 in. max.
DEPTH: 0 - 15 ft.

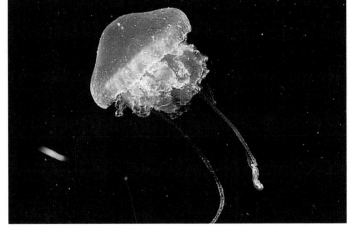

VISUAL ID: Saucer-shaped dome with numerous short, fringe-like tentacles around margin. Four-leaf-clover-shaped reproductive organs can be seen through translucent dome. Four frilly oral arms (not always obvious). Whitish, often shaded with pink or blue.

ABUNDANCE & DISTRIBUTION: Common Florida, Bahamas, Caribbean. Worldwide distribution. Can be abundant during brief periods of the year.

HABITAT & BEHAVIOR: Inhabit surface waters, often over reefs.

EFFECT ON DIVERS: Mildly toxic; can sting bare sensitive skin and cause slight itchy rash.

VISUAL ID: Bulb-shaped dome with short, forked oral arms around stout protruding feeding tube. No marginal tentacles. Milky, often with tints of blue or yellow, markings around margin of dome usually brown or white, can be yellow or lavender.

ABUNDANCE & DISTRIBUTION: Occasional Florida, Caribbean. Not reported Bahamas. Can be abundant at times.

HABITAT & BEHAVIOR: Inhabit surface waters near shore, often in harbors and bays, occasionally over reefs.

EFFECT ON DIVERS: None.

VISUAL ID: Marbled markings on white dome, with lappets around margin. Grape-like clustered oral arms, may equal in length the diameter of bell. Numerous filaments extend from arms.

ABUNDANCE & DISTRIBUTION: Rare Caribbean.

HABITAT & BEHAVIOR: Inhabit surface waters, occasionally over reefs.

EFFECT ON DIVERS: Toxic; contact with bare skin can produce an intense sting. May cause redness and welts.

NOTE: The pictured specimen may be *L. lucerna* which is found in the waters off Brazil or it may be an undescribed species. Laboratory examination of specimen required for positive identification.

MOON JELLY
Aurelia aurita
CLASS:
Jellyfishes
Scyphozoa

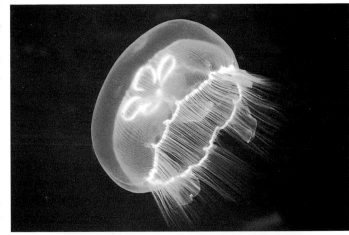

SIZE: 6 - 8 in.,
16 in. max.
DEPTH: 0 - 20 ft.

CANNONBALL JELLY
Stomolophus meleagris
CLASS:
Jellyfishes
Scyphozoa

SIZE: 4 - 6 in.,
7¼ in. max.
DEPTH: 0 - 20 ft.

MARBLED JELLY
Lychnorhiza sp.
CLASS:
Jellyfishes
Scyphozoa

SIZE: 4 - 6 in.
DEPTH: 0 - 15 ft.

VISUAL ID: Smooth, saucer-shaped dome with lappets around margin. Numerous tentacles, and four large, cauliflower-like liplobes around feeding snout. Usually lavender to purple (color of pictured specimen uncommon). Caribbean's largest jellyfish.

ABUNDANCE & DISTRIBUTION: Uncommon South Florida, Bahamas, Caribbean. Its appearance is sporadic and at times can be locally abundant.

HABITAT & BEHAVIOR: Inhabit surface waters. Juvenile pelagic fish often live within the protection of the tentacles. Feed on Moon Jellies, *Aurelia aurita,* [pg. 85]

EFFECT ON DIVERS: Highly toxic; contact with bare skin can produce an intense sting, redness, welts and blistering. Pour vinegar on affected area. Severe stings may cause muscle cramps and breathing difficulty, treat for shock and seek medical attention.

VISUAL ID: White to whitish translucent with numerous small warts on dome and four ruffled oral arms; 24, and occasionally up to 40, long tentacles attach to the dome's scalloped margin. Dome occasionally marked with 16 radiating bands of color.

ABUNDANCE & DISTRIBUTION: Rare to seasonally abundant Florida and Gulf of Mexico; also north to Cape Cod.

HABITAT & BEHAVIOR: Typically near surface drifting in bays, lagoons and estuaries, but occasionally in open water.

REACTION TO DIVERS: Mildly toxic; contact with bare skin may result in a mild itchy irritation, but a few individuals may suffer a severe reaction.

NOTE: Species identification is tentative because members of the genus inhabiting the Atlantic need further taxonomic study.

VISUAL ID: Brown, thimble-shaped dome. A few short tentacles around margin of dome.

ABUNDANCE & DISTRIBUTION: Occasional circumtropical.

HABITAT & BEHAVIOR: Inhabit surface waters; usually appear in swarms in springtime.

EFFECT ON DIVERS: Mildly toxic; contact with sensitive skin may produce a mild sting and redness. Blooms of this small jellyfish can blanket the upper layer of the water column during late spring. The Sea Thimble larvae, which seems to accompany swarm of adults, can cause a severe week-long rash to sensitive skin.

STINGING CAULIFLOWER
Drymonema dalmatinum
CLASS:
Jellyfishes
Scyphozoa

SIZE: 1 - 2½ ft.,
3 ft. max.
DEPTH: 0 - 20 ft.

SEA NETTLE
Chrysaora quinquecirrha
CLASS:
Jellyfishes
Scyphozoa

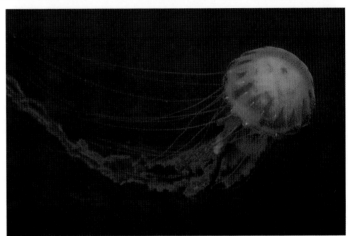

SIZE: Dome 4 - 10 in.wide;
Oral Arms 2 - 3½ ft.
DEPTH: Surface - 80 ft.

SEA THIMBLE
Linuche unguiculata
CLASS:
Jellyfishes
Scyphozoa

SIZE: ½ - ¾ in.
DEPTH: 0 - 10 ft.

VISUAL ID: Flattened, disc-like bell with grape-like clustered, branched oral arms. Small leaf-shaped or paddle-like appendages on oral arms. Arms about three quarters the length of dome radius. Usually yellowish brown with white markings. No marginal tentacles.

ABUNDANCE & DISTRIBUTION: Common Florida, Bahamas, Caribbean. May be locally abundant.

HABITAT & BEHAVIOR: Inhabit shallow sand flats in back reef areas and lagoons. Occasionally washed over nearby reefs. Rest on bottom with oral arms oriented upward to speed growth of symbiotic single-celled algae, called zoozanthellae, that grow in their tissues. Receive part of their nourishment from the zoozanthellae.

EFFECT ON DIVERS: Mildly toxic; contact with bare skin can produce sting. May cause redness and welt.

VISUAL ID: Flattened, disc-like dome with grape-like clustered, branched oral arms. Long leaf-shaped or ribbon-like appendages on oral arms. Arms about one half times length of dome radius. May be gray, purplish, greenish or yellow-brown with white markings. No marginal tentacles.

ABUNDANCE & DISTRIBUTION: Common Florida, Bahamas, Caribbean. May be abundant locally.

HABITAT & BEHAVIOR: Inhabit shallow mangrove bays and lagoons with mud and sand bottoms. Occasionally tidally washed over nearby reefs. Rest on bottom with oral arms oriented upward to speed growth of symbiotic single-celled algae, called zoozanthellae, that grow in their tissues. Receive part of their nourishment from the zoozanthellae.

EFFECT ON DIVERS: Mildly toxic; contact with bare skin can produce sting. May cause redness and welt.

VISUAL ID: Tall, translucent, rectangular-shaped dome with a tentacle hanging from each of the four corners of the dome at oral end. May have reddish or bluish tints.

ABUNDANCE & DISTRIBUTION: Occasional Florida, Bahamas, Caribbean.

HABITAT & BEHAVIOR: Inhabit shallow water at night, often over reefs. Attracted to light at night, often swarm.

EFFECT ON DIVERS: Highly toxic; contact with bare skin can produce an intense sting, redness and welts. Pour vinegar on affected area. Severe stings may cause muscle cramps and breathing difficulty, treat for shock and seek medical attention.

SIMILAR SPECIES: Warty Sea Wasp, *C. marsupialis,* smaller with shorter dome, covered with numerous nematocyst-bearing warts. Also attracted to light at night and highly toxic.

UPSIDEDOWN JELLY
Cassiopea frondosa
CLASS:
Jellyfishes
Scyphozoa

SIZE: 4 - 5 in.,
10 1/2 in. max.
DEPTH: 1 - 25 ft.

MANGROVE UPSIDEDOWN JELLY
Cassiopea xamachana
CLASS:
Jellyfishes
Scyphozoa

SIZE: 6 - 7 in.,
12 in. max.
DEPTH: 1 - 15 ft.

SEA WASP
Carybdea alata
CLASS:
Jellyfishes
Scyphozoa
ORDER:
Box Jellyfishes
Cubomedusae

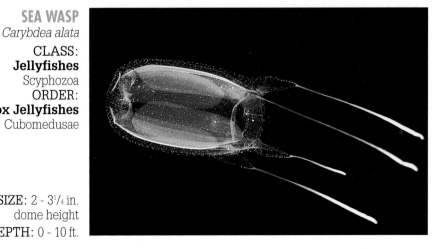

SIZE: 2 - 3 1/4 in.
dome height
DEPTH: 0 - 10 ft.

VISUAL ID: Largest of Caribbean anemones. Tentacles and body white, often with tints of gray, brown, yellow or green. Tentacles are long with slightly enlarged tips that may be pink, lavender, yellow, chartreuse or, occasionally, white.

ABUNDANCE & DISTRIBUTION: Common South Florida, Bahamas, Caribbean.

HABITAT & BEHAVIOR: Inhabit reef and lagoonal areas. Bodies are usually partially or completely hidden from view, in recesses. Tentacles are normally extended, but retract if disturbed. Diamond Blenny, *Malacoctenus boehlkei*, Pederson Cleaner Shrimp, *Periclimenes pedersoni*, [pg. 177], Spotted Cleaner Shrimp, *P. yucatanicus*, [pg. 177], Squat Anemone Shrimp, *Thor amboinensis*, [pg. 173], and Banded Clinging Crab, *Mitrax cinctimanus*, [pg. 221] are known to associate with this anemone.

EFFECT ON DIVERS: Not considered toxic, but may produce mild irritation to sensitive skin.

VISUAL ID: Hundreds of short, thick tentacles with rounded tips cover flattened oral disc. Tentacles and oral disc are green to brown.

ABUNDANCE & DISTRIBUTION: Common to occasional Bahamas, eastern and southern Caribbean; rare northwestern Caribbean.

HABITAT & BEHAVIOR: Inhabit shallow back reefs. Dense clusters may carpet an area. The following are known to associate with this anemone: Sun Anemone Shrimp, *Periclimenes rathbunae*, [pg. 177], Squat Anemone Shrimp, *Thor amboinensis*, [pg. 173] and Banded Clinging Crab, *Mithrax cinctimanus*, [pg. 221].

EFFECT ON DIVERS: Toxic; will sting bare skin and occasionally produce blistering.

GIANT ANEMONE
Condylactis gigantea
ORDER:
Anemones
Actiniaria

SIZE: 6 - 12 in. across
tentacles & body
DEPTH: 15 - 100 ft.

Giant Anemone
Color variations.

SUN ANEMONE
Stichodactyla helianthus
ORDER:
Anemones
Actiniaria

SIZE: Disc 4 - 6 in.
DEPTH: 3 - 30 ft.

VISUAL ID: Numerous knob-like tentacles cover flat oral disc. Tentacles and oral disc are light to dark gray and brown.

ABUNDANCE & DISTRIBUTION: Uncommon to rare from Jamaica to the Leeward and Windward Islands to Curacao.

HABITAT & BEHAVIOR: Inhabit areas of sand and coral rubble; occasionally reefs. The following are known to associate with this anemone: Spotted Cleaner Shrimp, *Periclimenes yucatanicus,* [pg. 177], Squat Anemone Shrimp, *Thor amboinensis,* [pg. 173] and Banded Clinging Crab, *Mithrax cinctimanus,* [pg. 221].

EFFECT ON DIVERS: Not considered toxic.

VISUAL ID: Numerous long, thin, pointed tentacles are translucent and marked with whitish "corkscrew-like" markings. Tentacles and body shades of gray, brown or green.

ABUNDANCE & DISTRIBUTION: Common Florida, Bahamas, Caribbean.

HABITAT & BEHAVIOR: Inhabit reefs and areas of sand and coral rubble. Bodies usually hidden from view in small recesses, frequently in openings of dead conch shells. If disturbed, will rapidly retract tentacles, often completely from view. Red Snapping Shrimp, *Alpeus armatus* [pg. 187] and Pederson Cleaning Shrimp, *Periclimenes pedersoni,* [pg. 177] are known to associate with this anemone.

EFFECT ON DIVERS: Mildly toxic; will sting sensitive skin.

VISUAL ID: Numerous nematocyst-bearing knobs on long, thin, pointed, translucent tentacles. Tentacles and body shades of gray to brown or green.

ABUNDANCE & DISTRIBUTION: Common Florida, Bahamas, Caribbean.

HABITAT & BEHAVIOR: Inhabit reefs and areas of sand and coral rubble, prefer clear water fore reefs. Bodies usually hidden in recesses. If disturbed, will rapidly retract tentacles, often completely from view.

EFFECT ON DIVERS: Toxic; will sting bare skin.

*NOTE: Formerly, inappropriately classified in the genus *Heteractis.* At printing, a proper genus has yet to be described.

ELEGANT ANEMONE
Actinoporus elegans
ORDER:
Anemones
Actiniaria

SIZE: Disc 7 - 9 in.
DEPTH: 10 - 60 ft.

CORKSCREW ANEMONE
Bartholomea annulata
ORDER:
Anemones
Actiniaria

SIZE: 4 - 7 in. across
exposed tentacles
DEPTH: 5 - 130 ft.

KNOBBY ANEMONE
* lucida
ORDER:
Anemones
Actiniaria

SIZE: Tentacles 3 - 4 in.
2¹/₂ - 4¹/₂ in. across
exposed tentacles
DEPTH: 5 - 100 ft.

VISUAL ID: Relatively large anemone with more than 200 short tentacles in several indistinct rows ring outer edge of oral disc. Tentacles often have several swollen tips and may be marked with stripes or rings. Lines and rows of bead-like warts radiate from slit mouth to tentacles. Colors and patterns highly variable.

ABUNDANCE & DISTRIBUTION: Occasional Bahamas, Caribbean.

HABITAT & BEHAVIOR: Inhabit shallow, back reef areas of sand and rocky rubble. Only oral disc visible above substrate, column buried in sand or cracks between rocky debris. Oral disc quickly retracts beneath surface if disturbed.

EFFECT ON DIVERS: Not considered toxic.

NOTE: This species was formerly classified in the genus *Phymanthus*.

VISUAL ID: Long, thin, pointed, transparent tentacles encircle brownish to bluish white oral disc. Often in groups, but may be solitary.

ABUNDANCE & DISTRIBUTION: Common to occasional Florida, Bahamas, Caribbean.

HABITAT & BEHAVIOR: Inhabit reefs, wrecks and rocky areas. Often attach to exposed surfaces, such as sides of wrecks.

EFFECT ON DIVERS: Not considered toxic.

NOTE: In Florida, has been reported by a junior name, *A. pallida*.

BEADED ANEMONE
Epicystis crucifer
ORDER:
Anemones
Actiniaria

SIZE: Disc 3 - 6 in.
DEPTH: 10 - 30 ft.

PALE ANEMONE
Aiptasia tagetes
ORDER:
Anemones
Actiniaria

SIZE: Disc 1 - 2 in.
DEPTH: 5 - 60 ft.

VISUAL ID: Tentacles with enlarged, "club-like" tips ring the protruding central oral opening. Tentacles and oral disc whitish, brown or lavender, often mottled and marked with flecks and splotches. Body column large and barrel-shaped, diameter about equal to that of oral disc.

ABUNDANCE & DISTRIBUTION: Common to occasional central, eastern and southern Caribbean; rare northwestern Caribbean, Bahamas. Not reported Florida.

HABITAT & BEHAVIOR: Inhabit caves and other dark recesses. Extend oral discs from under rocks and other protected areas. Bodies usually hidden, but occasionally exposed, especially in protected recesses.

EFFECT ON DIVERS: Not considered toxic.

VISUAL ID: Long pseudotentacles with slightly enlarged tips extend from fissure. Brown to dark gray to bluish green with shaded line and ring markings. Pseudotentacles tips are slightly enlarged, often darker and occasionally double lobed.

ABUNDANCE & DISTRIBUTION: Occasional Bahamas, Caribbean; rare South Florida.

HABITAT & BEHAVIOR: Inhabit narrow fissures in coral heads, with only the ends of pseudotentacles extended from openings. If disturbed, will retract pseudotentacles, often completely from view. Long, unbranched, true tentacles may be extended at night.

EFFECT ON DIVERS: Toxic; will sting bare skin.

VISUAL ID: Stubby, branching pseudotentacles have prominent, nematocyst-bearing knobs. Usually shades of brown to dark gray with lighter colored markings, occasionally in shades of blue-green.

ABUNDANCE & DISTRIBUTION: Common Florida, Bahamas, Caribbean.

HABITAT & BEHAVIOR: Inhabit reefs. Bodies hidden from view in recesses, and concealed by the branch-work bed of pseudotentacles. If disturbed, will rapidly retract pseudotentacles, often completely from view. Long, unbranched, true tentacles are only extended at night.

EFFECT ON DIVERS: Toxic; will sting bare skin.

CLUB-TIPPED ANEMONE
Telmatactis americana
ORDER:
Anemones
Actiniaria

SIZE: Disc 1 - 4 in.
DEPTH: 5 - 40 ft.

HIDDEN ANEMONE
Lebrunia coralligens
ORDER:
Anemones
Actiniaria

SIZE: 1¹/₂ - 2¹/₂ in.
tentacle spread
DEPTH: 3 - 40 ft.

BRANCHING ANEMONE
Lebrunia danae
ORDER:
Anemones
Actiniaria

SIZE: 3 - 10 in. across
exposed pseudotentacles
DEPTH: 5 - 130 ft.

Anemones

VISUAL ID: Whitish, translucent to transparent tentacles and body.
ABUNDANCE & DISTRIBUTION: Common to occasional Florida, Bahamas, Caribbean.
HABITAT & BEHAVIOR: Attach to blades of turtle grass.
EFFECT ON DIVERS: Highly toxic; will sting bare skin and occasionally produce blistering.
NOTE: Scientific name may be junior to and synonymous with *Bunodeopsis antilliensis*.

VISUAL ID: Shape of tentacles is distinctive; ends are enlarged and bulbous, and tipped with a thin, elongated, curling point. Transparent to translucent tentacles and body. Marked, ringed and banded in shades of green, tan and white.
ABUNDANCE & DISTRIBUTION: Common northern Gulf Coast of Florida.
HABITAT & BEHAVIOR: Inhabit reefs, wrecks and rocky areas.
EFFECT ON DIVERS: Not toxic.
NOTE: Although this anemone is relatively common, its living appearance has not been matched with a scientific identification. Collection of a photographed specimen and microscopic examination is necessary to establish visual identification. Possibly an undescribed species. Unfortunately, at the time of writing there are no taxonomists working with Caribbean anemones.

VISUAL ID: Short conical tentacles olive green, often with whitish patches and pink to purplish shading on the oral side. Reddish brown to brick red muscular column is covered with closely set vertical rows of bead-like warts. Oral disc red to reddish brown with fine lines radiating from mouth to the multiple rows of tentacles ringing outer edge.
ABUNDANCE & DISTRIBUTION: Occasional from North Carolina to Caribbean, including Bahamas and Gulf of Mexico.
HABITAT & BEHAVIOR: Inhabit shallow areas of sand, rocks and rubble where they attach to rocky substrate. Typically partially open during the day (pictured) and completely expanded at night. When tightly closed appears as a warty lump.
EFFECT ON DIVERS: Not considered toxic.
SIMILAR SPECIES: Warty Sea Anemone, *B. cavernatum*, is slightly smaller; columns range from olive green to muddy brown with multiple vertical rows of warts forming wide, often differently shaded stripes; tentacles blotched or banded.

TURTLE GRASS ANEMONE
Viatrix globulifera
ORDER:
Anemones
Actiniaria

SIZE: Disc ¼ - ¾ in.
DEPTH: 1 - 20 ft.

LIGHT BULB ANEMONE
Unidentified
ORDER:
Anemones
Actiniaria

SIZE: Disc 2 - 3 in.
DEPTH: 30 - 130 ft.

RED WARTY ANEMONE
Bunodosoma granulifera
ORDER:
Anemones
Actiniaria

SIZE: Disc 1½ - 3¼ in.
Column 2 - 5 in.
DEPTH: 0 - 30 ft.

VISUAL ID: Tan to brown, reddish brown, dark orange, red, purple or olive. Muscular column smooth when fully extended, has ring or rings of small dark spots just above point of attachment. Oral disc and rings of approximately 500 slender tentacles are often covered with white speckles.

ABUNDANCE & DISTRIBUTION: Occasional Florida, Bahamas, Caribbean.

HABITAT & BEHAVIOR: Commonly attach to shells inhabited by hermit crabs, but occasionally to the shells of large crabs, especially decorator crabs (see picture pg. 229), and occasionally to the shells of living mollusk. The anemones probably gain a feeding advantage by attaching to mobile crabs, which receive protection from the anemones' stinging nematocysts. When disturbed anemone extrudes bright orange to white threads loaded with stinging nematocysts through column pores.

VISUAL ID: Sunburst design on oral disc radiates from red slit mouth to base of tentacle rings around outer edge. Colors of design pattern variable including shades of tan, brown, orange and red.

ABUNDANCE & DISTRIBUTION: Photographed Los Frailes Islets Venezuela where the species occurs occasionally; range has yet to be established.

HABITAT & BEHAVIOR: Nestle in small cracks and recesses of reefs.

NOTE: Although this anemone is not uncommon, its living appearance has not been matched with a scientific description. Collection of a photographed specimen and microscopic examination of anatomical detail is required to establish visual identification. Possibly an undescribed species. Regrettably, at the time of this writing, no taxonomic biologists are working with this order in the tropical western Atlantic.

VISUAL ID: Pale to translucent tentacles with pale olive to white oral disc.

ABUNDANCE & DISTRIBUTION: Occasional Florida, Bahamas, Caribbean.

HABITAT & BEHAVIOR: Commonly grow in clumps of several to numerous individuals. May nestle in small cracks and recesses of reefs or attach to sponges or gorgonians.

NOTE: Species in the genus *Aiptasia* have the characteristics described above. Whether these commonly observed anemones represent one or more species from a single genus or multiple genera has not been determined. Collection of photographed specimens and microscopic examination of anatomical details are necessary to establish visual identification. Possibly an undescribed species. Regrettably, at the time of this writing, no taxonomic biologists are working with this order in the tropical western Atlantic.

HITCHHIKING ANEMONE
Calliactis tricolor
ORDER:
Anemones
Actiniaria

SIZE: Disc 1½ - 2¾ in.
Column 1 - 3 in.
DEPTH: 0 - 100 ft.

SUNBURST ANEMONE
Unidentified
ORDER:
Anemones
Actiniaria

SIZE: Disc 1 - 2 in.
DEPTH: 15 - 40 ft.

PALE CLUMPING ANEMONE
Aiptasia sp.
ORDER:
Anemones
Actiniaria

SIZE: Disc ½ - 1 in.
DEPTH: 10 - 100 ft.

VISUAL ID: Transparent to translucent brownish tentacles marked with white bands and speckles. Oral disc brownish translucent with white speckles; occasionally has white center around oral opening.

ABUNDANCE & DISTRIBUTION: Common Caribbean.

HABITAT & BEHAVIOR: Associate with sponges. Grow from folds and depressions in surface, and around bases.

NOTE: Although this anemone is relatively common, its living appearance has not been matched with a scientific identification. Collection of a photographed specimen and microscopic examination is necessary to establish visual identification. Possibly an undescribed species. Unfortunately, at the time of writing there are no taxonomists working with Caribbean anemones.

VISUAL ID: Large, tightly packed, knob-like outgrowths cover the body column. When contracted, usually during day, overall appearance resembles a head of cauliflower. When expanded, usually only at night, translucent tentacles protrude from upper part of body column and knob-like outgrowths appear as berry clusters on a tree trunk. Whitish gray areas on outgrowths are concentrations of defensive stinging nematocysts.

ABUNDANCE & DISTRIBUTION: Rare Florida, Bahamas, Caribbean.

HABITAT & BEHAVIOR: Inhabit sand, rocky outcroppings, mooring ropes, shipwrecks and reefs.

EFFECT ON DIVERS: Toxic; will sting bare skin.

Berried Anemone
Remain closed, in a mass about the size of a fist, during the day.

SPONGE ANEMONE
Unidentified
ORDER:
Anemones
Actinaria

SIZE: Disc ³/₄ - 1¹/₄ in.
DEPTH: 25 - 130 ft.

BERRIED ANEMONE
Alicia mirabilis
ORDER:
Anemones
Actiniaria

SIZE: 2 - 4 in. diameter
of closed body;
extended body
8 - 14 in.
DEPTH: 20 - 130 ft.

Berried Anemone
*Beginnging to open
at sunset.*

Zoanthids

VISUAL ID: Tapering tentacles with blunt tips numbering to 28 are brown, yellow-brown, light greenish brown or greenish yellow; oral disc somewhat darker. Body white to grayish white. Large communities inhabit surfaces of a wide variety of sponges.

ABUNDANCE & DISTRIBUTION: Common Florida, Bahamas, Caribbean, also Bermuda.

HABITAT & BEHAVIOR: Large numbers of individuals colonize several species of sponges. including: Branching Vase Sponge, *Callyspongia vaginalis*, [pg. 23], Pink Vase Sponge, *Niphates digitalis*, [pg. 27], Lavender Rope Sponge, *N. digitalis*, [pg. 37] and Red Boring Sponge, *Cliona delitrix*, [pg. 57].

VISUAL ID: Brilliant gold to yellow body and tentacles. Encrust surfaces of several species of sponges.

ABUNDANCE & DISTRIBUTION: Common Caribbean, Bahamas.

HABITAT & BEHAVIOR: Colonies grow in meandering, band-like rows. When polyps are closed, colonies appear as golden patches. Large numbers of individuals colonize several species of sponges. including: Thin Rope Sponge, *Rhaphidolphlus juniperinus*, [pg. 41], Green Finger Sponge, *Iotrochota birotulata*, [pg. 43] and Brown Tube Sponge, *Agelas conifera*, [pg. 21].

VISUAL ID: Body and tentacles dark maroon, burgundy or purple. Tentacles may be somewhat translucent. Large communities inhabit surfaces of several species of sponge.

ABUNDANCE & DISTRIBUTION: Common Caribbean.

HABITAT & BEHAVIOR: Inhabit sponges. Often grow on Brown Tube Sponges, *Agelas condifera*, [pg. 21] and Dark Volcano Sponges, *Calyx podatypa*, [pg. 33]. Most common sponge zoanthid at depths below 65 ft.

SPONGE ZOANTHID
Parazoanthus parasiticus
ORDER:
Zoanthids
Zoanthidea

SIZE: ¹/₄ in.
DEPTH: 25 - 100 ft.

GOLDEN ZOANTHID
Parazoanthus swiftii
ORDER:
Zoanthids
Zoanthidea

SIZE: ¹/₄ in.
DEPTH: 40 - 130 ft.

MAROON SPONGE ZOANTHID
Parazoanthus puertoricense
ORDER:
Zoanthids
Zoanthidea

SIZE: ¹/₄ in.
DEPTH: 40 - 100 ft.

VISUAL ID: Twenty brown to yellow-brown tapering tentacles in two rings around concave oral disc; disc brown, darker toward center with light colored slit mouth; body column whitish.

ABUNDANCE & DISTRIBUTION: Occasional Caribbean.

HABITAT & BEHAVIOR: Large colonies cover several species of deep dwelling sponges. Most commonly colonize the maroon fan-shaped sponge *Xestospongia* sp. but occasionally colonize other sponges including the Giant Barrel Sponge, *X. muta*, [pg. 29].

VISUAL ID: Twelve bright yellow tapering tentacles form two rings around oral disc; disc and body column darker yellow with pale slit mouth.

ABUNDANCE & DISTRIBUTION: Occasional Caribbean.

HABITAT & BEHAVIOR: Large colonies of individuals, spaced with considerable regularity, often cover the deep-dwelling maroon fan-shaped sponge *Xestospongia* sp.

VISUAL ID: Colonies encrust Feather Bush, *Deentitheca dendritica*, [pg. 75].

ABUNDANCE & DISTRIBUTION: Occasional Florida, Bahamas, Caribbean.

HABITAT & BEHAVIOR: Inhabit reefs where Feather Tree Hydroids grow.

EFFECT ON DIVERS: Only the Feather Tree Hydroid is known to sting humans.

BROWN SPONGE ZOANTHID
Parazoanthus catenularis

ORDER:
Zoanthids
Zoanthidea

SIZE: $1/8$ - $1/4$ in.
DEPTH: 60 - 150 ft.

YELLOW SPONGE ZOANTHID
Epizoanthus cutressi

ORDER:
Zoanthids
Zoanthidea

SIZE: $1/8$ - $1/4$ in.
DEPTH: 60 - 150 ft

HYDROID ZOANTHID
Parazoanthus tunicans

ORDER:
Zoanthids
Zoanthidea

SIZE: $1/4$ in.
DEPTH: 30 - 130 ft.

VISUAL ID: Grow in clusters. Flat oral disc is shades of brown, and often has blue and/or green overtones and white blotch in center. Two rings of thin, pointed tentacles around outer edge.

ABUNDANCE & DISTRIBUTION: Occasional Caribbean; rare South Florida.

HABITAT & BEHAVIOR: Inhabit coral reefs. Small clusters grow in secluded, protected areas of reef.

NOTE: Although this distinctive zoanthid is relatively common, its living appearance has never been matched with a scientific identification. Collection of a photographed specimen and microscopic examination are necessary to establish visual identification. Possibly an undescribed species. Unfortunately, at the time of writing there are no taxonomists working with Caribbean zoanthids.

VISUAL ID: Grow in dense mats. When circular oral discs are fully expanded, they often pack so tightly together that they become polygonal. Two rows of stubby tentacles around outer edge of oral disc. Colors and patterns vary, usually mottled in earthtones. On deeper reefs, occasionally fluoresce a dayglow-orange color which is not visible when lit by a hand light or strobe.

ABUNDANCE & DISTRIBUTION: Common Caribbean, Bahamas; occasional south Florida.

HABITAT & BEHAVIOR: Inhabit reef tops. Under stands of antler coral and in shallow cracks and crevices. If disturbed, tentacles curl inward and retract, forming a dome capped column [right].

SIMILAR SPECIES: Row Zoanthid, *Z. sociatus,* colonies tend to grow in rows from thin, band-like, occasionally branching bases. Oral disc small (about 1/4 in.). Bodies usually hidden in sand or algae. Rarely deeper than 15 ft.

BROWN ZOANTHID
Unidentified
ORDER:
Zoanthids
Zoanthidea

SIZE: Disc ¼ - ½ in.
DEPTH: 20 - 60 ft.

MAT ZOANTHID
Zoanthus pulchellus
ORDER:
Zoanthids
Zoanthidea

SIZE: Disc ¼ - ½ in.
DEPTH: 20 - 60 ft.

Mat Zoanthid
Color variation.

VISUAL ID: Brownish white colonies form mats that encrust substrate. Oral discs push against one another when fully expanded. Two rings of short tentacles around outer edge.

ABUNDANCE & DISTRIBUTION: Occasional South Florida, Caribbean, Bahamas; can be locally abundant.

HABITAT & BEHAVIOR: Inhabit shallow reefs; prefer areas with some water movement. If disturbed, tentacles curl inward and retract forming dome-like lumps [below].

SIMILAR SPECIES: Knobby Zoanthid, *Palythoa mammillosa,* colonies form small mats, rarely exceeding 4 inches across. Oral discs do not touch when fully expanded and are separated by polygonal dividing lines.

NOTE: Has been reported by junior name *P. caribaea.*

Sun Zoanthid
Occasionally grow in small clumps.

VISUAL ID: One of the largest zoanthids. Highly flattened oral disc is green to brown and often somewhat mottled. Short, light brown tentacles ring outer edge. May occur singly, in pairs or clumps.

ABUNDANCE & DISTRIBUTION: Occasional South Florida, Caribbean.

HABITAT & BEHAVIOR: Inhabit mid-range to deep reefs. Attach to rocky, and usually somewhat sheltered, substrate. Several may grow in close proximity, but do not form mats. If disturbed, edges will curl inward revealing underside of oral disc.

WHITE ENCRUSTING ZOANTHID
Palythoa caribaeorum
ORDER:
Zoanthids
Zoanthidea

SIZE: Disc ¼ - ½ in.
DEPTH: 10 - 40 ft.

White Encrusting Zoanthid
Polyps closed.

SUN ZOANTHID
Palythoa grandis
ORDER:
Zoanthids
Zoanthidea

SIZE: Disc ¾ - 1¼ in.
DEPTH: 40 - 120 ft.

Corallimorphs

VISUAL ID: Spherical, knob-like tentacles cover the oral disc, with elongated tentacles around edge. Completely extended and flattened disc reveals distinctive, radial, spoke-like arrangement of tentacles. Usually green overall, but may be, or have mixed in, shades of yellow, orange, brown and blue. Colors may fluoresce.

ABUNDANCE & DISTRIBUTION: Occasional Florida, Bahamas, Caribbean.

HABITAT & BEHAVIOR: Attach to solid reef structures. Often cover area in the form of mat-like communities, occasionally so compact that individual polyps are difficult to distinguish. Curl inward if disturbed.

VISUAL ID: Flattened oral disc with wart-like tentacles having forked extensions. These tentacles may be numerous and compacted together, or few and widely separated. Thin short tentacles around outer edge. Green overall, often has bluish overtones, and may be somewhat translucent.

ABUNDANCE & DISTRIBUTION: Occasional Florida, Bahamas, Caribbean.

HABITAT & BEHAVIOR: Attach to solid reef structures. Solitary, or grow in small groups, occasionally form mat-like communities so compacted that the individual polyps are difficult to distinguish. Curl inward if disturbed.

NOTE: This species was formerly classified in the genus *Rhodactis*.

Warty Corallimorph
Color variation.

**FLORIDA
CORALLIMORPH**
Ricordea florida
ORDER:
Corallimorphs
Corallimorpharian

SIZE: Disc 1¹/₂ - 2 in.
DEPTH: 15 - 100 ft.

WARTY CORALLIMORPH
Discosoma sanctithomae
ORDER:
Corallimorphs
Corallimorpharian

SIZE: Disc 2 - 3 ¹/₂ in.
DEPTH: 10 - 75 ft.

Warty Corallimorph
Color variation.

Corallimorphs

VISUAL ID: Tiny, widely separated, forked tentacles cover oral disc. Green, brown and bluish gray splotches cover oral disc. Often somewhat translucent.

ABUNDANCE & DISTRIBUTION: Uncommon Caribbean; rare South Florida.

HABITAT & BEHAVIOR: Attach to solid reef structures. Prefer secluded areas. Grow as solitary polyp, or in small groups. Curl inward if disturbed.

NOTE: This species was formerly classified in the genus *Rhodactis*.

VISUAL ID: Extremely flattened oral disc with short, squarish, irregular tentacles around edge. Light green to olive to dark brown oral disc, occasionally streaked or splotched.

ABUNDANCE & DISTRIBUTION: Rare Florida, Bahamas, Caribbean.

HABITAT & BEHAVIOR: Attach to solid reef structures. Prefer shaded, secluded areas and caves. Grow as solitary polyps.

NOTE: This species was formerly classified in the genus *Paradiscosoma*.

VISUAL ID: Cup-shaped oral disc with rectangular tentacles of varying length around edge. Numerous rows of small knob-like tentacles radiate from protruding mouth to disc edge including rectangular tentacles. Varying shades of green.

ABUNDANCE & DISTRIBUTION: Photographed in Dominica where the species is common; range has yet to be established.

HABITAT & BEHAVIOR: Grow in small colonies on walls and reefs in normally shaded areas.

NOTE: Although this corallimorph is common, its living appearance has not been matched with a scientific description. Collection of a photographed specimen and microscopic examination of anatomical details are necessary to establish visual identification. Possibly an undescribed species. Regrettably, at the time of this writing, no taxonomic biologists are working with this order in the tropical western Atlantic.

FORKED TENTACLE CORALLIMORPH
Discosoma carlgreni
ORDER:
Corallimorphs
Corallimorpharian

SIZE: Disc 1¹/₂ - 2 ¹/₂ in.
DEPTH: 10 - 60 ft.

UMBRELLA CORALLIMORPH
Discosoma neglectum
ORDER:
Corallimorphs
Corallimorpharian

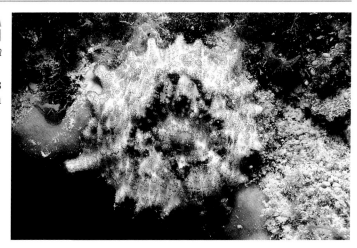

SIZE: Disc 1¹/₂ - 2 ¹/₂ in.
DEPTH: 30 - 90 ft.

CUP CORALLIMORPH
Unidentified
ORDER:
Corallimorphs
Corallimorpharian

SIZE: 2 - 3 in.
DEPTH: 15 - 100 ft.

Corallimorphs

VISUAL ID: Umbrella-shaped oral disc with short pointed tentacles around edge. Widely spaced rows of small tentacles radiate from protruding mouth to disc edge (these resemble the wire supports of an umbrella). Varying shades of green and somewhat translucent.

ABUNDANCE & DISTRIBUTION: Photographed in Jamaica where the species occurs occasionally; range has yet to be established.

HABITAT & BEHAVIOR: Grow in small colonies on walls and reefs in normally shaded, protected areas.

NOTE: Although this corallimorph is not uncommon, its living appearance has not been matched with a scientific description. Collection of a photographed specimen and microscopic examination of anatomical details are necessary to establish visual identification. Possibly an undescribed species. Regrettably, at the time of this writing, no taxonomic biologists are working with this order in the tropical western Atlantic.

VISUAL ID: Flattened oral disc with a fringe of tiny pointed tentacles around edge. Numerous rows of tiny polyps radiate from protruding mouth to disc edge. Light green mouth, dark brownish green disc with light green border.

ABUNDANCE & DISTRIBUTION: Photographed in Roatan where the species occurs occasionally; range has yet to be established.

HABITAT & BEHAVIOR: Individuals grow on reef in protected areas.

NOTE: Although this corallimorph is not uncommon, its living appearance has not been matched with a scientific description. Collection of a photographed specimen and microscopic examination of anatomical details are necessary to establish visual identification. Possibly an undescribed species. Regrettably, at the time of this writing, no taxonomic biologists are working with this order in the tropical western Atlantic.

VISUAL ID: Flattened oral disc with fringe of long, thin pointed tentacles around edge. On disc face are widely scattered long, thin pointed tentacles and rows of bluish white spots radiating from the protruding mouth.

ABUNDANCE & DISTRIBUTION: Photographed in Grand Cayman where the species is rare; range has yet to be established.

HABITAT & BEHAVIOR: Individuals grow on reefs in protected areas.

NOTE: The living appearance of this corallimorph has not been matched with a scientific description. Collection of a photographed specimen and microscopic examination of anatomical details are necessary to establish visual identification. Possibly an undescribed species. Regrettably, at the time of this writing, no taxonomic biologists are working with this order in the tropical western Atlantic.

PARACHUTE CORALLIMORPH
Unidentified
ORDER:
Corallimorphs
Corallimorpharian

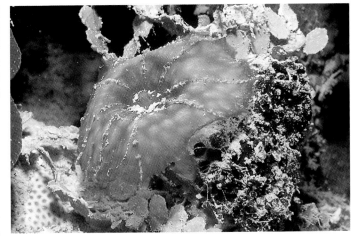

SIZE: 1¹/₂ - 2¹/₂ in.
DEPTH: 15 - 100 ft.

DISC CORALLIMORPH
Unidentified
ORDER:
Corallimorphs
Corallimorpharian

SIZE: 1 - 2 in.
DEPTH: 15 - 100 ft.

FRINGED CORALLIMORPH
Unidentified
ORDER:
Corallimorphs
Corallimorpharian

SIZE: 2 - 3 in.
DEPTH: 15 - 100 ft.

VISUAL ID: Bright orange body column and ball-like tips on nearly transparent tentacles. On rare occasion may be pale yellow, blue or white.

ABUNDANCE & DISTRIBUTION: Occasional to uncommon Bahamas, Caribbean.

HABITAT & BEHAVIOR: Inhabit reefs and sandy areas near reefs. Nocturnal, solitary polyps extend from recesses or sand. If disturbed or lighted, will retract.

NOTE: Because of their visual resemblance to anemones, this species is often called the "Orange Ball Anemone", which is a misnomer.

Banded Tube-Dwelling Anemone

VISUAL ID: Translucent brown-and-white banded outer tentacles, whitish oral disc and central tentacles.

ABUNDANCE & DISTRIBUTION: Occasional South Florida, Bahamas, Caribbean.

HABITAT & BEHAVIOR: Inhabit areas of sand and coral rubble. Nocturnal, solitary polyps extend from parchment-like tube buried in sand. If disturbed or lit by a diver's light, retract into tube.

NOTE: Identification is tentative. Because there are several similar appearing species, positive identification requires microscopic examination.

ORANGE BALL CORALLIMORPH
Pseudocorynactis caribbeorum
ORDER:
Corallimorphs
Corallimorpharian

SIZE: Disc 1 - 2 in.
Tentacles 1 - 2 in.
DEPTH: 20 - 80 ft.

Orange Ball Corallimorph
Blue variation.

BANDED TUBE-DWELLING ANEMONE
Arachnanthus nocturnus
ORDER:
Tube-Dwelling Anemones
Ceriantharia

SIZE: Disc ³/₄ - 1¹/₄ in.
Tentacles 1 - 2 in.
DEPTH: 10 - 80 ft.

VISUAL ID: Numerous long, tapering wispy tentacles encircle oral disc with numerous short tentacles around mouth. Shades of gray to pale lavender.

ABUNDANCE & DISTRIBUTION: Uncommon to rare Florida, Bahamas, Caribbean.

HABITAT & BEHAVIOR: Inhabits areas of sand and rubble. Solitary polyps extend from buried parchment-like tubes to catch drifting food. If disturbed retract into tubes.

NOTE: Identification is tentative. Collection of a photographed specimen and microscopic examination of anatomical details are necessary to establish positive visual identification.

VISUAL ID: Numerous long, tapering, transparent, wispy tentacles encircle oral disc; large circle of numerous reddish brown to pink and white short tentacles on central disc.

ABUNDANCE & DISTRIBUTION: Photographed in the Gulf of Mexico off the Florida panhandle coast where the species occurs occasionally; range has yet to be established.

HABITAT & BEHAVIOR: Inhabit areas of sand and rubble. Solitary polyps extend from buried parchment-like tubes to catch drifting food. If disturbed retract into tubes.

NOTE: Although this tube-dwelling anemone is not uncommon, its living appearance has not been matched with a scientific description. Collection of a photographed specimen and microscopic examination of anatomical details are necessary to establish visual identification. Possibly an undescribed species. Regrettably, at the time of this writing, no taxonomic biologists are working with this order in the tropical western Atlantic.

VISUAL ID: Numerous long, white, tapering tentacles encircle oral disc; tuft of short lavender tentacles on central disc.

ABUNDANCE & DISTRIBUTION: Photographed Isla Cubagua, Venezuela where the species is occasional; range has yet to be established.

HABITAT & BEHAVIOR: Inhabit areas of sand and rubble. Solitary polyps extend from buried parchment-like tubes to catch drifting food. If disturbed retract into tubes.

NOTE: Although this tube-dwelling anemone is not uncommon, its living appearance has not been matched with a scientific description. Collection of a photographed specimen and microscopic examination of anatomical details are necessary to establish visual identification. Possibly an undescribed species. Regrettably, at the time of this writing, no taxonomic biologists are working with this order in the tropical western Atlantic.

GIANT TUBE-DWELLING ANEMONE
Ceriantheomorphe brasiliensis
ORDER:
Tube-Dwelling Anemones
Ceriantharia

SIZE: 6 - 12 in.
DEPTH: 15 - 60 ft.

TRANSPARENT TUBE-DWELLING ANEMONE
Unidentified
ORDER:
Tube-Dwelling Anemones
Ceriantharia

SIZE: 3 - 5 in.
DEPTH: 15 - 60 ft.

LAVENDER TUBE-DWELLING ANEMONE
Unidentified
ORDER:
Tube-Dwelling Anemones
Ceriantharia

SIZE: 1 - 2 in.
DEPTH: 15 - 60 ft.

Tube-Dwelling Anemones

VISUAL ID: Pair of lines (often formed by dashes) run length of the numerous long, tapering tentacles that encircle oral disc; large circle of short tentacles on central disc with dark paired lines radiate to outer tentacle rings.

ABUNDANCE & DISTRIBUTION: Photographed Isla Cubagua, Venezuela where the species is common; range has yet to be established.

HABITAT & BEHAVIOR: Inhabits areas of sand and rubble. Solitary polyps extend from buried parchment-like tubes to catch drifting food. If disturbed retract into tubes.

NOTE: Although this tube-dwelling anemone is common, its living appearance has not been matched with a scientific description. Collection of a photographed specimen and microscopic examination of anatomical details are necessary to establish visual identification. Possibly an undescribed species. Regrettably, at the time of this writing, no taxonomic biologists are working with this order in the tropical western Atlantic.

VISUAL ID: Numerous long, tapering tentacles encircle oral disc; outer half of tentacles translucent and inner half maroon with a few large pale spots; most of disc smooth with only a small tuft of short tentacles around mouth.

ABUNDANCE & DISTRIBUTION: Photographed in Bahamas and St. Lucia where the species occurs occasionally; range has yet to be established.

HABITAT & BEHAVIOR: Inhabit areas of clean sand. Solitary polyps extend from buried parchment-like tubes to catch drifting food. If disturbed retract into tubes.

NOTE: Although this tube-dwelling anemone is not uncommon, its living appearance has not been matched with a scientific description. Collection of a photographed specimen and microscopic examination of anatomical details are necessary to establish visual identification. Possibly an undescribed species. Regrettably, at the time of this writing, no taxonomic biologists are working with this order in the tropical western Atlantic.

VISUAL ID: White to deep purple, kidney-shaped, leaf-like colony with short fleshy stalk and pale to yellowish brown polyps on upper surface; underside smooth. Colony noticeably wider than tall.

ABUNDANCE & DISTRIBUTION: Uncommon Gulf of Mexico and Caribbean; absent east Florida and Bahamas.

HABITAT & BEHAVIOR: Inhabit shallow sandy areas. Generally extended colonies above soft bottom on stalks; float free when dislodged. If covered by sand muscular stalk can push colony above surface.

SIMILAR SPECIES: Common Sea Pansy, *Renilla reniformis*, colonies nearly circular with sharp, deep indentions at point where long fleshy stalks attach.. Cape Hatteras to Caribbean.

LINED TUBE-DWELLING ANEMONE
Unidentified

ORDER:
Tube-Dwelling Anemones
Ceriantharia

SIZE: 3 - 4 in.
DEPTH: 15 - 60 ft.

WIDEBAND TUBE-DWELLING ANEMONE
Unidentified

ORDER:
Tube-Dwelling Anemones
Ceriantharia

SIZE: 1 - 2 in.
DEPTH: 6 - 60 ft.

MULLER'S SEA PANSY
Renilla muelleri

SUBCLASS:
Octocorallia
Alcyonaria
ORDER:
Sea Pens
Pennatulacea
SUBORDER:
Sessiliflorae
FAMILY:
Renillidae
SIZE: 1 - 2 in. high,
2 - 4 in. wide
DEPTH: 0 - 25 ft.

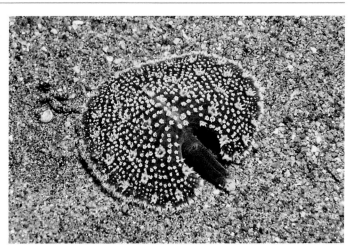

VISUAL ID: Feather-like structures emerging from sand or mud. Colonial animals with two basic parts: a buried muscular peduncle anchors the colony to the bottom; a central stalk with either branch-like or leaf-like structures extends in a single plane. The side structures bear numerous eight-tentacled feeding polyps. Some colonies are thin and tall with narrow central stalks, others are more robust with thick central stalks and peddle-like side branches. Colors vary. Although many species have distinctive shapes and colors, their living appearances have never been matched with microscopic examination of spicules (skeletal elements) to substantiate visual identifications. Regrettably, at the time of this writing, no taxonomic biologists are working with this order in the tropical western Atlantic.

ABUNDANCE & DISTRIBUTION: Uncommon Florida, Bahamas, Caribbean.

HABITAT & BEHAVIOR: Often in areas with some current where the polyps catch floating particles of food. Most species extend their bodies at night, by hydrostatic pressure, to feed. Water is drawn in or discharged through pores in small non-feeding polyps located between the larger feeding polyps.

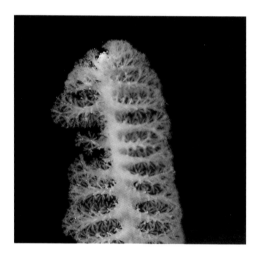 

FEATHER SEA PENS
Unidentified
ORDER:
Sea Pens
Pennatulacea
FAMILIES:
Virgulariidae
Pennatulidae

SIZE: photographed
specimen 2 ft. tall

Feather Sea Pens
*Unidentified species
photographed in 20 feet
of water in Tobago.*

Feather Sea Pens
Detail [left]

IDENTIFICATION GROUP 3
Phylum Ctenophora
(Tee-NOFF-for-uh / L. to bear combs)
Comb Jellies

Ctenophores comprise a small phylum of transparent, free-floating marine invertebrates that are often mistaken for jellyfish. However, there are a few distinct features that easily distinguish the group. Comb jellies are usually small, no more than one or two inches across, and have either two **tentacles** or lack them altogether. Their delicate body, which breaks apart easily when touched, often tends to be oval or pear-shaped, rather than having the open-dome shape of most jellyfish. Stinging nematocysts are absent in this phylum.

The phylum's most important visual distinction is the presence of eight rows or bands of hair-like cilia, called **combs**. Beating of the cilia in coordinated waves gives most of these animals their means of movement. This beating action appears as sets of iridescent lights moving along the comb rows.

Divers generally observe comb jellies just beneath the surface where the animals prey upon tiny planktonic animals. The best way to spot these animals is to look up toward the surface light, which makes them more visible as it passes through their transparent bodies. They occasionally appear in such large numbers that a haze is created across the surface. Ctenophores are noted for their bioluminescence. When disturbed at night, they produce a spectacular greenish-blue glow.

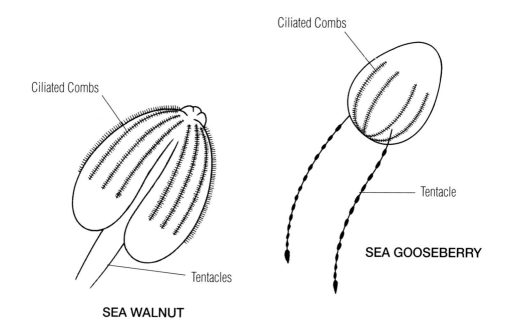

Ciliated Combs

Ciliated Combs

Tentacle

SEA GOOSEBERRY

Tentacles

SEA WALNUT

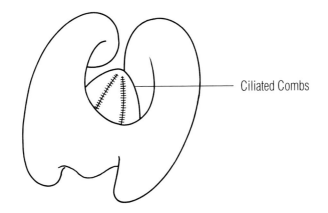

Ciliated Combs

WINGED COMB JELLY

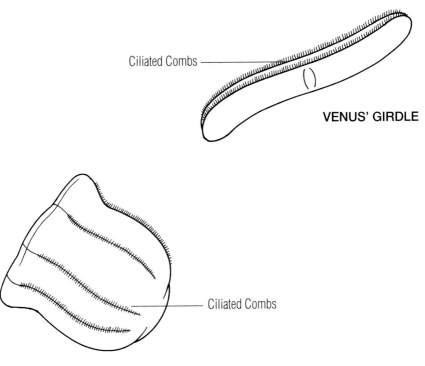

Ciliated Combs

VENUS' GIRDLE

Ciliated Combs

FLATTENED HELMET

Comb Jellies

VISUAL ID: Walnut or occasionally pear-shaped, with large oral lobes and some lateral compression. Often bespeckled with numerous small warts. Opalescent or translucent, frequently with a greenish amber cast.

ABUNDANCE & DISTRIBUTION: Common Florida, Bahamas, Caribbean.

HABITAT & BEHAVIOR: Float near surface. Often appear in large aggregations over reefs, in bays and harbors, especially in summer months. Bioluminescent; when disturbed at night produce a greenish blue light.

VISUAL ID: Largest comb jelly. Easily distinguished by numerous long, conical papillae. Transparent to translucent, occasionally with some yellowish markings, oral lobes tinted brown. Two short tentacles.

ABUNDANCE & DISTRIBUTION: Occasional Florida, Bahamas, Caribbean.

HABITAT & BEHAVIOR: During calm weather often float near surface of open water. May appear in large aggregations over reefs, especially in spring and summer. Bioluminescent; when disturbed at night produce a greenish blue light.

VISUAL ID: Distinguished by two large, prominent oral lobes and compressed body. Transparent to translucent. May have some milky warts on outer surface of oral lobes.

ABUNDANCE & DISTRIBUTION: Occasional Florida, Bahamas, Caribbean.

HABITAT & BEHAVIOR: Float near surface of open water, found deeper when water is rough. May appear in large aggregations, especially on calm days of spring and early summer. Actively swim with flapping movements of oral lobes, usually with two or three pulsations followed by a brief rest period. Bioluminescent; when disturbed at night produce a greenish blue light.

SEA WALNUT
Mnemiopsis mccradyi
CLASS:
Comb Jellies
Tentaculata

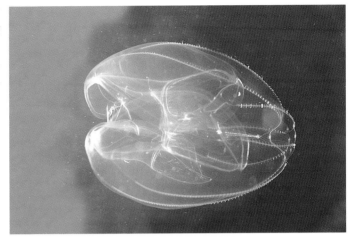

SIZE: 2 - 2½ in.,
4 in. max.
DEPTH: 0-15 ft.

WARTY COMB JELLY
Leucothea multicornis
CLASS:
Comb Jellies
Tentaculata

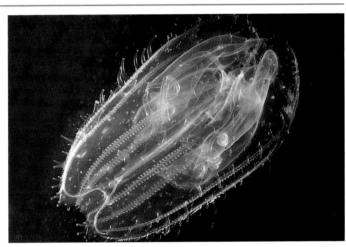

SIZE: 2 - 3 in.,
8 in. max.
DEPTH: 0 - 130 ft.

WINGED COMB JELLY
Ocyropsis crystallina
CLASS:
Comb Jellies
Tentaculata

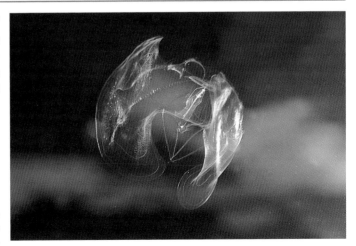

SIZE: 1 - 2 in.,
3½ in. max.
DEPTH: 1 - 15 ft.

Comb Jellies

VISUAL ID: Four conspicuous brown spots on large, prominent oral lobes, body compressed. Body and lobes whitish and translucent.

ABUNDANCE & DISTRIBUTION: Occasional Florida, Bahamas, Caribbean.

HABITAT & BEHAVIOR: Float near surface of open water, found deeper when water is rough. May appear in large aggregations after several days of calm. Actively swim with flapping movements of oral lobes, usually with two or three pulsations followed by a brief rest period. Bioluminescent; when disturbed at night produce a greenish blue light.

VISUAL ID: Transparent, narrow, elongated body with small oral lobes (about one-quarter of body's length). Pores in the combs of cilia contain a red, oily, dye-like substance that make the combs appear as rows of brilliant red dots. Extremely fragile.

ABUNDANCE & DISTRIBUTION: Occasional Florida, Bahamas, Caribbean.

HABITAT & BEHAVIOR: Inhabit open oceanic waters, only occasionally over reefs. Near surface only on calm days. Swim solely by means of the ciliated combs. When disturbed red dye is ejected into the water as a fluorescing cloud. Bioluminescent; when disturbed at night produce a greenish blue light.

VISUAL ID: Egg-shaped body, narrowing at the oral end. Comb rows extend from the aboral pole two-thirds to three-quarters the body's length. Two long tentacles with side branching filaments. When contracted, the filaments coil tightly into a tear-drop shape. Transparent to translucent with slight red pigmentation along edges of comb rows.

ABUNDANCE & DISTRIBUTION: Occasional Caribbean.

HABITAT & BEHAVIOR: Float near surface, found deeper when water is rough. Swim by means of the ciliated combs which they can reverse, causing a spinning action that spreads the tentacles in a corkscrew pattern. Filaments usually remain in coiled position, extending only when they contact food. Bioluminescent; when disturbed at night produce a greenish blue light.

NOTE: Positive identification of this genus cannot be confirmed without light-microscopic examination of the tentacles. Pictured specimen may be an undescribed species.

SPOT-WINGED COMB JELLY
Ocyropsis maculata
CLASS:
Comb Jellies
Tentaculata

SIZE: 1 ½ - 2½ in.,
4 in. max.
DEPTH: 0 - 15 ft.

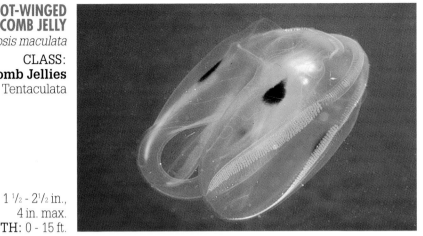

RED-SPOT COMB JELLY
Eurhamphaea vexilligera
CLASS:
Comb Jellies
Tentaculata

SIZE: 1 - 2 in.,
3 ½ in. max.
DEPTH: 1 - 130 ft.

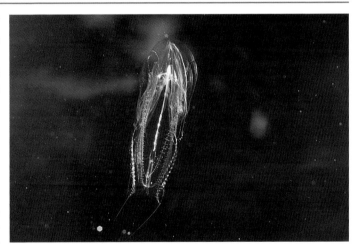

SEA GOOSEBERRY
Euplokamis sp.
CLASS:
Comb Jellies
Tentaculata

SIZE: ½ - ¾ in.
DEPTH: 1 - 130 ft.

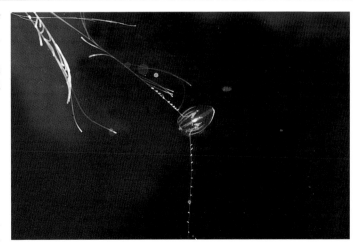

VISUAL ID: Long, ribbon-shaped body. Young are transparent; they become violet with age and often display a greenish blue fluorescence. Edge of body curves out from central axis. Similar, smaller species, Small Venus' Girdle [next], has straight edge extending from central axis.

ABUNDANCE & DISTRIBUTION: Occasional Florida, Bahamas, Caribbean.

HABITAT & BEHAVIOR: Inhabit open oceanic waters, only occasionally over deeper reefs. Swim with undulating movements of body. Bioluminescent; when disturbed at night produce a greenish blue light.

VISUAL ID: Transparent, ribbon-shaped body. Often display a blue to violet fluorescence. Edge of body straight from central axis. Similar, larger species, Venus' Girdle [previous], has curving edge extending from central axis.

ABUNDANCE & DISTRIBUTION: Occasional Florida, Bahamas, Caribbean.

HABITAT & BEHAVIOR: Inhabit open oceanic waters, occasionally over deeper reefs. Swim with undulating movements of body. Bioluminescent; when disturbed at night produce a greenish blue light.

NOTE: Formerly classified in the genus *Folia*.

VISUAL ID: Flat, helmet-shaped body. Transparent to translucent, often steely-blue, occasionally milky. Internal canals often pink to reddish brown. Young are spotted.

ABUNDANCE & DISTRIBUTION: Occasional Florida, Bahamas, Caribbean.

HABITAT & BEHAVIOR: Habitat ranges from shallow-water mangrove bays to oceanic open water. Swim rapidly, solely by means of its ciliated combs. Bioluminescent; when disturbed at night produce a greenish blue light.

VENUS' GIRDLE
Cestum veneris
CLASS:
Comb Jellies
Tentaculata

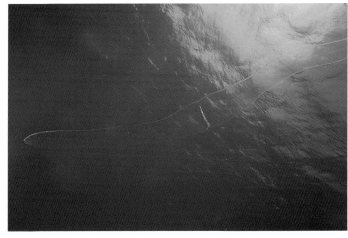

SIZE: 1 - 2 ft.,
5 ft. max.
DEPTH: 1 - 130 ft.

SMALL VENUS' GIRDLE
Velamen parallelum
CLASS:
Comb Jellies
Tentaculata

SIZE: 1 - 3 in.,
6 in. max.
DEPTH: 1 - 130 ft.

FLATTENED HELMET COMB JELLY
Beroe ovata
CLASS:
Comb Jellies
Nuda

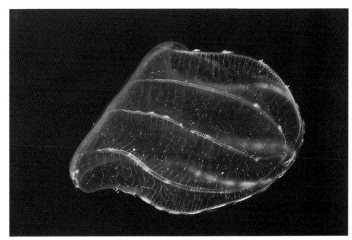

SIZE: 2 - 3 in.,
max. 6 in.
DEPTH: 1 - 130 ft.

IDENTIFICATION GROUP 4

Phylum Platyhelminthes

(Plat-ee-hell-MIN-theez / Gr. broad flat worm)

Flatworms

Flatworms are flat, elongated ovals, that range in length from one to five inches. The only animal on the reef that they could be confused with are the thick-bodied nudibranchs (shell-less snails) which, like flatworms, are often brightly colored and oval-shaped. Remembering that flatworms are thin and leaf-like alleviates confusion.

Most marine flatworms observed by divers are in the Class Turbellaria, Order Polycladida. Although not particularly uncommon, flatworms are rarely sighted because they spend the majority of their time under rocks and in dark recesses, scavenging for small invertebrates and the remains of dead animals. Their slow, gliding movement over the bottom is accomplished primarily by the beating of cilia on the underside. In larger species, muscular waves, or ripples, running the length of the body, assist in movement. On rare occasions they may be observed swimming in open water using an undulating motion.

Flatworms are simple animals, but the phylum is biologically significant. They are the most primitive animals to have similar right and left sides, a definite front and rear end, and a dorsal and ventral surface. The primitive beginnings of specialized body organs, a complex nervous system, and three tissue layers are present. One body-opening, located centrally on the underside, serves as both **mouth** and **anus.** On the heads of most reef species are rudimentary sensory organs in the form of **antennae.** Eye spots, that function simply in the detection of light, are developed in many species. Flatworms have the capacity to regenerate parts severed from their body, and often can regenerate another complete animal from only the severed part.

Phylum Rhynchocoela

(Rin-co-SEE-luh / L. stout belly)

Ribbon Worms

Ribbon worms are long, slender and somewhat flattened. Those occurring on tropical reefs are often brightly colored and striped. In many respects they are similar to flatworms, but are more highly organized, and have both mouth and anus. They are not uncommon reef inhabitants, but are rarely observed in the open. Ribbon worms hide under rocks, or beneath algae and in deep recesses, where they prey on small invertebrates.

134

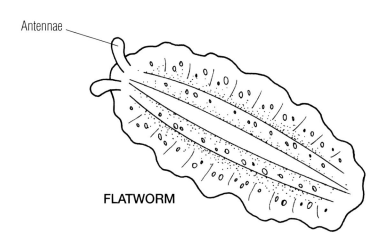

Antennae

FLATWORM

Antennae

Mouth & Anus

FLATWORM

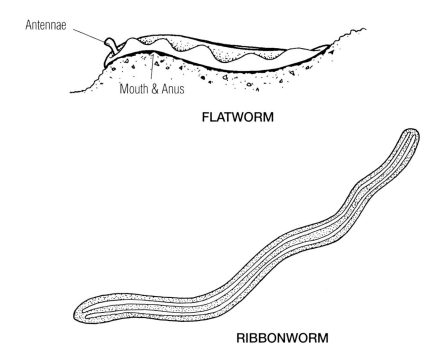

RIBBONWORM

135

VISUAL ID: Dark reddish brown with orange spots ringed in black, margin trimmed in black with white spots. Two short sensory antennae at head.

ABUNDANCE & DISTRIBUTION: Occasional South Florida, Bahamas, Caribbean.

HABITAT & BEHAVIOR: Inhabit coral reefs. Often hide under rocks and rubble. Occasionally swim in open water with an undulating motion of entire body.

VISUAL ID: White to light grayish brown or green with numerous, thin, dark brown lines crisscrossing body. Two short sensory antennae at head.

ABUNDANCE & DISTRIBUTION: Occasional Florida, Bahamas, Caribbean.

HABITAT & BEHAVIOR: Inhabit shallow areas of rocks and coral rubble, patch reefs, and around mangroves. Occasionally swim in open water with an undulating motion of entire body.

NOTE: Also commonly known as Crozier's Flatworm.

VISUAL ID: White, light gray or tan with brown, net-like pattern over body. Two short sensory antennae at head.

ABUNDANCE & DISTRIBUTION: Occasional Florida, Bahamas.

HABITAT & BEHAVIOR: Inhabit coral reefs. Often hide under rocks and rubble. Occasionally swim in open water with an undulating motion of entire body.

LEOPARD FLATWORM
Pseudoceros pardalis
CLASS:
Flatworms
Turbellaria
ORDER:
Polycladida

SIZE: 1 - 2 in.;
max 5 in.
DEPTH: 15 - 75 ft.

LINED FLATWORM
Pseudoceros crozieri
CLASS:
Flatworms
Turbellaria
ORDER:
Polycladida

SIZE: 1 - 2 in.
DEPTH: 1 - 35 ft.

NETTED FLATWORM
Pseudoceros texarus
CLASS:
Flatworms
Turbellaria
ORDER:
Polycladida

SIZE: 1 - 2 in.
DEPTH: 1 - 35 ft.

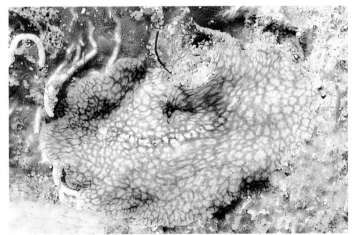

VISUAL ID: Dark brown central area, with scattered white spots and scalloped border. Margin of body is white with pale green to yellow edge. Two short sensory antennae at head.

ABUNDANCE & DISTRIBUTION: Uncommon to rare Florida, Bahamas, Caribbean.

HABITAT & BEHAVIOR: Inhabit shallow patch reefs, areas of sand, rubble and sea grass beds.

VISUAL ID: Navy blue to dark purple body, with narrow, orange to gold margin and dark purple edge. Two short sensory antennae at head.

ABUNDANCE & DISTRIBUTION: Rare Florida, Bahamas, Caribbean. Circumtropical. Common in some Indo-Pacific regions.

HABITAT & BEHAVIOR: Inhabit coral reefs and areas of rubble. Often hide under rocks and rubble. Occasionally swim in open water with an undulating motion of entire body.

VISUAL ID: Two red stripes running down back are bordered by three narrow white stripes. Belly is pale grayish white.

ABUNDANCE & DISTRIBUTION: Uncommon Florida, Bahamas, Caribbean.

HABITAT & BEHAVIOR: Inhabit reefs and areas of coral rubble. Hide under rocks, debris and recesses in reef.

NOTE: Many species of ribbon worms vary greatly in color and markings. Microscopic examination of tissue is required to determine genus and species.

BICOLORED FLATWORM
Pseudoceros bicolor
CLASS:
Flatworms
Turbellaria
ORDER:
Polycladida

SIZE: ½ - 1¾ in.
DEPTH: 1 - 35 ft.

SPLENDID FLATWORM
Pseudoceros splendidus
CLASS:
Flatworms
Turbellaria
ORDER:
Polycladida

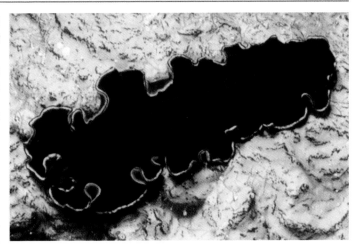

SIZE: 1 - 2 in.
DEPTH: 10 - 75 ft.

RED & WHITE STRIPED RIBBON WORM
Undescribed
PHYLUM:
Ribbon Worms
Rhynchocoela

SIZE: 3 - 10 in.
DEPTH: 1 - 130 ft.

IDENTIFICATION GROUP 5

Phylum Annelida

(Aah-NELL-id-uh / L. little rings)

Segmented Worms

Common earthworms, as well as many marine worms, are members of this phylum. Their distinguishing characteristic is repetitive segments which divide the worm's body. Marine worms that inhabit reefs belong to the class Polychaeta, and are commonly referred to as polychaetes.

Fireworms

CLASS: Polychaeta (Polly-KEY-tuh / Gr. many hairs)
ORDER: Amphinomida (Am-fin-NOME-ih-da / L. moving round about)
FAMILY: Amphinomidae (Am-fin-NOME-ih-dee / L. moving round about)

For defense, free-living fire worms have developed the sensory hairs on each segment into bundles of tiny, white, **sharp, detachable bristles**. Also, extending from the segments are clusters of reddish, irregular-branching **gill filaments**, part of their circulatory system. Located on the head is a fleshy plate, called a **caruncle**; its size and shape is often a clue for species identification. These somewhat flattened worms can grow to 12 inches in length. They prefer the cover of rocks during the day, but occasionally can be found crawling about the reef, where they feed on branched corals and gorgonians. When disturbed, fire worms flare their sharp, detachable bristles. These bristles can easily penetrate the skin and break off, causing a painful, long-lasting irritation.

Feather Duster Worms

CLASS: Polychaeta
ORDER: Sabellida (Suh-BELL-ih-da / L. sand)
FAMILY:Sabellidae (Suh-BELL-ih-dee / L. sand)

Feather dusters, also known as fan worms, do not appear to be worms at all, because their bodies are hidden inside **parchment-like tubes** attached to the reef. The flexible tube is constructed of fine sand held together with glue that is secreted by collar glands just below the head. Feather dusters have a highly modified head with a crown of feather-like appendages called **radioles** that are normally extended from the tube. These work as both gills, and for capturing plankton, which is moved to its mouth at the center of the feathery crown. The dramatic colors and patterns of the radioles are often the keys to visual identification. Feather duster worms are very sensitive to nearby movement and changes in light intensity and, if disturbed, instantly retract the crown.

Calcareous Tube Worms

CLASS: Polychaeta
ORDER: Sabellida (Sir-PYULE-ih-da / L. to creep)
FAMILY:Serpulidae (Sir-PYULE-ih-dee / L. to creep)

Serpulids build hard, **calcareous tubes** which are often hidden in or on rock, coral, or, occasionally, sponge. Their extended crown of colorful **radioles** form spirals and whorls. Like fan worms, the radioles are used to catch food, and will instantly retract when disturbed. A hardened structure, called an **operculum**, covers the tube opening when the worm withdraws. **Horn-like growths** that often extend from the operculum are useful in species identification.

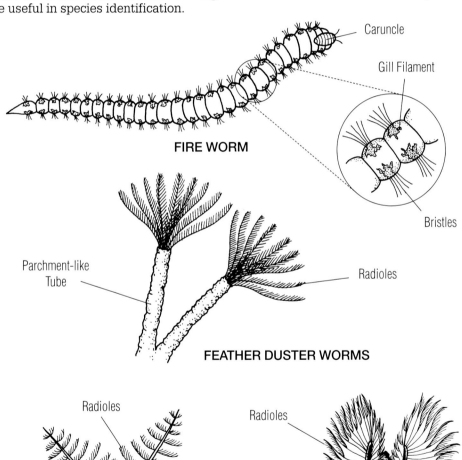

FIRE WORM

Caruncle

Gill Filament

Bristles

Parchment-like Tube

Radioles

FEATHER DUSTER WORMS

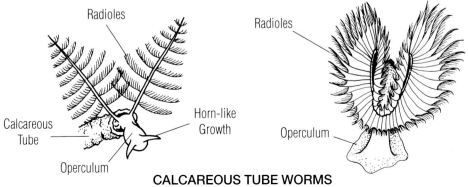

Radioles

Radioles

Calcareous Tube

Horn-like Growth

Operculum

Operculum

CALCAREOUS TUBE WORMS

Fireworms

VISUAL ID: Large, pleated and branched (beard-like) appendage of flesh on head, called a caruncle, distinguishes this species. Segments have short tufts of white bristles and stalks of red, branched-gill filaments. Color varies from shades of red to green to yellow and brown.

ABUNDANCE & DISTRIBUTION: Common Florida, Bahamas, Caribbean.

HABITAT & BEHAVIOR: Inhabit reefs, areas of reef rubble and sea grass beds. Often hide under rocks, slabs of coral and in recesses. Occasionally forage in open. Feed on a variety of attached marine invertebrates, including gorgonians, anemones and stony corals.

EFFECT ON DIVERS: When disturbed display bristles, which can easily penetrate and break off in skin, causing a painful burning sensation and irritating wound.

NOTE: Color pattern of juveniles [below] was confirmed by collection of pictured specimen and microscopic examination.

Bearded Fireworm Juvenile

VISUAL ID: Long, numerous bristles along sides are tipped or banded with red and/or orange. Caruncle is small, ribbed and divided longitudinally. Tufts of gill-filaments on each side of segments. Body color varies from pale green to shades of brown, often in patterned designs.

ABUNDANCE & DISTRIBUTION: Occasional Florida, Bahamas, Caribbean. Also along Pacific coast of Central America.

HABITAT & BEHAVIOR: In all marine habitats, especially in the areas of debris or reef rubble, occasionally on reefs. These voracious predators often forage in the open, can swim and will even take a fisherman's bait!

EFFECT ON DIVERS: When disturbed display bristles, which can easily penetrate and break off in skin, causing a very painful burning sensation and irritating wound.

BEARDED FIREWORM
Hermodice carunculata

ORDER:
Amphinomida
FAMILY:
Fireworms
Amphinomidae

SIZE: 4 - 6 in.,
12 in. max.
DEPTH: 1 - 130 ft.

Bearded Fireworm
Greenish variation.

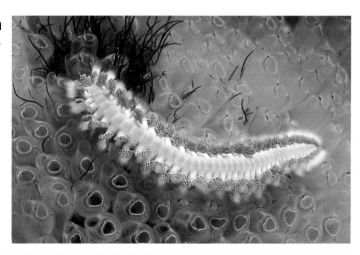

RED-TIPPED FIREWORM
Chloeia viridis

ORDER:
Amphinomida
FAMILY:
Fireworms
Amphinomidae

SIZE: 3 - 5 in.,
6 in. max.
DEPTH: 1 - 130 ft.

143

VISUAL ID: Caruncle is large, triangular and ribbed with scalloped edges. Segments have tufts of long whitish bristles and stalks of red, branched gill filaments. Single dark stripe centered on back runs length of body. Color varies from whitish to orangish.

ABUNDANCE & DISTRIBUTION: Occasional Venezuela and offshore islands.

HABITAT & BEHAVIOR: Inhabit reefs and areas of sand and rubble.

EFFECT ON DIVERS: When disturbed display bristles, which can easily penetrate and break off in skin, causing a painful burning sensation and irritating wound.

NOTE: Collection and scientific examination required for species identification. Possibly an undescribed species. The full range of this species is unknown.

VISUAL ID: This family of segmented worms is characterized by two paired rows of overlapping, plate-like scales, called elytra, that run down the back. Frequently in shades of brown to gray to black. Most species require microscopic examination to determine genus and species.

ABUNDANCE & DISTRIBUTION: Occasional Florida, Bahamas, Caribbean.

HABITAT & BEHAVIOR: Found in most marine habitats. Hide under rock slabs, coral and shell rubble, and in recesses.

REACTION TO DIVERS: Many species will roll into a tight ball when threatened.

VISUAL ID: Thousands of tiny white worms on inner walls of sponges.

ABUNDANCE & DISTRIBUTION: Common Florida, Bahamas, Caribbean.

HABITAT & BEHAVIOR: Inhabit sponges on which they feed by inserting their proboscis into individual cells. They are most commonly observed in Touch-Me-Not Sponges, *Neofibularia nolitangere,* [pg. 37].

NOTE: Until recently, sponge worms of this type were all thought to be *Syllis spongicola,* a species first described from the Mediterranean. Many scientists, however, now believe that there are several species instead, all in the genus *Haplosyllis.*

**SCALLOPED
FIREWORM**
Chloeia sp.
ORDER:
Amphinomida
FAMILY:
Fireworms
Amphinomidae

SIZE: 3 - 5 in.
DEPTH: 1 - 130 ft.

SCALE WORMS
Undescribed
ORDER:
Phyllodocida
FAMILY:
Scale Worms
Polynoidae

SIZE: 1 - 4 in.
DEPTH: 0 - 130 ft.

SPONGE WORMS
Haplosyllis sp.
ORDER:
Phyllodocida
FAMILY:
Sponge Worms
Syllidae

SIZE: $1/16$ - 1/8 in.
DEPTH: 10 - 130 ft.

Lugworms – Elongated Worms

VISUAL ID: Volcanic-cone-shaped mound in sand. The worms, which are never above the surface, reside in U-shaped burrows beneath sand. They are colored in shades of green to brown, with brownish red tufts of gill filaments.

ABUNDANCE & DISTRIBUTION: Common Florida, Bahamas, Caribbean.

HABITAT & BEHAVIOR: Inhabit sand flats, where hundreds of the conical mounds may be observed. Worms ingest sandy bottom material, digest organic debris, then blow excreted sand from burrows by water pressure, forming the conical mounds (see photograph).

VISUAL ID: Large dark brown to reddish brown with five long tentacles extending from the head segment. Body segments are separated by deep creases. Near the base of most body segments extend a small tuft of short bristles, a single long cirri and starting about seven segments back from the head are long feather-like gill structures.

ABUNDANCE & DISTRIBUTION: Uncommon Caribbean.

HABITAT & BEHAVIOR: Inhabit the maze of deep recesses in reefs. At night may forage in the open around the base of reefs.

REACTION TO DIVERS: Extremely sensitive to light; retreat rapidly into reef when illuminated by divers' lights.

NOTE: Identification is tentative because more taxonomic research needs to be done on this and several similar appearing species reported in the region.

VISUAL ID: Dark brown to reddish brown; five long, banded tentacles extend from the head segment, two more extend from the upper portion of the first body segment. Deep creases separate body segments. A small tuft of short bristles extends from most body segments. Long, feather-like gill structures begin about seven segments back from the head.

ABUNDANCE & DISTRIBUTION: Uncommon Florida; also Bermuda.

HABITAT & BEHAVIOR: Burrow beneath gravel, shell and coral rubble. At night extend head and first few body segments to feed.

REACTION TO DIVERS: Extremely sensitive to light; rapidly retreat when illuminated by divers' lights.

SOUTHERN LUGWORM
Arenicola cristata
ORDER:
Capitellida
FAMILY:
Lugworms
Arenicolidae

SIZE: 4 - 6 in.
DEPTH: 3 - 60 ft.

THE THING
Eunice roussaei
ORDER:
Eunicida
FAMILY:
Elongated Worms
Eunicidae

SIZE: 2 - 4 ft.,
max. 6 ft.
DEPTH: 10 - 100 ft.

LONG BRISILE EUNICE
Eunice longisetis
ORDER:
Eunicida
FAMILY:
Elongated Worms
Eunicidae

SIZE: 6 - 14 in., max. 18 in.
DEPTH: 8 - 60 ft.

Feather Duster Worms

VISUAL ID: Large crown of radioles arranged in a double circular pattern. Banded pattern comes in a variety of colors, including shades of brown, brownish red, reddish purple, gold, tan and white. Parchment-like tubes are often hidden in recesses or encased in coral. Largest of Caribbean feather dusters.

ABUNDANCE & DISTRIBUTION: Common to uncommon Florida, Bahamas, Caribbean

HABITAT & BEHAVIOR: Inhabit reefs, sand and gravel bottoms, pilings and wrecks. Often grow from coral heads.

REACTION TO DIVERS: Shy; instantly retract crowns into tubes when approached. If diver waits motionless, for several minutes, crowns may slowly extend and reopen.

VISUAL ID: Grow in clusters. Crowns of radioles arranged in circular patterns, extend from parchment-like tubes that are usually exposed. Crowns' color variable, although generally consistent within a geographical area; for example, tend to be violet in Cayman Islands, white in Cozumel, and light brown in Belize. Color usually more intense near mouth, shading to white around outer part of crown; occasionally display some banding.

ABUNDANCE & DISTRIBUTION: Common Caribbean, Bahamas.

HABITAT & BEHAVIOR: Inhabit reefs. Prefer areas with some water movement. Reproduce asexually and are, consequently, usually found in clusters.

REACTION TO DIVERS: Shy; instantly retract crowns into tubes when approached. If diver waits motionless, for several minutes, crowns may slowly extend and reopen.

NOTE: Specimens in all three photographs were collected and visual identification confirmed by microscopic examination.

Social Feather Duster
Color and marking variation.

148

MAGNIFICENT FEATHER DUSTER
Sabellastarte magnifica

ORDER:
Sabellida
FAMILY:
Feather Duster Worms
Sabellidae

SIZE: Crown 3 - 6 in.
DEPTH: 10 - 60 ft.

SOCIAL FEATHER DUSTER
Bispira brunnea

ORDER:
Sabellida
FAMILY:
Feather Duster Worms
Sabellidae

SIZE: Crown $^3/_4$ - $1^1/_4$ in.
DEPTH: 15 - 60 ft.

Social Feather Duster
Color and marking variation.

Feather Duster Worms

VISUAL ID: Circular crown of radioles often variegated [below right] or banded [below] in shades of brown, maroon and violet, although color is occasionally uniform [opposite]. Parchment-like tubes usually hidden. Dark eyespots are often visible on stems of radioles.

ABUNDANCE & DISTRIBUTION: Occasional Florida, Bahamas, Caribbean.

HABITAT & BEHAVIOR: Inhabit reefs and surrounding areas of rubble and sand. Often congregate in small groups. Tubes are usually hidden in sand, under rocks or in recesses.

REACTION TO DIVERS: Shy; instantly retract crowns into tubes when approached. If diver waits motionless, for several minutes, crowns may slowly extend and reopen.

NOTE: Specimens in all three photographs were collected and visual identifications confirmed by microscopic examination. Often reported by junior names *Sabella melanostigma* and *S. bipunctuta*.

Variegated Feather Duster
Color and marking variation.

VISUAL ID: Circular crown of radioles is nearly colorless to white, with three very faint maroon bands and darker ring just above mouth. Usually cluster in large groups, with parchment-like tubes protruding from the sand.

ABUNDANCE & DISTRIBUTION: Common Florida, Bahamas, Caribbean.

HABITAT & BEHAVIOR: Inhabit sandy areas around reefs where solid substrate or coral rock is at or near sand's surface. Tube bases often encased in coral rock.

REACTION TO DIVERS: Extremely sensitive to any movement. Even when approached from several feet away, instantly retract crowns into tubes. If diver waits motionless, for several minutes, crowns may slowly extend and reopen.

NOTE: Photographed specimens were collected and visual identification of genus determined by microscopic examination. Probably an undescribed species.

VARIEGATED FEATHER DUSTER

Bispira variegata

ORDER:
Sabellida
FAMILY:
Feather Duster Worms
Sabellidae

SIZE: Crown ³/₄ - 1¹/₄ in.
DEPTH: 20 - 75 ft

Variegated Feather Duster

Color and marking variation.

GHOST FEATHER DUSTERS

Anamobaea sp.

ORDER:
Sabellida
Feather Duster Worms
Sabellidae

SIZE: Crown ¹/₂ - ³/₄ in.
DEPTH: 15 - 60 ft.

Feather Duster Worms

VISUAL ID: Circular crown of radioles is yellow, and occasionally spotted or thinly banded with dark purple. Also reported white, red and/or purple on occasion. Parchment-like tubes usually hidden.

ABUNDANCE & DISTRIBUTION: Common to occasional Florida, Bahamas, Caribbean.

HABITAT & BEHAVIOR: Inhabit older areas of reefs without much living coral. Prefer shaded areas, often under ledges, rocks or in recesses. Tubes usually encased in coral rock.

REACTION TO DIVERS: Shy; instantly retract crowns into tubes when approached. If diver waits motionless, for several minutes, crowns may slowly extend and reopen.

NOTE: Photographed specimen was collected and visual identification confirmed by microscopic examination. Has previously been incorrectly reported as *Hypsicomus elegans*.

VISUAL ID: Circular crown of radioles is spotted and banded, in shades of white, brown and purple. Parchment-like tubes usually hidden.

ABUNDANCE & DISTRIBUTION: Common to occasional Florida, Bahamas, Caribbean.

HABITAT & BEHAVIOR: Inhabit older areas of reefs with little living coral. Prefer shaded areas, often under ledges, rocks and in recesses. Tubes usually encased in coral rock.

REACTION TO DIVERS: Shy; instantly retract crowns into tubes when approached. If diver waits motionless, for several minutes, crowns may slowly extend and reopen.

NOTE: Photographed specimen was collected and visual identification confirmed by microscopic examination. Has previously been reported by junior name *Protulides elegans*.

VISUAL ID: Circular crown of radioles form a pleated design. Yellowish with a white ring around outer edge and white band near mouth. About one inch of parchment-like tube is usually visible.

ABUNDANCE & DISTRIBUTION: Occasional Caribbean.

HABITAT & BEHAVIOR: Inhabit coral reefs, especially along walls. Prefer somewhat protected areas, often under ledges and in depressions along walls. Tubes usually encased in coral rock.

REACTION TO DIVERS: Shy; instantly retract crowns into tubes. If diver waits motionless, for several minutes, crowns may slowly extend and reopen.

NOTE: Photographed specimen was collected and identification made by microscopic examination. This was a previously unreported genus in the Caribbean and is probably an undescribed species.

YELLOW FANWORM
Notaulax occidentalis
ORDER:
Sabellida
FAMILY:
Feather Duster Worms
Sabellidae

SIZE: Crown ¾ - 1¼ in.
DEPTH: 10 - 70 ft.

BROWN FANWORM
Notaulax nudicollis
ORDER:
Sabellida
FAMILY:
Feather Duster Worms
Sabellidae

SIZE: Crown ¾ - 1¼ in.
DEPTH: 10 - 70 ft.

RUFFLED FEATHER DUSTER
Hypsicomus sp.
ORDER:
Sabellida
FAMILY:
Feather Duster Worms
Sabellidae

SIZE: Crown ¼ - ¾ in.
DEPTH: 25 - 75 ft.

Feather Duster Worms

VISUAL ID: Radioles arranged in an oval pattern, with a longitudinal split of the crown into mirrored halves. Color variable in shades of brown, orangish brown, maroon and violet, often with white spots and bands. Parchment-like tubes usually hidden.

ABUNDANCE & DISTRIBUTION: Common Florida, Bahamas, Caribbean.

HABITAT & BEHAVIOR: Inhabit reefs and adjacent areas. May be solitary or in small groups of three or four. Tubes often deeply encased in coral rock.

REACTION TO DIVERS: Shy; instantly retract crowns into tubes when approached. If diver waits motionless, for several minutes, crowns may slowly extend and reopen.

NOTE: Photographed specimens were collected and visual identification confirmed by microscopic examination.

VISUAL ID: Radioles of crown form circular pattern with a distinctive V-shaped fold into one side; the two inner radioles of the fold are long and tipped with ball-like eyespots.. Banded and spotted in shades of lavender or brown and white. Parchment-like tube usually hidden.

ABUNDANCE & DISTRIBUTION: Occasional South Florida, Bahamas, Caribbean.

HABITAT & BEHAVIOR: Inhabit reefs. Tubes usually in narrow, tight crevices or recesses. Multi-faceted eyespots on tips of radioles allow this worm to be unusually sensitive to movement.

REACTION TO DIVERS: Extremely sensitive to any movement. Even when approached from several feet away, instantly retract crowns into tubes. Do not extend crowns for several minutes after retraction. An extremely slow approach is required to view these worms closely.

NOTE: Photographed specimen was collected and identification of genus determined by microscopic examination. Probably an undescribed species.

SPLIT-CROWN FEATHER DUSTER
Anamobaea orstedii
ORDER:
Sabellida
FAMILY:
Feather Duster Worms
Sabellidae

SIZE: Crown 1½ - 2 in.
DEPTH: 15 - 75 ft.

Split-crown Feather Duster
Color and marking variations.

SHY FEATHER DUSTER
Megalomma sp.
ORDER:
Sabellida
FAMILY:
Feather Duster Worms
Sabellidae

SIZE: Crown ½ - 1 in.
DEPTH: 6 - 75 ft.

Feather Duster Worms – Calcareous Tube Worms

VISUAL ID: Radioles form distinctive horseshoe-shaped crown. Banded in shades of brown and white. Rows of black eyespots are visible on the radioles' stems. Parchment-like tube usually hidden.

ABUNDANCE & DISTRIBUTION: Common South Florida, Bahamas; occasional Caribbean.

HABITAT & BEHAVIOR: Inhabit reefs. Tubes usually in crevices or encased in sponges.

REACTION TO DIVERS: Shy; instantly retract crowns into tubes when approached. If diver waits motionless, for several minutes, crowns may slowly extend and reopen.

NOTE: Photographed specimen was collected and visual identification confirmed by microscopic examination.

VISUAL ID: Double fold of radioles form U-shaped crown. Long, heavy-stalked operculum has circular tip with no horns or heavy spikes; at the center is a star-shaped pattern of fine spines, that is often overgrown with algae. Colors and patterns of radioles variable, though most commonly in shades of red, orange, yellow and white. Tubes usually hidden.

ABUNDANCE & DISTRIBUTION: Abundant Florida, Bahamas, Caribbean.

HABITAT & BEHAVIOR: Inhabit all areas of reef. Tubes usually encased in living coral.

REACTION TO DIVERS: Shy; when approached instantly retract crowns into tube and close openings with operculum. If diver waits motionless, for several minutes, crowns may slowly extend and reopen.

NOTE: Specimens in all four photographs were collected and visual identifications confirmed by laboratory examination.

BLACK-SPOTTED FEATHER DUSTER
Branchiomma nigromaculata

ORDER:
Sabellida
FAMILY:
Feather Duster Worms
Sabellidae

SIZE: Crown ½ - 1 in.
DEPTH: 6 - 75 ft.

STAR HORSESHOE WORM
Pomatostegus stellatus

ORDER:
Sabellida
FAMILY:
Calcareous Tube Worms
Serpulidae

SIZE: Crown 1 - 1½ in.
DEPTH: 10 - 100 ft.

Star Horseshoe Worm
Color and marking variations.

Calcareous Tube Worms

VISUAL ID: Two spiraled crowns of radioles, with double-horned operculum between. Tubes usually hidden; a single sharp spike protrudes from edge of opening. Color and patterns of radioles variable, though most frequently shades of brown, orange, maroon and white.

ABUNDANCE & DISTRIBUTION: Abundant Florida, Bahamas, Caribbean.

HABITAT & BEHAVIOR: Inhabit all areas of reef. Tubes usually encased in living coral.

REACTION TO DIVERS: Shy; when approached instantly retract crowns into tube and close openings with operculum. If diver waits motionless, for several minutes, crown may slowly extend and reopen.

VISUAL ID: Double fold of white radioles with red spots form a deep, rounded, U-shaped crown. Tube hidden; opening has a trumpet-like flair. No operculum.

ABUNDANCE & DISTRIBUTION: Common Caribbean.

HABITAT & BEHAVIOR: Inhabit reefs. Prefer secluded, shaded areas, often in small recesses under lower edges of corals.

REACTION TO DIVERS: Shy; retract crowns into tubes instantly when approached. If diver waits motionless, for several minutes, crowns may slowly extend and reopen.

NOTE: Photographed specimen was collected and visual identification of genus confirmed by microscopic examination. Possibly an undescribed species.

VISUAL ID: Small fan-shaped crown of radioles is translucent with white markings. Circular operculum on long stalk. Tubes hidden.

ABUNDANCE & DISTRIBUTION: Common to occasional Florida, Bahamas, Caribbean.

HABITAT & BEHAVIOR: Live in association with Touch-Me-Not Sponges, *Neofibularia nolitangere,* [pg. 37]. Tubes become encased as their rate of extension matches that of host sponge's growth. Not found on all Touch-Me-Not Sponges, but when present they are usually numerous.

REACTION TO DIVERS: Shy; instantly retract crowns into tubes when approached. If diver waits motionless, for several minutes, crowns may slowly extend and reopen.

CHRISTMAS TREE WORM
Spirobranchus giganteus
ORDER:
Sabellida
FAMILY:
Calcareous Tube Worms
Serpulidae

SIZE: Crown 1 - 1½ in.
DEPTH: 10 - 100 ft.

RED-SPOTTED HORSESHOE WORM
Protula sp.
ORDER:
Sabellida
FAMILY:
Calcareous Tube Worms
Serpulidae

SIZE: Crown 1 - 1¼ in.
DEPTH: 15 - 60 ft.

TOUCH-ME-NOT FANWORM
Hydroides spongicola
ORDER:
Sabellida
FAMILY:
Calcareous Tube Worms
Serpulidae

SIZE: Crown ½ - 1 in.
DEPTH: 10 - 100 ft.

Calcareous Tube Worms

VISUAL ID: Tangles and twinings of tiny white tubes. Often encrust, but may grow in small clumps or disordered masses. Tiny crowns of radioles at tubes' heads are barely visible.

ABUNDANCE & DISTRIBUTION: Common Florida, Bahamas, Caribbean.

HABITAT & BEHAVIOR: Primarily inhabit reefs. Prefer shaded, protected areas. Often encrust areas around base of rope and tube sponges and under ledge overhangs [pictured]. Clumps often in areas of rubbles. The branches of black coral trees occasionally support disordered masses.

REACTION TO DIVERS: Shy; instantly retract crowns into tubes when approached. If diver waits motionless, for several minutes, crowns may slowly extend and reopen.

Sea Frost
Detail.

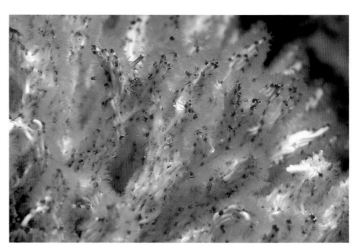

VISUAL ID: Tiny reddish fans on surface of Blushing Star Coral, *Stephanocenia michelini*. Tubes encased in coral.

ABUNDANCE & DISTRIBUTION: Occasional South Florida, Bahamas, Caribbean.

HABITAT & BEHAVIOR: Apparently always live in association with Blushing Star Coral (see note), which form medium-sized, rounded mounds.

REACTION TO DIVERS: Shy; instantly retract crowns into tubes when approached; the coral's tiny polyps also retract simultaneously. The overall effect is that the coral head appears to "blush" white. If diver waits motionless, for several minutes, crowns and coral polyps may slowly extend and reopen.

NOTE: Pictured specimens were collected and visual identification of genus determined by microscopic examination. Little is known about this worm, and it is probably an undescribed species.

SEA FROST
Filograna huxleyi
ORDER:
Sabellida
FAMILY:
**Calcareous
Tube Worms**
Serpulidae

SIZE: Crown $^1/_{16}$ in.
Tubes to 6 in.
DEPTH: 20 - 130 ft.

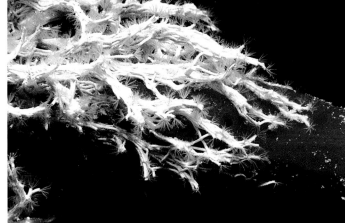

Sea Frost
Clumping pattern.

BLUSHING STAR CORAL FANWORM
Vermiliopsis n. sp.
ORDER:
Sabellida
FAMILY:
**Calcareous
Tube Worms**
Serpulidae

SIZE: Crown to $^1/_4$ in.
DEPTH: 10 - 130 ft.

Spaghetti Worms – Worm Rock

VISUAL ID: Long, smooth, transparent to translucent whitish tentacles extend from hiding place and spread over sand.

ABUNDANCE & DISTRIBUTION: Common Florida, Bahamas, Caribbean.

HABITAT & BEHAVIOR: Inhabit reefs and adjacent areas of sand and rubble. Hide under rocks, debris, coral heads and in cracks along the bases of reefs. Live in tubes constructed of fine sand and mucus.

REACTION TO DIVERS: Retract tentacles when disturbed.

NOTE: Photographed specimen was collected and identified by laboratory examination. There are several species of similar worms and identification beyond family often requires the disturbance of worm's habitat to see its body, a practice not encouraged.

VISUAL ID: Long, smooth, bluish or greenish translucent tentacles with whitish spots and rings. Tentacles extend from hiding place and spread over sand. Body grayish with whitish or pinkish bands.

ABUNDANCE & DISTRIBUTION: Common Florida, Bahamas, Caribbean.

HABITAT & BEHAVIOR: Inhabit reefs and adjacent areas of sand and rubble. Hide under rocks, debris, coral heads and in cracks along bases of reefs. Live in tubes constructed of fine sand and mucus.

REACTION TO DIVERS: Retract tentacles when disturbed.

NOTE: There are several species of similar worms and identification beyond family often requires the disturbance of worm's habitat to see its body, a practice not encouraged.

VISUAL ID: Long, often intertwining rows of fluted holes cover the surface of hard cement-like structures ranging in size from small encrustations to huge boulders and mounds. In some areas they collectively form shallow water reefs, known as worm reefs.

ABUNDANCE & DISTRIBUTION: Encrustations are common along Florida's east coast from Cape Canaveral to Key Biscayne, Florida. Large boulders and mounds forming worm reefs are best developed off St. Lucie and Martin counties, Florida.

HABITAT & BEHAVIOR: Aggregations of small tropical marine worms construct hard tube homes of sand grains cemented held together by a protein cement. Structures build by succeeding generations of worm larvae settling on existing tube masses.

NOTE: Formerly classified as species *lapidesa*.

SPAGHETTI WORM
Eupolymnia crassicornis
ORDER:
Terebellida
FAMILY:
Spaghetti Worms
Terebellidae

SIZE: Tentacles to 18 in.
DEPTH: 10 - 130 ft.

MEDUSA WORM
Loimia medusa
ORDER:
Terebellida
FAMILY:
Spaghetti Worms
Terebellidae

SIZE: Tentacles to 18 in.
DEPTH: 10 - 130 ft.

WORM ROCK
Phragmatopoma caudata
ORDER:
Terebellida
FAMILY:
Sabellariidae

SIZE: 1-1¹/₂ in.
DEPTH: 0 - 35 ft.

Phylum Arthropoda

(Are-THROP-uh-duh / Gr. jointed leg))

Class Crustacea
Shrimps, Lobsters, Crabs, Barnacles

Arthropods make up the largest phylum in the Animal Kingdom, with nearly two million described species. They include the insects and spiders, as well as many marine creatures. At this writing, many zoologists believe arthropods should be re-classified into several phyla and additional subdivisions. This text, however, uses the traditional classifications. The group's most distinguishing feature is jointed legs, coupled with an often elaborate exoskeleton. A cuticular material is secreted to form an array of plates and tubes which are connected by flexible membranes to allow movement. While the exoskeleton provides excellent protection, it has the drawback of restricting growth. To remedy this problem, all arthropods periodically molt — shedding their old covering and replacing it with a new, enlarged version. Because the animal is vulnerable to predators during this process, molting usually takes place in protected recesses of the reef.

The most frequently observed arthropods on the reef are in the Class Crustacea, and are distinguished among other things by **two pairs of antennae,** and three distinct body parts — head, thorax and abdomen. The largest order of crustaceans is the decapods. They have **five pairs of legs,** and include shrimp, lobsters, crabs and their relatives. The head and thorax of these animals are fused and covered by a dorsal shell called a **carapace.**

Shrimps

CLASS: Crustacea (Krus-STAY-shuh / L. covered by a hard shell)
ORDER: Decapoda (Deck-ah-POE-duh / Gr. ten legs)
SUBORDER: Natantia (Nuh-TAN-tee-uh / L. swimming)

The most distinguishing characteristic of shrimp is their **long, hair-like antennae** which help divers locate them in their daytime hiding places, just inside dark recesses and near the openings of sponges. They are often beautifully colored and patterned. Their bodies tend to be laterally compressed, with a well-developed **abdomen,** making them highly adapted for swimming. A number of species, called cleaning shrimp, feed by removing parasites and bacterial debris from fish. A few species find protection by living in association with anemones. Although normally secretive, most come out into the open to feed on the reef at night.

Lobsters

CLASS: Crustacea
ORDER: Decapoda
SUBORDER: Palinura (Pal-uh-NUR-uh / Gr. backwards by tail)

Lobsters are bottom-dwellers that use well-developed legs to crawl about. If danger approaches, they can swim backward with darting speed, using powerful strokes of a heavy, muscular abdomen and wide, flattened tail. Spiny lobsters have a pair of **long, conical antennae** that often give away their hiding places on reefs during the day. They do not have claws for protection; instead, they rely on sharp spikes that cover their carapace and antennae. Slipper lobsters are also clawless, but have flattened, **rounded plate-like antennae,** and a second pair of **thin, short antennae.** They rely on their shell and camouflage for protection.

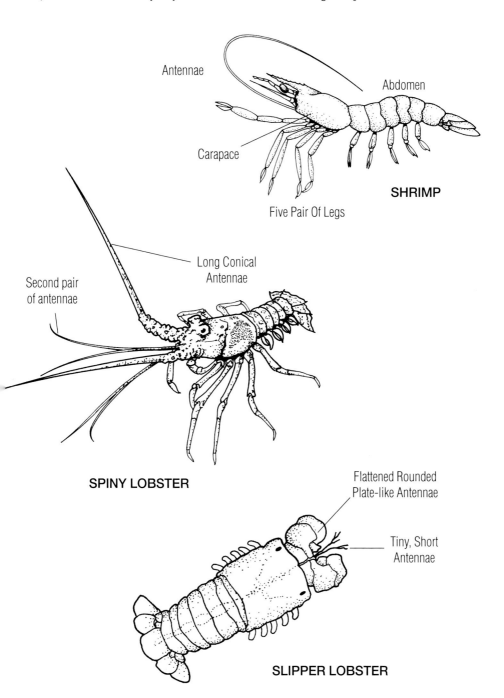

Antennae

Abdomen

Carapace

SHRIMP

Five Pair Of Legs

Long Conical
Antennae

Second pair
of antennae

SPINY LOBSTER

Flattened Rounded
Plate-like Antennae

Tiny, Short
Antennae

SLIPPER LOBSTER

Hermit Crabs & Porcelain Crabs

CLASS: Crustacea,
ORDER: Decapoda
SECTION: Anomura (An-oh-MURE-uh / Gr. irregular tail)

Hermit crabs use discarded **sea shells** as mobile homes. They occupy the shell by wrapping their long abdomen around the internal spirals of the shell and extend only head, antennae and legs from the opening. If threatened, they withdraw completely into the shell for protection. When they outgrow their homes, they simply move into a larger shell. This section also includes the porcelain crabs that look much like true crabs, but are distinguished by the presence of **long antennae** and **three pairs of walking legs.**

True Crabs

CLASS: Crustacea
ORDER: Decapoda
SECTION: Brachyura (Brack-ee-YOUR-uh / Gr. short tail)

Crabs have greatly reduced abdomens and tails, which are kept curled under their large, rounded, and often flattened carapace. Their first pair of legs have developed claws that are used for protection and for the manipulation of objects. If disturbed, these claws are raised toward the danger in a threatening manner. Using the remaining **four pairs of legs,** crabs can move rapidly in a sideways direction. Many species are quite small and secretive, and therefore difficult to find.

Mantis Shrimp

CLASS: CLASS: Crustacea
ORDER: Stomatapoda (Stow-ma-tuh-POE-duh / Gr. mouth-like leg)

Mantis shrimp inhabit both reefs and burrows in sandy areas. They resemble the praying mantis insect with their large, **stalked eyes** and long, **spiked foreclaws** which, when not in use, fold back into a claw slot in the leg. These powerful claws can slice a finger as well as capture prey. Species vary in length from a few inches to nearly a foot. These crustaceans are not decapods, and have only **three pairs of walking legs.** They are usually observed peering from the burrow entrance, but are occasionally spotted out in the open. They have an elongated body and **feather-like gills** attached to the lower abdomen.

Barnacles

CLASS: Crustacea
SUBCLASS: Cirripedia (Seer-uh-PED-ee-uh / L. curled or ringed legs)

Barnacles are gregarious crustaceans that permanently attach to a variety of substrate, including animals like whales and turtles. They have been described as shrimp-like animals that stand on their head and kick food into their mouths. Barnacles secrete a protective exoskeleton, composed of **shell plates.** Because they have shells they are often mistaken for mollusks. They can be distinguished by fan-like legs, called **cirri,** that extend from the shell and sweep the water for food. There are two basic types: **sessile barnacles** attach their shells directly to the substrate; the shells of **gooseneck barnacles,** are attached by an intervening **stalk.**

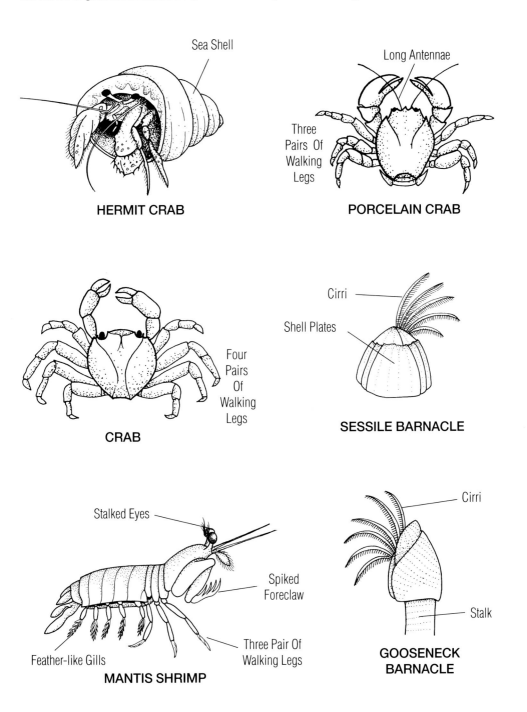

Sea Shell

HERMIT CRAB

Long Antennae

Three Pairs Of Walking Legs

PORCELAIN CRAB

Four Pairs Of Walking Legs

CRAB

Cirri

Shell Plates

SESSILE BARNACLE

Stalked Eyes

Spiked Foreclaw

Three Pair Of Walking Legs

Feather-like Gills

MANTIS SHRIMP

Cirri

Stalk

GOOSENECK BARNACLE

Shrimp

VISUAL ID: Red to reddish brown with white banding on legs, body and claws. Second pair of legs bear long, cylindrical, large claws with short somewhat slender pincers.
ABUNDANCE & DISTRIBUTION: Common Florida, Bahamas, Caribbean.
HABITAT & BEHAVIOR: Inhabit coral reefs.

VISUAL ID: Red and white banded body and claws, with bands occasionally bordered in purple. Two pairs of long, white, hair-like antennae. Walking legs and some parts of the body are often translucent. Third (middle) pair of legs are enlarged and bear large claws. Although the large claws break off easily, they can be regenerated and, as a consequence, are sometimes of unequal size.
ABUNDANCE & DISTRIBUTION: Common Florida, Bahamas, Caribbean.
HABITAT & BEHAVIOR: Inhabit reefs. Cleaning shrimp; perch near the openings of recesses or sponges.
REACTION TO DIVERS: When approached closely, retreat into protective recesses. If a bare hand is slowly extended toward the shrimp, it may leave its retreat and even attempt to clean fingers.
NOTE: Also commonly known as "Barber Pole Shrimp."

VISUAL ID: Yellow body and legs, with red and occasionally white bands on abdomen and claws. Two pairs of long white, hair-like antennae. Walking legs and some parts of the body are often translucent. Third (middle) pair of legs, which are enlarged, bear large claws. Although the large claws break off easily, they can be regenerated and, as a consequence, are sometimes of unequal size.
ABUNDANCE & DISTRIBUTION: Occasional to uncommon Florida, Bahamas, Caribbean.
HABITAT & BEHAVIOR: Inhabit reefs. Cleaning shrimp; perch near the openings of recesses or sponges.
REACTION TO DIVERS: When approached, retreat into protective recesses. If a bare hand is slowly extended toward the shrimp, it may leave its retreat and even attempt to clean fingers.

TWO CLAW SHRIMP
Brachycarpus biunguiculatus
ORDER:
Decapoda
SUBORDER:
Shrimp
Natantia
FAMILY:
Palaemonidae

SIZE: 1 - 2 ½ in.
DEPTH: 1 - 130 ft.

BANDED CORAL SHRIMP
Stenopus hispidus
ORDER:
Decapoda
SUBORDER:
Shrimp
Natantia
FAMILY:
Stenopodidae

SIZE: 1 ½ - 2 in.
DEPTH: 3 - 130 ft.

GOLDEN CORAL SHRIMP
Stenopus scutellatus
ORDER:
Decapoda
SUBORDER:
Shrimp
Natantia
FAMILY:
Stenopodidae

SIZE: ¾ - 1 ¼ in.
DEPTH: 10 - 130 ft.

Shrimp

VISUAL ID: Pale, pinkish white body and appendages with bold, bright red to reddish orange line markings.
ABUNDANCE & DISTRIBUTION: Occasional Florida, Bahamas, Caribbean.
HABITAT & BEHAVIOR: Inhabit reefs; often inside tube sponges. Cleaning shrimp.
REACTION TO DIVERS: Quite shy; retreat into sponge when approached.

VISUAL ID: Pale, orangish white body and appendages with fine, red to reddish orange, line markings. (Similar Peppermint Shrimp, *L. wurdemanni,* [previous] have wider, bold line markings.)
ABUNDANCE & DISTRIBUTION: Occasional Florida, rare Caribbean; also north to Virginia.
HABITAT & BEHAVIOR: Reclusive; inhabit deep crevices in reefs and rocky areas. Typically in pairs. Cleaning shrimp.
REACTION TO DIVERS: Wary; retreat into recesses when approached.

VISUAL ID: Two broad red stripes, with a narrow white stripe between, extend down back to tail. Pale cream to yellow body and legs. Two pairs of long, white, hair-like antennae.
ABUNDANCE & DISTRIBUTION: Occasional to uncommon Florida, Bahamas, Caribbean.
HABITAT & BEHAVIOR: Inhabit reefs. Cleaning shrimp that perch near the openings of recesses or sponges and slowly wave their antennae to attract fish. Pictured specimens are cleaning a Nassau Grouper, *Epinephalus striatus.*
REACTION TO DIVERS: When approached, retreat into protective recesses. If a bare hand is slowly extended toward the shrimp, they may leave their retreats and even attempt to clean fingers.

PEPPERMINT SHRIMP
Lysmata wurdemanni
ORDER:
Decapoda
SUBORDER:
Shrimp
Natantia
FAMILY:
Hippolytidae

SIZE: 1 - 1³/₄ in.
DEPTH: 3 - 90 ft.

HIDDEN CLEANER SHRIMP
Lysmata rathbunae
ORDER:
Decapoda
SUBORDER:
Shrimp
Natantia
FAMILY:
Hippolytidae

SIZE: ³/₄ - 1 in.,
1¹/₄ in. max.
DEPTH: 3 - 90 ft.

SCARLET-STRIPED CLEANING SHRIMP
Lysmata grabhami
ORDER:
Decapoda
SUBORDER:
Shrimp
Natantia
FAMILY:
Hippolytidae

SIZE: 1¹/₄ - 2 in.
DEPTH: 3 - 90 ft.

171

Shrimp

VISUAL ID: Slender, elongated body with long, pointed snout and prominent abdominal hump. Color varies from translucent to tan, gray, purple or green.
ABUNDANCE & DISTRIBUTION: Occasional Florida, Bahamas, Caribbean.
HABITAT & BEHAVIOR: Found in all shallow habitats. Color usually matches background, such as green on turtle grass, purple on sea plumes, etc.

VISUAL ID: Brown to gray body with three white saddles across back, and several spots on sides and tail. Saddles and spots are often outlined in dark brown and violet. Two pairs of short banded antennae. Large protruding eyes and upward pointing tail.
ABUNDANCE & DISTRIBUTION: Common South Florida, Bahamas, Caribbean.
HABITAT & BEHAVIOR: Live in association with a variety of anemones, especially the Giant Anemone, Sun Anemone and Elegant Anemone, *Actinoporus elegans*, [pg. 93].
REACTION TO DIVERS: When closely approached or molested, they retreat into the tentacles or under the anemone's body.
NOTE: Identification is probable. This genus was recently split into three groups according to minute anatomical differences; positive identification requires microscopic examination.

VISUAL ID: Tiny. Transparent to translucent with whitish carapace and belly; two narrow whitish bars encircle abdomen joining whitish belly; white eyes on short stocks.
ABUNDANCE & DISTRIBUTION: Occasional Florida, Bahamas, Caribbean.
HABITAT & BEHAVIOR: Live on gorgonians. Possibly prey on mucus excreted by hosts often move upside down clinging to underside of gorgonian branches [pictured].
REACTION TO DIVERS: Appear unconcerned; react only when molested.

ARROW SHRIMP
Tozeuma carolinense

ORDER:
Decapoda
SUBORDER:
Shrimp
Natantia
FAMILY:
Hippolytidae

SIZE: 1 - 1½ in.
DEPTH: 1 - 50 ft.

SQUAT ANEMONE SHRIMP
Thor amboinensis

ORDER:
Decapoda
SUBORDER:
Shrimp
Natantia
FAMILY:
Hippolytidae

SIZE: ¼ - ¾ in.
DEPTH: 10 - 60 ft.

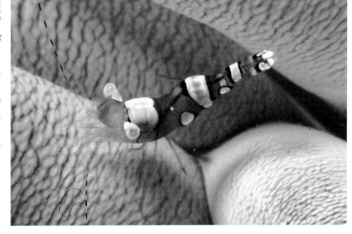

NICHOLSON'S SHRIMP
Hippolyte nicholsoni

ORDER:
Decapoda
SUBORDER:
Shrimp
Natantia
FAMILY:
Hippolytidae

SIZE: ¼ - 1 in.
DEPTH: 6 - 100 ft.

Shrimp

VISUAL ID: Rostrum flat with wide base and large eyes; abdominal segments lack spines and legs end in hooks. Most commonly translucent to transparent during day and shades of blue and green at night.

ABUNDANCE & DISTRIBUTION: Uncommon Florida Keys and northwestern Caribbean. Not reported balance of Caribbean, but the full extent of its range is not well established.

HABITAT & BEHAVIOR: Live on Slimy Sea Plume, *Pseudopterogorgia americana*, and possibly other sea plumes of the same genus.

REACTION TO DIVERS: Ignore divers unless molested.

VISUAL ID: Tiny. Typically color of host gorgonian; white eyes on short stocks.

ABUNDANCE & DISTRIBUTION: Occasional Florida, Bahamas, Caribbean.

HABITAT & BEHAVIOR: Live on gorgonians. Possibly prey on mucus excreted by hosts.

REACTION TO DIVERS: Appear unconcerned; react only when molested.

VISUAL ID: Tiny. Transparent to translucent with some greenish tinting; white eyes on transparent stocks; two or three faint whitish ring markings encircle body.

ABUNDANCE & DISTRIBUTION: Known only from Turks and Caicos Islands, where it is occasional. The range of this species is not well known, range may extend wherever Slimy Sea Plumes occur.

HABITAT & BEHAVIOR: Apparently live exclusively on Slimy Sea Plume, *Pseudopterogorgia americana*. Tend to move upside down clinging to the underside of gorgonian branches, [pictured].

REACTION TO DIVERS: Appear unconcerned; react only when molested.

SEA PLUME SHRIMP
Neopontonides chacei
ORDER:
Decapoda
SUBORDER:
Shrimp
Natantia
FAMILY:
Palaemonidae

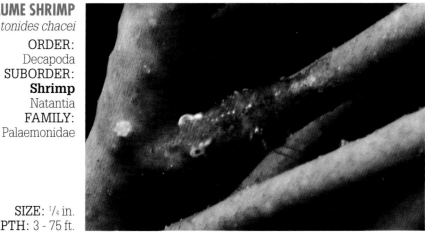

SIZE: ¹/₄ in.
DEPTH: 3 - 75 ft.

GORGONIAN SHRIMP
Periclimenes antillensis
ORDER:
Decapoda
SUBORDER:
Shrimp
Natantia
FAMILY:
Palaemonidae

SIZE: ¹/₄ - ¹/₂ in.
DEPTH: 50 - 150 ft.

SLIMY SEA PLUME SHRIMP
Periclimenes mclellandi
ORDER:
Decapoda
SUBORDER:
Shrimp
Natantia
FAMILY:
Palaemonidae

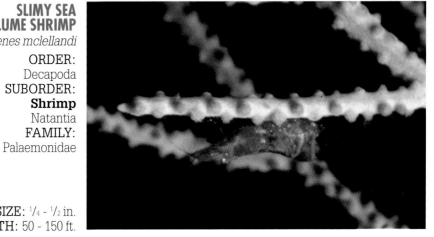

SIZE: ¹/₄ - ¹/₂ in.
DEPTH: 50 - 150 ft.

Shrimp

VISUAL ID: Transparent body and legs covered with purple to lavender spots. Two pairs of long, white, hair-like antennae. Rows of pinkish eggs are occasionally attached to belly [see photograph].

ABUNDANCE & DISTRIBUTION: Common South Florida, Bahamas, Caribbean.

HABITAT & BEHAVIOR: Live in association with a variety of anemones, especially Corkscrew Anemome, *Actinoporus elegans*, [pg. 93], Branching Anemones, *Lebrunia danae*, [pg. 97], Giant Anemone, *Condylactis gigantea*, [pg. 91] and Knobby Anemone, *lucida* [pg. 93]. Cleaning shrimp that perch on the tentacles of anemones, and sway their bodies and wave their antennae to attract fish.

REACTION TO DIVERS: Unafraid; if a bare hand is slowly extended, shrimp may swim out and attempt to clean fingers.

VISUAL ID: Body is transparent, with three or four tan and white saddle markings across back, and several white spots along sides. Legs and claws banded with white and purple, lavender or red. Two pairs of long, white, hair-like antennae with dark bands. Rows of pinkish eggs are occasionally attached to belly.

ABUNDANCE & DISTRIBUTION: Common South Florida, Bahamas, Caribbean.

HABITAT & BEHAVIOR: Live in association with a variety of anemones, especially Corkscrew Anemone, *Actinoporus elegans*, [pg. 93, Branching Anemones, *Lebrunia danae*, [pg. 97] and Giant Anemone, *Condylactis gigantea*, [pg. 91]. Cleaning shrimp that perch on the tentacles of anemones, and sway their bodies and wave their antennae to attract fish.

REACTION TO DIVERS: Unafraid.

NOTE: Identification is probable. Because there are several similar appearing species, positive identification requires microscopic examination.

VISUAL ID: Translucent to transparent with numerous brown and white spots, bands and other markings, including intricate design on carapace and abdominal segments.

ABUNDANCE & DISTRIBUTION: Occasional Florida, Bahamas Caribbean.

HABITAT & BEHAVIOR: Live in association with a number of anemones, but most commonly Sun Anemone, *Stichodactyla helianthus,* [pg.91].

REACTION TO DIVERS: Unafraid, ignore divers.

PEDERSON CLEANER SHRIMP
Periclimenes pedersoni
ORDER:
Decapoda
SUBORDER:
Shrimp
Natantia
FAMILY:
Palaemonidae

SIZE: ³/₄ - 1 in.
DEPTH: 10 - 60 ft.

SPOTTED CLEANER SHRIMP
Periclimenes yucatanicus
ORDER:
Decapoda
SUBORDER:
Shrimp
Natantia
FAMILY:
Palaemonidae

SIZE: ³/₄ - 1 in.
DEPTH: 10 - 60 ft.

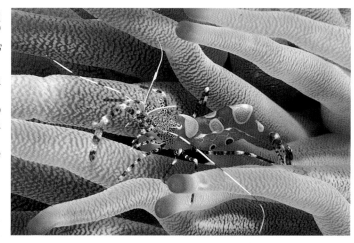

SUN ANEMONE SHRIMP
Periclimenes rathbunae
ORDER:
Decapoda
SUBORDER:
Shrimp
Natantia
FAMILY:
Palaemonidae

SIZE: ³/₄ - 1 in.
DEPTH: 3 - 60 ft.

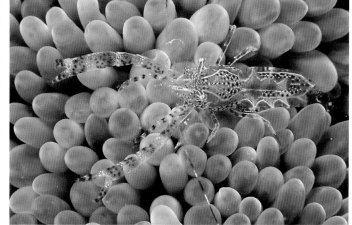

Shrimp

VISUAL ID: Translucent to transparent. Abdomen arched in middle, rostrum arched above and flat below, pincers of second legs larger than those of first.

ABUNDANCE & DISTRIBUTION: Occasional Florida, Bahamas, Caribbean and Gulf of Mexico. Also north to North Carolina and south to Brazil.

HABITAT & BEHAVIOR: Typically in shallow seagrass bed, but also inhabit reefs.

REACTION TO DIVERS: Ignore divers unless molested.

NOTE: Identification is tentative, collection and microscopic examination required to confirm identification.

VISUAL ID: Tiny. White stalked eyes with white stripe on upper back to tail; dark brown to black head belly and stripe from head to upper back; transparent midbody.

ABUNDANCE & DISTRIBUTION: Occasional Curacao and Bonaire. Range not well established, possibly exists wherever host crinoid is found.

HABITAT & BEHAVIOR: Live exclusively on Black & White Crinoid, *Nemaster grandis*, [pg. 357]

REACTION TO DIVERS: Appear unconcerned; react only when molested.

VISUAL ID: Tiny. Bright yellow stalked eyes with bright yellow stripe on upper back; orange head back and tail; orangish translucent to transparent midbody.

ABUNDANCE & DISTRIBUTION: Occasional eastern and southern Caribbean. Range not well established, probably possibly exists wherever host crinoid is found.

HABITAT & BEHAVIOR: Live exclusively on Golden Crinoid, *Davidaster rubiginosa*, [pg. 355].

REACTION TO DIVERS: Appear unconcerned; react only when molested.

LONGTAIL GRASS SHRIMP
Periclimenes longicaudatus
ORDER:
Decapoda
SUBORDER:
Shrimp
Natantia
FAMILY:
Palaemonidae

SIZE: ¹/₂ - ³/₄ in.
DEPTH: 0-90 ft.

BROWN FEATHERSTAR SHRIMP
Periclimenes meyeri
ORDER:
Decapoda
SUBORDER:
Shrimp
Natantia
FAMILY:
Palaemonidae

SIZE: ¹/₂ - ⁷/₈ in.
DEPTH: 30 - 130 ft.

ORANGE FEATHERSTAR SHRIMP
Periclimenes crinoidalis
ORDER:
Decapoda
SUBORDER:
Shrimp
Natantia
FAMILY:
Palaemonidae

SIZE: ¹/₂ - ⁷/₈ in.
DEPTH: 30 - 130 ft.

Shrimp

VISUAL ID: Tiny. Transparent to translucent with some brown markings; white eyes on dark stocks.
ABUNDANCE & DISTRIBUTION: Occasional southern Bahamas and Caribbean.
HABITAT & BEHAVIOR: Live exclusively on black corals *Antipathes gracilis* and *Cirrhipathes* sp.
REACTION TO DIVERS: Appear unconcerned; react only when molested.
NOTE: Not a well known species, possibly live on other species of black coral.

VISUAL ID: Large pale yellow eyes; long tapering carapace with flat rostrum, long claw arms, and abdominal segments without spines. Colors vary from olive to brown to dark gray to match associated Antipatharian. Occasionally with alternating light and dark bands.

ABUNDANCE & DISTRIBUTION: Occasional Caribbean and Gulf of Mexico. Not reported east Florida or Bahamas, but the entire extent of range is not well established.

HABITAT & BEHAVIOR: Live on stems of Wire Coral, *Cirrhipathes leutkeni*, the branches of Feather Black Coral, *Antipathes pennacea*, and possibly other Antipatharians.

REACTION TO DIVERS: Tend to ignore divers unless molested.

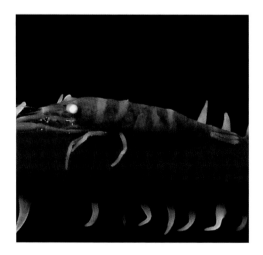

BLACK CORAL SHRIMP
Periclimenes antipathophilus
ORDER:
Decapoda
SUBORDER:
Shrimp
Natantia
FAMILY:
Palaemonidae

SIZE: ¹/₄ - ³/₈ in.
DEPTH: 50 - 150 ft.

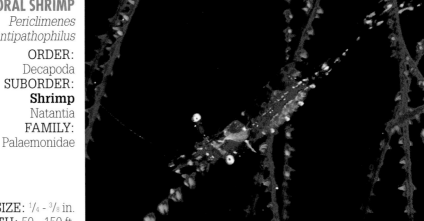

WIRE CORAL SHRIMP
Pseudopontonides principis
ORDER:
Decapoda
SUBORDER:
Shrimp
Natantia
FAMILY:
Palaemonidae

SIZE: ¹/₄ - ¹/₂ in.
DEPTH: 45 - 225 ft.

Wire Coral Shrimp
Color variations.

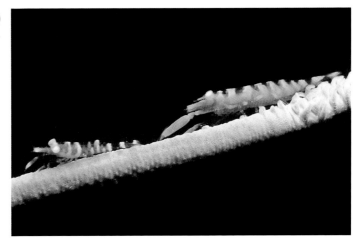

Shrimp

VISUAL ID: Tiny. Shades of orange to tan and dark brown with black bar across center of white tail; may have additional dark bar markings on body and banded legs. White eyes on stalks.
ABUNDANCE & DISTRIBUTION: Uncommon West Florida, Florida Keys and Bonaire. Range not well established, possibly exists wherever host Giant Basket Star occurs.
HABITAT & BEHAVIOR: Live exclusively on Giant Basket Star, *Astrophyton muricatum* [pg. 377].
REACTION TO DIVERS: Appear unconcerned; react only when molested.

VISUAL ID: Barrel-shaped body with dark brown bands with lines of yellow-gold between.
ABUNDANCE & DISTRIBUTION: Common eastern Caribbean; occasional to rare balance of Caribbean, Florida and Bahamas. Also circumtropical.
HABITAT & BEHAVIOR: Commonly live on sea cucumbers and occasionally other echinoderms.
REACTION TO DIVERS: Ignore divers unless molested.

VISUAL ID: Tiny. Broad, pale brownish gray stripe down back bordered with broad white stripes.
ABUNDANCE & DISTRIBUTION: Uncommon South Florida, Bahamas, Caribbean; also circumtropical.
HABITAT & BEHAVIOR: Live exclusively on Variegated Urchin, *Lytechinus variegates,* [pg. 383] where they feed on detritus caught on the urchin's spines, the hosts' skin and plankton.
REACTION TO DIVERS: Appear unconcerned; react only if molested.

BASKET STAR SHRIMP
Periclimenes perryae
ORDER:
Decapoda
SUBORDER:
Shrimp
Natantia
FAMILY:
Palaemonidae

SIZE: ¹/₂ in.
DEPTH: 15 - 90 ft.

BUMBLEBEE SHRIMP
*Gnathophyllum
americanum*
ORDER:
Decapoda
SUBORDER:
Shrimp
Natantia
FAMILY:
Gnathophyllidae

SIZE: ¹/₄ in.
DEPTH: 0 - 150 ft.

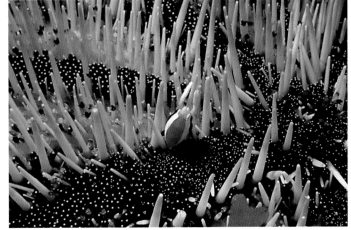

SQUAT URCHIN SHRIMP
Gnathophylloides mineri
ORDER:
Decapoda
SUBORDER:
Shrimp
Natantia
FAMILY:
Gnathophyllidae

SIZE: ¹/₄ - ⁷/₈ in. max.
DEPTH: 2 - 10 ft.

Shrimp

VISUAL ID: Body is red and may have white to tan bands and spots. Large black eyes.

ABUNDANCE & DISTRIBUTION: Abundant Florida Keys, Bahamas, Caribbean; occasional Palm Beach to Dade County, Florida.

HABITAT & BEHAVIOR: Inhabit coral reefs. Nocturnal; hide deep in reefs by day, and appear in large numbers at night. Eyes glow red when illuminated by a diver's light.

REACTION TO DIVERS: Shy; when approached retreat into protective recesses.

NOTE: Previously reported as *Rhynchocinetes ringens*, which has been reclassified in the genus *Cinetorynchus*. The species *C. ringens* only inhabits the eastern Atlantic.

VISUAL ID: Translucent to transparent body with red markings. Large bean-shaped eyes and tiny pincers on first three pair of walking legs.

ABUNDANCE & DISTRIBUTION: Occasional Florida, Bahamas, Caribbean. Also north to North Carolina, Bermuda and south to Brazil.

HABITAT & BEHAVIOR: Inhabit sand and seagrass beds.

NOTE: Identification is tentative, collection and microscopic examination required to confirm identification.

REACTION TO DIVERS: Ignore divers unless molested.

VISUAL ID: Members of this genus can be identified by their first legs: one bears a smooth, cylindrical, highly enlarged snapping claw; the other a much smaller claw. There are over 30 species in this genus; most require microscopic examination for identification.

ABUNDANCE & DISTRIBUTION: Common Florida, Bahamas, Caribbean.

HABITAT & BEHAVIOR: Found in all habitats. Hide in dark recesses. Several species live inside the canals of sponges. They use their powerful snapping claw to produce a loud popping sound which wards off intruders and helps capture food.

RED NIGHT SHRIMP
Cinetorhynchus manningi
ORDER:
Decapoda
SUBORDER:
Shrimp
Natantia
FAMILY:
Rhynchocinetidae

SIZE: 1¼ - 2 in.
DEPTH: 20 - 90 ft.

VELVET SHRIMP
Metapenaeopsis goodie
ORDER:
Decapoda
SUBORDER:
Shrimp
Natantia
FAMILY:
Penaeidae

SIZE: 1½ - 2 in.,
max. 2½ in
DEPTH: 6 - 900 ft.

LARGE-CLAW SNAPPING SHRIMP
Synalpheus sp.
ORDER:
Decapoda
SUBORDER:
Shrimp
Natantia
FAMILY:
Snapping Shrimp
Alpheidae

SIZE: ½ - ¾ in.
DEPTH: 1 - 130 feet.

Shrimp

VISUAL ID: Red and white banded antennae. Body ranges from bright red to orange to light brown, with white spots and markings. Blue markings often appear on tail. Each of their first legs bears a claw; one is a greatly enlarged snapping claw, the other is much smaller.

ABUNDANCE & DISTRIBUTION: Common South Florida, Bahamas, Caribbean

HABITAT & BEHAVIOR: Live with Corkscrew Anemone, *Bartholomea annulata,* [pg. 93]. Often only their antennae can be seen protruding from anemone. They use their powerful snapping claw to produce loud popping sounds which ward off intruders and help capture food.

REACTION TO DIVERS: When threatened with quick movements, often dart forward and snap large claw or pinch. If fingertips are held steady at the edge of the anemone the shrimp will pick cuticles gently.

NOTE: Also commonly known as "Pistol Shrimp." There are four similar species that are impossible to distinguish underwater: *A. armatus, A. immoculatus, A. polystictus* and *A roquensis.*

VISUAL ID: Members of this genus can be identified by two claws of unequal size. The larger claw is quite robust, appearing somewhat swollen and tipped with a relatively small, curved pincer. The smaller is less robust with long straight pincer. Beady eyes protrude from the carapace (not on stalks) and fan-shaped tail. There are about 25 species in this genus, most require microscopic examination for identification to species.

ABUNDANCE & DISTRIBUTION: Occasional Florida, Bahamas, Caribbean and Gulf of Mexico.

HABITAT & BEHAVIOR: Reclusive; inhabit recesses in reefs, under debris and in shells.

REACTION TO DIVERS: Shy; retreat quickly to cover when exposed.

RED SNAPPING SHRIMP
Alpheus spp.
ORDER:
Decapoda
SUBORDER:
Shrimp
Natantia
FAMILY:
Snapping Shrimp
Alpheidae

SIZE: 1 - 2 in.
DEPTH: 3 - 40 ft.

SNAPPING SHRIMP
Alpheus spp.
ORDER:
Decapoda
SUBORDER:
Shrimp
Natantia
FAMILY:
Snapping Shrimp
Alpheidae

SIZE: ³/₄ - 2 in.
DEPTH: 3 - 75 ft.

Snapping Shrimp
Color variations.

Shrimp – Spiny Lobsters

VISUAL ID: Carapace has three ridges on back running length of shell; nearly equal sized lobster-like pincers. Scientific literature does not indicate color, consequently it is unknown if the red and white markings on the pictured specimen is typical of the species.

ABUNDANCE & DISTRIBUTION: Rare Bahamas, Caribbean; also Bermuda.

HABITAT & BEHAVIOR: Inhabit areas of mixed rocks, sand and rubble. Hide during day in recesses and under debris.

REACTION TO DIVERS: Shy; rapidly retreat to protective cover upon approach.

VISUAL ID: Carapace has shaded areas of brown and tan with a few dark spots, while abdomen is brown and tan banded with a few light spots. They have sharp "horns" above their eyes and pair of long, conical antennae. **JUVENILE:** Dark brown body with lavender markings, brown and white banded legs, and a whitish band on tail.

ABUNDANCE & DISTRIBUTION: Common Florida, Bahamas, Caribbean. May be abundant in areas where they are not harvested.

HABITAT & BEHAVIOR: Inhabit reefs. Hide in protective recesses during day, and forage in the open at night. When disturbed, can swim backwards rapidly using powerful strokes of their tails. Females, during reproduction, carry clusters of tiny orange eggs under their abdomens and should be left undisturbed. Occasionally after winter storms, mass migrations of up to 50 individuals move in a single-file line across open terrain.

REACTION TO DIVERS: Wary; when approached retreat into protective recesses.

Caribbean Spiny Lobster
The species often gather in clusters.

THREE-RIDGE SNAPPING SHRIMP
Alpheopsis trigonus

ORDER:
Decapoda
SUBORDER:
Shrimp
Natantia
FAMILY:
Alpheidae

SIZE: 1 - 3 in.,
4 in. max.
DEPTH: 6 - 40 ft.

CARIBBEAN SPINY LOBSTER
Panulirus argus

ORDER:
Decapoda
SUBORDER:
Palinura
FAMILY:
Spiny Lobsters
Palinuridae

SIZE: 6 - 10 in.,
2 ft. max.
DEPTH: 3 - 200 ft.

**Caribbean
Spiny Lobster
Juvenile**

SIZE: Photographed
specimen about 1 in.

189

Spiny Lobsters

VISUAL ID: Body is brown to dark purple, and covered with numerous white spots. Last segment of legs has brown stripes.

ABUNDANCE & DISTRIBUTION: Occasional Florida, Bahamas, Caribbean.

HABITAT & BEHAVIOR: Inhabit reefs. Hide in protective recesses during the day, and forage in the open at night. When disturbed, can swim backwards rapidly using powerful strokes of their tails.

REACTION TO DIVERS: Wary; retreat into protective recesses when approached.

SIMILAR SPECIES: Smoothtail Spiny Lobster, *P. laevicauda,* distinguished by bluish green to purplish cast and large white spots along sides of abdomen. Rare.

NOTE: Also commonly known as the "Spanish Lobster."

VISUAL ID: Bright red with white bulls-eye design on side of carapace; legs and tips of large, equal sized claws banded; spines and a series of white spots on each abdominal segment.

ABUNDANCE & DISTRIBUTION: Rare Florida, Bahamas, Caribbean. Also south to Brazil, Bermuda and eastern Atlantic.

HABITAT & BEHAVIOR: Inhabit reefs. Primarily nocturnal, normally hide in deep dark recesses during day, but may occasionally peer out from under ledge overhangs or recesses opening.

REACTION TO DIVERS: Very shy; retreat into recess when approached.

VISUAL ID: Legs have wide red bands and a few narrow white bands and spots. Antennae are banded in red and gold. Body is marked in shades of red and gold. First legs of males modified into large claws.

ABUNDANCE & DISTRIBUTION: Uncommon South Florida, Bahamas, Caribbean

HABITAT & BEHAVIOR: Inhabit deep reefs. Hide in deep recesses and caves during the day, and forage near openings at night.

REACTION TO DIVERS: Wary; when approached retreat into protective recesses.

SPOTTED SPINY LOBSTER
Panulirus guttatus

ORDER:
Decapoda
SUBORDER:
Palinura
FAMILY:
Spiny Lobsters
Palinuridae

SIZE: 5 - 8 in.,
18 in. max.
DEPTH: 6 - 75 ft.

FLAMING REEF LOBSTER
Enoplometopus antellensis

ORDER:
Decapoda
SUBORDER:
Palinura
FAMILY:
Spiny Lobsters
Palinuridae

SIZE: ³/₄ in.,
max. 4¹/₂ in.
DEPTH: 30 - 600 ft.

RED BANDED LOBSTER
Justitia longimanus

ORDER:
Decapoda
SUBORDER:
Palinura
FAMILY:
Spiny Lobsters
Palinuridae

SIZE: 5 - 8 in.
DEPTH: 40 - 130 ft.

Spiny Lobsters

VISUAL ID: Reddish orange to reddish brown body and appendages, with no dramatic markings. Lacks large, numerous spines, but is somewhat hairy. Body is flatter than other spiny lobsters.

ABUNDANCE & DISTRIBUTION: Uncommon South Florida, Bahamas, Caribbean.

HABITAT & BEHAVIOR: Inhabit caves in deep coral reefs. Rarely venture far from cave, even at night.

REACTION TO DIVERS: Shy; when approached rapidly retreat deep inside cave.

VISUAL ID: Four or five purple spots on first segment of abdomen. Abdomen segments are relatively smooth compared with Ridged Slipper Lobster [next page]. Body reddish brown to orangish brown. Legs yellow with tiny brown spots. Flattened, plate-like antennae are smooth, and the forward portion of the second plate is squared-off (compare with Sculptured Slipper Lobster [below]).

ABUNDANCE & DISTRIBUTION: Occasional South Florida, Bahamas, Caribbean.

HABITAT & BEHAVIOR: Inhabit coral reefs. Hide in protective recesses during day, and forage in the open at night. When disturbed, can swim backwards rapidly using powerful strokes of their tails.

REACTION TO DIVERS: Wary; when approached retreat into protective recesses.

NOTE: Also commonly known as the "Shovel-nosed Lobster."

VISUAL ID: Numerous spines and stiff, bristol-like hairs project from edges of flattened antenna and carapace. Antenna and carapace have rough, cobblestone-like texture. Carapace low, wide and rounded. Mottled tan to yellow-brown and brown.

ABUNDANCE & DISTRIBUTION: Occasional Bahamas, Caribbean; uncommon South Florida. Circumtropical.

HABITAT & BEHAVIOR: Inhabit rocky areas and coral reefs. Hide in protective recesses during day, and forage in open at night. When disturbed, can swim backwards rapidly using powerful strokes of their tails.

REACTION TO DIVERS: Wary; when approached retreat into protective recesses.

COPPER LOBSTER
Palinurellus gundlachi

ORDER:
Decapoda
SUBORDER:
Palinura
FAMILY:
Spiny Lobsters
Palinuridae

SIZE: 5 - 8 in.
DEPTH: 60 - 130 ft.

SPANISH LOBSTER
Scyllarides aequinoctialis

ORDER:
Decapoda
SUBORDER:
Palinura
FAMILY:
Slipper Lobsters
Scyllaridae

SIZE: 6 - 12 in.
DEPTH: 30 - 130 ft.

SCULPTURED SLIPPER LOBSTER
Parribacus antarcticus

ORDER:
Decapoda
SUBORDER:
Palinura
FAMILY:
Slipper Lobsters
Scyllaridae

SIZE: 4 - 7 in.
DEPTH: 20 - 75 ft.

Slipper Lobsters

VISUAL ID: Numerous spikes project from edges of plate-like antennae. Carapace is relatively smooth, but with deep sculpturing on the abdomen. Numerous bristle-like hairs on body, especially along sides. Body tan to yellowish with red and blue shading [pictured].
ABUNDANCE & DISTRIBUTION: Occasional to uncommon Bahamas, Caribbean. Not known Florida.
HABITAT & BEHAVIOR: Inhabit coral reefs and areas of sand and sea grass. Hide in protective recesses during day, and forage in the open at night. When disturbed, can swim backwards rapidly using powerful strokes of their tails.
REACTION TO DIVERS: Wary; when approached retreat into protective recesses.

VISUAL ID: Red and white banded legs. Carapace and body cover by rough granules.
ABUNDANCE & DISTRIBUTION: Uncommon, Florida, Bahamas, Caribbean and Gulf of Mexico. Also, north to North Carolina and Bermuda.
HABITAT & BEHAVIOR: Typically inhabit areas of sand, mud, mixed rubble, and seagrass beds, but occasionally inhabit coral heads and patch reefs.
REACTION TO DIVERS: Wary; retreat when approached.

VISUAL ID: Tiny. Flattened, rounded plate-like antennae and a second pair of thin, short antennae. Exoskeleton transparent to translucent with whitish tinting. The physical appearance of juvenile slipper lobsters is not well known, thus identification only to family is possible.
ABUNDANCE & DISTRIBUTION: Rare Florida, Bahamas, Caribbean.
HABITAT & BEHAVIOR: Inhabit reefs, often in secluded small recesses.
REACTION TO DIVERS: Remain still, apparently relying on camouflage.
NOTE: Possibly the Sculptured Slipper Lobster, *Parribacus antarcticus*, because it is the only slipper lobster with a carapace wider than long and notched edges on antennae and carapace as seen on pictured specimen. However, these characteristics could change with maturity.

REGAL SLIPPER LOBSTER
Arctides guineensis

ORDER:
Decapoda
SUBORDER:
Palinura
FAMILY:
Slipper Lobsters
Scyllaridae

SIZE: 4 - 7 in.
DEPTH: 25 - 60 ft.

RIDGED SLIPPER LOBSTER
Scyllarides nodifer

ORDER:
Decapoda
SUBORDER:
Palinura
FAMILY:
Slipper Lobsters
Scyllaridae

SIZE: 5 - 8 in.,
max. 12 in.
DEPTH: 6 - 190 ft.

JUVENILE SLIPPER LOBSTER
Unidentified

ORDER:
Decapoda
SUBORDER:
Palinura
FAMILY:
Slipper Lobsters
Scyllaridae

SIZE: ¹/₂ - 1 in.
DEPTH: 20 - 70 ft.

Hermit Crabs

VISUAL ID: Long pincers and arms, egg-shaped carapace with eyes on short stalks and sharp spine between; abdomen crayfish like with well developed fan tail. Bright red to brown.

ABUNDANCE & DISTRIBUTION: Occasional Florida, Bahamas, Caribbean and Gulf of Mexico. Also north to North Carolina.

HABITAT & BEHAVIOR: Commonly near or on sponges in areas of mixed sand, rocks and rubble.

REACTION TO DIVERS: Tend to ignore divers.

NOTE: Several similar-appearing species are difficult to visual distinguish. Pictured specimens were collected and identified by magnified examination of small spines on carapace, antennae and mouth parts.

Stareye Hermit
Note recent molt in front of shell.

VISUAL ID: Blue to blue-green eyes, with dark pupils and distinctive star-like design. Legs are banded in a variety of colors that may include white, cream, red, lavender, orange and reddish brown. Claws often shaded in lavender. Numerous bristle-like hairs.

ABUNDANCE & DISTRIBUTION: Occasional Florida, Bahamas, Caribbean.

HABITAT & BEHAVIOR: In a wide variety of habitats, including reefs.

REACTION TO DIVERS: Wary; pull back into shell when approached. After quiet, motionless wait crab often reappears.

SIMILAR SPECIES: Bareye Hermit, *D. fucosus*, has a dark horizontal bar across the eye when viewed from the front. These two species are so similar in appearance that laboratory examination is required for positive identification.

196

COMMON SQUAT LOBSTER
Munida pusilla

ORDER
Decapoda
SECTION
Anomura
FAMILY
Squat Lobsters
Galatheidae

SIZE: Carapace ½ in.
DEPTH: 25 - 450 ft.

Common Squat Hermit
Brown variation.

STAREYE HERMIT
Dardanus venosus

ORDER:
Decapoda
SECTION:
Anomura
FAMILY:
Hermit Crabs
Diogenidae

SIZE: 3 - 5 in.
DEPTH: 2 - 130 ft.

Hermit Crabs

VISUAL ID: Large lavender-gray to reddish gray to reddish brown claws of nearly equal size (right slightly larger), with a surface texture resembling irregular, overlapping scales. Red and white banded antennae. Green or blue-green eyes. Largest Caribbean hermit crab.

ABUNDANCE & DISTRIBUTION: Occasional Florida, Bahamas, Caribbean.

HABITAT & BEHAVIOR: Inhabit sand and areas of sea grass, often near reefs. Occupy large shells, most commonly those of the Queen Conch, *Strombus gigas*, [pg. 261].

REACTION TO DIVERS: Wary; pull back into shell when approached. After a quiet wait crab often reappears.

VISUAL ID: Cream to tan legs and claws with red bands and large spots. Tentacles and eyestalks gold; eyes blue. Equal sized claws.

ABUNDANCE & DISTRIBUTION: Occasional Caribbean.

HABITAT & BEHAVIOR: In a wide variety of habitats, including reefs.

REACTION TO DIVERS: Wary; pull back into shell when approached. After a quiet wait crab often reappears.

NOTE: There are several similar appearing species and varieties of color variations within this species, positive identification may require laboratory examination.

VISUAL ID: Reddish with bright red eye stalks and small, brilliant blue eyes. (Similar Red Banded Hermit, P. erythrops [previous] has gold eye stalks.) Flattened equal sized claws.

ABUNDANCE & DISTRIBUTION: Occasional Florida, Bahamas, Caribbean.

HABITAT & BEHAVIOR: Most commonly on sand and rubble bottoms. Inhabit shells with narrow opening.

REACTION TO DIVERS: Wary; pull back into shell when approached. After a quiet wait crabs often reappear.

GIANT HERMIT
Petrochirus diogenes
ORDER
Decapoda
SECTION
Anomura
FAMILY
Hermit Crabs
Diogenidae

SIZE: 5 - 8 in.,
12 in. max.
DEPTH: 3 - 100 ft.

RED BANDED HERMIT
Paguristes erythrops
ORDER
Decapoda
SECTION
Anomura
FAMILY
Hermit Crabs
Diogenidae

SIZE: 2 - 3 in.,
4 in. max.
DEPTH: 2 - 130 ft.

BLUE-EYE HERMIT
Paguristes sericeus
ORDER
Decapoda
SECTION
Anomura
FAMILY
Hermit Crabs
Diogenidae

SIZE: 1 - 2½ in.
DEPTH: 30 - 450 ft.

Hermit Crabs

VISUAL ID: Carapace, legs, claws and eyestalks shades of red-brown to brown and covered with raised, scattered, white speckles. Equal sized claws.
ABUNDANCE & DISTRIBUTION: Occasional Caribbean.
HABITAT & BEHAVIOR: In a wide variety of habitats, including reefs.
REACTION TO DIVERS: Wary; pull back into shell when approached. After a quiet wait crab often reappears.
NOTE: There are two other species with similar coloration and appearance, *P. grayi* and *P. wassi.*

VISUAL ID: Bright red legs and carapace, may have some white spots. Greenish eyes on pale eyestalks.
ABUNDANCE & DISTRIBUTION: Common South Florida, Bahamas, Caribbean.
HABITAT & BEHAVIOR: Inhabit coral reefs. Often form small aggregations during the day.
REACTION TO DIVERS: Wary; pull back into shell when approached. After a quiet wait crab often reappears in opening.

VISUAL ID: Legs and claws, which may be shades of orange, red, maroon or dark reddish brown, are covered with fine white spots and tipped with white or yellow. Orange antennae and eyestalks. Tip of eyestalks white, eyes black. Left claw larger than right.
ABUNDANCE & DISTRIBUTION: Occasional South Florida, Bahamas, Caribbean.
HABITAT & BEHAVIOR: Inhabit coral reefs and rocky substrates. Often in small aggregations during day.
REACTION TO DIVERS: Wary; pull back into shell when approached. After a quiet wait crab often reappears in opening.

WHITE SPECKLED HERMIT
Paguristes punticeps
ORDER
Decapoda
SECTION
Anomura
FAMILY
Hermit Crabs
Diogenidae

SIZE: 3 - 5 in.
DEPTH: 2 - 130 ft

RED REEF HERMIT
Paguristes cadenati
ORDER
Decapoda
SECTION
Anomura
FAMILY
Hermit Crabs
Diogenidae

SIZE: $1/2$ - 1 in.
DEPTH: 25 - 95 ft.

ORANGECLAW HERMIT
Calcinus tibicen
ORDER
Decapoda
SECTION
Anomura
FAMILY
Hermit Crabs
Diogenidae

SIZE: $1/2$ - 1 in.
DEPTH: 1 - 100 ft.

VISUAL ID: Legs white to cream and boldly striped in shades of red or brown. Right claw greatly enlarged; base mottled gray, movable pincer is white.

ABUNDANCE & DISTRIBUTION: Occasional South Florida, Bahamas, Caribbean.

HABITAT & BEHAVIOR: Inhabit coral reefs.

REACTION TO DIVERS: Wary; pull back into shell when approached. After a quiet wait crab often reappears in opening.

VISUAL ID: Right claw is greatly enlarged, base is maroon to orange with large white dots; moveable pincer is white. Legs and left claw red to reddish brown. Eyestalks are white with maroon band, eyes are blue.

ABUNDANCE & DISTRIBUTION: Occasional South Florida, Bahamas, Caribbean.

HABITAT & BEHAVIOR: Inhabit coral reefs. When withdrawn inside shell, the wide pincer covers opening.

REACTION TO DIVERS: Wary; pull back into shell when approached. After a quiet wait crab often reappears in opening.

VISUAL ID: Red to orange and covered with large white and violet spots ringed in red.

ABUNDANCE & DISTRIBUTION: Occasional Florida, Bahamas, Caribbean.

HABITAT & BEHAVIOR: Found in a variety of habitats. May be free-living, but commonly associate with Giant Hermits [pg. 199], Stareye Hermits [pg. 197], and Queen Conchs, *Strombus gigas*, [pg. 261].

REACTION TO DIVERS: Shy; retreat to protective cover when approached.

RED-STRIPE HERMIT
Phimochirus holthuisi
ORDER
Decapoda
SECTION
Anomura
FAMILY
Hermit Crabs
Diogenidae

SIZE: ½ - 1 in.
DEPTH: 20 - 65 ft.

POLKADOTTED HERMIT
Phimochirus operculatus
ORDER
Decapoda
SECTION
Anomura
FAMILY
Hermit Crabs
Diogenidae

SIZE: ½ - 1 in.
DEPTH: 10 - 85 ft.

SPOTTED
PORCELAIN CRAB
Porcellana sayana
ORDER
Decapoda
SECTION
Anomura
FAMILY
Porcelain Crabs
Porcellanidae

SIZE: ½ - 1 in.
DEPTH: 10 - 100 ft

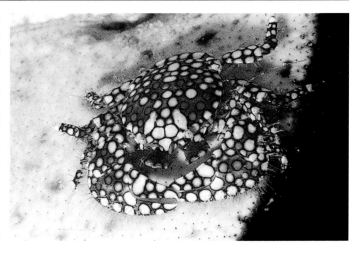

Porcelain Crabs

VISUAL ID: Body and appendages are mottled shades of green. Antennae long and translucent.
ABUNDANCE & DISTRIBUTION: Occasional Florida, Bahamas, Caribbean.
HABITAT & BEHAVIOR: Found in a variety of habitats, including reefs.
REACTION TO DIVERS: Shy; retreat to protective cover when approached.
NOTE: A small isopod is attached to the left side of photographed specimen's carapace.

VISUAL ID: Red with some darker spotting and long reddish translucent antennae. Very flat carapace; four large spines on forearm of pincer.
ABUNDANCE & DISTRIBUTION: Uncommon Caribbean. Also Brazil, West Africa and Ascension Island.
HABITAT & BEHAVIOR: Inhabit sand flats and areas of mixed sand and rubble. Hide under stones and narrow protective recesses.
REACTION TO DIVERS: Shy; retreat to cover when approached.

VISUAL ID: Four sharply pointed teeth along the inner edge of the first segment of the claw bearing leg. Carapace and legs have ridges that are usually marked with red. Undercolor variable from orange to brown or gray to white.
ABUNDANCE & DISTRIBUTION: Occasional Florida, Bahamas, Caribbean; also north to Cape Hatteras, North Carolina and south to Brazil.
HABITAT & BEHAVIOR: Reclusive; hide in narrow cracks or under stone slabs. Wide range of habitats from reefs to rocky areas mixed with rubble
REACTION TO DIVERS: Shy; rapidly retreat to cover when approached.

GREEN PORCELAIN CRAB

Petrolisthes armatus

ORDER
Decapoda
SECTION
Anomura
FAMILY
Porcelain Crabs
Porcellanidae

SIZE: ½ - 1 in.
DEPTH: 20 - 75 ft.

RED PORCELAIN CRAB

Petrolisthes marginatus

ORDER
Decapoda
SECTION
Anomura
FAMILY
Porcelain Crabs
Porcellanidae

SIZE: ½ - ¾ in.
DEPTH: 0 - 60 ft.

BANDED PORCELAIN CRAB

Petrolisthes galathinus

ORDER
Decapoda
SECTION
Anomura
FAMILY
Porcelain Crabs
Porcellanidae

SIZE: ½ - ¾ in.
DEPTH: 10 - 175 ft.

True Crabs

VISUAL ID: Smooth carapace in shades of orange, red or brown with white and yellow spots and markings. Legs are red with purple shading.

ABUNDANCE & DISTRIBUTION: Common Bahamas, Caribbean. Uncommon to rare in many locations due to overharvesting.

HABITAT & BEHAVIOR: Inhabit shallow coral reefs. Hide during day in protective recesses; forage in open at night.

REACTION TO DIVERS: Shy; when approached retreat into protective recesses.

NOTE: Also commonly known as "Coral Crab", "Red Coral Crab" and "Queen Crab".

VISUAL ID: Carapace is smooth and heavy. Claws are enlarged and stout. Juveniles are dark blue to purple and often spotted, claw tips are dark. Adults are reddish brown and spotted with gray or white, claw tips are dark brown to black.

ABUNDANCE & DISTRIBUTION: Common Florida, Bahamas, South Caribbean.

HABITAT & BEHAVIOR: Juveniles often inhabit reefs and rocky areas of moderate depth. Adults inhabit burrows in mud-bottom bays and harbors and are rarely observed by divers.

REACTION TO DIVERS: Retreat to protective recesses or burrows when approached.

NOTE: In Florida, Stone Crab claws are highly prized as food. Legally, only the claws may be taken, which the crabs regenerate. However, only one claw should be taken because it greatly improves the crab's chances of survival.

VISUAL ID: Yellowish to orangish white, with spots and irregular areas of varying sizes; the larger areas are red to orange with dark outlines. Carapace is smooth, rounded and hemispherical. Claws are flattened and have several longitudinal ridges.

ABUNDANCE & DISTRIBUTION: Occasional Florida, Bahamas, Caribbean.

HABITAT & BEHAVIOR: Inhabit shallow areas of sand, coral rubble, patch and fringing reefs.

REACTION TO DIVERS: Relatively unafraid, retreat if molested.

BATWING CORAL CRAB
Carpilius corallinus
ORDER:
Decapoda
SECTION:
True Crabs
Brachyura
FAMILY:
Mud Crabs
Xanthidae

SIZE: 3 ½ - 4 ¼ in.,
6 in. max.
DEPTH: 3 - 45 ft.

FLORIDA STONE CRAB
Menippe mercenaria
Juvenile
ORDER:
Decapoda
SECTION:
True Crabs
Brachyura
FAMILY:
Mud Crabs
Xanthidae

SIZE: Adults 2 ½ - 4 in.
Juveniles ¾ - 1 in.
DEPTH: 0 - 60 ft.

GAUDY CLOWN CRAB
Platypodiella spectabilis
ORDER:
Decapoda
SECTION:
True Crabs
Brachyura
FAMILY:
Mud Crabs
Xanthidae

SIZE: ¼ - ¾ in.
DEPTH: 1 - 35 ft.

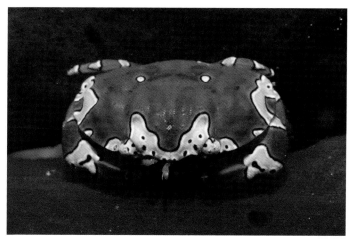

True Crabs

VISUAL ID: Red. Hairy with two lobes between eyes; small spines on pincers have pale tips; no coarse dark spines on carapace.
ABUNDANCE & DISTRIBUTION: Common Florida, Bahamas Caribbean and Gulf of Mexico. Also, north to North Carolina and south to Brazil.
HABITAT & BEHAVIOR: Inhabit reefs and areas of mixed rocks and coral rubble.
REACTION TO DIVERS: Shy; seek shelter when approached.

VISUAL ID: Carapace somewhat rectangular with three large black lateral spines followed by two smaller ones and tiny white spines on back; pincers and arms covered with numerous black and white spines
ABUNDANCE & DISTRIBUTION: Rare Florida, Caribbean. Also, north to Cape Hatteras.
HABITAT & BEHAVIOR: Wide range of habitats; in shallow water may shelter in fire coral.
REACTION TO DIVERS: Shy; seek shelter when approached.

VISUAL ID: Numerous reddish bumps with whitish undercolor on carapace and claws. Carapace wider than long.
ABUNDANCE & DISTRIBUTION: Occasional Florida, Bahamas and Caribbean; also Gulf of Mexico to Stetson Banks, north to Cape Lookout, North Carolina and South to Rio de Janeiro, Brazil.
HABITAT & BEHAVIOR: Inhabit areas of sand, gravel and rocky rubble.
REACTION TO DIVERS: Shy; retreat to cover when approached.

PLUMED HAIRY CRAB
Pilumnus floridanus
ORDER:
Decapoda
SECTION:
True Crabs
Brachyura
FAMILY:
Mud Crabs
Xanthidae

SIZE: ¹/₂ - ³/₄ in.
DEPTH: 0 - 450 ft.

THORNY MUD CRAB
Micropanope urinator
ORDER:
Decapoda
SECTION:
True Crabs
Brachyura
FAMILY:
Mud Crabs
Xanthidae

SIZE: ¹/₂ - ³/₄ in.
DEPTH: 0- 1,500 ft.

NODOSE RUBBLE CRAB
Paractaea rufopunctata
ORDER:
Decapoda
SECTION:
True Crabs
Brachyura
FAMILY:
Mud Crabs
Xanthidae

SIZE: ³/₄ - 1 in.
DEPTH: 0 - 600 ft.

VISUAL ID: Carapace appears to be eroded into numerous uneven ridges and bumps. Cream colored with red, maroon, orange and tan blotches and spots. Walking legs have yellowish tips.

ABUNDANCE & DISTRIBUTION: Occasional Florida, Bahamas, Caribbean.

HABITAT & BEHAVIOR: Inhabit small holes and recesses in shallow reefs, and algae-covered, rocky bottoms. Hide during day by wedging into holes, forage in open at night.

REACTION TO DIVERS: Generally remain motionless, relying on their camouflage for concealment.

VISUAL ID: Rough carapace covered with ridges and nodules. A "pinched-in" area located just behind front of carapace distinguishes this species. Color varies from pale yellow, pink, red, orange or brown, with a scattering of dark spots on front of carapace and upper claws. Encrustations on shell often hide true color.

ABUNDANCE & DISTRIBUTION: Occasional Florida, Bahamas, Caribbean.

HABITAT & BEHAVIOR: Inhabit sandy bottoms. Often hide by burying up to their eyes in sand.

REACTION TO DIVERS: Generally remain motionless, relying on their camouflage for concealment.

Rough Box Crab
Color variation.

ERODED MUD CRAB
Glyptoxanthus erosus

ORDER:
Decapoda
SECTION:
True Crabs
Brachyura
FAMILY:
Mud Crabs
Xanthidae

SIZE: 1¼ - 2 in.
DEPTH: 3 - 45 ft.

ROUGH BOX CRAB
Calappa gallus

ORDER:
Decapoda
SECTION:
True Crabs
Brachyura
FAMILY:
Box Crabs
Calappidae

SIZE: 1½ - 3 in.
DEPTH: 3 - 45 ft.

Rough Box Crab
Heavy encrustation on shell.

VISUAL ID: Network pattern of dark brown to reddish brown to lavender lines on carapace. Carapace wider than long with lateral spines; wide flattened pincers fold tightly against carapace.
ABUNDANCE & DISTRIBUTION: Occasional Florida, Bahamas, Caribbean. Also, Bermuda, north to North Carolina and south to Brazil.
HABITAT & BEHAVIOR: Inhabit sand flats and areas of mixed sand and rubble. Often bury in sand.
REACTION TO DIVERS: Shy; scurry away or bury in sand when approached.

VISUAL ID: Dark brown to reddish brown to lavender lines on carapace may form network pattern (Similar to Ocellated Box Crab, *C. ocellata*, [previous], but pattern on this species fades toward rear becoming a series of non-intersecting lines.) Carapace wider than long with lateral spines; wide flattened pincers fold tightly against carapace.
ABUNDANCE & DISTRIBUTION: Occasional Florida, Bahamas, Caribbean and Gulf of Mexico. Also, Bermuda and north to Massachusetts.
HABITAT & BEHAVIOR: Inhabit sand flats and areas of mixed sand and rubble. Often bury in sand.
REACTION TO DIVERS: Shy; scurry away or bury in sand when approached.

VISUAL ID: Tiny. Pale whitish carapace with brownish mottling and tiny eyes. Carapace wider than long.
ABUNDANCE & DISTRIBUTION: Occasional to uncommon Florida and northern Gulf of Mexico; also north to Vineyard Sound, Massachusetts.
HABITAT & BEHAVIOR: Live on sand dollars in the Family Mellitidae.
REACTION TO DIVERS: Appear unconcerned; retreat beneath sand dollar if molested.

OCELLATED BOX CRAB
Calappa ocellata
ORDER:
Decapoda
SECTION:
True Crabs
Brachyura
FAMILY:
Box Crabs
Calappidae

SIZE: 3 - 4 in.,
max. 5 in.
DEPTH: 0 - 250 ft.

FLAME BOX CRAB
Calappa flammea
ORDER:
Decapoda
SECTION:
True Crabs
Brachyura
FAMILY:
Box Crabs
Calappidae

SIZE: 3 - 4 in.,
max. 5 in.
DEPTH: 0 - 250 ft.

SANDDOLLAR
PEA CRAB
Dissodactylus mellitae
ORDER:
Decapoda
SECTION:
True Crabs
Brachyura
FAMILY:
Pea Crabs
Pinnotheridae

SIZE: $^1/_8$ - $^1/_2$ in.
DEPTH: 0 - 400 ft.

213

VISUAL ID: Pure white. Carapace is rounded and hemispherical. Legs hairy.
ABUNDANCE & DISTRIBUTION: Occasional Florida, Bahamas, Caribbean.
HABITAT & BEHAVIOR: Live among spines of Red Heart Urchin, *Meoma ventricosa ventricosa*, [pg. 387] for protection.

VISUAL ID: Brown to tan with two large, dark reddish brown spots ringed in white on rear of carapace. Rear pair of legs have developed into paddle-like appendages that are used for swimming.
ABUNDANCE & DISTRIBUTION: Occasional South Florida, Bahamas, Caribbean.
HABITAT & BEHAVIOR: Inhabit reefs and sea grass beds.
REACTION TO DIVERS: Wary; retreat to protective recesses when approached.

VISUAL ID: Carapace and appendages are shades of golden brown, and occasionally marked with white blotches. Rear pair of legs have developed into paddle-like appendages that are used for swimming.
ABUNDANCE & DISTRIBUTION: Occasional South Florida, Bahamas, Caribbean.
HABITAT & BEHAVIOR: Inhabit large floats of sargassum. May occasionally drop onto reefs.
REACTION TO DIVERS: Wary; retreat to protective recesses when approached.

HEART URCHIN PEA CRAB
Dissodactylus primitivus
ORDER:
Decapoda
SECTION:
True Crabs
Brachyura
FAMILY:
Pea Crabs
Pinnotheridae

SIZE: ¼ - ½ in.
DEPTH: 3 - 130 ft.

OCELLATE SWIMMING CRAB
Portunus sebae
ORDER:
Decapoda
SECTION:
True Crabs
Brachyura
FAMILY:
Swimming Crabs
Portunidae

SIZE: 2½ - 3½ in.
DEPTH: 15 - 90 ft.

SARGASSUM SWIMMING CRAB
Portunus sayi
ORDER:
Decapoda
SECTION:
True Crabs
Brachyura
FAMILY:
Swimming Crabs
Portunidae

SIZE: 2½ - 3½ in.
DEPTH: 20 - 60 ft.

VISUAL ID: Shades of brown with some blotches and mottling. Carapace wider than long with lateral spines of nearly equal length and eight small teeth (spines) between eyes. Four sharp spikes on forearms of pincers. Rear pair of legs have developed into paddle-like appendages that are used for swimming.

ABUNDANCE & DISTRIBUTION: Common Florida, Bahamas and Caribbean; also Gulf of Mexico, north to New Jersey and south to Brazil.

HABITAT & BEHAVIOR: Inhabit shallow inshore areas of sand, gravel and rocky rubble. Especially common in harbors and bays.

REACTION TO DIVERS: Shy; retreat to cover when approached.

VISUAL ID: Shades of reddish brown to yellowish brown blotched and mottled with red, dark brown, yellow or gray. Carapace wider than long with lateral spines, last spine longer than others that are of nearly equal length and forward pointing. Three large spines on "arm" of pincer become progressively larger toward pincer. Rear pair of legs have developed into paddle-like appendages that are used for swimming.

ABUNDANCE & DISTRIBUTION: Occasional Florida, Bahamas and Caribbean; also Bermuda, north to Vineyard Sound, Massachusetts and south to Brazil.

HABITAT & BEHAVIOR: Inhabit shallow areas of sand.

REACTION TO DIVERS: Shy; retreat to cover when approached.

VISUAL ID: Brown to brick red with some tan mottling, legs striped. Carapace wider than long with alternating large and small lateral spines often tipped with black; three to four sharp spines of forearm of pincer.

ABUNDANCE & DISTRIBUTION: : Occasional Florida, Bahamas Caribbean. Also, north to New Jersey, south to Brazil, west Africa and eastern Pacific.

HABITAT & BEHAVIOR: Inhabit mixed areas of sand, shell debris, rubble and coralline algae.

REACTION TO DIVERS: Shy; seek shelter when approached.

**BLOTCHED
SWIMMING CRAB**
Portunus spinimanus
ORDER:
Decapoda
SECTION:
True Crabs
Brachyura
FAMILY:
Swimming Crabs
Portunidae

SIZE: 2 - 3 in.,
4¹/₂ in. max.
DEPTH: 0 - 300 ft.

**REDHAIR
SWIMMING CRAB**
Portunus ordwayi
ORDER:
Decapoda
SECTION:
True Crabs
Brachyura
FAMILY:
Swimming Crabs
Portunidae

SIZE: 1 - 1¹/₂ in.,
2 in. max.
DEPTH: 0 - 1,200 ft.
(usually less than 20 ft.)

**BLACK POINT
SCULLING CRAB**
Portunus ordwayi
ORDER:
Decapoda
SECTION:
True Crabs
Brachyura
FAMILY:
Swimming Crabs
Portunidae

SIZE: 1¹/₂ - 2³/₄ in.,
max. 31/4 in.
DEPTH: 0 - 200 ft.

True Crabs

VISUAL ID: Members of this genus have a wide carapace with a long, sharp spine protruding from the widest point on each side; between this spine and eye is a row of pointed "teeth." Gray to brown with variable tints from blue to green. Positive identification usually requires microscopic examination.

ABUNDANCE & DISTRIBUTION: Common Florida, Bahamas, Caribbean.

HABITAT & BEHAVIOR: Generally inhabit shallow sand and mud bottoms. May be in sandy areas around patch reefs.

REACTION TO DIVERS: Aggressively rear back on hind legs with claws raised for attack when approached.

NOTE: Pictured species probably *C. ornatus,* distinguished by its greenish tint, white-tips on teeth and bluish legs with reddish tips. The Common Blue Crab, *C. sapidus,* known for its edibility, is the largest (6 - 8 in.), blue-gray with bright blue claws. There are several additional species and sub-species.

VISUAL ID: Carapace is flattened, discus-shaped and dark brown to olive with an iridescent green line around front. Brown legs are marked with yellow-gold bands.

ABUNDANCE & DISTRIBUTION: Common Florida, Bahamas, Caribbean. Also Pacific coast of Central America.

HABITAT & BEHAVIOR: Inhabit reefs and rocky areas. Often hide under Long-spined Urchins [pg. 287] for protection.

REACTION TO DIVERS: When approached, retreat under protective spines of urchins.

NOTE: Also commonly known as the "Urchin Crab."

VISUAL ID: Green carapace is covered with smooth, rounded nodules. Claws are smooth with blunt tips. Legs hairy.

ABUNDANCE & DISTRIBUTION: Common South Florida, Bahamas, Caribbean. Can be locally abundant.

HABITAT & BEHAVIOR: Inhabit shallow reefs and adjacent areas of coral rubble, sand and sea grass. Hide in small recesses and under coral debris.

REACTION TO DIVERS: Unafraid; normally allow close nonthreatening approach, retreating only if molested.

BLUE CRABS
Callinectes sp.
ORDER:
Decapoda
SECTION:
True Crabs
Brachyura
FAMILY:
Portunidae

SIZE: 4 - 6 in.
DEPTH: 5 - 50 ft.

NIMBLE SPRAY CRAB
Percnon gibbesi
ORDER:
Decapoda
SECTION:
True Crabs
Brachyura
FAMILY:
Grapsidae

SIZE: $^3/_4$ - $1^1/_4$ in.
DEPTH: 3 - 75 ft.

GREEN CLINGING CRAB
Mithrax sculptus
ORDER:
Decapoda
SECTION:
True Crabs
Brachyura
FAMILY:
Spider Crabs
Majidae

SIZE: $^1/_2$ - $^3/_4$ in.
DEPTH: 1 - 40 ft.

VISUAL ID: Smooth, blunt-tipped claws are cream colored and banded in dark reddish brown. Smooth carapace is cream colored with dark reddish brown markings and covered with rounded nodules. Legs hairy.

ABUNDANCE & DISTRIBUTION: Common South Florida, Bahamas, Caribbean.

HABITAT & BEHAVIOR: Inhabit coral reefs and adjacent areas. Usually live in association with anemones, especially Giant Anemone, *Condylactis gigantea*, [pg. 91] and Sun Anemone, *Stichodactyla helianthus*, [pg. 91].

REACTION TO DIVERS: Shy; retreat into protection of tentacles or under anemone when approached.

NOTE: Also commonly known as the "Anemone Crab."

VISUAL ID: Very smooth pincers with white tips; large spines on pincer arms and walking legs; rostrum short. Red granulated carapace (often difficult to see under a dense covering of dark bristles); pincers red to olive.

ABUNDANCE & DISTRIBUTION: Occasional Florida, Bahamas, Caribbean. Also, north to South Carolina and south to Brazil.

HABITAT & BEHAVIOR: In shallow habitats, often shelter in areas of fire coral and rubble. Generally nocturnal.

REACTION TO DIVERS: Shy; seek shelter when approached.

VISUAL ID: Red. Carapace with deep median furrows and short rostrum; forearm of pincer has four or five lobes or spines on outer margin and two on inner.

ABUNDANCE & DISTRIBUTION: Occasional Florida, Bahamas Caribbean. Also, south to Brazil.

HABITAT & BEHAVIOR: Typically inhabit shallow reefs and areas of mixed corals and rubble.

REACTION TO DIVERS: Shy; seek shelter when approached.

BANDED CLINGING CRAB
Mithrax cinctimanus

ORDER:
Decapoda
SECTION:
True Crabs
Brachyura
FAMILY:
Spider Crabs
Majidae

SIZE: $^1/_2$ - $^3/_4$ in.
DEPTH: 10 - 45 ft.

PAVED CLINGING CRAB
Mithrax verrucosus

ORDER:
Decapoda
SECTION:
True Crabs
Brachyura
FAMILY:
Spider Crabs
Majidae

SIZE: $^1/_2$ - $^3/_4$ in.
DEPTH: 0 - 30 ft.

NODOSE CLINGING CRAB
Mithrax coryphe

ORDER:
Decapoda
SECTION:
True Crabs
Brachyura
FAMILY:
Spider Crabs
Majidae

SIZE: $^3/_4$ - 1 in.
DEPTH: 0 - 300 ft.

VISUAL ID: Carapace has numerous grooves that form ridges and nodules; prominent pointed cone-shaped projections around sides; legs and carapace may have bands, stripes or spots. Colors variable: red, yellow-brown, and green. Smooth claws have blunt tips.

ABUNDANCE & DISTRIBUTION: Occasional South Florida, Bahamas, Caribbean; also Gulf of Mexico, north to North Carolina and Bermuda and south to Brazil.

HABITAT & BEHAVIOR: Inhabit reefs and adjacent areas of coral rubble and algae-covered, rocky bottoms. During the day hide in small holes and recesses.

REACTION TO DIVERS: Unafraid; normally allow close nonthreatening approach, retreating only when molested.

Red-Ridged Clinging Crab
Color variation.

VISUAL ID: Hairy carapace and appendages are reddish brown. Numerous spines on walking legs and claw arms. Claws are relatively narrow with blunt tips.

ABUNDANCE & DISTRIBUTION: Rare Florida, Bahamas, Caribbean.

HABITAT & BEHAVIOR: Inhabit rocky areas and reefs. Reclusive, hide in deep caves and recesses.

REACTION TO DIVERS: Shy; retreat deep into protective recesses when approached.

RED-RIDGED CLINGING CRAB
Mithrax forceps

ORDER:
Decapoda
SECTION:
True Crabs
Brachyura
FAMILY:
Spider Crabs
Majidae

SIZE: ½ - ¾ in.
DEPTH: 10 - 45 ft.

Red-Ridged Clinging Crab
Color variation.

HAIRY CLINGING CRAB
Mithrax pilosus

ORDER:
Decapoda
SECTION:
True Crabs
Brachyura
FAMILY:
Spider Crabs
Majidae

SIZE: 2 - 4 in.
DEPTH: 15 - 45 ft.

VISUAL ID: Reddish brown carapace and walking legs. Smooth claws purplish gray, with a single row of nodules running along the outer edge. Blunt claw tips. Numerous short spines and nodules cover legs. Largest species of Caribbean reef crab.

ABUNDANCE & DISTRIBUTION: Common to occasional Florida, Bahamas, Caribbean.

HABITAT & BEHAVIOR: Inhabit rocky areas and coral reefs. Often in caves or under ledge overhangs during the day; forage in the open at night. Frequently covered with algae and debris.

REACTION TO DIVERS: Relatively unafraid; retreat when closely approached.

NOTE: Also commonly known as "Reef Spider Crab," "Spiny Spider Crab," "Coral Crab" and "King Crab."

VISUAL ID: Golden-brown, triangular body with long pointed snout (rostrum). Carapace decorated with fine dark lines. Long, slender, spider-like legs. Claws often have violet tips.

ABUNDANCE & DISTRIBUTION: Abundant Florida, Bahamas, Caribbean.

HABITAT & BEHAVIOR: Found in a wide variety of habitats, including reefs.

REACTION TO DIVERS: Unafraid; retreat only if molested.

VISUAL ID: A decorator crab; the attachment of hydroids and other organisms to the legs at right angles is distinctive of this genus. A long rostrum extends from triangular carapace at head. Eye protrudes at right angles from sides of rostrum. Long, thin, spider-like legs.

ABUNDANCE & DISTRIBUTION: Common Florida, Bahamas, Caribbean.

HABITAT & BEHAVIOR: Inhabit reefs. Often on seafans and other gorgonians.

REACTION TO DIVERS: Unafraid; remain motionless, relying on their camouflage for concealment.

NOTE: Pictured species is probably the Shortfinger Neck Crab, *P. sidneyi,* which is distinguished by a blunt, scooped-out spine. Similar Curvedspine Neck Crab, *P. curvirostris,* is distinguished by a curved frontal spine, while the Unicorn Neck Crab, *P. gracilipes,* has a triangular frontal spine.

CHANNEL CLINGING CRAB
Mithrax spinosissimus

ORDER:
Decapoda
SECTION:
True Crabs
Brachyura
FAMILY:
Spider Crabs
Majidae

SIZE: 5 - 7 in.
DEPTH: 10 - 130 ft.

YELLOWLINE ARROW CRAB
Stenorhynchus seticornis

ORDER:
Decapoda
SECTION:
True Crabs
Brachyura
FAMILY:
Spider Crabs
Majidae

SIZE: 1¹/₂ - 2¹/₂ in.
DEPTH: 10 - 130 ft.

NECK CRABS
Podochela sp.

ORDER:
Decapoda
SECTION:
True Crabs
Brachyura
FAMILY:
Spider Crabs
Majidae

SIZE: 1¹/₂ - 2¹/₂ in.
DEPTH: 15 - 100 ft.

VISUAL ID: A decorator crab; the attachment of living sponge to its carapace and legs is distinctive of this species. Legs flattened. Light blue to purple claws with scattering of dark speckles.
ABUNDANCE & DISTRIBUTION: Common South Florida, Bahamas, Caribbean.
HABITAT & BEHAVIOR: Inhabit reefs.
REACTION TO DIVERS: Appear unconcerned; remain motionless, relying on their camouflage for concealment.

VISUAL ID: A decorator crab; the attachment of living sponge to carapace and legs is distinctive of this species. Claws banded in shades of brown (similar Cryptic Teardrop Crab, *P. mutica*, [previous] distinguished by light blue to purple claws with scattering of dark speckles).
ABUNDANCE & DISTRIBUTION: Occasional southern Caribbean; also south to Brazil.
HABITAT & BEHAVIOR: Inhabit reefs.
REACTION TO DIVERS: Appear unconcerned; remain motionless, relying on their camouflage for concealment.

VISUAL ID: A decorator crab; the attachment of massive amounts of sponge, other organisms and debris distinguishes this species. Red claws speckled and white banded. Two horn-like projections extend from front of head.
ABUNDANCE & DISTRIBUTION: Common South Florida, Bahamas, Caribbean.
HABITAT & BEHAVIOR: Inhabit reefs.
REACTION TO DIVERS: Unafraid; remain motionless, relying on their camouflage for concealment.
NOTE: This species is also commonly known as the "Two-Horned Spider Crab".

CRYPTIC TEARDROP CRAB
Pelia mutica
ORDER:
Decapoda
SECTION:
True Crabs
Brachyura
FAMILY:
Spider Crabs
Majidae

SIZE: $^1/_2$ - $^3/_4$ in.
DEPTH: 20 - 130 ft.

SOUTHERN TEARDROP CRAB
Pelia rotunda
ORDER:
Decapoda
SECTION:
True Crabs
Brachyura
FAMILY:
Spider Crabs
Majidae

SIZE: $^1/_4$ - $^1/_2$ in.
DEPTH: 6 - 130 ft.

SPECK-CLAW DECORATOR CRAB
Microphrys bicornuta
ORDER:
Decapoda
SECTION:
True Crabs
Brachyura
FAMILY:
Spider Crabs
Majidae

SIZE: $^1/_2$ - $^3/_4$ in.
DEPTH: 20 - 130 ft.

VISUAL ID: Triangular carapace with three large spines on rear, two long horns on rostrum, eyes arise from socket-like pits. Dull yellow to orange, red and red-brown.

ABUNDANCE & DISTRIBUTION: Occasional Florida, Bahamas Caribbean.

HABITAT & BEHAVIOR: Inhabit reefs and adjacent areas. Usually covered with sponge.

REACTION TO DIVERS: Remain still apparently relying on sponge camouflage.

VISUAL ID: Long tapering rostrum forked; large spine over eye; four large lateral spines on carapace. Dull red to orange and orange-brown.

ABUNDANCE & DISTRIBUTION: Occasional Florida, Bahamas, Caribbean and Gulf of Mexico. Also, north to North Carolina.

HABITAT & BEHAVIOR: Inhabit reefs. Young decorate with algae, sponge, and occasionally carry Hermit Crab Anemones, *Calliactis tricolor*, (pictured) and tunicates (below right). Large adults, if decorated at all, only decorate rostrum.

REACTION TO DIVERS: Unafraid; ignore divers.

**Furcate
Spider Crab**
Decoration variation.

SPONGY DECORATOR CRAB
Marcocoeloma trispinosum

ORDER:
Decapoda
SECTION:
True Crabs
Brachyura
FAMILY:
Sponge Crabs
Dromiidae

SIZE: 1 - 2 in.
DEPTH: 10 - 250 ft.

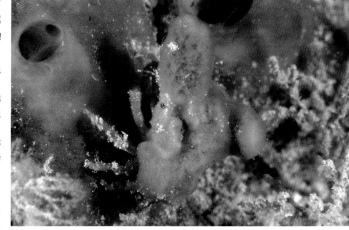

FURCATE SPIDER CRAB
Stenocionops furcatus coelata

ORDER:
Decapoda
SECTION:
True Crabs
Brachyura
FAMILY:
Sponge Crabs
Dromiidae

SIZE: ³/₄ in.,
max. 5¹/₂ in.
DEPTH: 0 - 350 ft.

Furcate Spider Crab
Decoration variation.

VISUAL ID: Red to brownish red overall including pincer tips. Eyes on long white stalks. Short felt-like hair covers carapace, legs and pincers.

ABUNDANCE & DISTRIBUTION: Rare eastern and southern Caribbean.

HABITAT & BEHAVIOR: Cut and shape sponge "caps" which they hold in place with two pair of short upturned rear legs. During the day typically remain stationary hiding under sponge caps; feed at night. Disturbed by direct beam from divers' lights.

REACTION TO DIVERS: Shy; remain still apparently relying on sponge camouflage, at night rapidly retreat from light.

VISUAL ID: Tips of pincers red; color of body and claws highly variable. Short felt-like hair covers carapace, legs and pincers; large spine to side of eye and spines along lateral margin (may be obscured by encrustations).

ABUNDANCE & DISTRIBUTION: Occasional Florida, Bahamas Caribbean and Gulf of Mexico. Also, south to Brazil and Bermuda.

HABITAT & BEHAVIOR: Cut and shape sponge "caps" which they hold in place with two pair of short upturned rear legs. During the day typically remain stationary hiding under sponge caps; feed at night. Disturbed by direct beam from divers' lights.

REACTION TO DIVERS: Shy; remain still apparently relying on sponge camouflage, at night rapidly retreat from light.

ANTILLES SPONGE CRAB
*Cryptodromiopsis
antillensis*
ORDER:
Decapoda
SECTION:
True Crabs
Brachyura
FAMILY:
Sponge Crabs
Dromiidae

SIZE: 1 - 2 in.,
max. 2$\frac{1}{2}$ in.
DEPTH: 0 - 130 ft.

REDEYE SPONGE CRAB
Dromia erythropus
ORDER:
Decapoda
SECTION:
True Crabs
Brachyura
FAMILY:
Sponge Crabs
Dromiidae

SIZE: 2 - 3 in.,
max. 3$\frac{1}{4}$ in.
DEPTH: 0 - 1,200 ft.

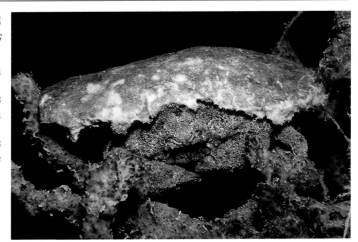

Redeye Crab
*Color and sponge
"cap" variations.*

True Crabs

DISCUSSION: A large number of crabs camouflage by using a wide range of marine life and debris. The material is often attached to tiny hooks on their carapaces, snouts and legs. Often the covering conceals identifying physical characteristics so completely that the species and, at times, even the genus cannot be determined without collection and scientific examination. Some of the most commonly used "decorations" include sponges, hydroids, sea anemones, zoanthids, tunicates and both leafy and hairy algae. The stinging capsules of hydroids, sea anemones and zoanthids serve the additional role of defense against predators. These attached organisms often remain alive and occasionally even reproduce.

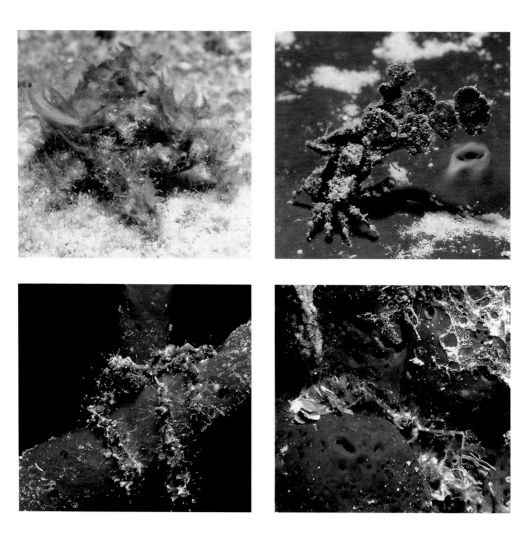

DECORATOR CRABS
Unidentified
ORDER:
Decapoda
SECTION:
True Crabs
Brachyura

Mantis Shrimp

VISUAL ID: Large, double-lobed eyes on stalks. Cream colored, with darkish bands crossing body; occasionally have patches of gold and black maze-like markings. Tail is distinctively covered with spinules and nodules, giving the surface a scaly appearance. Claws have eight to 11 sharp spines. The largest mantis shrimp in Florida and the Caribbean.

ABUNDANCE & DISTRIBUTION: Occasional Florida, Bahamas, Caribbean.

HABITAT & BEHAVIOR: Inhabit burrows on flat sand bottoms.

REACTION TO DIVERS: Aggressive if molested; claws can inflict deep, painful gashes. Known as "thumb-splitters" by Caribbean fishermen.

VISUAL ID: Large double-lobed eyes on stalks. Mottled in shades of dark brown to reddish brown to tan.

ABUNDANCE & DISTRIBUTION: Occasional South Florida, Bahamas, Caribbean.

HABITAT & BEHAVIOR: Inhabit burrows in sandy areas on coral reefs.

REACTION TO DIVERS: Aggressive if molested; claws can inflict deep, painful gashes. Known as "thumb-splitters" by Caribbean fishermen.

NOTE: Identification is tentative and based on eye shape, coloration and habitat. Specimen must be fully visible for positive identification.

VISUAL ID: Four sharp spikes protrude from outer edges of last two plates. Final or tail plate has a medial ridge. Claw has no spines and its base is enlarged. Stalked eyes have a single lobe. Color varies, but commonly cream with brown or green shading and mottling.

ABUNDANCE & DISTRIBUTION: Occasional South Florida, Bahamas, Caribbean.

HABITAT & BEHAVIOR: Inhabit reefs and adjacent areas. Often burrow under rocks in sand. Forage in cracks and recesses, under ledges and in other protected areas.

REACTION TO DIVERS: Shy; retreat to protective recesses when approached.

SCALY-TAILED MANTIS
Lysiosquilla scabricauda
ORDER:
Mantis Shrimp
Stomatopoda
FAMILY:
Spearing
Mantis Shrimp
Lysiosquillidae

SIZE: 4 - 6 in.,
1 ft. max.
DEPTH: 10 - 100 ft.

REEF MANTIS
Lysiosquilla glabriuscula
ORDER:
Mantis Shrimp
Stomatopoda
FAMILY:
Spearing
Mantis Shrimp
Lysiosquillidae

SIZE: 4 - 7 in.
DEPTH: 15 - 75 ft.

SWOLLEN-CLAW
MANTIS
Neogonodactylus oerstedii
ORDER:
Mantis Shrimp
Stomatopoda
FAMILY:
Smashing
Mantis Shrimp:
Gonodactylidae

SIZE: 1 - 2 in.
DEPTH: 1 - 75 ft.

Mantis Shrimp

VISUAL ID: Uniformly dark coloration is distinctive. Eyes have a single lobe.

ABUNDANCE & DISTRIBUTION: Occasional Caribbean.

HABITAT & BEHAVIOR: Inhabit reefs. Forage in cracks and recesses, under ledges and in other protected areas.

REACTION TO DIVERS: Shy; retreat to protective recesses when approached.

NOTE: Identification from photograph is probable. Positive identification cannot be confirmed without collected specimen.

VISUAL ID: Can change color and markings to match habitat; from black to brown, green, tan and white with mottling, speckling, spots, or stripes. In western Atlantic commonly pale to dark olive with white stripe down back.

ABUNDANCE & DISTRIBUTION: Common to occasional Florida, Bahamas Caribbean. Also circumtropical.

HABITAT & BEHAVIOR: Most commonly inhabit seagrass beds where they excavate U-shaped burrows, that often extend under coral or other debris. Also inhabit areas of coral and shell rubble and patch reefs.

REACTION TO DIVERS: Remain stationary apparently relying on sponge camouflage.

Ciliated False Squilla
Color variation.

DARK MANTIS
Neogonodactylus curacaoensis

ORDER:
Mantis Shrimp
Stomatopoda
FAMILY:
Smashing Mantis Shrimp
Gonodactylidae

SIZE: 1¼ - 2 in.
DEPTH: 25 - 75 ft.

CILIATED FALSE SQUILLA
Pseudosquilla ciliate

ORDER:
Mantis Shrimp
Stomatopoda
FAMILY:
Spearing Mantis Shrimp
Pseudosquillidae

SIZE: 1½ - 2½,
max. 3½ in.
DEPTH: 0 - 380 ft.

Ciliated False Squilla
Color variation.

VISUAL ID: Gray to dark brown; oval body formed by overlapping plates and fan-shaped tail.

ABUNDANCE & DISTRIBUTION: Common Florida, Bahamas, Caribbean.

HABITAT & BEHAVIOR: Cymothoids, as family members are known, are not true parasites. Instead of dining on the tissue of a hosts, single individuals or mated pairs attach to the head region of reef fishes with several pairs of hook-like legs and benignly scavenge specks of floating food from the water. Isopods begin life as tiny, one-eighth-inch, free-swimming males. Once associated with a fish, they lose their ability to swim and remain where they settle for life. To increase their odds of finding mates, males have the ability to transform into females. When a male settles on a host with a female already in place, it mates with the larger female. Later, after the female dies; the males change sex and await the arrival of a young male. If a mate is not present at settlement, a male accelerates growth and changes into a female. The largest and darkest individuals are invariably brooding females, sometimes incubating more than 100 juveniles inside their bulky ventral pouches.

NOTE: To date, 12 species from two genera have been classified from the Caribbean. The nine members of genus *Anilocra* are broadly distributed, but the different species tend to inhabit specific regions.

VISUAL ID: The tiny shrimp of this genus appear as small clouds of white to transparent specks hovering over reef. Often mistaken for fish larva. Close observation reveals a typical shrimp shape.

ABUNDANCE & DISTRIBUTION: Common South Florida, Bahamas, Caribbean.

HABITAT & BEHAVIOR: Inhabit reefs. Frequently hover near urchins and anemones where they hide when threatened. Occasionally over sea grass beds. Often swim in open, near surface at night.

NOTE: There are three primary Atlantic reef species, *M. columbiae*, *M. gracile*, and *M. integrum*. Microscopic examination of specimen is required for species identification.

CYMOTHOID ISOPODS

Anilocra spp.
Renocila spp.

ORDER:
Isopods
Isopoda
FAMILY:
Cymothoid Isopods
FAMILY:
Cymothoidae

SIZE: ½ - 3 in.

MYSID SHRIMP

Mysidium spp.
ORDER:
Mysid Shrimp
Mysidacea

SIZE: ¹/₁₆ - ¹/₈ in.
DEPTH: 15 - 65 ft.

Barnacles

VISUAL ID: Sessile barnacles permanently affix at the base of their shells to the substrate. The outer shell is composed of one to eight plates, depending upon genus; most genera observed by divers have six. Openings protected by two paired movable plates. When feeding, six cirri are repeatedly flicked in and out from opening. Identification of species is generally based on structures not observable underwater.

ABUNDANCE & DISTRIBUTION: Common worldwide.

HABITAT & BEHAVIOR: Attach to wide range of surfaces. Commonly on dock pilings, buoys, ship bottoms and shipwrecks. Often well camouflaged by other organisms, such as sponges, fire corals, hydroids and algae that attach and overgrow their shells.

NOTE: Photographed specimens were collected and by laboratory examination determined to include two species, *Megabalanus tintinnabulum* and *Balanus trigonus*.

VISUAL ID: Members of this genus permanently attach to the substrate in large clumps. The genus is recognized by the barnacles' large size, reddish net pattern and shallow depth. A number of species in the genus look similar requiring the collection and scientific examination of the shell structure for species identification.

ABUNDANCE & DISTRIBUTION: Common worldwide.

HABITAT & BEHAVIOR: Attach to wide range of surfaces, often on rocky substrate.

VISUAL ID: Body encased in flattened formation of five smooth, translucent, white to bluish white shell plates. Attached to substrate by stalk that may reach nearly one inch in length when fully extended.

ABUNDANCE & DISTRIBUTION: Common worldwide.

HABITAT & BEHAVIOR: Normally attach to floating objects such as driftwood, buoys and ship bottoms.

SIMILAR SPECIES: Grooved Goose-Neck Barnacle, *L. anserifera*, shell plates have fine radiating grooves, short stalk. Scaled Goose-Neck Barnacle, *L. pectinata*, shell plates are ridged with scales and occasionally spines.

NOTE: Visual identification was confirmed by collection of pictured specimens and laboratory examination.

SESSILE BARNACLES

SUBCLASS:
Barnacles
Cirripedia
ORDER:
Thoracica

SIZE: ¹/₄ - 1¹/₂ in.
DEPTH: 0 - 130 ft.

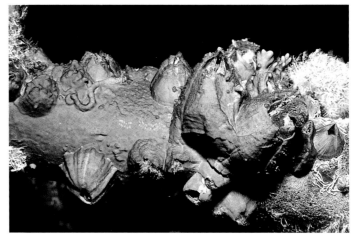

RED NETTED BARNACLE
Megabalanus sp.

SUBCLASS:
Barnacles
Cirripedia
ORDER:
Thoracica

SIZE: ³/₄ - 1¹/₂ in.
DEPTH: 0 - 60 ft.

SMOOTH GOOSE-NECK BARNACLE
Lepas anatifera

SUBCLASS:
Barnacles
Cirripedia
ORDER:
Thoracica
FAMILY:
Lepadidae

SIZE: ¹/₄ - 1¹/₂ in.
DEPTH: 0 - 130 ft.

VISUAL ID: Shell and stalk grayish black to reddish brown. Shells have pronounced hump where they join on back and dual knob-like tips at top.

ABUNDANCE & DISTRIBUTION: Occasional Caribbean.

HABITAT & BEHAVIOR: Attach to branches of Feather Black Coral, *Antipathes pennacea* and Bushy Black Coral, *A. salix.* Grow in small clusters.

NOTE: There are several similar appearing species of barnacles that associate with black corals. The pictured specimens were collected and identification made by laboratory examination.

VISUAL ID: Small thin body with four pair of long thin spider-like legs. Blue, blue-green, green and yellow spots and markings.

ABUNDANCE & DISTRIBUTION: Photographed in Cayman Islands where it is uncommon. The extent of its range has yet to be established.

HABITAT & BEHAVIOR: Inhabit reefs; on gorgonians, hydroids, bryozoans and other reef growth. Mouth at end of long proboscis is used to suck juices from cnidarians and other soft-bodied animals. Some species are able to swim by alternately flapping their long legs.

REACTION TO DIVERS: Ignore divers unless molested.

NOTE: The living appearance of this sea spider has not been matched with a scientific description. Collection of a photographed specimen and microscopic examination of anatomical detail is necessary to establish visual identification. Possibly an undescribed species. This is one of smallest species of several sea spiders that inhabit the Caribbean.

VISUAL ID: Gray to brown. Carapace is smooth and horseshoe-shaped. Tail is long and spike-like.

ABUNDANCE & DISTRIBUTION: Common Florida.

HABITAT & BEHAVIOR: Inhabit shallow areas with soft or sandy bottoms, often in areas of sea grass and other algal growth.

BLACK CORAL BARNACLE
Oxynaspis gracilis
SUBCLASS:
Barnacles
Cirripedia
ORDER:
Thoracica
FAMILY:
Heteralepidae

SIZE: ¹/₄ - ¹/₂ in.
DEPTH: 45 - 130 ft.

CARIBBEAN SEA SPIDER
Anoplodactulus sp.
CLASS:
Sea Spiders
Pycnogonida

SIZE: ¹/₄ - ¹/₂ in.
DEPTH: 0 - 60 ft.

HORSESHOE CRAB
Limulus polyphemus
CLASS:
Merostomata
SUBCLASS:
Horseshoe Crab
Xiphosura

SIZE: 10 - 20 in.
DEPTH: 1 - 15 ft.

IDENTIFICATION GROUP 7

Phylum Ectoprocta

(Eck-toe-PROCK-tuh / Gr. outside anus)

Bryozoans

Bryozoans are tiny, colonial animals called zooids. **Zooids** have polyp-like **tentacles** encircling the mouth; but, unlike polyps, they have a complete digestive system, including an anus that lies outside the ring of tentacles. These animals form a colonial skeleton with chambers that partition and separate one zooid from the next. These skeletal **chambers** may be **oval, tubular, vase** or **rectangular-shaped** and are usually less than 1/16 inch across. The colonies of different species vary greatly in appearance. Some look like a clump of **seaweed** or moss, while others grow as **lacy fans;** some species simply form **encrustations**. Colonies are generally white, although shades of brown, yellow, red and purple occur. Because the composition of building materials varies among species, colonies can be flexible or rigid. Rigid colonies, though calcareous, are often extremely fragile.

Because of the many variables, members of the phylum are not easily recognized as a group. Observing zooids joined together to form a colonial structure is often the best clue in recognizing a formation as bryozoan. Some species can be identified by the colony's pattern of growth, while others can be distinguished only by the shape of the individual zooids, which often requires microscopic examination.

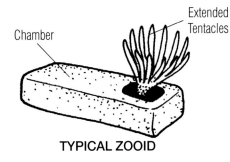

TYPICAL ZOOID

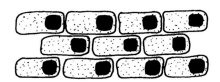

RECTANGULAR SHAPED ENCRUSTING
ZOOID CHAMBERS

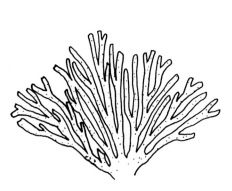

LACY FAN COLONY

SEAWEED-LIKE
COLONY

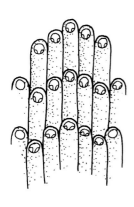

**OVAL SHAPED
ZOOID CHAMBERS**

**TUBULAR SHAPED
ZOOID CHAMBERS**

**VASE SHAPED
ZOOID CHAMBERS**

Phylum Phoronida

(fo-RON-i-da / L. surname of Io, in mythology)

Horseshoe Worms

Phoronids are a small group of marine animals consisting of only two genera that include about 12 species. They are small, worm-like animals that live on the bottom of shallow coastal waters. Individuals secrete a leathery or chitinous tube within which the body moves freely, but never leaves. Only the feeding head and anus are extended from the tube. The tube may be anchored to rocks, pilings or buried in sand or mud. The feeding head is composed of two parallel ridges curved into the shape of a horseshoe, the ends (called horns) may extend upward in rolled spirals. The mouth is located between the two ridges. Extending from the ridges are numerous hollow, slender ciliated tentacles used for feeding. If disturbed, the animal can completely withdraw the feeding head into the tube. Horseshoe worms are uncommon and rarely observed by divers.

TYPICAL HORSESHOE WORM

Bryozoans

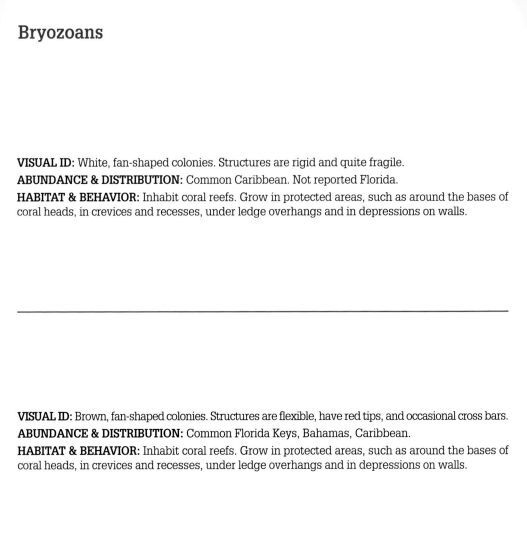

VISUAL ID: White, fan-shaped colonies. Structures are rigid and quite fragile.
ABUNDANCE & DISTRIBUTION: Common Caribbean. Not reported Florida.
HABITAT & BEHAVIOR: Inhabit coral reefs. Grow in protected areas, such as around the bases of coral heads, in crevices and recesses, under ledge overhangs and in depressions on walls.

VISUAL ID: Brown, fan-shaped colonies. Structures are flexible, have red tips, and occasional cross bars.
ABUNDANCE & DISTRIBUTION: Common Florida Keys, Bahamas, Caribbean.
HABITAT & BEHAVIOR: Inhabit coral reefs. Grow in protected areas, such as around the bases of coral heads, in crevices and recesses, under ledge overhangs and in depressions on walls.

VISUAL ID: Tan, fan-shaped colonies. Structures are flexible and somewhat crunchy to the touch.
ABUNDANCE & DISTRIBUTION: Common Gulf Coast of Florida. Genus is worldwide. (See note)
HABITAT & BEHAVIOR: Attach to hard substrate. Numerous colonies often grow in patches.
NOTE: This is the only genus to form tan, fan-like structures along the Gulf Coast of Florida. Species identification, however, requires laboratory examination of specimen.

WHITE FAN BRYOZOAN
Reteporellina evelinae
CLASS:
Bryozoans
Gymnolaemata

SIZE: Colony 1 - 2 in.
DEPTH: 25 - 100 ft.

BROWN FAN BRYOZOAN
Canda simplex
CLASS:
Bryozoans
Gymnolaemata

SIZE: Colony ³/₄ - 1¹/₄ in.
DEPTH: 25 - 130 ft.

TAN FAN BRYOZOAN
Scrupocellaria sp.
CLASS:
Bryozoans
Gymnolaemata

SIZE: Colony ³/₄ - 1¹/₄ in.
DEPTH: 15 - 100 ft.

Bryozoans

VISUAL ID: Purple, fan-shaped colonies. Structures are flexible with somewhat widely spaced branches.

ABUNDANCE & DISTRIBUTION: Occasional Caribbean; uncommon Florida.

HABITAT & BEHAVIOR: Inhabit reefs. Grow in protected areas, such as around the bases of coral heads, in crevices and recesses, under ledge overhangs and in depressions on walls.

SIMILAR SPECIES: Purple Fan Bryozoan, *B. neritina,* is impossible to visually distinguish from the Purple Reef Fan, but can generally be differentiated by habitat and location. Tend to grow in bays and harbors rather than reefs; occasional Florida, rare Caribbean.

VISUAL ID: Tangled masses of white, thin, cylindrical branches. Calcareous structures are rigid and quite fragile.

ABUNDANCE & DISTRIBUTION: Occasional Florida, Bahamas, Caribbean.

HABITAT & BEHAVIOR: Inhabit deep walls. Grow under ledge overhangs, attach to rope sponges and branches of black coral trees.

NOTE: Visual identification confirmed by microscopic examination of small sample collected from pictured specimen.

VISUAL ID: White, branching, ribbon-shaped colonies. These calcareous structures are rigid and quite fragile. The tiny, rectangular zooid chambers are distinctive of this genus.

ABUNDANCE & DISTRIBUTION: Uncommon Caribbean.

HABITAT & BEHAVIOR: Inhabit deep walls. Grow under ledge overhangs, attach to rope sponges and branches of black coral trees.

NOTE: Because there are several similar appearing species in this genus, species identification requires microscopic examination.

PURPLE REEF FAN
Bugula minima
CLASS:
Bryozoans
Gymnolaemata
ORDER:
Cheilostomata

SIZE: Colony 1 - 2 in.
DEPTH: 25 - 100 ft.

WHITE TANGLED BRYOZOAN
Bracebridgia subsulcata
CLASS:
Bryozoans
Gymnolaemata
ORDER:
Cyclostomata

SIZE: Colony 1 - 5 in.
DEPTH: 50 - 130 ft.

TANGLED RIBBON BRYOZOAN
Membranipora sp.
CLASS:
Bryozoans
Gymnolaemata
ORDER:
Cheilostomata

SIZE: Colony 1 - 5 in.
DEPTH: 50 - 130 ft.

Bryozoans

VISUAL ID: Bushy, flexible, seaweed-like colonies are light orangish brown to tan. Primary branches of the colony are the long axis for secondary branches that form a spiral pattern.

ABUNDANCE & DISTRIBUTION: Common North Florida; occasional South Florida. Not reported Caribbean.

HABITAT & BEHAVIOR: Attach to substrate in wide range of habitats, including dock pilings, sea grass beds, shipwrecks and rocky reefs.

VISUAL ID: Bushy, flexible, seaweed-like colonies are white to light gray or tan. Circular, fan-like structures tip the secondary branches.

ABUNDANCE & DISTRIBUTION: Common Florida; occasional Bahamas, Caribbean. Circumtropical.

HABITAT & BEHAVIOR: Attach to substrate in wide range of habitats, including dock pilings, sea grass beds, shipwrecks and rocky reefs.

NOTE: Visual identification confirmed by examination of small sample collected from pictured specimen.

VISUAL ID: Dark purple to reddish purple to brownish purple tuft or bush-like, flexible branching colonies with small pearly-white beads along the branches.

ABUNDANCE & DISTRIBUTION: Uncommon Florida, Bahamas, Caribbean, but can be locally abundant; also circumtropical.

HABITAT & BEHAVIOR: Typically in harbors and bays where it fouls ships, pilings, buoys, but also occasionally on reefs and rocky outcroppings.

NOTE: Visual identification confirmed by examination of small sample collected from pictured specimen.

SPIRAL-TUFTED BRYOZOAN
Bugula turrita
CLASS:
Bryozoans
Gymnolaemata
ORDER:
Cheilostomata

SIZE: Colonies to 1 ft.
DEPTH: 1 - 90 ft.

SEAWEED BRYOZOAN
Caulibugula dendrograpta
CLASS:
Bryozoans
Gymnolaemata
ORDER:
Cheilostomata

SIZE: Colonies to 1¹/₂ ft.
DEPTH: 10 - 130 ft.

PURPLE TUFT BRYOZOAN
Bugula neritina
CLASS:
Bryozoans
Gymnolaemata

SIZE: Colony 1 - 2 in.
DEPTH: 0 - 40 ft.

Bryozoans

VISUAL ID: Thin, encrusting colonies are red to pink and occasionally gold. In natural light usually fluoresce pale green. Calcified, relatively large, tooth-shaped zooid chambers give the surface of the colony a beaded texture.

ABUNDANCE & DISTRIBUTION: Common Caribbean. Possibly in Florida Keys and Bahamas.

HABITAT & BEHAVIOR: Inhabit reefs. Encrust in protected areas, such as around the bases of coral heads, in crevices and recesses, under ledge overhangs and in depressions on walls.

VISUAL ID: Pearly red color is distinctive. Encrusting colonies are calcified and composed of large, rectangular zooids with rounded ends that lay in an overlapping, shingle-like pattern.

ABUNDANCE & DISTRIBUTION: Occasional Florida, Bahamas, Caribbean. Circumtropical.

HABITAT & BEHAVIOR: Encrust in dead areas of reefs, especially around the bases of coral heads, under ledge overhangs and in shallow recesses.

NOTE: Visual identification confirmed by examination of small sample collected from pictured specimen.

VISUAL ID: Peachy-orange color is distinctive. Encrusting colonies are calcified and composed of rectangular zooids laying in long rows.

ABUNDANCE & DISTRIBUTION: Occasional Florida, Bahamas, Caribbean; also north to Maine and south to Brazil.

HABITAT & BEHAVIOR: Encrust hard rocky surfaces, often mixed with encrusting coralline algae and other encrusting bryozoans.

NOTE: Visual identification confirmed by examination of small sample collected from pictured specimen.

BLEEDING TEETH BRYOZOAN
Trematooecia aviculifera
CLASS:
Bryozoans
Gymnolaemata
ORDER:
Cheilostomata

SIZE: Colony ½ - 3 in.
DEPTH: 25 - 100 ft.

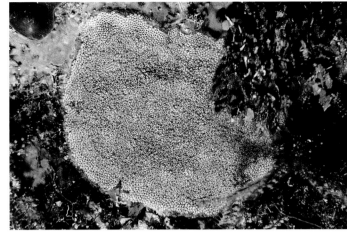

PEARLY RED ENCRUSTING BRYOZOAN
Steginoporella magnilabris
CLASS:
Bryozoans
Gymnolaemata

SIZE: Colonies 1 - 3 in.
DEPTH: 15 - 130 ft.

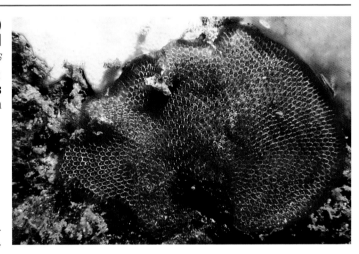

PEACH ENCRUSTING BRYOZOAN
Hippoporina verrilli
CLASS:
Bryozoans
Gymnolaemata

SIZE: Colony 2 - 10 in.
DEPTH: 6 - 80 ft.

Bryozoans

VISUAL ID: Pearly Orange Encrusting Bryozoan: Pearly orange color is distinctive. The thin, calcified encrusting colonies are composed of tiny zooids. Purple Encrusting Bryozoan: Purple color is distinctive. The thin, calcified encrusting colonies are composed of tiny zooids. Green coloration in picture comes from algae growth.

ABUNDANCE & DISTRIBUTION: Common Florida, Bahamas, Caribbean. Circumtropical.

HABITAT & BEHAVIOR: Encrust boat bottoms, dock pilings, and mangrove roots, but are also occasionally common on mid-range reefs.

NOTE: Pictured specimens were collected and visual identifications confirmed by laboratory examination. Purple Encrusting Bryozoan cannot be identified to species because of incomplete classification data for this and several similar appearing species. It is possibly *S. serialis* or *S. violacea*, but could also be an undescribed species.

VISUAL ID: Purplish brown, calcified encrusting colonies that often form tubular, branching, horn-like structures.

ABUNDANCE & DISTRIBUTION: Occasional Florida, Bahamas, Caribbean.

HABITAT & BEHAVIOR: Generally inhabit harbors, bays and mangrove environments in the Caribbean, but may be found on reefs. In North Florida waters they inhabit deep rocky reefs.

VISUAL ID: Twin spiral ridge structures of two and a half to three whorls with of 600-1000 tentacles extend above the bottom on thin stem-like bodies. Nearly translucent to pink, peach, dark reddish and black. Individuals cluster in circular aggregations around tube dwelling anemones.

ABUNDANCE & DISTRIBUTION: Rare Florida, Bahamas, Caribbean; also north to Georgia and tropical waters around the world.

HABITAT & BEHAVIOR: Inhabit areas of sand and soft sediment. Cluster around and always associate with tube-dwelling anemones lodging their chitinous tubes in the meshes of the felt-like tubes of the anemones. Hermaphroditic; when reproducing embryos cluster in the upper whorls of the spiral structures. [pictured]

PEARLY ORANGE ENCRUSTING BRYOZOAN
Hippopodina feegeensis

PURPLE ENCRUSTING BRYOZOAN
Schizoporella sp.

CLASS:
Bryozoans
Gymnolaemata
ORDER:
Cheilostomata
SUBORDER:
Ascophora
SIZE: Colonies 1 - 3 in.
DEPTH: 2 - 75 ft

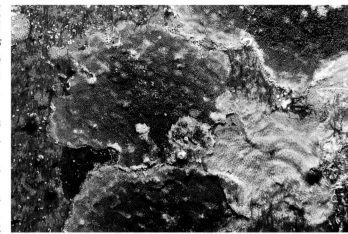

TUBULAR-HORN BRYOZOAN
Schizoporella violacea

CLASS:
Bryozoans
Gymnolaemata
ORDER:
Cheilostomata
SUBORDER:
Ascophora

SIZE: Colony 1 - 4 in.
DEPTH: 1 - 100 ft.

SPIRAL-HORN PHORONID
Phoronis australis

PHYLUM:
Horseshoe Worms
Phoronida

SIZE: Body length 2 - 8 in.,
tentacled head $^{1}/_{2}$ - 1 in.
DEPTH: 0 - 110 ft.

Phylum Mollusca

(Moe-LUS-kuh / L. soft body)

Gastropods, Shell-less Snails, Chitons, Bivalves, Octopi, Squid

The Latin name Mollusca means soft body, which appropriately describes these animals because they lack a true skeleton. A majority of phylum members have an external shell for protection. Shells are made of calcium carbonate secreted from a specialized layer of the animals' outer tissues, called the **mantle.**

Gastropods

CLASS: Gastropoda (Gas-tro-POE-duh / L. stomach foot)
SUBCLASS: Prosobranchia (Pro-so-BRAHNK-key-uh / Gr. forward gills)

Snails are, by far, the largest class of mollusks, containing more than 35,000 species. Typically, each animal secretes a tubular whorl that forms an ever-enlarging **cone-shaped shell** as the snail grows. Species are identified by their shells' shape, sculpturing, color pattern, or a combination of these features.

Normally, the snail's soft body is completely hidden within the shell. Occasionally, however, a tube-like mouth called the **proboscis,** and **two tentacles,** are seen extending from the shell's opening. **Eyes** are usually located at the base of these tentacles. A short leathery pad or **foot** is extended to slowly drag the snail about. Many species have a hard, cuticular disc, called an **operculum,** attached to the foot. This covers the opening of the shell when the animal withdraws. A few species, such as Flamingo Tongues and Cowries, extend their mantle over the entire shell as camouflage.

Shell-less Snails

CLASS: Gastropoda
SUBCLASS: Opisthobranchia (Oh-PISS-toe-BRAHNK-key-uh / Gr. back or rear gills)

Most members of this subclass lack an external shell, although several orders have reduced-external, or poorly-developed internal, shells. The body is typically a thick, elongated oval only a few inches in length. The mantle, which often has colorful, ornate designs, covers the animal's back. At the head are one or two pairs of tentacles; some have foot corner extensions that appear as an additional pairs of tentacles. Many opisthobranchs have specialized diets, feeding on only a single species of marine invertebrate or plant. Finding their food source is often the secret to locating many species. Several orders may be encountered on the reef; their similarity in appearance, however, makes them difficult to distinguish.

Headshield slugs, Order Cephalaspidea, have a distinctive **shield-shaped head.** They all have an internal or external shell.

Sea hares, Order Anaspidea, are large opisthobranchs with a **pair of rolled rhinophores** (sensory tentacles), **a pair of rolled tentacles** and **mantle skin flaps** on their backs. Most are colored in shades of green and brown, a few are black. They have a small internal shell and internal gills. Sea hares feed on algae. When disturbed, many species discharge a purple ink in defense.

Sidegill slugs, Order Notaspidea, have a **mantle skirt** that covers the gill on the body's right side. They usually have an internal shell and **one pair of rolled rhinophores** (sensory tentacles) that resemble dowel with a rounded tip. Members of this order feed primarily on tunicates.

Sea slugs, Order Sacoglossa, is a diverse order united by a sac in the alimentary canal that collects discarded teeth. Visually they vary greatly, although most are shades of green. Sea slugs respire by absorbing oxygen through their skin. Some can be identified by **skin ruffles** on their backs that increase the absorption area. They have **one pair of rolled rhinophores** (sensory tentacles) that resemble a rolled sheet of paper. All sea slugs have a shell, which may be external or internal and is usually reduced in size. Members of this order feed on algae.

Nudibranchs, Order Nudibranchia (L. naked gill), can be recognized by their external gills. Many species have developed true secondary gills, as in the Family Chromodoridae (Gr. colorful sea goddess). Their structure takes the form of a crown of feather-like appendages surrounding the anus, called **anal gills.** Others have developed appendages to increase skin area for the absorption of oxygen. These may take the form of skin ruffles, or fringe-like projections on the back, called cerata. Nudibranchs have a pair of **rhinophores** (sensory tentacles) on their heads; a second pair of **oral tentacles** is also present, although not obvious in some species. A few have foot corner extensions that resemble a third pair of tentacles. Members of this order have no shell and are carnivores.

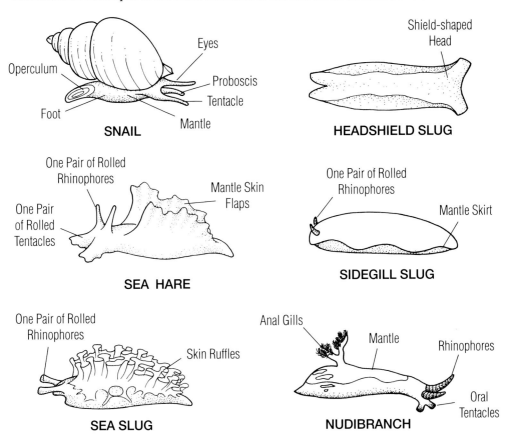

SNAIL

HEADSHIELD SLUG

SEA HARE

SIDEGILL SLUG

SEA SLUG

NUDIBRANCH

Chitons

CLASS: **Amphineura** (Am-fee-NUR-uh / L. nerves all around)

Chitons are easily recognized by their oval shape, formed by eight transverse, overlapping, **calcareous plates.** Around the edge is a fleshy border, called a girdle. The **girdle's** color, markings and texture are often important keys to species identification. Only an inch or two in length, they attach firmly to rocks with a large, muscular foot. Movement is imperceptibly slow as they graze on algae. Chitons generally inhabit shallow intertidal or subtidal water, but are occasionally found on reefs.

Bivalves

CLASS: **Bivalvia** (Buy-VALVE-ee-uh / L. two doors)

The soft-bodied animals of this class are protected by two shells, called **valves,** that are hinged together by a ligament. Special muscles, called abductors, contract to close the valves and relax to open. Species are identified by their valves' sculpturing, color pattern, or a combination of these features. When open, some species extend a curtain-like **mantle** that can be brightly colored. The mantle of a few species have **tentacles,** and **eye spots** for the detection of movement. Bivalves are filter-feeders. Water is drawn into a siphon, passed through a complex gill-filter to extract food and oxygen, and expelled out a second siphon.

Squid, Octopuses

CLASS: **Cephalopoda** (Sef-uh-low-POE-duh / Gr. head and foot)

Cephalopods have long arms with powerful suction cups that are used to catch prey and bring it to the mouth. All are carnivores that have a pair of powerful, beak-like jaws to crush or tear prey. Of all the invertebrate animals, they have the most highly evolved nervous system, including eyes similar in structure to those of vertebrates. Octopi and squid have no external shell, unlike their close relative, the chambered nautilus. Cephalopods can propel themselves rapidly by expelling water from a mantle cavity with a water-jet action. They can change body colors swiftly and dramatically, often to blend with their surroundings. This is accomplished by the expansion or contraction of specialized pigment cells called chromatophores.

Squid, Order Teuthoidea, can be recognized by the **eight arms** and **two longer tentacles** that stream behind their elongated body as they swim. Running along the sides are stabilizing **swim fins.** Squid are often seen in groups, moving over the reef in close formation. They prey primarily on fish.

Octopuses, Order Octopoda, have **eight arms** of about equal length, and a globular or bag-like body. They are primarily bottom-dwellers that use their arms and suction cups to move about; however, they have the ability to jet themselves backwards by rapidly expelling water from their mantle cavity. A cloud of dark ink is sometimes discharged to cover their escape. Crustaceans and shelled molluscs make up their basic diet.

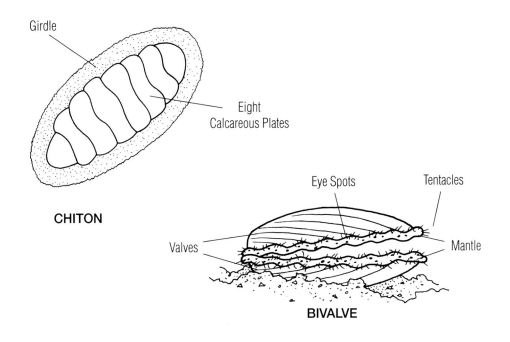

Girdle

Eight
Calcareous Plates

CHITON

Eye Spots

Tentacles

Valves

Mantle

BIVALVE

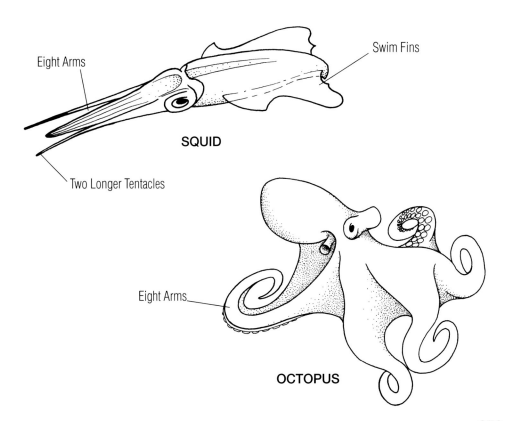

Eight Arms

Swim Fins

SQUID

Two Longer Tentacles

Eight Arms

OCTOPUS

259

VISUAL ID: Large shell has short conical spire with blunt spikes. Shell's exterior is orangish (not always apparent because of algal growth and debris); aperture rosy pink. Mottled gray head with large proboscis and long eye stalks. Eye at tip of stalk, tentacles below. Long, claw-like operculum.

ABUNDANCE & DISTRIBUTION: Abundant to uncommon South Florida, Bahamas, Caribbean. Has become uncommon in many areas because of over-harvesting.

HABITAT & BEHAVIOR: Inhabit sea grass beds and sand flats, often around patch reefs. Pictured species relatively young, shell becomes thicker with age. Often more abundant between 40 - 100 feet because of difficulty in harvesting.

REACTION TO DIVERS: When approached, retract proboscis and eye stalks into shell. If diver waits, motionlessly, animal often reappears after a short time.

VISUAL ID: Thick, whitish exterior shell, cream colored lip and aperture. Short conical spire with large rounded spikes. Green head with large proboscis. Long, greenish cream colored eye stalks with eye at tip and tentacle below. Long, claw-like operculum.

ABUNDANCE & DISTRIBUTION: Common to uncommon South Florida, Bahamas, Caribbean.

HABITAT & BEHAVIOR: Inhabit sea grass beds and sand flats, often around patch reefs.

REACTION TO DIVERS: When approached, retract proboscis and eye stalks into shell. If diver waits, motionlessly, animal often reappears after a short time.

VISUAL ID: Shell has short conical spire with two spikes on last whorl, aperture's upper lip is expanded and extends upward. Exterior mottled browns and purples (not always apparent because of algal growth and debris); aperture reddish. Long eye stalks with tentacles attached below eyes at tips. Long, claw-like operculum.

ABUNDANCE & DISTRIBUTION: Common South Florida, occasional Bahamas, Caribbean.

HABITAT & BEHAVIOR: Inhabit sea grass beds and sand flats, often around patch reefs.

REACTION TO DIVERS: When approached, retract proboscis and eye stalks into shell. If diver waits, motionlessly, animal often reappears after a short time.

QUEEN CONCH
Strombus gigas
CLASS:
Gastropods
Gastropoda
SUBCLASS:
Prosobranchia
FAMILY:
Conchs
Srombidae

SIZE: 6 - 9 in.,
12 in. max.
DEPTH: 3 - 100 ft.

MILK CONCH
Strombus costatus
CLASS:
Gastropods
Gastropoda
SUBCLASS:
Prosobranchia
FAMILY:
Conchs
Srombidae

SIZE: 4 - 6 in.
DEPTH: 3 - 40 ft.

HAWKWING CONCH
Strombus raninus
CLASS:
Gastropods
Gastropoda
SUBCLASS:
Prosobranchia
FAMILY:
Conchs
Srombidae

SIZE: 2^1/$_2$ - 3^1/$_2$ in.,
4^1/$_2$ in. max.
DEPTH: 3 - 80 ft.

VISUAL ID: Shell has knob-like spikes on next-to-last whorl of spire, and short, pointed spikes on final whorl. Aperture's upper lip slants downward. Exterior orangish brown and may be mottled and/or banded; aperture reddish cream. Mottled brown head with large white-tipped proboscis and long, whitish eye stalks. Long, claw-like operculum.

ABUNDANCE & DISTRIBUTION: Abundant West Florida; common East Florida. Not reported Caribbean.

HABITAT & BEHAVIOR: Inhabit sea grass beds and sand flats, often around shallow patch and fringing reefs.

REACTION TO DIVERS: When approached, retract proboscis and eye stalks into shell. If diver waits, motionlessly, animal often reappears after a short time.

SIMILAR SPECIES: West Indian Fighting Conch, *S. pugilis,* is distinguished by longer, more pointed spikes on last two whorls of spire, upper aperture lip "U"-shaped. Common Caribbean, occasional South Florida.

VISUAL ID: Shell has long, narrow extension of aperture's upper lip. Exterior is orangish, often blotched with white; aperture reddish cream. Mottled brown head with large proboscis and long eye stalks. Eye at tip of stalk, tentacle below. Long, claw-like operculum.

ABUNDANCE & DISTRIBUTION: Rare South Florida, Bahamas, Caribbean.

HABITAT & BEHAVIOR: Inhabit sea grass beds and sand flats, often around shallow patch and fringing reefs.

REACTION TO DIVERS: When approached, retract proboscis and eye stalks into shell. If diver waits, motionlessly, animal often reappears after a short time.

VISUAL ID: Shell has short spire of five or six whorls, the last few have a single or double row of short sharp spines, and large inflated body whorl; dark brown to dark gray or black undercolor with bluish white or yellow bands. Bluish white mantle with dark speckles and markings. Dark tear-shaped operculum..

ABUNDANCE & DISTRIBUTION: Occasional Florida and Gulf of Mexico.

HABITAT & BEHAVIOR: Inhabit shallow areas, including intertidal zones, of rocks and sand, commonly in mangroves.

FLORIDA FIGHTING CONCH
Strombus alatus

CLASS:
Gastropods
Gastropoda
SUBCLASS:
Prosobranchia
FAMILY:
Conchs
Srombidae

SIZE: 2¹/₂ - 3¹/₂ in.,
5 in. max.
DEPTH: 3 - 20 ft.

ROOSTERTAIL CONCH
Strombus gallus

CLASS:
Gastropods
Gastropoda
SUBCLASS:
Prosobranchia
FAMILY:
Conchs
Srombidae

SIZE: 3¹/₂ - 5 in.
DEPTH: 3 - 20 ft.

CROWN CONCH
Melongena corona

CLASS:
Gastropods
Gastropoda
SUBCLASS:
Prosobranchia
Crown Conchs
Melongenidae

SIZE: 2 - 5 in.
DEPTH: 0 - 35 ft.

VISUAL ID: Shell has long conical spire with small knobs. Exterior grayish white to salmon or tan; orangish aperture. Body cream to reddish orange. Shell often flaky. Long, claw-like operculum.

ABUNDANCE & DISTRIBUTION: Abundant to common Florida and Gulf of Mexico.

HABITAT & BEHAVIOR: Inhabit areas of sand, sea grass and patch reefs. Large adults tend to inhabit deeper waters.

REACTION TO DIVERS: When approached, retract into shell. If diver waits, motionlessly, animal often reappears after a short time.

NOTE ABOUT JUVENILES: Orange shell and red body to 3$\frac{1}{2}$ inches, usually in depths less than 30 feet.

VISUAL ID: Spindle-shaped shell with many broken, dark spiral stripes. Variable blotched color pattern, often in shades of gray, green or brown; in Florida, occasionally reddish orange. Body black to reddish-brown with white speckles. Tear-shaped operculum is brown.

ABUNDANCE & DISTRIBUTION: Occasional Florida, Bahamas, Caribbean.

HABITAT & BEHAVIOR: Inhabit shallow sand and grass bottoms, prefer quiet water of bays. Occasionally found in deeper water.

VISUAL ID: Long, pointed spiral shell is variegated in shades ranging from cream to dark brown. Yellow and black banded tentacles. Body mottled reddish brown.

ABUNDANCE & DISTRIBUTION: Occasional Southeast Florida, Caribbean. Has become rare in many areas because of over-collecting.

HABITAT & BEHAVIOR: Inhabit sandy bottoms and reefs. Hide in reef recesses during day. Feed on sea cucumbers at night, in the open at night.

FLORIDA HORSE CONCH
Pleuroploca gigantea

CLASS:
Gastropods
Gastropoda
SUBCLASS:
Prosobranchia
FAMILY:
Tulip Shells
Fasciolariidae

SIZE: 10 - 14 in.,
30 in. max.
DEPTH: 3 - 100 ft.

TRUE TULIP
Fasciolaria tulipa

CLASS:
Gastropods
Gastropoda
SUBCLASS:
Prosobranchia
FAMILY:
Tulip Shells
Fasciolariidae

SIZE: 3 - 6 in.,
10 in. max.
DEPTH: 0 - 35 ft.

ATLANTIC TRITON'S TRUMPET
Charonia variegata

CLASS:
Gastropods
Gastropoda
SUBCLASS:
Prosobranchia
FAMILY:
Tritons
Ranellidae

SIZE: 10 - 14 in.,
18 in. max.
DEPTH: 20 - 60 ft.

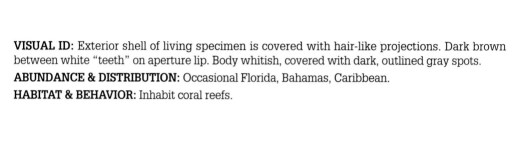

VISUAL ID: Exterior shell of living specimen is covered with hair-like projections. Dark brown between white "teeth" on aperture lip. Body whitish, covered with dark, outlined gray spots.
ABUNDANCE & DISTRIBUTION: Occasional Florida, Bahamas, Caribbean.
HABITAT & BEHAVIOR: Inhabit coral reefs.

VISUAL ID: Shell has long spire of four or five stout whorls and squat body whorl with wide ridges and valleys crossed by transverse encircling ribs; pale brown to yellowish brown to cream. Brownish white mantle with brown spots and markings.
ABUNDANCE & DISTRIBUTION: Occasional Florida Keys and Caribbean; also south to Brazil.
HABITAT & BEHAVIOR: Inhabit areas of rock and sand.

VISUAL ID: Shell has short spire and large, inflated helmet-like body whorl with transverse encircling ribs; pale yellow to whitish with pale brown squarish spots arranged in encircling whorls. Yellowish cream to white mantle with black line markings on eye tentacles.
ABUNDANCE & DISTRIBUTION: Common Florida, Bahamas, Caribbean; also north to North Carolina, Bermuda and south to Brazil.
HABITAT & BEHAVIOR: Inhabit sandy areas.

ATLANTIC HAIRY TRITON
Cymatium pileare
CLASS:
Gastropods
Gastropoda
SUBCLASS:
Prosobranchia
FAMILY:
Tritons
Ranellidae

SIZE: 1½ - 3½ in.,
4 in. max.
DEPTH: 20 - 80 ft.

LIP TRITON
Cymatium labiosum
CLASS:
Gastropods
Gastropoda
SUBCLASS:
Prosobranchia
FAMILY:
Tritons
Ranellidae

SIZE: ½ - 1 in.
DEPTH: 20 - 80 ft.

SCOTCH BONNET
Phalium granulatum
CLASS:
Gastropods
Gastropoda
SUBCLASS:
Prosobranchia
FAMILY:
Helmet Shells
Cassidae

SIZE: 2 - 4 in.
DEPTH: 20 - 80 ft.

Gastropods

VISUAL ID: Exterior shell in shades of reddish brown in a wavy, netted pattern, with seven or eight dark stripes over outer lip. Flattened lip around aperture forms distinct triangle.

ABUNDANCE & DISTRIBUTION: Common to occasional Florida, Bahamas, Caribbean. Has become rare in many areas because of over-collecting.

HABITAT & BEHAVIOR: Inhabit shallow sand flats, often around patch and fringing reefs. During day usually burrow in sand with only small part of upper shell exposed. Hunt in open at night for sea urchins, which they attack with surprising speed, unimpeded by spines.

SIMILAR SPECIES: King Helmet, *C. tuberosa*, flattened lip around aperture is triangular, fine netted growth lines on shell, smaller shell, four inches maximum. Emperor or Queen Helmet, *C. madagascariensis*, flattened lip forms a rounded triangle, large shell to 12 inches.

VISUAL ID: Shell has short spire and large, inflated body whorl with numerous encircling ribs; pale to medium brown markings on white undercolor. Pale gray mantle with gray mottling.

ABUNDANCE & DISTRIBUTION: Occasional South Florida, Bahamas, Caribbean; also Bermuda and south to Brazil.

HABITAT & BEHAVIOR: Inhabit sandy areas around coral reefs.

VISUAL ID: Thick shell; short conical spire has blunt spikes; cream with blackish to reddish brown markings and shadings, distinctive series of lines, resembling a musical score, encircle mid-shell. Whitish to goldish mantle with black speckles and markings. Brown tear-shaped operculum.

ABUNDANCE & DISTRIBUTION: Occasional from Dominican Republic east through island chain then south to South America.

HABITAT & BEHAVIOR: Inhabit shallow areas of sand, mud, rocks and rubble. May forage with mantle extended during the day.

KING HELMET
Cassis tuberosa
CLASS:
Gastropods
Gastropoda
SUBCLASS:
Prosobranchia
FAMILY:
Helmet Shells
Cassidae

SIZE: 4 - 6 in.,
7 in. max.
DEPTH: 10 - 35 ft.

ATLANTIC PARTRIDGE TUN
Tonna maculosa
CLASS:
Gastropoda
SUBCLASS:
Prosobranchia
FAMILY:
Tuns
Tonnidae

SIZE: 5 - 6 in.
DEPTH: 60 - 200 ft.

MUSIC VOLUTE
Voluta musica
CLASS:
Gastropoda
SUBCLASS:
Prosobranchia
FAMILY:
Volutes
Volutidae

SIZE: 1¹/₂ - 3 in.
DEPTH: 0 - 50 ft.

Gastropods

VISUAL ID: Thick, rough wrinkled shell has a large body whorl and pointed conical spire of approximately five whorls; rough, often hollow, spikes protrude from spire, back of body whorl and around aperture; grayish. Commonly encrusted with coralline algae and barnacles.
ABUNDANCE & DISTRIBUTION: Occasional Caribbean; can be abundant in localized areas.
HABITAT & BEHAVIOR: Inhabit shallow areas of sand, silt, rocks and rubble.

VISUAL ID: Long, lustrous cylindrical shell with shout pointed spire of about four whorls; light brown netted pattern over creamy to white exterior. May occasionally have two or three dark bands; rarely all white with no markings.
ABUNDANCE & DISTRIBUTION: Common Florida, Bahamas, Caribbean.
HABITAT & BEHAVIOR: Inhabit sandy areas near shallow patch and back reefs. Crawl about, partially buried in sand, while searching for prey. The shell's lustrous finish is produced by the fleshy mantle, which can cover the entire outer surface.

VISUAL ID: Long, lustrous cylindrical shell with short pointed conical spire of four or five whorls; brownish cream to pale gray undercolor with numerous brown triangular markings.
ABUNDANCE & DISTRIBUTION: Common Florida; also north to South Carolina.
HABITAT & BEHAVIOR: Inhabit shallow areas of sand, silt, rocks and rubble. The shell's lustrous finish is produced by the fleshy mantle, which can be slid up over the entire surface. Often forage with mantle extended.

WEST INDIAN MUREX
Chicoreus brevifrons
CLASS:
Gastropoda
SUBCLASS:
Prosobranchia
FAMILY:
Murex Shells
Muricidae

SIZE: 4 - 6 in.
DEPTH: 10 - 80 ft.

NETTED OLIVE
Oliva reticularis
CLASS:
Gastropods
Gastropoda
SUBCLASS:
Prosobranchia
FAMILY:
Olive Shells
Olividae

SIZE: 1 - 1$\frac{1}{2}$ in.,
2 in. max.
DEPTH: 5 - 25 ft.

LETTERED OLIVE
Oliva sayana
CLASS:
Gastropoda
SUBCLASS:
Prosobranchia
FAMILY:
Olive Shells
Olividae

SIZE: 1 - 2$\frac{1}{2}$ in.
DEPTH: 0 - 30 ft.

Gastropods

VISUAL ID: Lustrous white shell with white spots and blotches, three faint, diffuse, yellowish bands. Translucent mantel blotched with white.

ABUNDANCE & DISTRIBUTION: Common Caribbean.

HABITAT & BEHAVIOR: Inhabit sand and sea grass bottoms, often near fringing reefs. The shell's lustrous finish is produced by the fleshy mantle, which can cover the entire outer surface. May forage about with mantle extended during the day.

VISUAL ID: Shell with short, blunt conical spire and teardrop-shaped body whorl; lustrous brownish cream to pinkish gray with numerous white spots and blotches. Brownish cream to pinkish gray translucent mantle with numerous white spots.

ABUNDANCE & DISTRIBUTION: Occasional southeast Florida and Caribbean.

HABITAT & BEHAVIOR: Typically inhabit soft sand around coral reefs. The shell's lustrous finish is produced by the fleshy mantle, which can cover the entire outer surface. Often forage with mantle extended.

VISUAL ID: Shell has short, blunt conical spire and elongate teardrop-shaped body whorl. Lustrous brownish cream. Grayish translucent to transparent mantle with numerous white speckles, a white blotch and a single line marking on foot, orangish and white spots on proboscis.

ABUNDANCE & DISTRIBUTION: Occasional Caribbean.

HABITAT & BEHAVIOR: Inhabit shallow coral reefs and surrounding sand. The shell's lustrous finish is produced by the fleshy mantle, which can cover the entire outer surface. Often forage with mantle extended.

GLOWING MARGINELLA
Marginella pruniosum
CLASS:
Gastropods
Gastropoda
SUBCLASS:
Prosobranchia
FAMILY:
Marginellidae
Marginellidae

SIZE: ¼ - ½ in.
DEPTH: 5 - 20 ft.

WHITE-SPOT MARGINELLA
Marginella guttata
CLASS:
Gastropoda
SUBCLASS:
Prosobranchia
FAMILY:
Marginellas
Marginellidae

SIZE: ½ - 1 in.
DEPTH: 3 - 30 ft.

OBLONG MARGINELLA
Marginella oblongum
CLASS:
Gastropoda
SUBCLASS:
Prosobranchia
FAMILY:
Marginellas
Marginellidae

SIZE: ½ - 1 in.
DEPTH: 0 - 40 ft.

VISUAL ID: Shell has short, blunt conical spire and teardrop-shaped body whorl; orange with two narrow whitish bands encircling the middle of the body whorl. Whitish transparent mantle with white spots and orange and white speckles.

ABUNDANCE & DISTRIBUTION: Uncommon southeast Florida and Caribbean.

HABITAT & BEHAVIOR: Inhabit shallow areas of sand, mud, rocks, rubble and algae. The shell's lustrous finish is produced by the fleshy mantle, which can be slipped over the entire outer surface. Often forage with mantle extended.

VISUAL ID: High, conical spire. Exterior usually covered with various growths including Red Coralline Algae.

ABUNDANCE & DISTRIBUTION: Common Caribbean; occasional South Florida.

HABITAT & BEHAVIOR: Inhabit grass beds and shallow reefs, often hide under rocks.

SIMILAR SPECIES: American Starsnail, *L. americanum,* is virtually indistinguishable, common Southeast Florida.

VISUAL ID: Width of lower whorl is half that of shell's overall length. Shallow-water specimens tend to have whitish spire with numerous small, dark, spiraled markings and prominent short spikes on spire. Deep-water specimens tend to have orange-brown to rust-brown mottling on spire, with less pronounced short spikes.

ABUNDANCE & DISTRIBUTION: Abundant South Florida, Bahamas, Caribbean.

HABITAT & BEHAVIOR: Inhabit wide range of marine environments including intertidal pools, sea grass beds and reefs. More common in shallow water.

SIMILAR SPECIES: There are numerous similar and easily confused species, all of which are somewhat more elongated.

ORANGE MARGINELLA
Valvarina sp.
CLASS:
Gastropoda
SUBCLASS:
Prosobranchia
FAMILY:
Marginellas
Marginellidae

SIZE: ½ - 1 in.
DEPTH: 0 - 40 ft.

WEST INDIAN STARSNAIL
Lithopoma tectum
CLASS:
Gastropods
Gastropoda
SUBCLASS:
Prosobranchia
FAMILY:
Turbans
Turbinidae

SIZE: 1 - 1½ in.,
2 in. max.
DEPTH: 5 - 25 ft.

STOCKY CERITH
Cerithium litteratum
CLASS:
Gastropods
Gastropoda
SUBCLASS:
Prosobranchia
FAMILY:
Ceriths
Cerithiidae

SIZE: ¾ - 1¼ in.,
1¾ in. max.
DEPTH: Intertidal - 100 ft.

VISUAL ID: Numerous whorls of chocolate-brown lines on sharp spire. Exterior in varying shades of light brown.
ABUNDANCE & DISTRIBUTION: Rare Florida Keys, Caribbean.
HABITAT & BEHAVIOR: Inhabit sandy areas and shallow coral reefs.

VISUAL ID: Stout, elongate spiral shell of approximately six non-overlapping whorls with nine or ten blade-like, longitudinal ribs on each whorl; brilliant white. White translucent mantle.
ABUNDANCE & DISTRIBUTION: Common Florida and Gulf of Mexico; also north to New York.
HABITAT & BEHAVIOR: Inhabit shallow areas of sand, often near shallow reefs.

VISUAL ID: Ribs run around shell from slit-like groove on back . White to tan to brownish-pink with three pairs of large, irregular, brownish spots on back. Grayish translucent to transparent mantle often with yellow to orange or red spots.
ABUNDANCE & DISTRIBUTION: Common Florida. Occasional Bahamas, Caribbean.
HABITAT & BEHAVIOR: Inhabit intertidal zones to deep reefs.

**CHOCOLATE-LINED
TOPSNAIL**
Calliostoma javanicum
CLASS:
Gastropods
Gastropoda
SUBCLASS:
Prosobranchia
FAMILY:
Pearly Top Shell
Trochidae

SIZE: ³/₄ - 1 in.,
1¹/₄ in. max.
DEPTH: 2 - 35 ft.

**ANGULATE
WENTLETRAP**
Epitonium angulatum
CLASS:
Gastropoda
SUBCLASS:
Prosobranchia
FAMILY:
Wentletraps
Epitoniidae

SIZE: ¹/₂ - 1 in.
DEPTH: 0 - 90 ft.

COFFEE BEAN TRIVIA
Trivia pediculus
CLASS:
Gastropods
Gastropoda
SUBCLASS:
Prosobranchia
FAMILY:
Erato Shails
Eratoidae

SIZE: ³/₄ - 1 in.,
1¹/₄ in. max.
DEPTH: 2 - 80 ft.

VISUAL ID: Shell has short, pointed, somewhat convex spire of seven to eight whorls with large cone-shaped body whorl; yellowish brown with white and brown blotches, occasionally encircled with several lines composed of dashes [pictured]; a wide pale band often encircles central body whorl. Pale brown mantle and orange snout.

ABUNDANCE & DISTRIBUTION: Common Florida; also north to North Carolina.

HABITAT & BEHAVIOR: Inhabit shallow areas of sand, often near shallow reefs.

EFFECT ON DIVERS: Cone shells secrete neurotoxic venom that is delivered by a single radular tooth that resembles a small harpoon. Although the venom of some Indo-Pacific cone shells can be fatal, the wounds of western Atlantic species are painful, but not life threatening. Handle with care!

VISUAL ID: Shell has short pointed spire of approximately seven whorls with large cone-shaped body whorl; brick red with numerous encircling lines of spots and several centrally located, pale, elongate blotches. Red, lightly speckled mantle.

ABUNDANCE & DISTRIBUTION: Rare eastern Caribbean.

HABITAT & BEHAVIOR: Inhabit shallow areas of sand, often near shallow reefs.

EFFECT ON DIVERS: Cone shells secrete neurotoxic venom that is delivered by a single radular tooth that resembles a small harpoon. Although the venom of some Indo-Pacific cone shells can be fatal, the wounds of western Atlantic species are painful, but not life threatening. Handle with care!

VISUAL ID: Shell has short, blunt spire of seven to eight knobbed whorls and a large cone-shaped body whorl; commonly mottled and blotched in shades of yellow, red, purple or chocolate brown and white, uncommonly solid shade of brown. Maroon mantle with numerous dark speckles.

ABUNDANCE & DISTRIBUTION: Common South Florida and Caribbean; also south to Brazil.

HABITAT & BEHAVIOR: : Inhabit coral reefs.

EFFECT ON DIVERS: Cone shells secrete neurotoxic venom that is delivered by a single radular tooth that resembles a small harpoon. Although the venom of some Indo-Pacific cone shells can be fatal, the wounds of western Atlantic species are painful, but not life threatening. Handle with care!

FLORIDA CONE
Conus floridanus
CLASS:
Gastropoda
SUBCLASS:
Prosobranchia
FAMILY:
Cone Shells
Conidae

SIZE: 1 - 1¹/₂ in.
DEPTH: 0 - 50 ft.

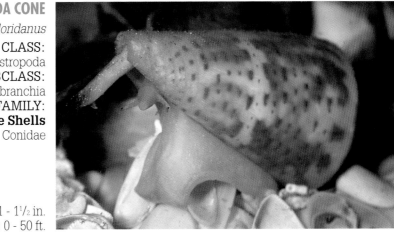

MATCHLESS CONE
Conus cedonulli
CLASS:
Gastropoda
SUBCLASS:
Prosobranchia
FAMILY:
Cone Shells
Conidae

SIZE: 1 - 2 in.
DEPTH: 3 - 50 ft.

CROWN CONE
Conus regius
CLASS:
Gastropoda
SUBCLASS:
Prosobranchia
FAMILY:
Cone Shells
Conidae

SIZE: 1 - 2¹/₄ in.
DEPTH:10 - 80 ft.

Gastropods

VISUAL ID: Bulbous-shaped shell (compare with more elongated shell of similar Measled Cowrie [next]). Covered with white spots, the larger of which often have brown centers. Lustrous shell in shades of brown, often has indistinct lighter and darker bands. Shell of young is banded and has no spots. Black, gray and brown mottled mantle with occasional white blotches and numerous fleshy, spike-like projections.

ABUNDANCE & DISTRIBUTION: Occasional to rare Florida, Caribbean.

HABITAT & BEHAVIOR: Inhabit reefs, often on underside of ledge overhangs and in recesses. Camouflage by extending mantle over shell. (Note the partial extension of mantle in photograph.) The shell's lustrous finish is produced by the fleshy mantle, which can cover the entire outer surface.

VISUAL ID: Shell somewhat elongated (compare with more bulbous shell of similar Atlantic Deer Cowrie [previous]). Covered with whitish spots, the larger of which often have brown centers, especially around sides. Lustrous shell, in shades of brown, often has indistinct lighter and darker bands. Shell of young is banded and has no spots. Grayish mottled mantle and numerous fleshy, spike-like projections.

ABUNDANCE & DISTRIBUTION: Occasional to rare Southeast Florida, Caribbean.

HABITAT & BEHAVIOR: Inhabit reefs, often on underside of ledge overhangs and in recesses. Also found near protective rocks in shallow water. Camouflage by extending mantle over shell. The shell's lustrous finish is produced by the fleshy mantle, which can cover the entire outer surface.

VISUAL ID: Lustrous, medium-brown to mauve shell with dark-brown to black flecks. Mantle mottled in shades of brown and mauve, and covered with numerous fleshy warts with forked extensions.

ABUNDANCE & DISTRIBUTION: Common to uncommon Southeast Florida, Caribbean.

HABITAT & BEHAVIOR: Inhabit coral reefs, often on undersides of ledge overhangs and in recesses. Camouflage by extending mantle over shell. The shell's lustrous finish is produced by the fleshy mantle, which can cover the entire outer surface.

ATLANTIC DEER COWRIE
Cypraea cervus

CLASS:
Gastropoda
SUBCLASS:
Prosobranchia
FAMILY:
Cowries
Cypraeidae

SIZE: 2 - 3 in.,
5 in. max.
DEPTH: 1 - 40 ft.

MEASLED COWRIE
Cypraea zebra

CLASS:
Gastropoda
SUBCLASS:
Prosobranchia
FAMILY:
Cowries
Cypraeidae

SIZE: 2 - 3¹/₂ in.,
4 in. max.
DEPTH: 6 - 35 ft.

ATLANTIC GRAY COWRIE
Cypraea cinerea

CLASS:
Gastropoda
SUBCLASS:
Prosobranchia
FAMILY:
Cowries
Cypraeidae

SIZE: ¹/₂ - 1 in.,
1¹/₂ in. max.
DEPTH: 20 - 50 ft.

Gastropods

VISUAL ID: Lustrous, yellow-brown shell with lighter spots. Mantle medium to dark-brown with numerous, lighter colored, fleshy warts with forked projections.

ABUNDANCE & DISTRIBUTION: Occasional Florida, Bahamas, Caribbean.

HABITAT & BEHAVIOR: Inhabit areas of reef rubble, often under rocks and in other sheltered locations. Camouflage by extending mantle over shell. (Note the partial extension of mantle in photograph.) The shell's lustrous finish is produced by the fleshy mantle, which can cover the entire outer surface.

VISUAL ID: White mantle covered with gray to black, usually rounded spots, with darker outlines. Shell is porcelain white.

ABUNDANCE & DISTRIBUTION: Occasional to rare Florida, Bahamas.

HABITAT & BEHAVIOR: Attach to and feed on gorgonians in all types of habitats. Often cover themselves with sea grass and other debris as a shield against strong light.

NOTE: Also commonly known as McGinty's Cyphoma. The shell's lustrous finish is produced by the fleshy mantle, which can cover the entire outer surface.

VISUAL ID: Cream-white mantle covered with orangish, often somewhat rectangular spots with black outlines. Shell is lustrous reddish cream to white.

ABUNDANCE & DISTRIBUTION: Common Florida, Bahamas, Caribbean.

HABITAT & BEHAVIOR: Attach to and feed on gorgonians in all types of habitats. Mantle normally extended over shell. The shell's lustrous finish is produced by the fleshy mantle, which can cover the entire outer surface.

ATLANTIC YELLOW COWRIE
Cypraea spurca acicularis

CLASS:
Gastropoda
SUBCLASS:
Prosobranchia
FAMILY:
Cowries
Cypraeidae

SIZE: ¹/₂ - 1 in.,
1¹/₂ in. max.
DEPTH: 15 - 50 ft.

SPOTTED CYPHOMA
Cyphoma macgintyi

CLASS:
Gastropods
Gastropoda
SUBCLASS:
Prosobranchia
FAMILY:
Simnias
Ovulidae

SIZE: ³/₄ - 1 in.
DEPTH: 20 - 80 ft.

FLAMINGO TONGUE
Cyphoma gibbosum

CLASS:
Gastropods
Gastropoda
SUBCLASS:
Prosobranchia
FAMILY:
Simnias
Ovulidae

SIZE: ³/₄ - 1 in.
DEPTH: 6 - 45 ft.

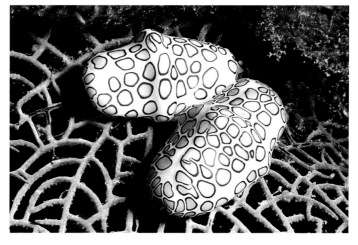

VISUAL ID: White mantle with numerous finger print-like designs of black and gold. Shell white to cream, often with a few yellowish markings.

ABUNDANCE & DISTRIBUTION: Uncommon to rare South Florida, Caribbean.

HABITAT & BEHAVIOR: Attach to and feed on gorgonians in all types of habitats. Often cover themselves with sea grass and other debris.

VISUAL ID: Mantle has fine network of lines and white spots; various shades of purple, yellow or green. Small, thin elongate shell with, narrow slit-like aperture running entire length; glossy, in various colors including lavender, yellow, green or white, with white border around aperture.

ABUNDANCE & DISTRIBUTION: Common Florida, Bahamas, Caribbean.

HABITAT & BEHAVIOR: Attach to and feed upon purple or yellow sea fans, and occasionally other gorgonians, including sea rods and sea whips. Change mantle color to match gorgonian.

NOTE: Although common, rarely observed because of its small size and excellent camouflage.

VISUAL ID: An unmarked mantle of either purple, yellow or green. Small, thin elongate shell with long, narrow slit-like aperture running entire length; glossy white to yellowish, pink or purple.

ABUNDANCE & DISTRIBUTION: Common Florida, Bahamas, Caribbean; also north to North Carolina.

HABITAT & BEHAVIOR: Attach to and feed on purple or yellow sea fans and on occasion other gorgonians, including sea rods and sea whips. Can change color to match gorgonian.

NOTE: Although common, rarely observed because of their small size and excellent camouflage.

FINGERPRINT CYPHOMA
Cyphoma signatum
CLASS:
Gastropods
Gastropoda
SUBCLASS:
Prosobranchia
FAMILY:
Simnias
Ovulidae

SIZE: ³/₄ - 1 in.
DEPTH: 6 - 45 ft.

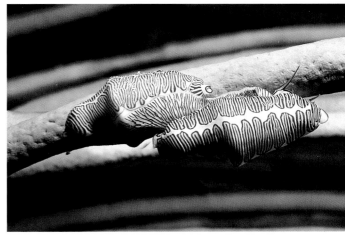

WEST INDIAN SIMNIA
Cymbovula acicularis
CLASS:
Gastropods
Gastropoda
SUBCLASS:
Prosobranchia
FAMILY:
Simnias
Ovulidae

SIZE: ¹/₂ in.
DEPTH: 5 - 50 ft.

SINGLE-TOOTH SIMNIA
Simnia uniplicata
CLASS:
Gastropoda
SUBCLASS:
Prosobranchia
FAMILY:
Simnia Shells
Ovulidae

SIZE: ¹/₄ - ³/₄ in.
DEPTH: 6 - 40 ft.

Worm Snails – Headshield Slugs

VISUAL ID: Circular shell opening (about $^3/_{16}$ in.) protrudes slightly from sponge or dead coral surface. The animal's head, with two small tentacles, can be seen in the opening. Color varies, often yellow, orange or black. Shell (rarely visible) is a long tube with several curves, the tip is spiraled. Tube is marked with rings of reddish-brown to gray and muddy-white, the last quarter inch and spiraled tip are white.

ABUNDANCE & DISTRIBUTION: Common Florida, Bahamas, Caribbean.

HABITAT & BEHAVIOR: Grow in sponges and dead coral heads. Often grow in intertwining clumps in shallow water. On deeper reefs, more commonly solitary, although several individuals may inhabit a single sponge. Commonly found growing in Touch-Me-Not Sponge, *Neofibularia nolitangere*, [pg.37]. Feed by sending out mucus thread [note photograph].

NOTE: Identification was made by collection of pictured specimen. This and several similar species can often be identified only by collection.

VISUAL ID: Thin black line design on polished, cream shell. Body translucent white with opaque white patches.

ABUNDANCE & DISTRIBUTION: Uncommon Florida, Bahamas, Caribbean. However, can be common in localized areas.

HABITAT & BEHAVIOR: Inhabit sandy areas, hide under rocks during day. Forage at night for polychaete worms.

VISUAL ID: Body and shell mottled brown with whitish flecks. Shell sculptured with widely spaced parallel grooves.

ABUNDANCE & DISTRIBUTION: Occasional Florida, Bahamas, Caribbean; also in eastern Pacific from southern Mexico to Chile and Galapagos.

HABITAT & BEHAVIOR: Inhabit areas of sand, gravel and mud. Bury during day, forage at night for algae.

FLORIDA WORMSNAIL
Vermicularia knorrii
CLASS:
Gastropods
Gastropoda
SUBCLASS:
Prosobranchia
FAMILY:
Worm Snails
Turritellidae

SIZE: Tube 3 - 5 in.
DEPTH: 5 - 60 ft.

MINIATURE MELO
Micromela undata
SUBCLASS:
Opisthobranchia
ORDER:
Headshield Slugs
Cephalaspidea
FAMILY:
Hydatinidae

SIZE: $1^{1}/_{4}$ - $1^{3}/_{4}$ in.,
$2^{1}/_{2}$ in. max.
DEPTH: 0 - 14 ft.

STRIATE BUBBLE
Bulla striata
SUBCLASS:
Opisthobranchia
ORDER:
Headshield Slugs
Cephalaspidea
FAMILY:
Bullidae

SIZE: 1 - $1^{1}/_{2}$ in.,
$2^{1}/_{2}$ in. max.
DEPTH: 0 - 100 ft.

VISUAL ID: Rows of brilliant blue spots on mantle. Body finely lined in shades of olive and brown.
ABUNDANCE & DISTRIBUTION: Occasional Florida, Bahamas, Caribbean.
HABITAT & BEHAVIOR: Inhabit rocky areas. Feed on other opisthobranchs, especially Lettuce Sea Slug, *Tridachia crispata,* [pg. 301].

VISUAL ID: Orange, blue and black stripes, white patch mid-back.
ABUNDANCE & DISTRIBUTION: Occasional Florida, Bahamas, Caribbean.
HABITAT & BEHAVIOR: Inhabit sandy areas. Feed on other headshield slugs.

VISUAL ID: Olive-brown to tan with numerous very thin brown lines and small iridescent blue rings or spots. Long tapered tail.
ABUNDANCE & DISTRIBUTION: Uncommon Florida, Bahamas, Caribbean.
HABITAT & BEHAVIOR: Inhabit areas of rocky rubble and open sand. Feed on algae. When disturbed will discharge a scarlet fluid.

MYSTERIOUS HEADSHIELD SLUG

Navanax aenigmaticus

SUBCLASS:
Opisthobranchia
ORDER:
Headshield Slugs
Cephalaspidea
FAMILY:
Aglajidae

SIZE: 1¼ - 1¾ in.,
2½ in. max.
DEPTH: 3 - 30 ft.

LEECH HEADSHIELD SLUG

Chelidonura hirundinina

SUBCLASS:
Opisthobranchia
ORDER:
Headshield Slugs
Cephalaspidea
FAMILY:
Aglajidae

SIZE: ½ - ¾ in.,
1 in. max.
DEPTH: 3 - 60 ft.

BLUE-RING SEA HARE

Stylocheilus longicauda

SUBCLASS:
Opisthobranchia
ORDER:
Sea Hares
Anaspidea
FAMILY:
Notarchidae

SIZE: ¾ - 1¼ in.,
3 in. max.
DEPTH: 0 - 100 ft.

VISUAL ID: Mantel skin flaps and tips of rolled rhinophores and rolled tentacles edged with black to dark blue are distinctive of this species. Brown to green occasionally mottled, with white speckles.
ABUNDANCE & DISTRIBUTION: Uncommon Florida, Caribbean, Bahamas; world-wide in tropical to warm temperate waters.
HABITAT & BEHAVIOR: Inhabit sand and rocky rubble areas with abundant algal growth.

VISUAL ID: Irregular skin flaps on back, interior edge lined with black or blue. Pale brown overall, with numerous white blotches and spots. Tips of rhinophores and oral tentacles darkened.
ABUNDANCE & DISTRIBUTION: Uncommon Caribbean. Circumtropical.
HABITAT & BEHAVIOR: Inhabit areas of rocky rubble and open sand. Feed on algae.

VISUAL ID: Light brown to green with irregular light spots outlined in black.
ABUNDANCE & DISTRIBUTION: Occasional to common Florida, Bahamas, Caribbean. Circumtropical and subtropical.
HABITAT & BEHAVIOR: Prefer grassy flats with scattered rocks. Feed on algae. When disturbed will discharge a harmless, thick, purple fluid.

FRECKLED SEA HARE
Aplysia parvula
SUBCLASS:
Opisthobranchia
ORDER:
Sea Hares
Anaspidea
FAMILY:
Aplysiidae

SIZE: 1 - 1¹/₂ in.
2¹/₂ in. max.
DEPTH: 10 - 40 ft.

WHITE-SPOTTED SEA HARE
Aplysia parvula
SUBCLASS:
Opisthobranchia
ORDER:
Sea Hares
Anaspidea
FAMILY:
Aplysiidae

SIZE: ³/₄ - 1 in.,
1¹/₂ in. max.
DEPTH: 0 - 20 ft.

SPOTTED SEA HARE
Aplysia dactylomela
SUBCLASS:
Opisthobranchia
ORDER:
Sea Hares
Anaspidea
FAMILY:
Aplysiidae

SIZE: 3 - 6 in.,
12 in. max.
DEPTH: 0 - 120 ft.

Sea Hares

VISUAL ID: Numerous hair-like skin papillae extend from body which is blackish to brown, tan, white or pale lavender, often with white to gold spots.

ABUNDANCE & DISTRIBUTION: Uncommon Caribbean. Can be common in localized areas. Circumtropical

HABITAT & BEHAVIOR: Inhabit sea grass beds. Feed on algae. During breeding season individuals form long lines while copulating.

Ragged Sea Hare
Copulating mound.
Note color variations.

VISUAL ID: Pale green compact muscular body covered with rough, pebble-like papillae; short rolled rhinophores and oral tentacles.

ABUNDANCE & DISTRIBUTION: Uncommon Florida, Bahamas, Caribbean.

HABITAT & BEHAVIOR: Inhabit sand and rocky rubble areas with abundant algal growth.

RAGGED SEA HARE
Bursatella leachii

SUBCLASS:
Opisthobranchia
ORDER:
Sea Hares
Anaspidea
FAMILY:
Aplysiidae

SIZE: 5 - 7 in.,
10 in. max.
DEPTH: 1 - 50 ft.

Ragged Sea Hare Young
Skin papillae less hair-like than those of adults.

WARTY SEACAT
Dolabrifera dolabrifera

SUBCLASS:
Opisthobranchia
ORDER:
Sea Hares
Anaspidea
FAMILY:
Aplysiidae

SIZE: 1 - 2½ in.
DEPTH: 15 - 30 ft.

VISUAL ID: Dark maroon to nearly black, occasionally with some spotting, speckles and streaks. Large, muscular mantle with skin flaps on back.

ABUNDANCE & DISTRIBUTION: Uncommon Florida, Bahamas, Caribbean.

HABITAT & BEHAVIOR: Inhabit bottoms with abundant algal growth. Occasionally spread mantle skin flaps like wings and swim vigorously. If disturbed may emit clouds of harmless dark purple ink as they swim away. Lay string-like tangles of bright reddish pink eggs.

VISUAL ID: Numerous warts on back. Varies from dark reddish-brown to light golden-brown, occasionally pale yellow to white.

ABUNDANCE & DISTRIBUTION: Uncommon Caribbean, rare Bahamas and South Florida; Also inhabit the eastern tropical Pacific.

HABITAT & BEHAVIOR: Inhabit rocky shallows and areas of reef rubble. Hide in recesses.

VISUAL ID: Orange, smooth, somewhat translucent body.

ABUNDANCE & DISTRIBUTION: Occasional Caribbean. Circumtropical.

HABITAT & BEHAVIOR: Hide under reef rubble, especially flat slabs of coral. When disturbed may secrete sulphuric acid in defense.

NOTE: Pictured individual is laying eggs.

ATLANTIC BLACK SEAHARE
Aplysia morio
SUBCLASS:
Opisthobranchia
ORDER:
Sea Hares
Anaspidea
FAMILY:
Aplysiidae

SIZE: 4 - 10 in.,
max. 14 in.
DEPTH: 10 - 80 ft.

WARTY SIDEGILL SLUG
Pleurobranchus areolatus
SUBCLASS:
Opisthobranchia
ORDER:
Sidegill Slugs
Notaspidea
FAMILY:
Pleurobranchidae

SIZE: 2 - 4 in.,
6¹/₂ in. max.
DEPTH: 0 - 80 ft.

APRICOT SIDEGILL SLUG
Berthellina engeli
SUBCLASS:
Opisthobranchia
ORDER:
Sidegill Slugs
Notaspidea
FAMILY:
Pleurobranchidae

SIZE: 1 - 2¹/₂ in.,
3¹/₄ in. max.
DEPTH: 0 - 100 ft.

VISUAL ID: Shades of green, with numerous black and white speckles. Outer edges of skin flaps on back are yellow to orange with black border.
ABUNDANCE & DISTRIBUTION: Occasional Florida, Bahamas, Caribbean.
HABITAT & BEHAVIOR: Inhabit reefs and other areas where they camouflage by blending with various algae, upon which they feed.

VISUAL ID: Brown line along outer edge of skin ruffles. Color varies from green to orange to yellow.
ABUNDANCE & DISTRIBUTION: Occasional Florida, Bahamas, Caribbean.
HABITAT & BEHAVIOR: Inhabit reefs and other areas where they camouflage by blending with *Caulerpa* species of algae, upon which they feed.

VISUAL ID: Shades of light green to brown with darker, fine, net-like pattern. Rhinophores and skin flap borders are whitish. Scattered small, pointed skin papillae. Have smooth, thin external shell that is often covered with folds of skin.
ABUNDANCE & DISTRIBUTION: Occasional Florida, Bahamas, Caribbean.
HABITAT & BEHAVIOR: Inhabit bays and other calm water areas, often under docks. Found blending in with Sea Grape Alga, *Caulerpa racemosa,* upon which they feed. Secrete milky white liquid when disturbed.

ORNATE ELYSIA
Elysia ornata
SUBCLASS:
Opisthobranchia
ORDER:
Sea Slugs
Sacoglossa
FAMILY:
Elysiidae

SIZE: 1 - 1¹/₂ in.,
2 in. max.
DEPTH: 0 - 100 ft.

BROWN-LINED ELYSIA
Elysia subornata
SUBCLASS:
Opisthobranchia
ORDER:
Sea Slugs
Sacoglossa
FAMILY:
Elysiidae

SIZE: ³/₄ - 1¹/₄ in.,
1¹/₂ in. max.
DEPTH: 1 - 100 ft.

RETICULATED SEA SLUG
Oxynoe antillarum
SUBCLASS:
Opisthobranchia
ORDER:
Sea Slugs
Sacoglossa
FAMILY:
Oxynoidae

SIZE: ¹/₂ - ³/₄ in.,
1¹/₂ in. max.
DEPTH: 0 - 35 ft.

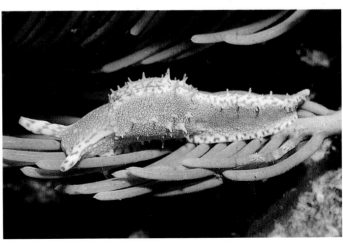

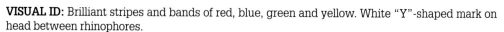

VISUAL ID: Brilliant stripes and bands of red, blue, green and yellow. White "Y"-shaped mark on head between rhinophores.
ABUNDANCE & DISTRIBUTION: Rare Florida, Bahamas, Jamaica and Cayman Islands.
HABITAT & BEHAVIOR: Inhabit areas of reef rubble and sand near shallow patch reefs.

VISUAL ID: Green body with numerous thin white stripes; black line on white outer edge of skin ruffles.
ABUNDANCE & DISTRIBUTION: Photographed in Guanaja, Honduras where the species is rare. Also reported from Belize; full range has yet to be established.
HABITAT & BEHAVIOR: Inhabit turtle grass beds, probably feed on the grass blades.

VISUAL ID: Thin black lines and a few iridescent blue spots on shell. Body and shell are shades of green to brown.
ABUNDANCE & DISTRIBUTION: Occasional Caribbean. Circumtropical.
HABITAT & BEHAVIOR: Inhabit bays and other calm water areas, often under docks. Found blending in with Sea Grape Alga, *Caulerpa racemosa,* upon which they feed. Secrete milky white liquid when disturbed.

PAINTED ELYSIA
Elysia picta
SUBCLASS:
Opisthobranchia
ORDER:
Sea Slugs
Sacoglossa
FAMILY:
Elysiidae

SIZE: ½ - 1 in.,
1¼ in. max.
DEPTH: 0 - 20 ft.

STRIPED ELYSIA
Elysia pratensis
SUBCLASS:
Opisthobranchia
ORDER:
Sea Slugs
Sacoglossa
FAMILY:
Elysiidae

SIZE: ¼ - ¾ in.
DEPTH: 0 - 25 ft.

LINED-SHELL
SEA SLUG
Lobiger souverbiei
SUBCLASS:
Opisthobranchia
ORDER:
Sea Slugs
Sacoglossa
FAMILY:
Oxynoidae

SIZE: ¾ - 1 in.,
1½ in. max.
DEPTH: 0 - 35 ft.

VISUAL ID: Numerous large, leaf-like cerata on back. Translucent with burgundy and white spots and markings.Cerata often bordered with white.

ABUNDANCE & DISTRIBUTION: Rare Florida, Bahamas, Caribbean.

HABITAT & BEHAVIOR: Found in a variety of habitats where algae is present. Can drop cerata when disturbed.

VISUAL ID: Numerous skin ruffles on back resemble leaf lettuce. Color extremely variable, generally shades of green [opposite], occasionally pale to white with red, blue and green tints [below right], uncommonly blue [below middle]. Large pale spots along side.

ABUNDANCE & DISTRIBUTION: Common Florida, Bahamas, Caribbean.

HABITAT & BEHAVIOR: Inhabit reefs and other areas where they camouflage by blending with various algae they eat.

NOTE: Fomerly classified as genus *Tridachia*.

HARLEQUIN GLASS-SLUG
Cyerce cristallina
SUBCLASS:
Opisthobranchia
ORDER:
Sea Slugs
Sacoglossa
FAMILY:
Caliphyllidae

SIZE: 1 - 1¹/₂ in.,
3 in. max.
DEPTH: 3 - 45 ft.

LETTUCE SEA SLUG
Elysia crispata
SUBCLASS:
Opisthobranchia
ORDER:
Sea Slugs
Sacoglossa
FAMILY:
Elysiidae

SIZE: 1 - 2 in.,
4 in. max.
DEPTH: 0 - 40 ft.

Lettuce Sea Slug
Color variations.

Young
[far left]

VISUAL ID: Black and white stripes run length of back; pale blue foot; markings resembling a smiling face on head.

ABUNDANCE & DISTRIBUTION: Photographed in Dominica where the species is rare; range has yet to be established.

HABITAT & BEHAVIOR: Inhabit sandy areas with gorgonians and sea pens upon which they feed. Generally nocturnal, often bury beneath the sand during day.

NOTE: The living appearance of this nudibranch has not been matched with a scientific description. Collection of a photographed specimen and microscopic examination of anatomical details may be necessary to establish visual identification. Possibly an undescribed species. Regrettably, at the time of this writing, no taxonomic biologists are working with this order in the tropical western Atlantic.

VISUAL ID: Tentacles transparent to translucent white. Head is opaque white to base of white-tipped rhinophores. Numerous translucent, fringe-like cerata on back; color varies with color of food consumed.

ABUNDANCE & DISTRIBUTION: Rare Florida, Bahamas, Caribbean.

HABITAT & BEHAVIOR: Feed on opisthobranch eggs. Found in varied habitats where eggs are seasonally present. Most striking in coloration after consuming the scarlet eggs of the Caribbean Spanish Dancer.

VISUAL ID: Numerous translucent, fringe-like cerata on back with brown and white markings. Tentacles and rhinophores white-tipped.

ABUNDANCE & DISTRIBUTION: Occasional Florida, Bahamas, Caribbean. Can be abundant in localized areas.

HABITAT & BEHAVIOR: Inhabit rocky intertidal areas.

SMILING ARMINA
Armina sp.
SUBCLASS:
Opisthobranchia
ORDER:
Nudibranchs
Nudibranchia
SUBORDER:
Arminacea
FAMILY:
Arminidae

SIZE: $^3/_4$ - $1^1/_4$ in.
DEPTH: 5 - 40 ft.

LONG-EARED NUDIBRANCH
Favorinus auritulus
SUBCLASS:
Opisthobranchia
ORDER:
Nudibranchs
Nudibranchia
SUBORDER:
Aeolidacea

SIZE: $^1/_4$ - $^1/_2$ in.,
$^3/_4$ in. max.
DEPTH: 0 - 45 ft.

LYNX NUDIBRANCH
Phidiana lynceus
SUBCLASS:
Opisthobranchia
ORDER:
Nudibranchs
Nudibranchia
SUBORDER:
Aeolidacea

SIZE: $^1/_2$ - $^3/_4$ in.,
$1^1/_4$ in. max.
DEPTH: 0 - 8 ft.

Nudibranchs

VISUAL ID: Foremost tentacles are very long, about half the length of the body. Along either side of back are tufts of cerata. Shades of translucent brown with white markings and fine speckles.

ABUNDANCE & DISTRIBUTION: Occasional Bahamas, Caribbean.

HABITAT & BEHAVIOR: Inhabit living reefs. Feed on hydroids.

NOTE: The living appearance of this nudibranch has not been matched with a scientific description. Collection of a photographed specimen and microscopic examination of anatomical details may be necessary to establish visual identification. Possibly an undescribed species. Regrettably, at the time of this writing, no taxonomic biologists are working with this order in the tropical western Atlantic.

VISUAL ID: The back is white with numerous fringe-like cerata; border of mantel bright blue with a black inner margin.

ABUNDANCE & DISTRIBUTION: Photographed in Dominica where the species is uncommon; range has yet to be established.

HABITAT & BEHAVIOR: Inhabit sandy areas with gorgonians and rocky outcroppings.

NOTE: The living appearance of this nudibranch has not been matched with a scientific description. Collection of a photographed specimen and microscopic examination of anatomical details may be necessary to establish visual identification. Possibly an undescribed species. Regrettably, at the time of this writing, no taxonomic biologists are working with this order in the tropical western Atlantic.

VISUAL ID: Reddish body; numerous fringe-like cerata marked with white tips and purple rings on back.

ABUNDANCE & DISTRIBUTION: Rare continental coastal waters Belize to Brazil, also Tobago.

HABITAT & BEHAVIOR: Inhabit sandy areas mixed with sea grasses near mangroves.

LONG-HORN NUDIBRANCH
Austraeolis catina
SUBCLASS:
Opisthobranchia
ORDER:
Nudibranchs
Nudibranchia
SUBORDER:
Aeolidacea

SIZE: ³/₄ - 1¹/₄ in.,
1³/₄ in. max.
DEPTH: 30 - 100 ft.

BLUE-STREAK NUDIBRANCH
Unidentified
SUBCLASS:
Opisthobranchia
ORDER:
Nudibranchs
Nudibranchia
SUBORDER:
Aeolidacea

SIZE: ³/₄ - 1¹/₄ in.
DEPTH: 5 - 40 ft.

PURPLE-RING NUDIBRANCH
Flabellina marcusorum
SUBCLASS:
Opisthobranchia
ORDER:
Nudibranchs
Nudibranchia
SUBORDER:
Aeolidacea

SIZE: ³/₄ - 1¹/₄ in.
DEPTH: 3 - 40 ft.

VISUAL ID: Numerous fringe-like cerata on back vary from black to gray to white. Body translucent cream to white. Head often flushed with red or orange.

ABUNDANCE & DISTRIBUTION: Occasional Florida, Bahamas, Caribbean. Can be locally abundant.

HABITAT & BEHAVIOR: Inhabit live and dead reef areas around Christmas Tree Hydroids, *Halocordyle disticha,* [pg. 71] upon which they feed. Undischarged stinging nematocysts of prey are engulfed but not digested; instead, they are transported to the cerata for use in their own defense.

VISUAL ID: Numerous fringe-like cerata on back. Color patterns as well as the forms of their bodies vary greatly.

ABUNDANCE & DISTRIBUTION: Uncommon Florida, Bahamas, Caribbean. Also in Brazil.

HABITAT & BEHAVIOR: Varied habitats including mangrove estuaries, areas of reef rubble and living reefs. Feed on wide range of cnidarians including tentacles of Upside-Down Jellyfish, *Cassiopea frondosa,* [pg. 89] and hydroids. Undischarged stinging nematocysts of prey are engulfed but not digested; instead, they are transported to the cerata for use in their own defense.

NOTE: Positive visual identification is nearly impossible; internal examination is usually required.

VISUAL ID: Numerous fringe-like cerata with white speckles. Most commonly orange, also bluish and gray.

ABUNDANCE & DISTRIBUTION: Occasional Caribbean.

HABITAT & BEHAVIOR: Inhabit living reefs. Feed on sea rods of the genus *Plexaurella*.

CHRISTMAS TREE HYDROID NUDIBRANCH
Learchis poica
SUBCLASS:
Opisthobranchia
ORDER:
Nudibranchs
Nudibranchia
SUBORDER:
Aeolidacea

SIZE: ³/₄ - 1 in.,
1¹/₄ in. max.
DEPTH: 1 - 60 ft.

FRINGE-BACK NUDIBRANCH
Dondice occidentalis
SUBCLASS:
Opisthobranchia
ORDER:
Nudibranchs
Nudibranchia
SUBORDER:
Aeolidacea

SIZE: 1 - 1¹/₄ in.,
1³/₄ in. max.
DEPTH: 0 - 100 ft.

WHITE-SPECKLED NUDIBRANCH
Paleo jubatus
SUBCLASS:
Opisthobranchia
ORDER:
Nudibranchs
Nudibranchia
SUBORDER:
Aeolidacea

SIZE: 1¹/₂ - 2 in.,
2¹/₂ in. max.
DEPTH: 10 - 100 ft.

Nudibranchs

VISUAL ID: Orangish, somewhat translucent body; numerous fringe-like cerata on back; rhinophores and oral tentacles tipped with lighter shade of orange.

ABUNDANCE & DISTRIBUTION: Photographed off Isla Cubagua, Venezuela where the species is uncommon; range has yet to be established.

HABITAT & BEHAVIOR: Inhabit areas of rubble, course sand and gravel near gorgonian stands.

NOTE: The living appearance of this nudibranch has not been matched with a scientific description. Collection of a photographed specimen and microscopic examination of anatomical details is probably necessary to establish visual identification. Possibly an undescribed species. Regrettably, at the time of this writing, no taxonomic biologists are working with this order in the tropical western Atlantic.

VISUAL ID: Blue to blue-green body; numerous gold fringe-like cerata on back.

ABUNDANCE & DISTRIBUTION: Photographed in St. Vincent where the species is rare; range has yet to be established.

HABITAT & BEHAVIOR: Inhabit areas of sand and sea grasses.

VISUAL ID: Dark brown to black body with green spots; anal gill structure bright orange with black filaments.

ABUNDANCE & DISTRIBUTION: Photographed in Los Testigos, Venezuela where the species is rare; range has yet to be established.

HABITAT & BEHAVIOR: Inhabit rocky reef areas with encrusting sponges, possibly its food.

NOTE: The living appearance of this nudibranch has not been matched with a scientific description. Collection of a photographed specimen and microscopic examination of anatomical details may be necessary to establish visual identification. Possibly an undescribed species in either genus *Roboastra* or *Tambja*. Regrettably, at the time of this writing, no taxonomic biologists are working with this order in the tropical western Atlantic.

ORANGE NUDIBRANCH
Unidentified
SUBCLASS:
Opisthobranchia
ORDER:
Nudibranchs
Nudibranchia
SUBORDER:
Aeolidacea

SIZE: ³/₄ - 1¹/₄ in.
DEPTH: 3 - 40 ft.

GOLD-FRINGED NUDIBRANCH
Cerberilla cf. tanna
SUBCLASS:
Opisthobranchia
ORDER:
Nudibranchs
Nudibranchia
SUBORDER:
Aeolidacea
FAMILY:
Aeolidiidae

SIZE: ³/₄ - 1¹/₄ in.
DEPTH: 3 - 40 ft.

ORANGE-GILL DORIS
Unidentified
SUBCLASS:
Opisthobranchia
ORDER:
Nudibranchs
Nudibranchia
SUBORDER:
Doridacea
FAMILY:
Polyceridae

SIZE: ³/₄ - 1¹/₄ in.
DEPTH: 15 - 60 ft.

Nudibranchs

VISUAL ID: Navy blue to deep purple with brilliant yellow-gold stripes and markings. Large crown of feather-like anal gills.

ABUNDANCE & DISTRIBUTION: Occasional to common Florida.

HABITAT & BEHAVIOR: Inhabit reefs, feed upon sponges.

VISUAL ID: Yellow-gold anal gills, purple rhinophores. Yellow-gold body with numerous purple spots. Mantle border of white skin ruffles.

ABUNDANCE & DISTRIBUTION: Uncommon Caribbean rare South Florida.

HABITAT & BEHAVIOR: Inhabit shallow rocky areas and reefs, feed on sponges.

VISUAL ID: Purple spots scattered over brown back and sides, white mantle border.

ABUNDANCE & DISTRIBUTION: Uncommon, Northwest Caribbean, Venezuala; also south to Brazil.

HABITAT & BEHAVIOR: Inhabit reef in areas where algae overgrows dead corals, especially branches of Staghorn Coral, *Acropora cervicornis*.

FLORIDA REGAL SEA GODDESS
Hypselodoris edenticulata
SUBCLASS:
Opisthobranchia
ORDER:
Nudibranchs
Nudibranchia
SUBORDER:
Doridacea
FAMILY:
Chromodoridae

SIZE: 1½ - 4 in.,
DEPTH: 20 - 130 ft.

GOLD-CROWNED SEA GODDESS
Hypselodoris acriba
SUBCLASS:
Opisthobranchia
ORDER:
Nudibranchs
Nudibranchia
SUBORDER:
Doridacea
FAMILY:
Chromodoridae

SIZE: 1¼ - 1¾ in.,
2½ in. max.
DEPTH: 10 - 35 ft.

PURPLE-SPOTTED SEA GODDESS
Hypselodoris marci
SUBCLASS:
Opisthobranchia
ORDER:
Nudibranchs
Nudibranchia
SUBORDER:
Doridacea
FAMILY:
Chromodoridae

SIZE: 1 - 1½ in.,
2 in. max.
DEPTH: 12 - 45 ft.

VISUAL ID: Thin gold lines down black back, whitish mantle border with gold line trim. Occasional blue spots on back.

ABUNDANCE & DISTRIBUTION: Occasional Caribbean.

HABITAT & BEHAVIOR: Inhabit living reefs, prefer areas of moderate current. Feed on Blue Sponge, *Dysidea janiae.*

VISUAL ID: Black spots on white mantle border. Yellow-gold stripes on back and sides.

ABUNDANCE & DISTRIBUTION: Uncommon, known only from South Florida, Belize and Roatan, Honduras. Most numerous in Miami's Biscayne Bay.

HABITAT & BEHAVIOR: Live in association with sponges of the genus *Dysidea* .

VISUAL ID: Three yellow lines running down length of back are distinctive of this species. Other markings and colors are highly variable. Often mottled in shades of pale brown, gray and white; yellow streaks on back and sides; series of black spots around outer edge of back.

ABUNDANCE & DISTRIBUTION: Uncommon Florida, Caribbean; also south to Brazil, Mediterranean and West Africa.

HABITAT & BEHAVIOR: Inhabit sandy areas mixed with rubble and rocky outcroppings.

GOLD-LINE SEA GODDESS

Hypselodoris ruthae

SUBCLASS:
Opisthobranchia
ORDER:
Nudibranchs
Nudibranchia
SUBORDER:
Doridacea
FAMILY:
Chromodoridae

SIZE: ³/₄ - 1 in.,
1¹/₂ in. max.
DEPTH: 1 - 65 ft.

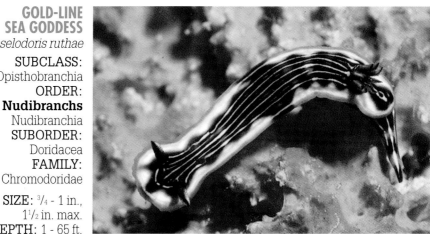

BLACK-SPOTTED SEA GODDESS

Hypselodoris bayeri

SUBCLASS:
Opisthobranchia
ORDER:
Nudibranchs
Nudibranchia
SUBORDER:
Doridacea
FAMILY:
Chromodoridae

SIZE: 1 - 1¹/₂ in.,
2 in. max.
DEPTH: 1 - 50 ft.

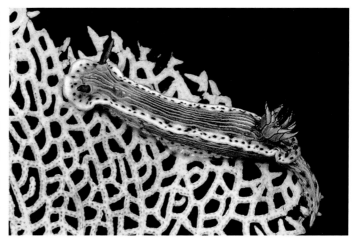

YELLOW-STREAKED SEA GODDESS

Hypselodoris picta

SUBCLASS:
Opisthobranchia
ORDER:
Nudibranchs
Nudibranchia
SUBORDER:
Doridacea
FAMILY:
Chromodoridae

SIZE: ³/₄ - 1¹/₄ in.
DEPTH: 3 - 40 ft.

VISUAL ID: Purple anal gills and rhinophores. White with black markings on back, yellow mantle border.
ABUNDANCE & DISTRIBUTION: Uncommon South Florida, Bahamas, Caribbean.
HABITAT & BEHAVIOR: Inhabit living reefs. Feed on sponges.

VISUAL ID: Blue with red mantle border.
ABUNDANCE & DISTRIBUTION: Uncommon Florida, Bahamas.
HABITAT & BEHAVIOR: Prefer areas of moderate current. Found on sponges of the genus Dysidea, sometimes in large numbers.

VISUAL ID: Reddish-brown, white mantle border with gold stripe around edge.
ABUNDANCE & DISTRIBUTION: Rare Caribbean.
HABITAT & BEHAVIOR: Hide under coral slabs in calm, protected areas.

PURPLE-CROWNED SEA GODDESS
Chromodoris kempfi
SUBCLASS:
Opisthobranchia
ORDER:
Nudibranchs
Nudibranchia
SUBORDER:
Doridacea
FAMILY:
Chromodoridae

SIZE: $^1/_2$ - $^3/_4$ in.,
1 in. max.
DEPTH: 25 - 75 ft.

RED-LINE BLUE SEA GODDESS
Chromodoris nyalya
SUBCLASS:
Opisthobranchia
ORDER:
Nudibranchs
Nudibranchia
SUBORDER:
Doridacea
FAMILY:
Chromodoridae

SIZE: $^1/_2$ - $^3/_4$ in.,
$1^1/_2$ in. max.
DEPTH: 6 - 30 ft.

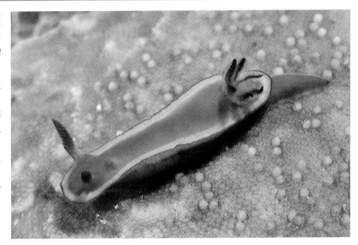

BROWN SEA GODDESS
Chromodoris grahami
SUBCLASS:
Opisthobranchia
ORDER:
Nudibranchs
Nudibranchia
SUBORDER:
Doridacea
FAMILY:
Chromodoridae

SIZE: $^3/_4$ - 1 in.,
$1^1/_2$ in. max.
DEPTH: 1 - 10 ft.

VISUAL ID: Back reddish-brown with two white blotches between rhinophores and anal gills, white mantle border. Numerous, scattered bluish spots of different sizes. Overall pattern of colored areas and spots extremely variable.

ABUNDANCE & DISTRIBUTION: Occasional Florida, Bahamas, Caribbean.

HABITAT & BEHAVIOR: Hide under coral slabs and rubble in calm, protected rocky and sandy areas.

VISUAL ID: Rhinophores and anal gills tipped with red. White body, red mantle border with yellow edge.

ABUNDANCE & DISTRIBUTION: Uncommon, known only from South Florida and northeastern Bahamas. Most numerous in Miami's Biscayne Bay. Also in eastern tropical and subtropical Pacific.

HABITAT & BEHAVIOR: Inhabit reefs and rocky areas. Feed on sponges.

NOTE: This nudibranch probably became established in South Florida by passing through the Panama Canal on a ship bottom or in a ballast tank.

VISUAL ID: Cream to tan, covered with reddish-brown spots and blotches.

ABUNDANCE & DISTRIBUTION: Occasional Florida, Bahamas, Caribbean.

HABITAT & BEHAVIOR: Hide under coral slabs in live reef areas. If disturbed can swim with an undulating head-to-tail motion.

HARLEQUIN BLUE SEA GODDESS

Chromodoris clenchi

SUBCLASS:
Opisthobranchia
ORDER:
Nudibranchs
Nudibranchia
SUBORDER:
Doridacea
FAMILY:
Chromodoridae

SIZE: ³/₄ - 1 in.,
1¹/₂ in. max.
DEPTH: 1 - 14 ft.

RED-TIPPED SEA GODDESS

Glossodoris sedna

SUBCLASS:
Opisthobranchia
ORDER:
Nudibranchs
Nudibranchia
SUBORDER:
Doridacea
FAMILY:
Chromodoridae

SIZE: 1 - 1³/₄ in.,
3 in. max.
DEPTH: 10 - 50 ft.

BROWN-SPECKLED DORIS

Aphelodoris antillensis

SUBCLASS:
Opisthobranchia
ORDER:
Nudibranchs
Nudibranchia
SUBORDER:
Doridacea
FAMILY:
Asteronitidae

SIZE: ¹/₂ - 1 in.,
1¹/₄ in. max.
DEPTH: 6 - 12 ft.

VISUAL ID: Distinctive dome shape. Patterns and color variable, ranging from white [below] to orange [below right] to black [opposite]. Vein-like markings usually in mantle border. Soft and slimy to the touch.

ABUNDANCE & DISTRIBUTION: Occasional Florida, Bahamas, Caribbean.

HABITAT & BEHAVIOR: Hide under coral slabs in shallow water habitats. Feed on sponges.

Slimy Doris
White variation.

VISUAL ID: Color variable, cream or beige with dark brown spots to almost solid dark brown.

ABUNDANCE & DISTRIBUTION: Occasional Florida, Bahamas, Caribbean.

HABITAT & BEHAVIOR: Hide under coral slabs in many habitats, usually shallow, but occasionally to 100 feet. Small individuals can swim with undulating head-to-tail motion. Large individuals shed pieces of mantle when disturbed.

SLIMY DORIS
Dendrodoris krebsii

SUBCLASS:
Opisthobranchia
ORDER:
Nudibranchs
Nudibranchia
SUBORDER:
Doridacea
FAMILY:
Dendrodorididae

SIZE: 1$^1/_2$ - 2$^1/_2$ in.,
6 in. max.
DEPTH: 3 - 15 ft.

Slimy Doris
Orange variation.

BROWN DORIS
Discodoris evelinae

SUBCLASS:
Opisthobranchia
ORDER:
Nudibranchs
Nudibranchia
SUBORDER:
Doridacea
FAMILY:
Discodorididae

SIZE: 1$^1/_4$ - 1$^3/_4$ in.,
4 in. max.
DEPTH: 12 - 30 ft.

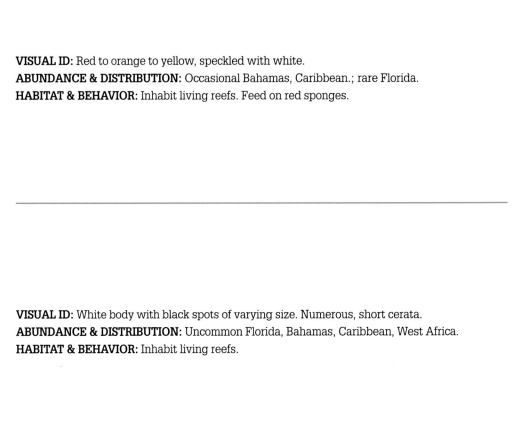

VISUAL ID: Red to orange to yellow, speckled with white.
ABUNDANCE & DISTRIBUTION: Occasional Bahamas, Caribbean.; rare Florida.
HABITAT & BEHAVIOR: Inhabit living reefs. Feed on red sponges.

VISUAL ID: White body with black spots of varying size. Numerous, short cerata.
ABUNDANCE & DISTRIBUTION: Uncommon Florida, Bahamas, Caribbean, West Africa.
HABITAT & BEHAVIOR: Inhabit living reefs.

VISUAL ID: Mottled, varies from almost totally white to orange, red and dark purple. When disturbed, rolls out mantle border skin-folds to reveal bright red band.
ABUNDANCE & DISTRIBUTION: Uncommon Caribbean.
HABITAT & BEHAVIOR: Inhabit living reefs. When disturbed, can swim with undulating movement of mantle border skin-folds.
NOTE: Closely related to the Spanish Dancer, *H.sanguineus,* found in the Indo-Pacific.

LEATHER-BACKED DORIS
Platydoris angustipes
SUBCLASS:
Opisthobranchia
ORDER:
Nudibranchs
Nudibranchia
SUBORDER:
Doridacea
FAMILY:
Platydorididae

SIZE: 1 - 2 in.,
4¹/₂ in. max.
DEPTH: 0 - 35 ft.

BLACK-SPOTTED
NUDIBRANCH
Phyllidiopsis papilligera
SUBCLASS:
Opisthobranchia
ORDER:
Nudibranchs
Nudibranchia
SUBORDER:
Doridacea
FAMILY:
Phyllidiidae
SIZE: 1 - 2 in.,
4¹/₂ in. max.
DEPTH: 50 - 100 ft.

CARIBBEAN
SPANISH DANCER
Hexabranchus morsomus
SUBCLASS:
Opisthobranchia
ORDER:
Nudibranchs
Nudibranchia
SUBORDER:
Doridacea
FAMILY:
Hexabranchidae

SIZE: 2 - 3 in.,
4³/₄ in. max.
DEPTH: 20 - 100 ft.

VISUAL ID: Two or more paired, large, flattened cerata on each side. Rhinophores large and paddle-like. Translucent, light olive-brown to orangish-brown.
ABUNDANCE & DISTRIBUTION: Seasonally common Florida, Bahamas.
HABITAT & BEHAVIOR: Inhabit floats of on sargassum weed. Feed on hydroids that grow on sargassum branches.

VISUAL ID: Rows of light brown cerata (branchial gills) down each side, covered with clusters of whitish hemispherical bumps. Dark brown body.
ABUNDANCE & DISTRIBUTION: Occasional Florida, Bahamas, Caribbean. Also in Brazil.
HABITAT & BEHAVIOR: Live in association with Feather Bush Hydroid, *Dentitheca dendritica*, [pg. 75] upon which they feed. Color and size make them difficult to spot, presence is often given away by more obvious creamy yellow spiral egg case deposited on hydroid branches.

VISUAL ID: Tips of cerata (branchial gills) highly branched. Varies from red to orange to yellow with darker net pattern, occasionally spotted with white.
ABUNDANCE & DISTRIBUTION: Occasional Caribbean.
HABITAT & BEHAVIOR: Inhabit areas of moderate current with reef rubble bottoms that are populated by hydroids, upon which they feed.

SARGASSUM NUDIBRANCH
Scyllaea pelagica
SUBCLASS:
Opisthobranchia
ORDER:
Nudibranchs
Nudibranchia
SUBORDER:
Dendronotacea
FAMILY:
Scyllaeidae

SIZE: ¹/₂ - ³/₄ in.,
2 in. max.
DEPTH: 0 - 2 ft.

GRAPE-CLUSTER NUDIBRANCH
Doto uva
SUBCLASS:
Opisthobranchia
ORDER:
Nudibranchs
Nudibranchia
SUBORDER:
Dendronotacea
FAMILY:
Dotoidae

SIZE: ¹/₄ - ¹/₂ in. max.
DEPTH: 15 - 60 ft.

TASSELED NUDIBRANCH
Bornella calcarata
SUBCLASS:
Opisthobranchia
ORDER:
Nudibranchs
Nudibranchia
SUBORDER:
Dendronotacea
FAMILY:
Bornellidae

SIZE: ³/₄ - 1¹/₂ in.,
4³/₄ in. max.
DEPTH: 30 - 120 ft.

VISUAL ID: Cerata (branchial gills) highly branched. Varies from grayish white to orange (note colors of three individuals in picture).

ABUNDANCE & DISTRIBUTION: Uncommon Florida, Bahamas, Caribbean. Can be locally common.

HABITAT & BEHAVIOR: Inhabit living reefs. Feed on sea rod gorgonians of the genus *Plexaurella*, commonly found under colonies that have fallen over.

VISUAL ID: Translucent with white network pattern on smooth back; branched cerata (branchial gills) along sides.

ABUNDANCE & DISTRIBUTION: Uncommon Florida, Bahamas, Caribbean; also north to Georgia.

HABITAT & BEHAVIOR: Inhabit shallow reefs and sandy areas with stands of gorgonians, sea whips and hydroids.

VISUAL ID: Irregular rows of short, scaly spines project from around outer border of valves. Valves flattish and sculptured with concentric growth plates radiating from the hinge. Small wings at end of hinge. Shades of brown, often mottled.

ABUNDANCE & DISTRIBUTION: Common South Florida, Bahamas, Caribbean.

HABITAT & BEHAVIOR: Attach to rocks, wrecks and, occasionally, sea fans. Well camouflaged, often overgrown by a variety of organisms.

REACTION TO DIVERS: Snap shut when approached. This movement often attracts attention to oyster.

NOTE: Member of famous pearl-oyster family. Occasionally produce small pearls, rarely of value from Florida waters, occasionally of value from southern Caribbean. Interiors are covered with lustrous mother-of-pearl.

TUFTED NUDIBRANCH
Tritoniopsis frydis
SUBCLASS:
Opisthobranchia
ORDER:
Nudibranchs
Nudibranchia
SUBORDER:
Dendronotacea
FAMILY:
Tritoniidae

SIZE: $1/2$ - $11/4$ in.,
$13/4$ in. max.
DEPTH: 30 - 120 ft.

CRISSCROSS TRITONIA
Tritonia bayeri
SUBCLASS:
Opisthobranchia
ORDER:
Nudibranchs
Nudibranchia
SUBORDER:
Dendronotacea
FAMILY:
Tritoniidae

SIZE: $1/4$ - $3/4$ in.
DEPTH: 5 - 50 ft.

ATLANTIC PEARL-OYSTER
Pinctada radiata
CLASS:
Bivalves
Bivalvia
FAMILY:
Pearl Oysters
Pteriidae

SIZE: 2 - 3 in.
DEPTH: 6 - 65 ft.

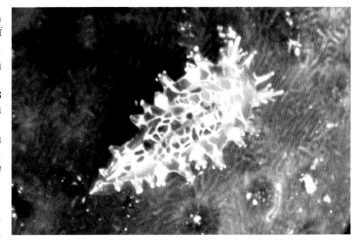

VISUAL ID: Brilliant red to orange-red mantle. Tentacles often reddish orange, especially in shallow water and white in deeper water. Whitish to brownish valves sculptured with many fine, radiating ribs.

ABUNDANCE & DISTRIBUTION: Common Florida, Bahamas, Caribbean.

HABITAT & BEHAVIOR: Inhabit narrow cracks, crevices and recesses. Valves usually hidden with only mantle and tentacles exposed. Often attach to substrate by byssal threads. Can swim with jerky movements by repeatedly snapping valves open and shut.

REACTION TO DIVERS: Snap valves shut and retreat into recesses if threatened.

VISUAL ID: White to lavender mantle and tentacles. White to tan valves deeply sculptured with many radiating, sharply spined ribs.

ABUNDANCE & DISTRIBUTION: Common Florida, Bahamas, Caribbean.

HABITAT & BEHAVIOR: Hide under stones in shallow water. Can swim with jerky movements by repeatedly snapping valves open and shut.

REACTION TO DIVERS: Snap valves shut and retreat into dark, protected areas if threatened.

VISUAL ID: Numerous raised rings encircle white to pinkish tentacles; mantle red, orange or occasionally white. White valves of unequal size are sculptured with small, uneven, radiating ribs.

ABUNDANCE & DISTRIBUTION: Occasional Florida, Bahamas, Caribbean.

HABITAT & BEHAVIOR: Inhabit shallow waters, often under rocks. Can swim with jerky movements by repeatedly snapping valves open and shut.

REACTION TO DIVERS: Snap valves shut and retreat to dark, protected areas if threatened.

ROUGH FILECLAM
Lima scabra
CLASS:
Bivalves
Bivalvia
FAMILY:
File Shells
Limidae

SIZE: 2 - 3¹/₂ in.
DEPTH: 3 - 130 ft.

SPINY FILECLAM
Lima lima
CLASS:
Bivalves
Bivalvia
FAMILY:
File Shells
Limidae

SIZE: 2 - 3¹/₂ in.
DEPTH: 3 - 25 ft.

ANTILLEAN FILECLAM
Lima pellucida
CLASS:
Bivalves
Bivalvia
FAMILY:
File Shells
Limidae

SIZE: ³/₄ - 1 in.
DEPTH: 5 - 25 ft.

VISUAL ID: Numerous scattered spines, to two inches in length, cover surface. Color varies, including white, yellow, orange, red and purple. Mantle patterned in brown, gold and white [below right].

ABUNDANCE & DISTRIBUTION: Common Florida, Bahamas, Caribbean.

HABITAT & BEHAVIOR: Inhabit reefs, often attach under ledge overhangs. Well camouflaged, often overgrown by a variety of organisms [below right].

REACTION TO DIVERS: Snap valves shut when approached. With slow, patient approach, valves may remain open, allowing close observation of mantle.

**Atlantic
Thorny-oyster**
*Open valve with
exposed mantle.*

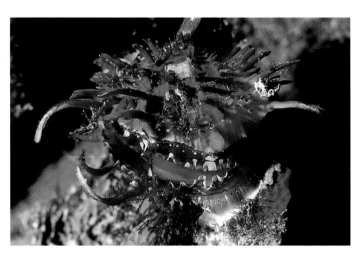

VISUAL ID: Long, wing-like structure extends along valve hinge. Dark brown to black.

ABUNDANCE & DISTRIBUTION: Common Florida, Bahamas, Caribbean.

HABITAT & BEHAVIOR: Attach to stalks of gorgonians, most commonly sea plumes. Well camouflaged, often overgrown by a variety of organisms.

ATLANTIC THORNY-OYSTER
Spondylus americanus

CLASS:
Bivalves
Bivalvia
FAMILY:
Spiny Oysters
Spondylidae

SIZE: 3 - 4 in.,
5½ in. max.
DEPTH: 50 - 130 ft.

Atlantic Thorny-oyster
Open valve with exposed mantle.

ATLANTIC WING-OYSTER
Pteria colymbus

CLASS:
Bivalves
Bivalvia
FAMILY:
Pearl Oysters
Pteriidae

SIZE: 2 - 3 in.
DEPTH: 10 - 100 ft.

VISUAL ID: White fan-shaped valves with eight to ten heavy ribs, some lined with short knobs. White-speckled tentacles are translucent to reddish.

ABUNDANCE & DISTRIBUTION: Occasional Florida, Bahamas, Caribbean.

HABITAT & BEHAVIOR: Hide under rocks and in recesses. Often attach to substrate by byssal threads. Can swim with jerky movements by repeatedly snapping valves open and shut. Shells often encrusted with marine growth.

REACTION TO DIVERS: Snap valves shut and retreat into recesses if threatened.

VISUAL ID: Valves interlock in zig-zag pattern.

ABUNDANCE & DISTRIBUTION: Common Florida, Bahamas, Caribbean.

HABITAT & BEHAVIOR: Attach to gorgonians, dead corals and substrate. Well camouflaged, often overgrown by a variety of organisms, especially encrusting sponge [pictured], hydroids and algae.

REACTION TO DIVERS: Close valves when disturbed.

NOTE: Formerly classified as *Lopha frons.*

VISUAL ID: Valve opening is long, irregular and often twisted. Yellowish, with a few light radial rays.

ABUNDANCE & DISTRIBUTION: Common to occasional Florida, Bahamas, Caribbean.

HABITAT & BEHAVIOR: Attach to rocks, under ledge overhangs, wrecks and other substrata. Prefer habitats with high sedimentation. Hundreds of individuals often encrust a large area. Usually covered with sediment, other debris and encrusting sponge.

SIMILAR SPECIES: Bicolor Purse-Oyster, *I. bicolor,* heavy, irregular growth plates form concentric pattern; most commonly attach to rocks in tidal areas, occasionally found on shallow reefs.

KNOBBY SCALLOP
Chlamys imbricata
CLASS:
Bivalves
Bivalvia
FAMILY:
Scallops
Pectinidae

SIZE: 1 - 1³/₄ in.
DEPTH: 10 - 25 ft.

FROND OYSTER
Dendostrea frons
CLASS:
Bivalves
Bivalvia
FAMILY:
Oysters
Ostreidae

SIZE: 1¹/₂ - 2¹/₂ in.
DEPTH: 20 - 130 ft.

LISTER PURSE-OYSTER
Isognomon radiatus
CLASS:
Bivalves
Bivalvia
FAMILY:
Purse Shells
Isognomonidae

SIZE: 1 - 2¹/₂ in.
DEPTH: 10 - 60 ft.

VISUAL ID: Flat and thin with smooth, rounded valve openings. Interior stained with brown, purple or black.

ABUNDANCE & DISTRIBUTION: Common to occasional Florida, Bahamas, Caribbean.

HABITAT & BEHAVIOR: Grow in clusters on mangrove roots, dock pilings, shipwrecks and rocks. Prefer areas with high sedimentation. Usually covered with encrusting sponge and sediment. Occasionally on reefs; may attach to gorgonians.

VISUAL ID: Thin, fan-shaped valves. Amber to gray, somewhat translucent. Rows of short projections radiate from base.

ABUNDANCE & DISTRIBUTION: Common Caribbean, occasional Bahamas, Florida.

HABITAT & BEHAVIOR: Wide variety of habitats. Bury in mud or sand, or inhabit narrow openings in reefs, with valves only slightly exposed.

REACTION TO DIVERS: Close when disturbed.

VISUAL ID: Smooth, highly polished valves vary in color and pattern. Most commonly white with a yellowish tint and rays of pink. May have concentric markings of yellow, pink or lavender, with or without rays, or may be one solid color. Slight incurve of valves' central lips are distinctive.

ABUNDANCE & DISTRIBUTION: Common Caribbean, rare Florida, Bahamas.

HABITAT & BEHAVIOR: Inhabit shallow sand flats, where they bury beneath the surface. Valves of non-living specimens are often found in great numbers.

FLAT TREE-OYSTER
Isognomon alatus
CLASS:
Bivalves
Bivalvia
FAMILY:
Purse Shells
Isognomonidae

SIZE: 1 - 3 in.
DEPTH: 0 - 40 ft.

AMBER PENSHELL
Pinna carnea
CLASS:
Bivalves
Bivalvia
FAMILY:
Pen Shells
Pinnidae

SIZE: 4 - 6 in.,
10 in. max.
DEPTH: 6 - 50 ft.

SUNRISE TELLIN
Tellina radiata
CLASS:
Bivalves
Bivalvia
FAMILY:
Tellins
Tellinidae

SIZE: 1$\frac{1}{2}$ - 2$\frac{1}{2}$ in.,
3 in. max.
DEPTH: 0 - 25 ft.

Chitons

VISUAL ID: Girdle is gray with bands of black, and covered with short, coarse, hair-like spines. Plates are brown when not eroded or encrusted.
ABUNDANCE & DISTRIBUTION: Abundant Caribbean.
HABITAT & BEHAVIOR: Inhabit rocky shorelines; attach to rocks and solid substrate.
NOTE: Often used by natives as bait, and on some islands as food.

VISUAL ID: Girdle is marbled in bluish gray, covered with round scales. Plates gray, often with tints or markings of green and olive. Elongated oval shape.
ABUNDANCE & DISTRIBUTION: Common to uncommon Caribbean, except off coast of Central America. This and two similar species are visually indistinguishable, positive identification requires microscopic examination. However, they can often be identified by their distribution.
HABITAT & BEHAVIOR: Inhabit rocky shorelines and reefs. Attach to rocks and solid substrata.
SIMILAR SPECIES: Florida Slender Chiton, *S. floridana,* Florida and Central American Coast to Panama., Slender Chiton, *S., bahamensis,* only member of genus in Bahamas, also in Florida Keys and Yucatan to Honduras.

VISUAL ID: Girdle is crimson, with lighter spots and occasional bands, and is textured like granular sugar. Plates are ornately sculptured and patterned in gray, greenish brown and, often, crimson.
ABUNDANCE & DISTRIBUTION: Uncommon Florida, Bahamas, Caribbean.
HABITAT & BEHAVIOR: Inhabit shallow, rocky inshore areas and reefs. Attach to rocks and solid substrate.

FUZZY CHITON
Acanthopleura granulata
CLASS:
Chitons
Amphineura

SIZE: 1¹/₂ - 3¹/₂ in.
DEPTH: Intertidal

CARIBBEAN SLENDER CHITON
Stenoplax purpurascens
CLASS:
Chitons
Amphineura

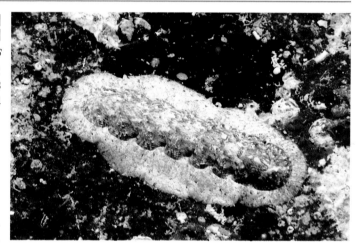

SIZE: 1 - 2 in.
DEPTH: 0 - 20 ft.

ORNATE CHITON
Tonicia schammi
CLASS:
Chitons
Amphineura

SIZE: ¹/₂ - ³/₄ in.
DEPTH: 10 - 45 ft.

VISUAL ID: Small size. Pair of small rounded fins on each side of rear body do not join; two rows of suckers on arms. Large pigmented chromatophores often visible, but can rapidly contract to become translucent [right].

ABUNDANCE & DISTRIBUTION: Uncommon Florida, Bahamas and Caribbean.

HABITAT & BEHAVIOR: Inhabit shallow seagrass beds and patch reefs.

REACTION TO DIVERS: Appear unconcerned; allow a close approach.

Caribbean Reef Squid

At night, when blinded by divers' lights or cornered, often raise arms in a defensive posture.

VISUAL ID: Entire length of oblong body is bordered by a thin fin which forms a point at the rear. Color varies: during day often shades of bluish gray to brown with white spots on back; at night, generally mottled and spotted in shades of white, brown, green and lavender, may be iridescent. Arms are shorter than body.

ABUNDANCE & DISTRIBUTION: Common South Florida, Bahamas, Caribbean.

HABITAT & BEHAVIOR: Inhabit shallow waters, often swim over reefs and turtle grass beds.

REACTION TO DIVERS: Wary; generally retreat slowly, but will jet away rapidly if chased. May allow close approach with slow, nonthreatening movements.

NOTE: This is the only squid commonly encountered over Caribbean reefs. Attracted to lights at night. When disturbed, often spread arms in a defensive pose.

GRASS SQUID
Pickfordiateunthis pulchella

CLASS:
Cephalopoda
ORDER:
Squid
Teuthoidea
FAMILY:
Grass Squid
Pickfordiateuthidae

SIZE: ½ to 1 in.
DEPTH: 3 - 45 ft.

Grass Squid

Displaying large pigmented chromatophores.

CARIBBEAN REEF SQUID
Sepioteuthis sepioidea

CLASS:
Cephalopoda
ORDER:
Squid
Teuthoidea
FAMILY:
Inshore Squid
Loliginidae

SIZE: 6 - 12 in.
DEPTH: 0 - 60 ft.

Squid

VISUAL ID: Triangular-shaped fins extend from rear half of body. Adult males can be distinguished by red, flame-like markings on side of body. Juveniles [pictured] have short arms and tentacles of about equal length, large eyes and elongated body.

ABUNDANCE & DISTRIBUTION: Common Florida, Bahamas, Caribbean.

HABITAT & BEHAVIOR: An inshore, open-water species, rarely found over reefs. Egg clusters attach to reefs. After hatching, young may remain around reefs for a few weeks or months.

NOTE: This identification is probable, but cannot be confirmed without a specimen. The fin's shape, location and body length confirm that it is an arrow squid, Family Loliginidae. The juveniles of several squid species (less than 4 inches in total length) may be observed over a reef and adjacent areas. Their color patterns are not distinctive, making juveniles difficult to distinguish from pictures alone.

VISUAL ID: Large elongate body with rounded, somewhat triangular, fins that extend nearly half the body's length before ending in a point. Variable color and markings in shades from brown to bluish gray; often display orange spots.

ABUNDANCE & DISTRIBUTION: Although common Florida, Bahamas, Caribbean and Gulf of Mexico rarely observed by divers.

HABITAT & BEHAVIOR: Inhabit deep water (350 - 900 ft.) during the winter; move inshore late summer and autumn. Rest near bottom during day; feed at night on shrimps and other squid.

VISUAL ID: Compact body with a rounded fin on each side of rear quarter of body ends in a rounded tip that creates a nearly oval outline. Color varies from shades of bluish gray to brown; often display black spots.

ABUNDANCE & DISTRIBUTION: Uncommon Florida, Bahamas, Caribbean; also Gulf of Mexico, north to Maine and south to Brazil.

HABITAT & BEHAVIOR: Inhabit inshore waters including shallow estuaries and bays where they feed on zooplankton, small crustaceans and fish.

ARROW SQUID
Juvenile
Loligo plei
CLASS:
Cephalopoda
SUBORDER:
Squid
Teuthoidea
FAMILY:
Inshore Squid
Loliginidae

SIZE: 8 - 18 in.
DEPTH: 0 - 130 ft.

LONGFIN SQUID
Loligo pealei
CLASS:
Cephalopoda
ORDER:
Squid
Teuthoidea
FAMILY:
Inshore Squid
Loliginidae

SIZE: Body 8 - 14 in.,
max. 18 in.
DEPTH: 10 - 1,500 ft.

ATLANTIC BRIEF SQUID
Lolliguncula brevis
CLASS:
Cephalopoda
ORDER:
Squid
Teuthoidea
FAMILY:
Inshore Squid
Loliginidae

SIZE: Body 3 - 4 in.,
max. 5 in.
DEPTH: Surface to 70 ft.

VISUAL ID: Small size. Very large eye; tentacles nearly as long as body. Triangular fins on each side of rear body end in a point. Five light organs around lower third of eye, outer two are large, central three appear as small spots. Covered with small dark spots and speckles; color varies from pale shades of bluish gray to brown.

ABUNDANCE & DISTRIBUTION: Uncommon Florida, Bahamas, Caribbean.

HABITAT & BEHAVIOR: Generally inhabit open ocean over continental slopes where they are common. Occasionally migrate to shallow water to feed at night.

VISUAL ID: Frequently display pale to intense iridescent blue-green cast, often with brown mottling. Dark ring around eye is generally evident [below], no dark edges around suckers (compare with similar Common Octopus [next]). Skin relatively smooth with small, scattered wart-like skin papillae. Arms 4-6 times body length. Eggs large, up to $5/8$ inch long, and usually number less than 1000.

ABUNDANCE & DISTRIBUTION: Common Florida, Bahamas, Caribbean.

HABITAT & BEHAVIOR: Inhabit coral reefs, reside in recesses or sponges. Most common octopus found in the open on reefs at night, never out in daytime. Often spread bodies in distinctive parachute pattern to attack and engulf prey [note juvenile below right].

**Caribbean
Reef Octopus**
*Note dark ring
around eye.*

GIANTEYE SQUID
Abralia veranyi
CLASS:
Cephalopoda
ORDER:
Squid
Teuthoidea
FAMILY:
Enope Squid
Enoploteuthidae

SIZE: ³/₄ - 1¹/₄ in.,
1¹/₂ in.max.
DEPTH: Surface to 600 ft.

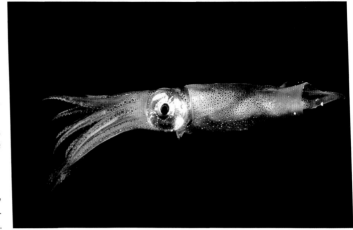

CARIBBEAN REEF OCTOPUS
Octopus briareus
CLASS:
Cephalopoda
ORDER:
Octopuses
Octopoda

SIZE: 12 - 20 in.
DEPTH: 15 - 75 ft.

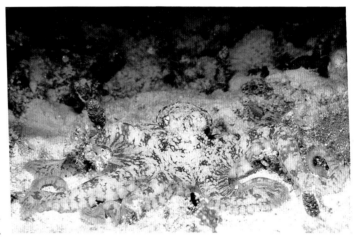

**Caribbean
Reef Octopus
Juvenile**

VISUAL ID: Edges of suckers dark, no dark ring around eye (compare with similar Caribbean Reef Octopus [previous]). Skin texture is a reticulated pattern of patches and thin grooves. Color and patterns highly variable, often mottled reddish-brown with frontal white spots. Arms 3 - 4 times body length. Eggs very small, less than 1/8 inch and numbering over 100,000.

ABUNDANCE & DISTRIBUTION: Occasional Florida, Bahamas, Caribbean.

HABITAT & BEHAVIOR: Inhabit sea grass beds, areas of sand and rubble, and coral reefs. Reside in holes in hard substrata. Area around hole littered with shells and debris. This is the only octopus commonly found in the open on reefs during the day.

Common Octopus

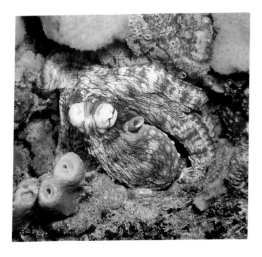

COMMON OCTOPUS
Octopus vulgaris
CLASS:
Cephalopoda
ORDER:
Octopuses
Octopoda

SIZE: 15 - 28 in.,
3 ft. max.
DEPTH: 15 - 75 ft.

Common Octopus

When moving in open water, often display broad black and white striped pattern thought to possibly mimic the initial phase of the Queen Parrotfish.

Common Octopus

VISUAL ID: Very long arms, third pair longest (although not always apparent). Usually brown to bluish gray; often has row of widely spaced white spots on arms; occasionally display tints of blue, especially on and around the suckers.

ABUNDANCE & DISTRIBUTION: Occasional Florida, Bahamas and Caribbean; also Gulf of Mexico.

HABITAT & BEHAVIOR: Inhabit sand, rubble and mud bottoms. Often hide within small burrows in the substrate; occasionally extend their heads from the openings. Have been observed foraging in open during day; may attempt to camouflage identity by mimicking the shape and movements of flounder.

REACTION TO DIVERS: When first approached remain still apparently relying on camouflage. If not threatened may continue to forage; jet away when frightened.

Atlantic Longarm Octopus
Jetting away in typical octopus fashion.

ATLANTIC LONGARM OCTOPUS
Octopus defilippi
CLASS:
Cephalopoda
ORDER:
Octopuses
Octopoda

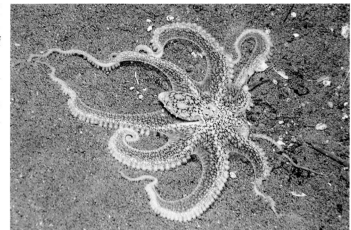

SIZE: 8 - 14 in.
DEPTH: 4 - 600 ft.

Atlantic Longarm Octopus
Post-larval juvenile with large chromatophores.

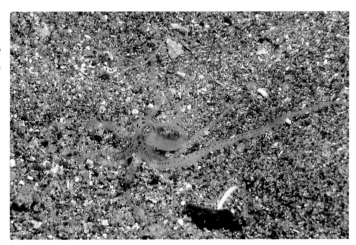

Atlantic Longarm Octopus
Mimicking flounder while moving. [right]

Peering from burrow
[far left]

Resting on bottom.
[left]

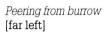

Octopuses

VISUAL ID: A blue ring creates a false eye marking, called an ocellus, below the true eye. Skin texture forms a reticulated pattern of patches and thin grooves. Color extremely variable, often mottled. Eggs small, less than 1/4 inch.

ABUNDANCE & DISTRIBUTION: Occasional Florida, Bahamas, Caribbean and Flower Gardens, Gulf of Mexico. Very common Haiti.

HABITAT & BEHAVIOR: Inhabit shallow coral reefs.

SIMILAR SPECIES: Mexican Four-Eyed Octopus, *O. maya,* distinguished by false eye that does not have a blue ring. Distribution restricted to southern Gulf of Mexico, including Isla Mujeres off northeastern Yucatan.

VISUAL ID: Numerous white oval spots, on brick red or bright red to brownish gray background. Usually display large, wart-like skin papillae on mantle. Arms 4-6 times body length. Eggs small, less than 1/8 inch.

ABUNDANCE & DISTRIBUTION: Uncommon Florida, Bahamas, Caribbean. Also circumtropical and subtropical.

HABITAT & BEHAVIOR: Inhabit sand flats and rubble areas adjacent to reefs. Forage along reef edge for shrimp and crabs When threatened turn bright red and display bold white spots.

VISUAL ID: A dark stripe running down each arm is usually visible. White frontal spots and white streak on mantle. Skin texture forms a reticulated pattern of patches in thin grooves. Color and patterns variable, often mottled reddish brown to brownish gray. May display wart-like skin papillae on mantle. Eggs small, less than 1/8 inch, are carried by female in her arms.

ABUNDANCE & DISTRIBUTION: Rare Florida, Bahamas, Caribbean.

HABITAT & BEHAVIOR: Inhabit sea grass beds, muddy bottoms and sand flats adjacent to reefs. Forage in open for crustaceans. Can rapidly bury themselves by diving into mud or sand.

CARIBBEAN TWO-SPOT OCTOPUS
Octopus filosusi
CLASS:
Cephalopoda
ORDER:
Octopuses
Octopoda

SIZE: 8 - 10 in.
DEPTH: 15 - 35 ft.

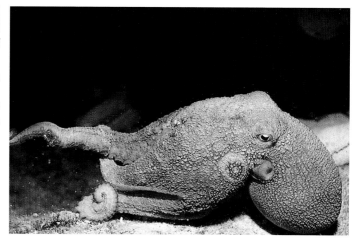

WHITE SPOTTED OCTOPUS
Octopus macropus
CLASS:
Cephalopoda
ORDER:
Octopuses
Octopoda

SIZE: 12 - 20 in.
DEPTH: 15 - 75 ft.

BROWNSTRIPE OCTOPUS
Octopus burryi
CLASS:
Cephalopoda
ORDER:
Octopuses
Octopoda

SIZE: 6 - 12 in.
DEPTH: 15 - 75 ft.

VISUAL ID: Red to orangish brown, coloration relatively uniform, rarely mottled. Small size helps distinguish this octopus. Skin texture is smooth. Eggs are small, less than $1/4$ inch and number up to 2,000.

ABUNDANCE & DISTRIBUTION: Rare Florida, Bahamas, Caribbean.

HABITAT & BEHAVIOR: Inhabit sand or mud bottoms and areas adjacent to reefs. Often reside in empty shells and bottles.

SIMILAR SPECIES: There is a common, yet undescribed and easily confused species in South and Gulf Coast Florida, along the Central American coast to Venezuela. Inhabit shallow grass beds. Can be distinguished by its dark brown to brownish gray color. The egg size of brooding females that measure up to $1/2$ inch are distinctive from the eggs of *O. joubini* eggs that are less than $1/4$ inch.

VISUAL ID: Females (pictured): Large, long front arms trail thin translucent, veil-like webs. Reddish violet to violet or purple upper body becomes cream colored below.

ABUNDANCE & DISTRIBUTION: Rare worldwide in subtropical and tropical waters.

HABITAT & BEHAVIOR: Inhabit surface waters. Swim by jet propulsion; feed primarily on fish.

VISUAL ID: Long, cylindrical, bluish translucent mass of egg strings laid in a double helix.

ABUNDANCE & DISTRIBUTION: Uncommon Florida, Bahamas, Caribbean; also worldwide in tropical-subtropical waters.

HABITAT & BEHAVIOR: The eggs of nearly all oceanic squid are laid in free-floating masses, which are either without form or structured as long, cylindrical tubes. Most inshore squid and octopuses lay eggs in masses attached to the substrate.

ATLANTIC PYGMY OCTOPUS
Octopus joubini

CLASS:
Cephalopoda
ORDER:
Octopuses
Octopoda

SIZE: 2 - 4 in.,
6 in. max.
DEPTH: 3 - 35 ft.

VIOLET BLANKET OCTOPUS
Tremoctopus violaceus

CLASS:
Cephalopoda
ORDER:
Octopuses
Octopoda

SIZE: Females 3 - 6 ft.;
Males 2 - 3 ft.
DEPTH: 0 - 35 ft.

EGG CASE DIAMOND BACK SQUID
Thysanoteuthis rhombus

CLASS:
Cephalopoda
ORDER:
Squid
Teuthoidae

SIZE: Length 2 - 4 ft.;
diameter 4 - 8 in.
DEPTH: Near surface.

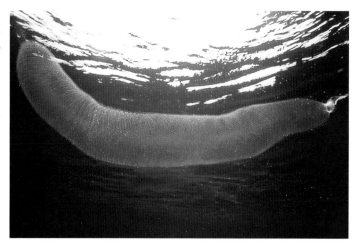

Phylum Echinodermata

(Ee-KINE-oh-DER-ma-tuh / Gr. spiny skin)

Sea Stars, Sea Urchins & Sea Cucumbers

All echinoderms are marine and have a hard, internal skeleton composed of small calcareous plates called ossicles. Often, the ossicles have projections that give the body surface a spiny appearance. Members of the phylum have five body sections of equal size that are arranged around a central axis. Most have hundreds of small tube feet, called podia, that work in unison, either to move the animal over the bottom, or to capture food.

Feather Stars

CLASS: Crinoidea (Cry-noy-DEE-uh / L. a lily)

Feather stars, also known as crinoids, are the most ancient of echinoderms. These animals have changed little according to fossil records, and are sometimes referred to as "living fossils." They have small, flattened pentagon-shaped bodies with five arms that immediately fork one or more times, giving them a total of **ten or more long arms** in multiples of five. Numerous short appendages extend along both sides of each arm creating a structure that resembles a feather. Skeletal ossicles give the arms a jointed appearance. Arms are used to sweep the water for particles of food. They adhere tightly, like Velcro, to anything that comes into contact with them and break easily. Fortunately, broken arms can be regenerated. Some crinoids can move short distances by swimming with coordinated arm movements, but most walk on jointed legs called cirri. Some species anchor inside narrow crevices with only their arms visible; others position themselves high atop coral heads and other reef structures.

Sea Stars

CLASS: Asteroidea (Ass-ter-OY-dee-uh / Gr. star form)

Asteroids have long been known as starfish, but a more modern and appropriate common name is sea stars. They usually have **five arms,** although a few species have more. The arms are triangular, merging at the base into the central disc. Broken arms can be regenerated, and in some species a new animal can form from a severed member. The mouth is located centrally on the undersurface, with anus on the top. Two or four rows of podia, tipped with suction discs, extend from the mouth down each arm. They are used both for movement and capturing prey. Some sea stars can invert their stomachs through their mouths to envelop and consume prey.

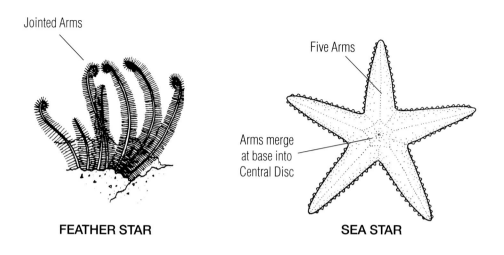

Jointed Arms

FEATHER STAR

Five Arms

Arms merge
at base into
Central Disc

SEA STAR

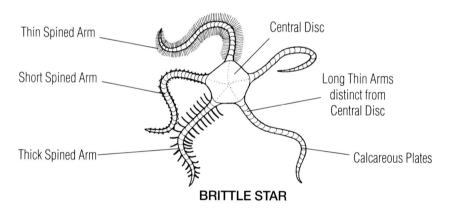

Thin Spined Arm

Short Spined Arm

Thick Spined Arm

Central Disc

Long Thin Arms
distinct from
Central Disc

Calcareous Plates

BRITTLE STAR

Brittle & Basket Stars

CLASS: Ophiuroidea (Oh-fee-ER-OY-dee-uh / Gr. serpent tail in appearance)

Both orders in this class have **long, thin arms** that, unlike sea stars, do not widen as they approach the central disc. The central disc is a flattened, smooth and somewhat rounded pentagon. The mouth, centrally located on the underside, opens into the stomach; there is no intestine or anus.

Brittle stars, Order Ophiurae, have a small **central disc** that rarely exceeds one inch in diameter, and five arms with numerous **spines** arranged in rows. The spines of different species can be distinct: they can be short or long, thin or thick, pointed or blunt. The tops of the arms are lined with large **calcareous plates** that allow only lateral movement. This armor results in arms that break off easily, giving rise to the common name. Severed arms, however, can be regenerated. In spite of their brittleness and restricted mobility, the arms allow the animal to move more rapidly than other members of the phylum. During the day brittle stars are occasionally seen clinging to sponges and gorgonian, but they generally hide under rocks and inside crevices, waiting for night before moving into the open to feed.

Basket stars, Order Euryalae, have **five arms that repeatedly subdivide into numerous branches,** resembling coiling tentacles. Unlike brittle stars, basket stars lack heavy arm shields and therefore can move their arms in all directions. During the day, the animals commonly cling to gorgonians, curling their network of arms into a tight ball. At night, they climb to the tops of gorgonians or other reef outcroppings, and spread their arms into the current to form a plankton net. Tiny, fine spines and tube feet work to transfer captured food to the mouth.

BASKET STAR

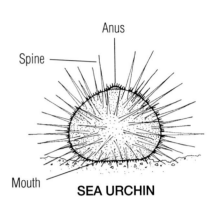

SEA URCHIN

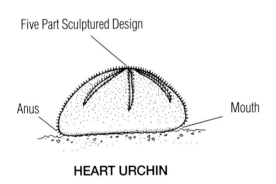

HEART URCHIN

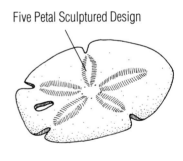

SAND DOLLAR

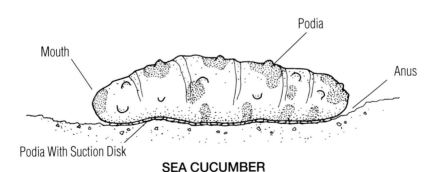

SEA CUCUMBER

Sea Urchins, Heart Urchins, Sand Dollars & Sea Biscuits

CLASS: Echinoidea (Eck-ih-NOY-dee-uh / L. spiny)

A skeleton of ten fused calcareous plates, covered with numerous spines, encases the body of echinoids. They are characterized into two basic groups, regular and irregular.

Sea urchins, regular echinoids, typically have **spherical bodies with long protective spines** and tube feet. The **mouth** is centrally located on the underside and the **anus on the top.** The mouth is a complicated arrangement of five teeth, called Aristotle's Lantern, used for scraping algae and other organic food from rocks. The spines of some species are long, sharp and needle-like, while others are stubby and blunt. Long, pointed spines easily puncture the skin, and are difficult to remove because the shaft is covered with recurved spinelets that function as miniature fish hooks. This causes a rather painful wound which should be treated to prevent infection.

Heart urchins, Order Spatangoida, are irregular echinoids. Their bodies are non-spherical, shaped more like an **oval dome.** The mouth, which lacks Aristotle's Lantern, is in front, the **anus at the rear.** On top is a distinct **five-part sculptured design.** The body is covered with short, tightly packed spines well-adapted for burrowing; tube feet are degenerate or absent. They spend most of their lives buried in sand or mud where they feed on organic material. Although common, heart urchins are seldom seen. If the animal is spotted in the open at all, it is usually at night. Skeletal remains are occasionally found on the sand.

Sand dollars and sea biscuits, Order Clypeasteroida, are also irregular echinoids. Their bodies are disc-shaped, with a five-petal sculptured design on the back. The mouth, which has an Aristotle's Lantern, is centered on the underside, with the anus toward the rear. The very short, compacted spines that cover the body appear as fuzz, and are well adapted for burrowing. Like heart urchins, they live under the sand and are rarely sighted in the open. Their skeletal remains, rather than the living animals, are usually found.

Sea Cucumbers

CLASS: Holothuroidea (Hoe-low-ther-OY-dee-uh / Gr. plant-like in appearance)

Sea cucumbers have **sausage-shaped** bodies, with a **mouth in front and anus at the rear.** The five body-sections common to all echinoderms are not visible in these animals, but are part of their internal structure. They also have no external spines or arms, and the skeletal plates are reduced to microscopic size and buried in the leathery body wall. The shape of these hidden plates is the key to scientific classification, and thus many species cannot be positively identified underwater. **Podia** on the underside are tipped with suction discs; those on the back have been modified into a variety of shapes and sizes. These are often the visual clue to underwater identification. Sea cucumbers are usually sighted slowly crawling across sand or reef, scooping up organic debris.

Feather Stars

VISUAL ID: Twenty arms, most commonly orange, occasionally greenish or black with yellow-or orange-tipped side branches.

ABUNDANCE & DISTRIBUTION: Abundant to common Caribbean; occasional Bahamas. Not reported Florida; uncommon south Florida and western Gulf of Mexico.

HABITAT & BEHAVIOR: Inhabit coral reefs. Hide bodies in recesses, exposing only arms.

NOTE: Formerly classified in genus *Nemaster.*

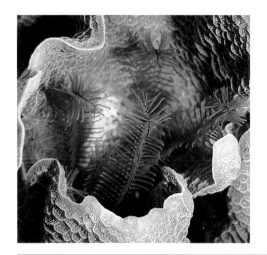

VISUAL ID: Side branches appear to be beaded. Twenty arms, color widely variable. Side branches are most commonly silver-gray, occasionally with black tips.

ABUNDANCE & DISTRIBUTION: Occasional Caribbean, Bahamas; uncommon South Florida and Gulf of Mexico.

HABITAT & BEHAVIOR: Inhabit deeper coral reefs. Hide bodies in recesses, exposing only arms.

NOTE: Formerly classified in genus *Nemaster.*

GOLDEN CRINOID
Davidaster rubiginosa
CLASS:
Feather Stars
Crinoidea

SIZE: Arms 7 - 10 in.
DEPTH: 20 - 130 ft.

Golden Crinoid
Greenish variation.

Greenish variation.
[far left]

Black with yellow-tip variation. [near left]

BEADED CRINOID
Davidaster discoidea
CLASS:
Feather Stars
Crinoidea

SIZE: Arms 5 - 8 in.
DEPTH: 60 - 130 ft.

VISUAL ID: Forty black arms, with white-tipped side branches.

ABUNDANCE & DISTRIBUTION: Common southern Caribbean; occasional to uncommon central Caribbean; rare northern Caribbean. Not reported Florida, Bahamas.

HABITAT & BEHAVIOR: Inhabit coral reefs. Attach to tops of tall sponges, coral heads and other pinnacles, where they are completely exposed.

VISUAL ID: Ten red and white banded arms and side arms.

ABUNDANCE & DISTRIBUTION: Common Caribbean; occasional Bahamas; rare Dry Tortugas, Florida. More common below 40 feet.

HABITAT & BEHAVIOR: Inhabit coral reefs. Commonly attach to branches of sea plumes, sea rods and sea whips. Unique ability to coordinate arm movements enables this species to swim in open water.

VISUAL ID: Cream to yellow, with brown, purplish, greenish, gray or black bands. Five long, tapered, limp arms. Numerous spines create velvet-like appearance.

ABUNDANCE & DISTRIBUTION: Occasional Florida, Caribbean; also north to North Carolina and south to Argentina.

HABITAT & BEHAVIOR: Inhabit sand or sandy mud bottoms. Burrow beneath surface, but often forage in the open at night.

BLACK & WHITE CRINOID
Nemaster grandis
CLASS:
Feather Stars
Crinoidea

SIZE: Arms 7 - 10 in.
DEPTH: 30 - 130 ft.

SWIMMING CRINOID
Analcidometra armata
CLASS:
Feather Stars
Crinoidea

SIZE: Arms 2¹/₂ - 3¹/₂ in.
DEPTH: 10 - 450 ft.

BANDED SEA STAR
Luidia alternata
CLASS:
Sea Stars
Asteroidea

SIZE: 6 - 12 in.
DEPTH: 10 - 160 ft.

Sea Stars

VISUAL ID: Conspicuous border of whitish spines on five long, tapered arms. White, cream, gray or brown with darker central stripe that is occasionally indistinct. Covered with a beaded or net-like pattern.

ABUNDANCE & DISTRIBUTION: Common Florida; occasional Bahamas, Caribbean; also Bermuda, north to New Jersey and south to Brazil.

HABITAT & BEHAVIOR: Inhabit sand bottoms around reefs. Burrow beneath surface, but occasionally forage in the open.

VISUAL ID: Nine long, tapered arms. Bluish gray to purple to tan, darker at central disc and center of arms.

ABUNDANCE & DISTRIBUTION: Uncommon Caribbean; rare Florida; also south to Brazil.

HABITAT & BEHAVIOR: Inhabit shallow sand or sandy mud bottoms. Burrow to feed, rarely seen in the open on bottom.

VISUAL ID: Five long tubular arms of equal length with rounded tips; small pits on surface are arranged in rows running length of arms. Red to reddish tan or reddish orange with dark red mottling or irregular banding.

ABUNDANCE & DISTRIBUTION: Rare Florida Keys; occasional east coast Central America. Distribution of this species is not well documented, possibly in other locations.

HABITAT & BEHAVIOR: Inhabit areas of coral rubble and shallow patch reefs. Hide under rubble.

STRIPED SEA STAR
Luidia clathrata

CLASS:
Sea Stars
Asteroidea

SIZE: 6 - 10 in.
DEPTH: 0 - 130 ft.

NINE-ARMED SEA STAR
Luidia senegalensis

CLASS:
Sea Stars
Asteroidea

SIZE: 6 - 12 in.
DEPTH: 0 - 150 ft.

MOTTLED RED SEA STAR
Copidaster lymani

CLASS:
Sea Stars
Asteroidea

SIZE: 4 - 8 in.,
12³/₄ in. max.
DEPTH: 15 - 110 ft.

Sea Stars

VISUAL ID: Five long tubular arms of equal length with reddish upturned tips. Squarish nodules on surface are arranged in rows that run length of arms. (Similar Common Comet Star [next] usually has arms of unequal length and surface nodules are rounded and distributed randomly.) Color varies from red to brownish red, orange or pale yellow, usually blotched with brown, maroon, purple or blue. Young (pictured) are dull purplish red.

ABUNDANCE & DISTRIBUTION: Uncommon Florida Keys, Caribbean; also, south to Brazil.

HABITAT & BEHAVIOR: Inhabit areas of coral and rock rubble between shallow patch reefs. Cryptic; commonly cling to the underside of rocks and rubble.

VISUAL ID: Four to seven slender, tubular arms with rounded tips. Rounded nodules on surface are distributed randomly. Arms often of unequal length. Orangish brown to tan, occasionally dull red to purple.

ABUNDANCE & DISTRIBUTION: Common Florida; occasional to uncommon Bahamas, Caribbean.

HABITAT & BEHAVIOR: Inhabit reefs. An arm that is broken off will regenerate another sea star by forming a new disc and arms. The buds of new arms form a star-like pattern at the trailing end of a regenerating arm, giving rise to the common name.

Common Comet Star
Five-armed variety; one arm lost.

COMET STAR
Ophidiaster guildingii
CLASS:
Sea Stars
Asteroidea

SIZE: 2 - 4 in.
DEPTH: 4 - 20 ft.

COMMON COMET STAR
Linckia guildingii
CLASS:
Sea Stars
Asteroidea

SIZE: 5 - 8 in.
DEPTH: 20 - 130 ft.

Common Comet Star
New individual regenerating from a severed arm.

VISUAL ID: Five arms are bordered with bead-like marginal plates which, when viewed from above, appear to be spineless. Brown, purple or maroon, with contrasting marginal plates of light yellow or tan.

ABUNDANCE & DISTRIBUTION: Common Florida; occasional to uncommon Bahamas, Caribbean; also north to Chesapeake Bay, Virginia.

HABITAT & BEHAVIOR: Inhabit sand and mud bottoms. Often burrow beneath surface.

VISUAL ID: Five arms bordered with marginal plates have short, outward-pointing spines. At base between arms, two, or occasionally four spines, are turned distinctively inward. Uniformly reddish brown to brown or gray.

ABUNDANCE & DISTRIBUTION: Uncommon Florida Keys, Bahamas, Caribbean; also north to North Carolina and south to Brazil.

HABITAT & BEHAVIOR: Inhabit sandy bottoms. Often burrow into sand. Most common between 15 and 65 feet.

**Two-Spined
Sea Star**
Color variation.

BEADED SEA STAR
Astropecten articulatus

CLASS:
Sea Stars
Asteroidea

SIZE: 4 - 6 in.
DEPTH: 0 - 540 ft.

TWO-SPINED SEA STAR
Astropecten duplicatus

CLASS:
Sea Stars
Asteroidea

SIZE: 5 - 8 in.
DEPTH: 3 - 1,800 ft.

Two-Spined Sea Star
Color variation.

Sea Stars

VISUAL ID: Reddish orange to orangish yellow spines form irregular ridges running arms' length, valleys (papular areas) bluish white.

ABUNDANCE & DISTRIBUTION: Common to occasional both Florida coasts; uncommon southern Caribbean. Not reported central or northern Caribbean.

HABITAT & BEHAVIOR: Inhabit rocky reefs and sand flats. Occasionally on dock pilings and other similar structures.

VISUAL ID: Five long, slightly tapered, equal-length tubular arms with bluntly rounded tips. Conical spines on surface are usually arranged in rows that run length of arms, but are occasionally scattered. Most commonly orange or orange-brown spines with tufts of maroon to violet papulae between, also reported to be red, red-brown, yellow-brown, violet and purple.

ABUNDANCE & DISTRIBUTION: Occasional Florida Keys and Bahamas.

HABITAT & BEHAVIOR: Inhabit areas of sand, rubble, algae growth, seagrass beds, rocky coastlines and sediment bottoms adjacent to mangroves.

VISUAL ID: Small central disc with five arms of equal length tapered slightly until near tips. Rows of thorn-like spines run length of arms. Uniform shades of red.

ABUNDANCE & DISTRIBUTION: Uncommon Florida Keys, Bahamas and Caribbean; also, south to Brazil.

HABITAT & BEHAVIOR: Inhabit areas of coral and rock rubble between shallow patch reefs. Cryptic; commonly cling to the underside of rocks and rubble. Also cling to mangrove roots.

ORANGE-RIDGED SEA STAR
Echinaster spinulosus

CLASS:
Sea Stars
Asteroidea

SIZE: 4 - 5 in.
DEPTH: 0 - 130 ft.

CONICAL SPINED SEA STAR
Echinaster sentus

CLASS:
Sea Stars
Asteroidea

SIZE: 4 - 7 in.
DEPTH: 0 - 40 ft.

THORNY SEA STAR
Echinaster echinophorus

CLASS:
Sea Stars
Asteroidea

SIZE: 1¹/₂ - 3 in.
DEPTH: 0 - 180 ft.

Sea Stars

VISUAL ID: Thick, short arms, heavy body. Knobby spines form net-like geometric design of contrasting color. Orangish brown to tan.

ABUNDANCE & DISTRIBUTION: Common to occasional Florida, Bahamas, Caribbean; also Bermuda, north to North Carolina and south to Brazil.

HABITAT & BEHAVIOR: Inhabit shallow sea grass beds and sand flats.

VISUAL ID: Thick, stud-like spines on tubular arms and small central disc. Brownish white with wide brown band on each arm.

ABUNDANCE & DISTRIBUTION: Rare Belize and Cozumel.

HABITAT & BEHAVIOR: Inhabit shallow areas of coral rubble.

NOTE: Species of the genus *Mithrodia* are known primarily from deep water, well below safe scuba diving depths and are rarely reported in the Caribbean. This specimen, photographed in shallow water, at night, off Belize, cannot be identified to species from the picture alone and may be a rare undescribed species. If observed, a sighting report should be made to REEF at *www.reef.org*.

366

CUSHION SEA STAR
Oreaster reticulatus

CLASS:
Sea Stars
Asteroidea

SIZE: 8 - 14 in.
DEPTH: 3 - 120 ft.

**Cushion Sea Star
Juvenile**

Color variations.
[left]

STUDDED SEA STAR
Mithrodia sp.

CLASS:
Sea Stars
Asteroidea

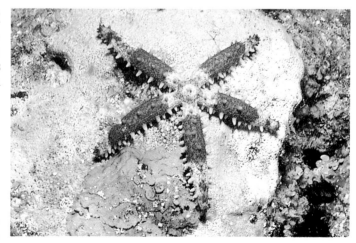

SIZE: 5 in.
DEPTH: 15 - 25 ft.

Sea Stars – Brittle Stars

VISUAL ID: Five wide, short, triangular arms emerge from central disc. Color widely variable, including white, tan, yellow, red, blue and olive.
ABUNDANCE & DISTRIBUTION: Uncommon to rare Florida, Bahamas, Caribbean; also Bermuda and south to Brazil.
HABITAT & BEHAVIOR: Inhabit reefs. Secretive; hide under rocks, coral rubble or in crevices. Can burrow into sand.
SIMILAR SPECIES: Tiny Blunt-Armed Star, *A. hartmeyeri,* grow to only one-half inch. Have somewhat longer, more distinct, arms. White to pinkish white. Caribbean only.

VISUAL ID: Bright red, may have white markings near center of disc and black markings around tips of arms.
ABUNDANCE & DISTRIBUTION: Rare Florida, Bahamas, Caribbean.
HABITAT & BEHAVIOR: Hide under corals and reef rubble near deep drop-offs.
NOTE: Previously classified as *Porania regularis.*

VISUAL ID: Tiny; irregular areas of cream to pink, purple and reddish brown central disc and occasionally banded arms. Arm plates bear tiny spines.
ABUNDANCE & DISTRIBUTION: Occasional Bahamas and Caribbean. Not reported in Florida.
HABITAT & BEHAVIOR: During day wrap arms tightly around branches of Rose Lace Coral, *Stylaster roseus,* at night arms open to feed.

BLUNT-ARMED SEA STAR
Asterina folium
CLASS:
Sea Stars
Asteroide

SIZE: $^1\!/_2$ -1 in.
DEPTH: 0 - 50 ft.

RED MINIATURE SEA STAR
Poraniella echinulata
CLASS:
Sea Stars
Asteroidea

SIZE: $^1\!/_2$ -1$^1\!/_4$ in.
DEPTH: 10 - 1,000 ft.

ROSE LACE CORAL BRITTLE STAR
Sigsbeia conifera
CLASS:
Brittle Stars
Ophiuroidae
FAMILY:
Hemieuryalidae

SIZE: Disc $^1\!/_8$ - $^3\!/_8$ in.
DEPTH: 15 - 100 ft.

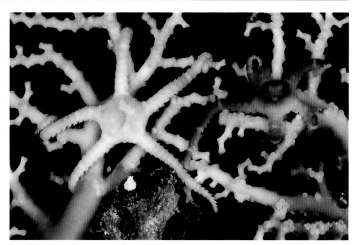

Brittle Stars

VISUAL ID: Numerous long, thin glassy spines cover arms. Distinct dark central line runs the length of arms. Yellow, brown, gray or black; color of arms and spines may be different.

ABUNDANCE & DISTRIBUTION: Common Caribbean, Bahamas; occasional to uncommon South Florida; also Bermuda and south to Brazil.

HABITAT & BEHAVIOR: Live on sponges, fire coral and occasionally gorgonians.

Sponge Brittle Star
Juvenile
Black and gray variety.

VISUAL ID: Reticulated network of fine dark lines on bone white to bluish disc. Arms whitish to pale yellow with brownish bands and short spines.

ABUNDANCE & DISTRIBUTION: Common central and South Florida, Bahamas, Caribbean; also Bermuda and south to Brazil.

HABITAT & BEHAVIOR: Inhabit sandy areas around reefs. Hide under slabs of coral and rubble.

SPONGE BRITTLE STAR
Ophiothrix suensonii

CLASS:
Brittle Stars
Ophiuroidea
ORDER:
Ophiurae

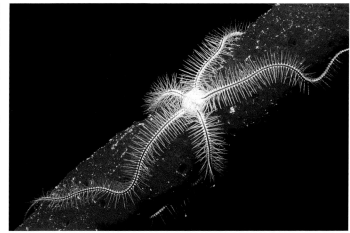

SIZE: Disc ¹/₂ - ³/₄ in.
Arms 2¹/₂ - 3¹/₂ in.
DEPTH: 10 - 200 ft.

Sponge Brittle Star
On Fire Coral.

RETICULATED BRITTLE STAR
Ophionereis reticulata

CLASS:
Brittle Stars
Ophiuroidea
ORDER:
Ophiurae

SIZE: Disc ¹/₂ - ³/₄ in.
DEPTH: 0 - 725 ft.

Brittle Stars

VISUAL ID: Numerous long, pointed spines cover arms. Distinctive, thin central stripe of pale pigment extends down arm, becoming more conspicuous near tip. Shades of brown.
ABUNDANCE & DISTRIBUTION: Uncommon Florida Keys, Bahamas, Northwest Caribbean.
HABITAT & BEHAVIOR: Inhabit fore reefs. Associate with living corals.

VISUAL ID: Heavy, blunt dorsal spines on arms, especially near disc. Mottled to banded brown, gray and black. Never show reddish hues.
ABUNDANCE & DISTRIBUTION: Common Florida, Bahamas, Caribbean; also Bermuda and south to Brazil.
HABITAT & BEHAVIOR: Inhabit reefs and areas of coral rubble. Hide under rocks and in dark recesses.
SIMILAR SPECIES: Red Brittle Star, *O. wendti,* dorsal spines long, thin and pointed. Usually has rust or reddish hues, occasionally bright red.

VISUAL ID: Red and cream bands on smooth arms. Disc may be solid, patterned or mottled with the same colors.
ABUNDANCE & DISTRIBUTION: Occasional South Florida, Bahamas, Caribbean.
HABITAT & BEHAVIOR: Inhabit deeper areas of fore reef. Forage about bottom in open at night. Have been observed, on rare occasions, climbing sea fans.

SPINY BRITTLE STAR
Ophiocoma paucigranulata
CLASS:
Brittle Stars
Ophiuroidea
ORDER:
Ophiurae

SIZE: Disc ³/₄ -1 in.
Arms 4 - 6 in.
DEPTH: 5 - 80 ft.

BLUNT-SPINED BRITTLE STAR
Ophiocoma echinata
CLASS:
Brittle Stars
Ophiuroidea
ORDER:
Ophiurae

SIZE: Disc ³/₄ -1¹/₄ in.
Arms 4 - 6 in.
DEPTH: 10 - 80 ft.

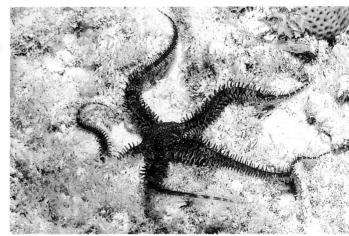

RUBY BRITTLE STAR
Ophioderma rubicundum
CLASS:
Brittle Stars
Ophiuroidea
ORDER:
Ophiurae

SIZE: Disc ¹/₂ - ³/₄ in.
Arms 3- 4 in.
DEPTH: 3 - 100 ft.

Brittle Stars

VISUAL ID: Arms usually banded gray and white, occasionally green or brown and white. Disc color variable, olive-green, gray, brown or white, often with white and/or black spots. Short spines give arms serrated appearance.

ABUNDANCE & DISTRIBUTION: Common Florida, Bahamas, Caribbean; also Bermuda, north to north Carolina and south to Brazil.

HABITAT & BEHAVIOR: Inhabit shallow to mid-range reefs. Hide under rocks, coral heads and in recesses.

SIMILAR SPECIES: Short-Armed Brittle Star, *O. brevicaudum,* relatively short, lightly banded arms, inhabit very shallow water areas of rubble. Short-Spined Brittle Star, *O. brevispinum,* disc shades of green, often green with banded arms, inhabit sea grass beds.

VISUAL ID: Pink disc, yellow arms. Colors may be bright and intense or pale.

ABUNDANCE & DISTRIBUTION: Occasional to rare Belize, Cayman Islands and Grand Turk.

HABITAT & BEHAVIOR: Inhabit deeper reefs and sloping drop-offs. Hide under rocks, coral heads and in recesses. Have been observed climbing sea plumes.

NOTE: This is a recently described species and its geographical distribution is not well-known. It is apparently rare or absent in most locations. Sightings should be reported to REEF at *www.reef.org.*

VISUAL ID: Ten circular radial shields (calcareous plates) with distinctive black outlines are arranged around the edge of the central disc. Arm plates have an irregular reticulate pattern, and small, blunt spines. Shades of gray to brown; arms often banded. Juveniles pale pink to rose or lavender.

ABUNDANCE & DISTRIBUTION: Occasional Florida, Bahamas, Caribbean; also south to Brazil.

HABITAT & BEHAVIOR: Wide range of habitats from mangrove estuaries to seagrass beds and coral reefs. Typically hide under rocks and in crevices and recesses.

BANDED-ARM BRITTLE STAR
Ophioderma appressum
CLASS:
Brittle Stars
Ophiuroidea
ORDER:
Ophiurae

SIZE: Disc $^3/_4$ -1 in.
Arms 4 - 6 in.
DEPTH: 0 - 160 ft.

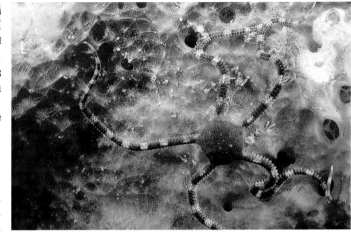

GAUDY BRITTLE STAR
Ophioderma ensiferum
CLASS:
Brittle Stars
Ophiuroidea
ORDER:
Ophiurae

SIZE: Disc $^1/_2$ - $^3/_4$ in.
Arms 3 - 4 in.
DEPTH: 50 - 100 ft.

CIRCLE MARKED BRITTLE STAR
Ophioderma cinereum
CLASS:
Brittle Stars
Ophiuroidea
ORDER:
Ophiurae

SIZE: Disc $^1/_2$ - $1^1/_4$ in.,
max. $1^1/_2$ in.
Arms 4 - 6 in.,
max. $8^1/_4$ in.
DEPTH: 0 - 80 ft.

Basket Stars

VISUAL ID: Reddish arms are finely banded and branch only once or twice.

ABUNDANCE & DISTRIBUTION: Occasional South Florida, Caribbean.

HABITAT & BEHAVIOR: Inhabit steep, deeper fore reefs. Large groups cling to gorgonians, especially sea rods. Wrap tightly around gorgonian during day, unfurling at night to feed.

VISUAL ID: Numerous thin, branched arms which, when extended, form a fan-shaped plankton net. Orange to tan to dark brown. Juveniles are usually tan and lavender [below right], but can also be black.

ABUNDANCE & DISTRIBUTION: Common South Florida, Bahamas, Caribbean; also north to North Carolina and south to Brazil.

HABITAT & BEHAVIOR: Inhabit reefs. Coil into a tight ball during day, and hide in dark recesses or attach to sponges and gorgonians. Feed at night by orienting to face current and spreading arms to filter planktonic animals.

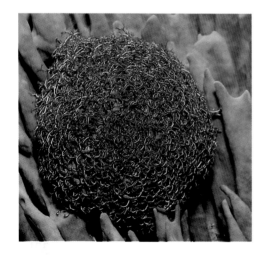

SEA ROD
BASKET STAR
Schizostella bifurcata

CLASS:
Basket Stars
Ophiuroidea
ORDER:
Phrynophiurida

SIZE: Disc ½ -1 in.
Arms 1 - 2 in.
DEPTH: 40 - 150 ft.

GIANT
BASKET STAR
Astrophyton muricatum

CLASS:
Basket Stars
Ophiuroidea
ORDER:
Phrynophiurida

SIZE: Disc 1 -1¾ in.
Arms 1 - 1½ ft.
DEPTH: 2 - 230 ft.

Giant Basket Star
Juvenile

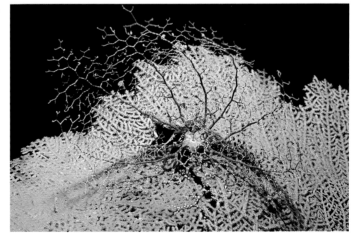

*Coiled daytime appearance
on Giant Barrel Sponge.*
[far left]

*Coiled daytime appearance
on Bipinnate Sea Plume.* [left]

Sea Urchins

VISUAL ID: Numerous long, thin, sharp spines. Usually all black, occasionally have some grayish white spines. Young have black and white banded spines.

ABUNDANCE & DISTRIBUTION: Abundant to common South Florida, Bahamas, Caribbean; also Bermuda and south to Brazil.

HABITAT & BEHAVIOR: Found in all habitats. Hide during day in sheltered locations. Feed in the open on algae at night.

EFFECT ON DIVERS: Spines easily puncture the skin and break off in the flesh, causing a painful wound. The embedded spines give off a purple dye, causing a slight discoloration under the skin. Treat area for infection; embedded spines will dissolve within a few days. Victim with numerous wounds may need treatment for shock.

NOTE: A Caribbean-wide epidemic in 1983-1984, which began near Panama and spread eastward, wiped out up 90 percent of populations across the region. The species is making a slow comeback.

VISUAL ID: Adults uniform dark purple or black. Spines much shorter and more slender than similar appearing Long Spine Urchin [previous]. Gaps between spines at joints of major plates. Juvenile [pictured] body is pinkish cream to tan, with spines of greenish tan, banded in reddish brown hues. Rows of brilliant blue spots near base of spines.

ABUNDANCE & DISTRIBUTION: Rare Florida, Caribbean; also north to South Carolina.

HABITAT & BEHAVIOR: Prefer deep-water habitats, rarely within depth range of scuba.

EFFECT ON DIVERS: Spines easily puncture the skin and break off in the flesh, causing a painful wound.

VISUAL ID: Pointed spines have violet to dark brown tips, greenish shaft and white ring around base. Body reddish to maroon.

ABUNDANCE & DISTRIBUTION: Occasional to uncommon South Florida, Bahamas, Caribbean.

HABITAT & BEHAVIOR: Inhabit shallower reefs. Hide during day in sheltered locations, often in Lettuce Coral, *Agaricia tenuifolia*. Feed on algae, in the open at night.

EFFECT ON DIVERS: Spines can produce puncture wound.

LONG-SPINED URCHIN
Diadema antillarum
CLASS:
Sea Urchins
Echinoidea
FAMILY:
Diadematidae

SIZE: Body 2 - 3 in.
Spines 4 - 8 in.
DEPTH: 0 - 165 ft.

MAGNIFICENT URCHIN
Astropyga magnifica
CLASS:
Sea Urchins
Echinoidea
FAMILY:
Diadematidae

SIZE: Body 2 - 5 $^3/_4$ in.
Spines 2$^1/_2$ - 4$^1/_2$ in.
DEPTH: 30 - 290 ft.

REEF URCHIN
Echinometra viridis
CLASS:
Sea Urchins
Echinoidea
FAMILY:
Echinometridae

SIZE: Body 1$^1/_4$ -2 in.
Spines 1 - 1$^1/_2$ in.
DEPTH: 0 - 130 ft.

Sea Urchins

VISUAL ID: Short, thick, pointed spines. Black to olive [pictured] to reddish brown and red.

ABUNDANCE & DISTRIBUTION: Common to uncommon Florida, Bahamas, Caribbean; also Bermuda, north to North Carolina and south to Brazil.

HABITAT & BEHAVIOR: Most common in shallow rocky and tidal areas, but occasionally much deeper. Bore holes in substrate, which they occupy during day. Feed on algae in the open (near their holes) at night.

EFFECT ON DIVERS: Spines can produce a puncture wound.

NOTE: Individuals in Caribbean tend to be much smaller than those in Florida.

Rock-Boring Urchin
Black color variation.

VISUAL ID: Long pointed spines with sharp tips. Variable from reddish gray to pale red, pale purple, pale brown and almost black.

ABUNDANCE & DISTRIBUTION: Two populations: (1) Occasional Massachusetts to Florida, Cuba and Gulf coast to Yucatan; (2) Occasional Panama to French Guiana and north to Barbados.

HABITAT & BEHAVIOR: Inhabit Turtle Grass and algae beds, coral reefs and rock, sand and rubble bottoms. Hide during day under rocks, rubble and other bottom debris, forage in open at night. (Similar appearing Rock-Boring Urchin [previous] distinguished during day by occupying bore holes in shallow limestone rock.)

ROCK-BORING URCHIN
Echinometra lucunter lucunter
CLASS:
Sea Urchins
Echinoidea
FAMILY:
Echinometridae

SIZE: Body 1¼ -3 in.
Spines ³/₄ - 1¼ in.
DEPTH: 0 - 150 ft.

Rock-Boring Urchin
Red color variation.

COMMON ARBACIA URCHIN
Arbacia punctulata
CLASS:
Sea Urchins
Echinoidea
FAMILY:
Echinometridae

SIZE: 2 - 4 in.
DEPTH: 0 - 750 ft.

Sea Urchins

VISUAL ID: Mixed in with spines are podia, and stalked, jaw-like structures that appear as purple balls. Body and spines usually white, occasionally green to brown.

ABUNDANCE & DISTRIBUTION: Occasional Caribbean; rare South Florida. Not reported Bahamas.

HABITAT & BEHAVIOR: Inhabit shallower reefs. Hide in sheltered locations, often around Staghorn Coral, *Acropora cervicornis,* and Lettuce Coral, *Agaricia tenuifolia.*

EFFECT ON DIVERS: Spines can produce puncture wound.

VISUAL ID: Densely covered with short spines, which part somewhat to form grooves at joints of major plates. Body and spines commonly white to green in Caribbean. May be red, purple, green, olive or white in Florida and Bahamas. Podia usually white.

ABUNDANCE & DISTRIBUTION: Common to occasional Florida, Bahamas, Caribbean; also Bermuda, north to North Carolina and south to Brazil.

HABITAT & BEHAVIOR: Inhabit sea grass beds and reefs. Often cover themselves with sea grass and other debris to shelter from light. The Squat Urchin Shrimp, *Gnathophyllodes mineri,* [pg. 183] lives among the urchins' spines.

EFFECT ON DIVERS: Spines can produce puncture wound.

JEWEL URCHIN
Lytechinus williamsi
CLASS:
Sea Urchins
Echinoidea
FAMILY:
Toxopneustidae

SIZE: Body 1 - 2 in.
Spines ½ -1¼ in.
DEPTH: 15 - 300 ft.

VARIEGATED URCHIN
Lytechinus variegatus
CLASS:
Sea Urchins
Echinoidea
FAMILY:
Toxopneustidae

SIZE: Body 2 - 3 in.
Spines ½ - ¾ in.
DEPTH: 0 - 164 ft.

Variegated Urchin
Color variations.

Sea Urchins – Heart Urchins

VISUAL ID: Densely covered with short, white spines. Body usually black, but can be dark purple or reddish brown.

ABUNDANCE & DISTRIBUTION: Abundant to uncommon Florida, Bahamas, Caribbean.

HABITAT & BEHAVIOR: Inhabit sea grass beds, occasionally on shallow reefs. Often cover themselves with sea grass and other debris.

NOTE: Numbers greatly reduced in some locations by natives who harvest them and eat their roe.

VISUAL ID: Thick, cylindrical, blunt spines. Body light to dark reddish brown. Spines often covered with various organisms and algae.

ABUNDANCE & DISTRIBUTION: Common to uncommon Florida, Bahamas, Caribbean; also north to North Carolina and south to Brazil.

HABITAT & BEHAVIOR: Inhabit sea grass beds, areas of reef rubble and reefs. Often hide in sheltered locations.

VISUAL ID: Elongate oval dome covered with tan hair-like spines; underside flat. Long, translucent needle-like spines extend from back.

ABUNDANCE & DISTRIBUTION: Occasional Florida, Bahamas, Caribbean; also south to Brazil.

HABITAT & BEHAVIOR: Inhabit sandy areas where seagrass and other growth is sparse or absent. A burrowing species rarely observed on the surface. Raise long spines defensively if disturbed.

WEST INDIAN SEA EGG

Tripneustes ventricosus

CLASS:
Sea Urchins
Echinoidea
FAMILY:
Toxopneustidae

SIZE: Body 4 - 5 in.
Spines ¹/₂ -³/₄ in.
DEPTH: 0 - 30 feet.

SLATE-PENCIL URCHIN

Eucidaris tribuloides

CLASS:
Sea Urchins
Echinoidea
FAMILY:
Cidaridas

SIZE: Body 1¹/₂ - 2 in.
Spines 1¹/₂ - 2 in.
DEPTH: 0 - 164 ft.

LONG-SPINED SEA BISCUIT

Plagiobrissus grandis

CLASS:
Echinoidea
ORDER:
Heart Urchins
Spatangoida
FAMILY:
Brissidae

SIZE: 4 - 7 in.,
max. 8 in.
DEPTH: 1 - 210 ft.

Heart Urchins – Sand Dollars

VISUAL ID: Dome-shaped with flat underside and pentagonal petal design on back. Densely covered with short, brown spines.

ABUNDANCE & DISTRIBUTION: Common Florida, Bahamas, Caribbean.

HABITAT & BEHAVIOR: Inhabit sandy areas, often around reefs. Burrow beneath sand during day, may emerge at night. Heart Urchin Pea Crab, *Dissodactylus primitivus,* [pg. 215] lives within the protection of its spines. Broken remains are often on sand.

VISUAL ID: Large brown to red-brown biscuit-shaped body with raised pentagonal petal design on back. Body covered with short, close set spines.

ABUNDANCE & DISTRIBUTION: Common to occasional South Florida, Gulf of Mexico and Caribbean.

HABITAT & BEHAVIOR: Most commonly inhabit shallow Turtle Grass, *Thalassia testudinum,* beds and adjacent areas of sand and rubble. Usually cover body with grass blades and fragments of rock and shell rubble, but do not burrow beneath surface as similar-appearing Red Heart Urchin [previous].

VISUAL ID: Disc-shaped. (Unlike similar species, has no notches in disc margin and no holes in body.) Densely covered with fine spines. Pentagonal petal design on back. Living specimens are shades of brown; shells of dead specimens are gray.

ABUNDANCE & DISTRIBUTION: Occasional Florida, Bahamas, Caribbean; also north to North Carolina and south to Brazil.

HABITAT & BEHAVIOR: Inhabit shallow, sandy areas around reefs. Burrow beneath sand during day, occasionally come out at night. Broken remains are often on sand.

RED HEART URCHIN
Meoma ventricosa
ventricosa

CLASS:
Echinoidea
ORDER:
Heart Urchins
Spatangoida
FAMILY:
Brissidae

SIZE: 4 - 6 in.
DEPTH: 3 - 130 ft.

INFLATED SEA BISCUIT
Clypeaster rosaceus

CLASS:
Sea Urchins
Echinoidea
FAMILY:
**Sea Biscuits &
Sand Dollars**
Clypeasteridae

SIZE: 4 - 8 in.
DEPTH: 0 - 935 ft.

SAND DOLLAR
Clypeaster subdepressus

CLASS:
Echinoidea
ORDER:
Sand Dollars
Clypeasteroida

SIZE: 3 - 4 in.,
6 in. max.
DEPTH: 0 - 104 ft.

Sand Dollars

VISUAL ID: Disc has a single elongated oval hole in body between the two slightly longer petals of the pentagonal petal design on back. Two conspicuous notches in disc margin opposite these petals with three smaller indentations opposite the three shorter petals. Living specimens are dark brown to dark purple and densely covered with fine spines.

ABUNDANCE & DISTRIBUTION: North Carolina south to Florida, Bahamas and Gulf of Mexico.

HABITAT & BEHAVIOR: Inhabit areas of course sand, gravel, or crushed shell rubble. Burrow beneath surface during day, occasionally in open at night. Broken remains are often on sand.

SIMILAR SPECIES: Notched Key-Hole Sand Dollar, *E. michelini,* is distinguished by five notches of equal size in disc margin. N.C. to Florida, Gulf of Mexico and Cozumel, but not reported in Bahamas. Five-Notched Sand Dollar, *E. emarginata,* has five notches in disc around margin, and a single oval hole through body; Caribbean.

VISUAL ID: Disc has five, elongated oval holes. Pentagonal petal design on back. Living specimens are shades of yellow-brown to brown or gray and densely covered with fine spines.

ABUNDANCE & DISTRIBUTION: Occasional Caribbean; also, south to Brazil.

HABITAT & BEHAVIOR: Inhabit shallow sandy areas around reefs. Burrow beneath sand during day, occasionally in open at night. Broken remains are often on sand.

SIMILAR SPECIES: Two very similar species are best distinguished by location. *M. isometra* Massachusetts to south Florida and Bahamas, but not Florida Keys. *M. tenuis* eastern Gulf of Mexico.

VISUAL ID: Disc-shaped with six, elongated oval holes in body. Densely covered with fine spines. Pentagonal petal design on back. Living specimens are shades of brown; young silvery gray; dead specimens are gray.

ABUNDANCE & DISTRIBUTION: Occasional Florida, Bahamas, Caribbean; also north to North Carolina and south to Uruguay.

HABITAT & BEHAVIOR: Inhabit shallow sandy areas around reefs. Burrow beneath sand during day, occasionally in open at night. Broken remains are often on sand.

NOTE: Formerly classified in genus *Mellita.*

NOTCHED SAND DOLLAR
Encope aberrans
CLASS:
Sea Urchins
Echinoidea
FAMILY:
Sand Dollars
Mellitidae

SIZE: 3 - 6 in.
DEPTH: 30 - 300 ft.

FIVE-KEYHOLE
SAND DOLLAR
Mellita quinquiesperforata
CLASS:
Sea Urchins
Echinoidea
FAMILY:
Sand Dollars
Mellitidae

SIZE: 3 - 6 in.
DEPTH: 3 - 150 ft.

SIX-KEYHOLE
SAND DOLLAR
Leodia sexiesperforata
CLASS:
Echinoidea
ORDER:
Sand Dollars
Clypeasteroida

SIZE: 2 - 3½ in.,
4 in max.
DEPTH: 0 - 80 ft.

Sea Cucumbers

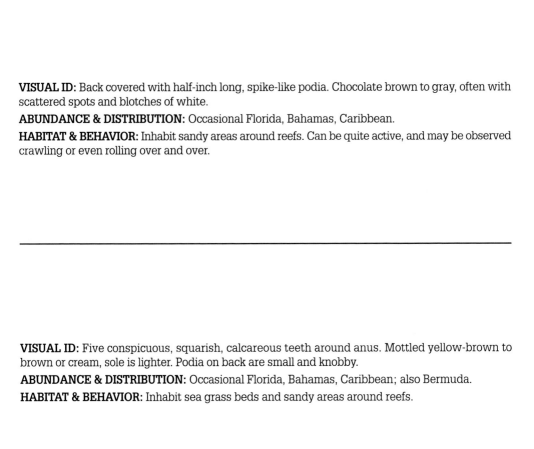

VISUAL ID: Back covered with half-inch long, spike-like podia. Chocolate brown to gray, often with scattered spots and blotches of white.
ABUNDANCE & DISTRIBUTION: Occasional Florida, Bahamas, Caribbean.
HABITAT & BEHAVIOR: Inhabit sandy areas around reefs. Can be quite active, and may be observed crawling or even rolling over and over.

VISUAL ID: Five conspicuous, squarish, calcareous teeth around anus. Mottled yellow-brown to brown or cream, sole is lighter. Podia on back are small and knobby.
ABUNDANCE & DISTRIBUTION: Occasional Florida, Bahamas, Caribbean; also Bermuda.
HABITAT & BEHAVIOR: Inhabit sea grass beds and sandy areas around reefs.

VISUAL ID: Large cone-like podia on back. Reddish brown to tan, podia often a lighter shade.
ABUNDANCE & DISTRIBUTION: Uncommon Caribbean.
HABITAT & BEHAVIOR: Inhabit reef rubble patches and sandy areas around reefs.

FURRY
SEA CUCUMBER
Astichopus multifidus

CLASS:
Sea Cucumbers
Holothuroidea

SIZE: 10 - 16 in.
DEPTH: 10 - 120 ft.

FIVE-TOOTHED
SEA CUCUMBER
Actinopygia agassizii

CLASS:
Sea Cucumbers
Holothuroidea

SIZE: 8 - 10 in.
DEPTH: 0 - 125 ft.

CONICAL
SEA CUCUMBER
Eostichopus arnesoni

CLASS:
Sea Cucumbers
Holothuroidea

SIZE: 10 - 16 in.
DEPTH: 25 - 75 ft.

391

Sea Cucumbers

VISUAL ID: Three rows of podia on sole, the center row is wider and split by a seam. Earth-tone colors and patterns highly variable. Small, knob-like podia on back are often a contrasting shade or color.

ABUNDANCE & DISTRIBUTION: Occasional Florida, Bahamas, Caribbean; also Bermuda, north to South Carolina and south to Brazil.

HABITAT & BEHAVIOR: Inhabit sea grass beds, shallow reef rubble patches, and sandy areas around reefs.

**Three-Rowed
Sea Cucumber**
Color variation.

**Three-Rowed
Sea Cucumber**
Color variation.

THREE-ROWED SEA CUCUMBER

Isostichopus badionotus

CLASS:
Sea Cucumbers
Holothuroidea

SIZE: 10 - 16 in.
DEPTH: 0 - 200 ft.

**Three-Rowed
Sea Cucumber
Juvenile**

**Three-Rowed
Sea Cucumber**
Color variation.

Sea Cucumbers

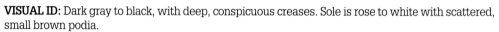

VISUAL ID: Dark gray to black, with deep, conspicuous creases. Sole is rose to white with scattered, small brown podia.

ABUNDANCE & DISTRIBUTION: Common Caribbean; occasional Bahamas; uncommon Florida Keys.

HABITAT & BEHAVIOR: Inhabit sea grass beds and sandy areas around reefs. Most common between 10 - 35 feet.

VISUAL ID: Thin, elongated body, often somewhat flask-shaped. Thin podia on back, and long, disc-tipped podia on sole. Variable coloration, may be yellow, reddish orange, brown, gray or purplish.

ABUNDANCE & DISTRIBUTION: Uncommon Florida, Bahamas, Caribbean, also circumtropical.

HABITAT & BEHAVIOR: Inhabit reefs and areas of reef rubble.

VISUAL ID: Maroon to red or yellowish red undercolor with brown mottling; upper body covered with small tube feet and numerous cone-shaped papillae that may be white with yellow tips. Distinctly flattened sole with numerous tube feet, often with yellow to yellowish tips.

ABUNDANCE & DISTRIBUTION: Occasional Florida, Bahamas, Caribbean; also south to southern Brazil.

HABITAT & BEHAVIOR: Occur in a variety of habitats from shallow lagoons where marine grasses are abundant to hard rock substrates and coral reefs. The numerous tube feet on the sole tenaciously grip hard substrates.

NOTE: Identification is tentative due to variations in color, markings. A microscopic examination of ossicles (skeletal elements embedded in the skin) is required for positive identification.

DONKEY DUNG
SEA CUCUMBER
Holothuria mexicana

CLASS:
Sea Cucumbers
Holothuroidea

SIZE: 10 - 14 in.
DEPTH: 0 - 120 ft.

SLENDER
SEA CUCUMBER
Holothuria impatiens

CLASS:
Sea Cucumbers
Holothuroidea

SIZE: 8 - 12 in.
DEPTH: 2 - 90 ft.

HARLEQUIN
SEA CUCUMBER
Holothuria grisea

CLASS:
Sea Cucumbers
Holothuroidea

SIZE: 6 - 8 in.,
max. 10 in.
DEPTH: 2 - 40 ft.

Sea Cucumbers

VISUAL ID: Slender, tubular body tapers significantly toward ends; body has numerous folds and is covered with conical podia often with pointed tips. Color ranges from uniform shades of light to dark gray, brown, yellow, or red or can be mottled or blotched.

ABUNDANCE & DISTRIBUTION: Occasional but can be locally abundant, central east coast Florida to Florida Bay, Bahamas and Caribbean.

HABITAT & BEHAVIOR: Inhabit shallow sand flats, seagrass beds, algae patches and mangrove forests.

VISUAL ID: Brownish to grayish white with two rows of light to dark brown blotches on back (often obscured by thin layer of sand grains coating body). Thick body near center tapers slightly to bluntly rounded ends. Numerous small poda cover body.

ABUNDANCE & DISTRIBUTION: Occasional Florida, Bahamas, Caribbean; also Bermuda.

HABITAT & BEHAVIOR: Inhabit shallow sandy rubble areas. Cryptic; cling to the underside of rocks, sponges coral rubble and other debris, occasionally burrow beneath rocks.

VISUAL ID: Mouth surrounded by eight long, slender, highly branched tentacles and a single shorter pair about $1/3$ to $1/4$ the length of longer tentacles. The cylindrical curved body is usually hidden from view.

ABUNDANCE & DISTRIBUTION: Uncommon Central and South Florida and Caribbean; also, Bermuda and south to Brazil.

HABITAT & BEHAVIOR: Wide range of habitats from soft sediment bottoms to areas of rocky rubble to reefs. Burrow into soft sediments or tenacious cling with tube feet to the underside of rocks in rubble areas; on reefs wedge into small cracks and holes. Tentacles extend to snag drifting food and are alternately inserted into mouth to remove catch.

FLORIDA SEA CUCUMBER
Holothuria floridana

CLASS:
Sea Cucumbers
Holothuroidea

SIZE: 3 - 8 in.,
max. 10 in.
DEPTH: 3 - 15 ft.

GRUB SEA CUCUMBER
Holothuria cubana

CLASS:
Sea Cucumbers
Holothuroidea

SIZE: 2 - 4 in.,
max. 6 in.
DEPTH: 0 - 30 ft.

HIDDEN SEA CUCUMBER
Pseudothyone belli

CLASS:
Sea Cucumbers
Holothuroidea

SIZE: ¹/₂ - 1 in.,
max. 2 in.
DEPTH: 0 - 120 ft.

Sea Cucumbers

VISUAL ID: Long, worm-like, body appears to be segmented with three large bead-like knobs on each. A mop-like crown of long, thick, feathery tentacles usually extends from around mouth. Shades of gray, brown, green or yellow, often with light and/or dark stripes and, occasionally, variegated with small white blotches. Body soft and fragile, skin sticky. They have no tube feet.

ABUNDANCE & DISTRIBUTION: Occasional South Florida, Bahamas, Caribbean.

HABITAT & BEHAVIOR: Hide under coral slabs, rubble and in recesses during the day. Often in open at night.

REACTION TO DIVERS: Highly contractile, when disturbed constrict dramatically. Will stick if touched.

**Tiger Tail
Sea Cucumber**
*Entire animal
exposed at night.*

VISUAL ID: Long, thin body extends from recess in reef. Mouth, on underside, has short, ruffled tentacles. Mottled brown to cream. Scattered, pointed podia.

ABUNDANCE & DISTRIBUTION: Occasional Florida, Bahamas, Caribbean.

HABITAT & BEHAVIOR: Inhabit coral reefs. Posterior firmly attaches in recess, while oral end of elongated body extends out, sweeping the reef for food, primarily at night. When disturbed, rapidly retracts body into recess.

BEADED SEA CUCUMBER

Euapta lappa

CLASS:
Sea Cucumbers
Holothuroidea

SIZE: 10 - 15 in.,
max 3 ft.
DEPTH: 0 - 80 ft.

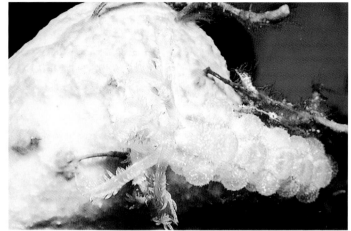

Beaded Sea Cucumber

Color variation.

TIGER TAIL SEA CUCUMBER

Holothuria thomasi

CLASS:
Sea Cucumbers
Holothuroidea

SIZE: 3 - 6 ft.
DEPTH: 10 - 100 ft.

Phylum Chordata
Subphylum Urochordata

(Core-DOT-uh / Gr. string / Your-oh-CORE-dot-uh / Gr. tail string)

Tunicates

Most chordates have backbones and are called vertebrates; urochordates do not have backbones, but are included because they have four important characteristics that are shared by all members of the phylum — at some point in their life cycle all have a tail, dorsal central nerve cord, pharyngeal gill clefts and notochord. The latter functions as a support system for the dorsal nerve cord and is replaced by bone in vertebrates. The subphylum's common name, tunicate, comes from a body covering of cellulose material called a **tunic**.

Tunicates

CLASS: Ascidiacea (Ah-sid-EE-aa-see-uh / Gr. little bottle)

Although tunicates are among the most common marine invertebrates, they are probably the least recognized. In most cases, they are simply overlooked, ignored or mistaken for sponges. They are attached to the substrate at one end; at the opposite end they have two siphons. Water is drawn in through the **spore** or buccal **siphon,** pumped through a **gill net** in the body, where food and oxygen are extracted, and then discharged through an **excurrent** or atrial **siphon**. Body shape, as well as size, varies considerably among species; some are only a quarter inch in length while others may exceed five inches. Tunicates come in a dazzling array of colors that is often enhanced by a translucent quality of the tunic.

When the animal is disturbed, muscular bands rapidly close the siphons. This ability easily distinguishes tunicates from sponges, which either cannot close their openings, or do so very slowly. In spite of their sponge-like appearance, tunicates are complicated animals with nervous, digestive, reproductive and circulatory systems.

Solitary tunicates are called **simple ascidians,** and include most of the larger species. Many of the smaller species grow in varying degrees of colonialism and are called **compound tunicates.** In some species individuals are joined only at their bases, while in more intimate associations, numerous individuals are completely embedded in a **common tunic** and the individuals are recognizable only by their two siphons. The most specialized colonies are those in which the individuals are not only imbedded in a common tunic, but their excurrent siphons open into a large common chamber or cloaca. Some of these colonies form geometric designs with the **incurrent siphons** evenly spaced around a **central outflow opening** or cloacal orifice. Others have incurrent siphons scattered randomly around larger **outflow openings.** Compound colonies often cover an area, appearing much like an encrusting sponge.

Pelagic Tunicates

CLASS: Thaliacea (Thal-ee-AA-see-uh / Gr. to flourish or bloom)

Members of this class are pelagic, free-swimming tunicates found in open water that occasionally swim over reefs. They are translucent-to-transparent animals thatresemble a jet engine pod in both appearance and function. The **incurrent** or buccal and **excurrent** or atrial **siphons** are at opposite ends of the pod. Water is pushed through the body by muscular contractions, moving the animal by water jet propulsion. Orange **cerebral ganglions** can usually be seen at the top, near the buccal siphon.

Members of the genera Salpa and Doliolumn are solitary adults that reproduce by asexual budding. Occasionally, buds are seen connected in long chains or other patterns. When mature, an individual detaches and swims free.

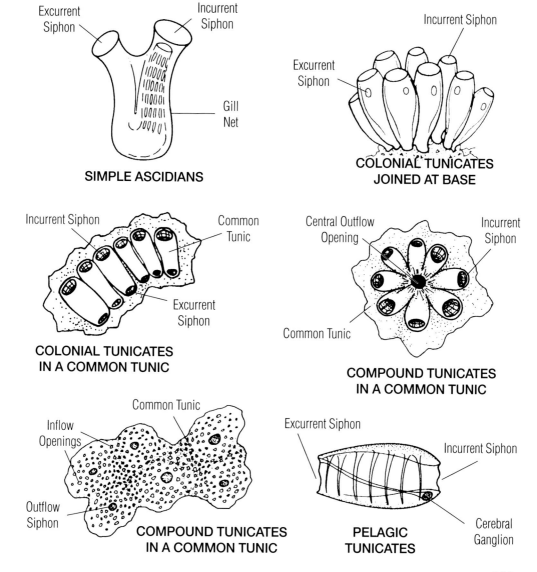

Excurrent Siphon — Incurrent Siphon — Gill Net

SIMPLE ASCIDIANS

Incurrent Siphon — Excurrent Siphon

COLONIAL TUNICATES JOINED AT BASE

Incurrent Siphon — Common Tunic — Excurrent Siphon

COLONIAL TUNICATES IN A COMMON TUNIC

Central Outflow Opening — Incurrent Siphon — Common Tunic

COMPOUND TUNICATES IN A COMMON TUNIC

Common Tunic — Inflow Openings — Outflow Siphon

COMPOUND TUNICATES IN A COMMON TUNIC

Excurrent Siphon — Incurrent Siphon — Cerebral Ganglion

PELAGIC TUNICATES

Tunicates

VISUAL ID: Lavender to dark purple or brown, may appear black at depth. Heavy, thick, gelatinous body. Solitary.

ABUNDANCE & DISTRIBUTION: Occasional South Florida, Bahamas, Caribbean.

HABITAT & BEHAVIOR: Inhabit coral reefs. Hide most of body in tight crevice or hole, exposing only small part of upper body and siphons.

REACTION TO DIVERS: Relatively unafraid; close siphons only when closely approached or molested.

VISUAL ID: Body globular, with two large protruding siphons. Just inside the incurrent siphon is a ring of bristle-like, unbranched tentacles. Mottled in shades of brown.

ABUNDANCE & DISTRIBUTION: Occasional South Florida, Bahamas, Caribbean.

HABITAT & BEHAVIOR: Inhabit coral reefs. Their bodies are often covered and camouflaged by algae.

REACTION TO DIVERS: Shy; close siphons and contract body when approached.

SIMILAR SPECIES: Two species, without common names, *Microcosmus exasperatus* and *Pyura vittata*, can be distinguished from the Giant Tunicate by the branched tentacles inside their incurrent siphon.

VISUAL ID: Long tubular incurrent siphon extends from crevice or recess in reef. Yellow to yellow-green to green to gray-green.

ABUNDANCE & DISTRIBUTION: Occasional Caribbean.

HABITAT & BEHAVIOR: Inhabit reefs. Hide bodies and excurrent siphons in crevices or recesses.

REACTION TO DIVERS: Somewhat shy; close incurrent siphon when approached, but rarely retract unless molested.

REEF TUNICATE
Rhopalaea abdominalis
CLASS:
Tunicates
Ascidiacea

SIZE: $^3/_4$ - 1 $^1/_2$ in.
DEPTH: 25 - 75 ft.

GIANT TUNICATE
Polycarpa spongiabilis
CLASS:
Tunicates
Ascidiacea

SIZE: 3 - 4 in.
DEPTH: 25 - 100 ft.

GREEN TUBE TUNICATE
Ascidia sydneiensis
CLASS:
Tunicates
Ascidiacea

SIZE: Siphon
length 2 - 4 in.,
width $^3/_4$ - 1 $^1/_2$ in.
DEPTH: 30 - 130 ft.

Tunicates

VISUAL ID: Bodies transparent and often shaded with white, red or purple. On occasionally translucent. Siphon rims and internal body parts are typically carmine to purple, although there may be some variations.

ABUNDANCE & DISTRIBUTION: Common to occasional Florida, Bahamas, Caribbean.

HABITAT & BEHAVIOR: Inhabit reefs and walls. Grow in clusters ranging from a few individuals to nearly 1,000. Often attach to gorgonians, black coral trees and sponges.

REACTION TO DIVERS: Relatively unafraid; close siphons only when closely approached or molested.

NOTE: May have other color phases not reported in scientific literature.

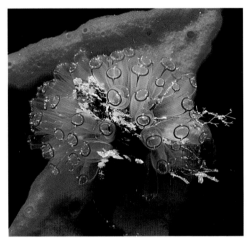

VISUAL ID: Bodies dense blue, siphon rims white. Smallest member of this genus in Caribbean.

ABUNDANCE & DISTRIBUTION: Occasional Caribbean.

HABITAT & BEHAVIOR: Inhabit reefs.

REACTION TO DIVERS: Relatively unafraid; close siphons only when closely approached or molested.

NOTE: May have other color phases not reported in scientific literature; for example, the first picture on next page appears to be a greenish yellow variety of this species.

PAINTED TUNICATE
Clavelina picta
CLASS:
Tunicates
Ascidiacea

SIZE: $^1/_2$ - $^3/_4$ in.
DEPTH: 15 - 100 ft

Painted Tunicate
Color variations.

BLUE BELL TUNICATE
Clavelina puerto-secensis
CLASS:
Tunicates
Ascidiacea

SIZE: $^1/_4$ - $^1/_2$ in.
DEPTH: 20 - 100 ft.

Tunicates

VISUAL ID: Members of this genus can generally be identified by their shape, location of siphons, and trait of growing in clusters. Colors and markings of many species, however, are neither consistent or well established in scientific literature. Positive identification requires microscopic examination of internal body parts.

ABUNDANCE & DISTRIBUTION: Common Florida, Bahamas, Caribbean.

HABITAT & BEHAVIOR: Inhabit reefs and attach to a variety of substrate.

NOTE: Pictured specimens, opposite, are possibly a color variety of Blue Bell Tunicate [previous page]; and specimens, on right page below, are probably a color variety of Painted Tunicate [previous page].

VISUAL ID: Bodies and internal parts transparent to translucent orange, occasionally yellow or pink. Both siphons protrude from top. Grow in clusters ranging from several to hundreds of individuals.

ABUNDANCE & DISTRIBUTION: Common Florida, Bahamas, Caribbean.

HABITAT & BEHAVIOR: Inhabit areas of mangrove and turtle grass, occasionally on shallow reefs. Attach to roots of mangroves, stems of turtle grass. On reefs they attach to gorgonians, sponges and areas of dead coral.

REACTION TO DIVERS: Relatively unafraid; close siphons only when closely approached or molested.

NOTE: A few Painted Tunicates [previous page] in shades of red and lavender are also in photograph.

BULB TUNICATES
Clavelina sp.
CLASS:
Tunicates
Ascidiacea

SIZE: ¹/₄ - ³/₄ in.
DEPTH: 15 - 130 ft.

Bulb Tunicates
Color variations.

MANGROVE TUNICATE
Ecteinascidia turbinata
CLASS:
Tunicates
Ascidiacea

SIZE: ¹/₂ - 1 in.
DEPTH: 1 - 40 ft.

Tunicates

VISUAL ID: Tiny individuals grow in clusters, their tunics joining at the bases to form a common tunic that encrusts areas of the substrate. Reported to be yellow-green, green, orange and purple. May have other color varieties. Interiors of siphons are often contrasting shades or colors.

ABUNDANCE & DISTRIBUTION: Common Florida, Bahamas, Caribbean.

HABITAT & BEHAVIOR: Inhabit reefs and walls. Often encrust areas of dead coral and the surface of large sponges.

REACTION TO DIVERS: Unafraid; close siphons only when molested.

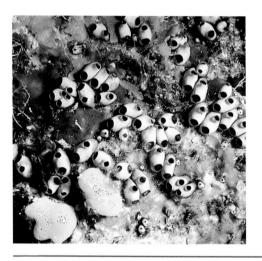 

VISUAL ID: Small individuals with thick tunics growing in close association are distinctive of this species. Usually brown upper body, paler below, any intervening tunic tissue also pale. Occasionally pale siphons and mottled.

ABUNDANCE & DISTRIBUTION: Occasional Florida, Bahamas, Caribbean.

HABITAT & BEHAVIOR: Inhabit reefs. Often attach in areas of dead coral and shipwrecks. Frequently covered and camouflaged by algae.

REACTION TO DIVERS: Relatively unafraid; close siphons only when closely approached or molested.

NOTE: Identification is tentative. Because there are several similar appearing genera and species, positive identification requires microscopic examination of internal body parts.

ENCRUSTING SOCIAL TUNICATES
Symplegma viride

CLASS:
Tunicates
Ascidiacea

SIZE: $\frac{1}{4}$ in.
DEPTH: 15 - 100 ft.

Encrusting Social Tunicates
Color variations.

MOTTLED SOCIAL TUNICATES
Polyandrocarpa tumida

CLASS:
Tunicates
Ascidiacea

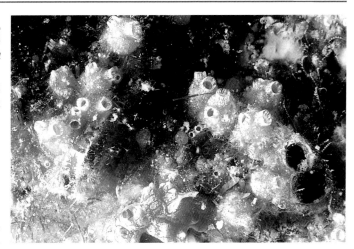

SIZE: $\frac{1}{4}$ - $\frac{1}{2}$ in.
DEPTH: 25 - 75 ft.

Tunicates

VISUAL ID: Numerous small individuals embedded in a firm, common berry-like, tunic that attaches to the substrate by a short stalk. Vary from violet to red to orange. Individuals are recognizable only by their two siphon openings that are often outlined in a darker shade.
ABUNDANCE & DISTRIBUTION: Occasional Florida, Bahamas, Caribbean.
HABITAT & BEHAVIOR: Inhabit reefs. Often grow in areas of dead coral and algae.
REACTION TO DIVERS: Unafraid; close siphons only when molested.
NOTE: This growth form of the genus is probably an undescribed species. It is closely related and could possibly be the same as an Indo-Pacific species.

VISUAL ID: Numerous small individuals embedded in a black, firm, globular common tunic. Individuals are recognizable only by their two siphon openings that protrude slightly from the surface, and are outlined with white.
ABUNDANCE & DISTRIBUTION: Occasional Florida, Bahamas, Caribbean.
HABITAT & BEHAVIOR: Inhabit reefs. Often grow in areas of dead coral and algae.
REACTION TO DIVERS: Unafraid; close siphons only when molested.
NOTE: Identification is tentative. Because there are several similar appearing genera and species, positive identification requires microscopic examination of internal body parts.

VISUAL ID: Numerous small tunicates embedded in a white, firm, globular common tunic. Each individual forms slight depression in the surface of the colony and can be recognized by the two siphon openings that protrude slightly.
ABUNDANCE & DISTRIBUTION: Occasional Florida, Bahamas, Caribbean.
HABITAT & BEHAVIOR: Inhabit reefs. Often grow in areas of dead coral and algae.
REACTION TO DIVERS: Unafraid; close siphons only when molested.
NOTE: Identification of genus is tentative, could also be *Polycitor* or *Stomozoa*. Because of the similarity in appearance of these genera and many similar species, positive identification requires microscopic examination of internal body parts.

STRAWBERRY TUNICATE
Eudistoma sp.
CLASS:
Tunicates
Ascidiacea

SIZE: Colony 1 - 1 ½ in.
DEPTH: 20 - 100 ft.

BLACK CONDOMINIUM TUNICATE
Eudistoma obscuratum
CLASS:
Tunicates
Ascidiacea

SIZE: Colony 1 - 4 in.
DEPTH: 25 - 75 ft.

WHITE CONDOMINIUM TUNICATES
Eudistoma sp.
CLASS:
Tunicates
Ascidiacea

SIZE: Colony 1 - 4 in.
DEPTH: 25 - 75 ft.

Tunicates

VISUAL ID: Brick red with yellow markings is characteristic of this species, although they are also reported in a wide range of colors, from black to bright orange. Tiny, elongated individuals growing in a common tunic cluster around central outflow openings. Each individual can be recognized by the small opening of its incurrent siphon.

ABUNDANCE & DISTRIBUTION: Occasional Florida, Bahamas, Caribbean.

HABITAT & BEHAVIOR: Colonies encrust areas of dead coral, shipwrecks, dock pilings and even turtle grass blades.

REACTION TO DIVERS: Unafraid; close siphons only when molested.

VISUAL ID: Several species of this genus can be recognized by their long, curved and meandering rows of individuals on either side of hallway-like central chambers that have occasional outflow openings. These rows often form circular patterns with centers composed of translucent tunic. Usually brightly colored, often orange of green. In the margin of the colony tiny, finger-shaped blood vessels, may be discernable, radiating toward the edge.

ABUNDANCE & DISTRIBUTION: Occasional Florida, Bahamas, Caribbean.

HABITAT & BEHAVIOR: Colonies encrust areas of dead coral, shipwrecks, dock pilings and gorgonian stalks.

REACTION TO DIVERS: Generally unafraid; close siphons only when molested.

NOTE: Because there are several similar appearing species in a variety of colors and patterns, positive identification requires microscopic examination of internal body parts.

VISUAL ID: Members of this genus are somewhat elongated, grow in a common tunic, and cluster in circular patterns around central outflow openings. Each individual can be recognized by the small opening of its incurrent siphon. The arrangement of individuals in the tunic and their color patterns often form geometric designs. Colors and markings of many species are not consistent or well established in scientific literature. Positive identification requires microscopic examination of internal body parts.

ABUNDANCE & DISTRIBUTION: Occasional Florida, Bahamas, Caribbean.

HABITAT & BEHAVIOR: Colonies encrust areas of dead coral, shipwrecks, dock pilings and gorgonian stalks.

REACTION TO DIVERS: Generally unafraid; close siphons only when molested.

FLAT TUNICATE
Botrylloides nigrum
CLASS:
Tunicates
Ascidiacea

SIZE: ¹/₄ in. or less.
DEPTH: 3 - 100 ft.

ROW ENCRUSTING TUNICATES
Botrylloides sp.
CLASS:
Tunicates
Ascidiacea

SIZE: ¹/₄ in. or less
DEPTH: 5 - 100 ft.

GEOMETRIC ENCRUSTING TUNICATES
Botryllus sp.
CLASS:
Tunicates
Ascidiacea

SIZE: ¹/₄ in. or less
DEPTH: 5 - 100 ft.

Tunicates

VISUAL ID: Mottled in a variety of colors including shades of brown, pink, red, and even blue. The colonies form cushions that are soft, not firm like those of genus Eudistoma [pg. 411]. Tiny individuals, growing in a common tunic, form circular or ovular patterns around central outflow openings. Each individual can be recognized by the small opening of its incurrent siphon.

ABUNDANCE & DISTRIBUTION: Occasional Florida, Bahamas, Caribbean.

HABITAT & BEHAVIOR: Colonies encrust areas of dead coral, shipwrecks, some species of living coral and gorgonian stalks.

REACTION TO DIVERS: Unafraid; close siphons only when molested.

VISUAL ID: Tiny individuals, in a common tunic, form circular or ovular patterns around a single outflow opening. These orange or purple button-like colonies usually grow in small clusters.

ABUNDANCE & DISTRIBUTION: Occasional Florida, Bahamas, Caribbean.

HABITAT & BEHAVIOR: Inhabit reefs. Encrust areas of dead coral, often between encrusting colonies of sponge.

REACTION TO DIVERS: Relatively unafraid; close siphons only when closely approached or molested.

VISUAL ID: Numerous tiny individuals are embedded in a soft, thin, globular tunic. Their excurrent siphons empty into a swollen, interior chamber that has random, large, outflow openings. Has many color varieties including yellow, orange, green, brown, and gray. Other unreported color varieties are possible. Usually has white outlines around the tiny incurrent siphons. Only this genus in the Family Didemnidae [next page] lacks spicules in their tunic which accounts for the soft structure. May appear, at first glance, as an encrusting sponge; note the visual similarity to red encrusting sponge in the photograph.

ABUNDANCE & DISTRIBUTION: Common Caribbean.

HABITAT & BEHAVIOR: Inhabit reefs. Encrust in protected areas, often under ledge overhangs and in shallow depressions on walls.

REACTION TO DIVERS: Unafraid; when molested, close siphons and dramatically deflate and retract.

414

MOTTLED ENCRUSTING TUNICATE
Distaplia bermudensis
CLASS:
Tunicates
Ascidiacea

SIZE: ¼ in. or less
DEPTH: 25 - 65 ft.

BUTTON TUNICATES
Distaplia corolla
CLASS:
Tunicates
Ascidiacea

SIZE: ¼ in. or less.
DEPTH: 25 - 75 ft.

GLOBULAR ENCRUSTING TUNICATE
Diplosoma glandulosum
CLASS:
Tunicates
Ascidiacea

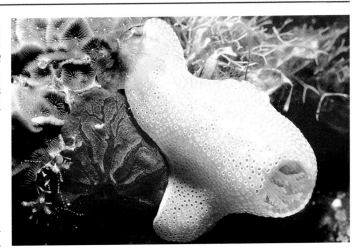

SIZE: Colonies 1 - 4 in.
DEPTH: 25 - 100 ft.

Tunicates

VISUAL ID: Distinguished from many similar appearing species by dense spicules embedded in the tunic that appear as tiny, white specks over the surface. Commonly orange, occasionally white. Numerous individuals are embedded in the thin, encrusting tunic. Their excurrent siphons empty into an interior chamber that has one or several outflow openings. Those with multiple outflow openings often form meandering chains. May appear, at first glance, as an encrusting sponge.

ABUNDANCE & DISTRIBUTION: Common Caribbean; occasional South Florida, Bahamas.

HABITAT & BEHAVIOR: Inhabit coral reefs. Attach to a variety of substrate, especially common on Orange Elephant Ear Sponges [pg. 53].

REACTION TO DIVERS: Unafraid; when molested, close siphons and dramatically deflate and retract.

VISUAL ID: Dark gray. Numerous tiny individuals are embedded in a soft, thin tunic. Their excurrent siphons empty into an inflated internal chamber that has random, large outflow openings. Dark, tiny incurrent siphons are scattered over the surface of the tunic. May appear, at first glance, as an encrusting sponge.

ABUNDANCE & DISTRIBUTION: Occasional Caribbean.

HABITAT & BEHAVIOR: Inhabit reefs. Encrust protected areas, often under ledge overhangs and in shallow depressions on walls. Occasionally overgrow live areas of reefs.

REACTION TO DIVERS: Unafraid; when molested, close siphons and dramatically deflate and retract.

VISUAL ID: Numerous tiny individuals are embedded in a tough, leathery tunic. Their excurrent siphons empty into thin internal chambers that have relatively small outflow openings. Tiny incurrent siphons are scattered over the surface of the tunic. At first glance, they appear to be encrusting sponges. Usually shades of gray, but can be blue-green, green or white.

ABUNDANCE & DISTRIBUTION: Common Florida, Bahamas, Caribbean.

HABITAT & BEHAVIOR: Inhabit shallow reefs. Encrust and often overgrow living corals.

REACTION TO DIVERS: Unafraid; close siphons only when molested.

WHITE SPECK TUNICATE
Didemnum conchyliatum
CLASS:
Tunicates
Ascidiacea
FAMILY:
Didemnidae

SIZE: Colony ¹/₄ - 2 in.
DEPTH: 20 - 100 ft.

BLACK OVERGROWING TUNICATE
Didemnum vanderhorsti
CLASS:
Tunicates
Ascidiacea
FAMILY:
Didemnidae

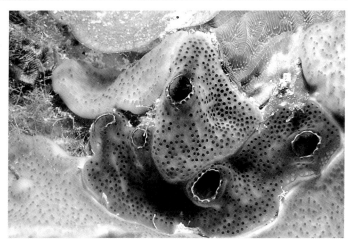

SIZE: Colony 1 - 4 in.
DEPTH: 20 - 75 ft.

OVERGROWING MAT TUNICATE
Trididemum solidum
CLASS:
Tunicates
Ascidiacea
FAMILY:
Didemnidae

SIZE: Colony 3 - 12 in.
DEPTH: 10 - 40 ft.

Tunicates – Pelagic Tunicates

VISUAL ID: Members of the Family Didemnidae are generally typified by numerous tiny individuals embedded in a thin tunic that is usually firm and opaque. Their incurrent siphons are scattered over the tunic's surface. The excurrent siphons empty into an internal chamber that has large outflow openings. Colors, markings and physical appearance of genera and species, however, are neither consistent or well established in scientific literature. Positive identification requires microscopic examination. There are five Caribbean genera, *Trididemnum, Didemnum, Leptoclinides, Lissoclinum,* and *Diplosoma*. At first glance, they often appear as an encrusting sponge.

ABUNDANCE & DISTRIBUTION: Common Florida, Bahamas, Caribbean.

HABITAT & BEHAVIOR: Inhabit reefs. Encrust and occasionally overgrow living parts of reefs.

REACTION TO DIVERS: Unafraid; when molested, close siphons and dramatically deflate and retract.

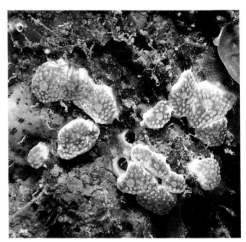

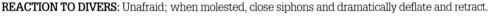

VISUAL ID: Transparent individuals that resemble a jet engine pod. Often joined in chains and other formations next page].

ABUNDANCE & DISTRIBUTION: Occasional worldwide.

HABITAT & BEHAVIOR: Swim in open water by water-jet action. Many species reproduce by budding, forming long chains and other formations of individuals.

REACTION TO DIVERS: None.

NOTE: Pictured individual, opposite, is a salp. Members of the genus *Salpa* can be distinguished by transparent muscular bands that do not completely encircle the body, while the bands of the genus *Doliolumn* encircle the body.

OVERGROWING TUNICATES

CLASS:
Tunicates
Ascidiacea
FAMILY:
Didemnidae

SIZE: Colonies 1 - 4 in.
DEPTH: 20 - 100 ft.

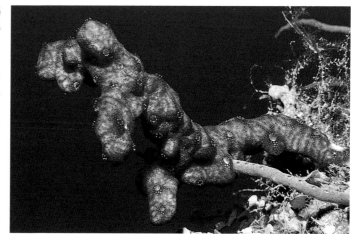

Overgrowing Tunicates
Color and shape variations.

PELAGIC TUNICATES
Salpa sp.
CLASS:
Pelagic Tunicates
Thaliacea

SIZE: 1 - 2 in.
DEPTH: 10 - 130 ft.

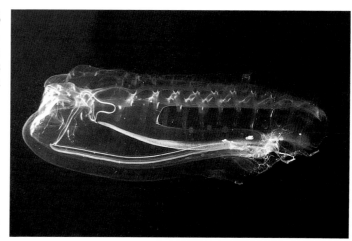

Pelagic Tunicates

Pelagic Tunicates: Chains and other formations

Budding reproduction in process.
[middle left]

Circular formation
[middle right]

Chain formations
[right, bottom left and right]

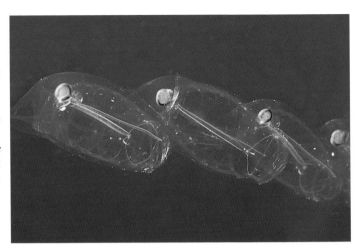

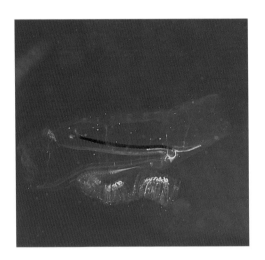

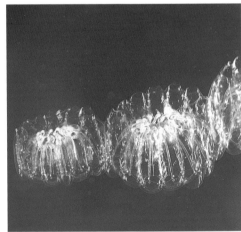

COMMON/SCIENTIFIC NAME INDEX

A

Abralia veranyi, 341
Acanthopleura granulata, 335
Actinoporus elegans, 93
Actinopyga agassizii, 391
Aequorea aequorea, 79
Agalma okeni, 81
Agelas clathrodes, 53
   conifera, 23
   wiedenmyeri, 23
Aglaophenia latecarainata, 69
Aiptasia tagetes, 95
Alicia mirabilis, 103
Alpheopsis trigonus, 189
Alpheus spp. 187
Amphimedon compressa, 43
Analcidometra armata, 357
Anamobaea sp. 151
   orsttedii, 155
Anemones
   Beaded, 95
   Berried, 103
   Branching, 97
   Club-Tipped, 97
   Corkscrew, 93
   Elegant, 93
   Giant, 91
   Hidden, 97
   Hitchhiking, 101
   Knobby, 93
   Light Bulb, 99
   Pale, 95
   Pale Clumping, 101
   Red Warty, 99
   Sponge, 103
   Sun, 91
   Sunburst, 101
   Turtle Grass, 99
   Warty, 98
Anilocra spp. 239
Anoplodactulus sp. 243
Aphelodoris antillensis, 317
Aplysia dactylomela, 291
   parvula, 291
   sp. 291
Aplysina archeri, 19
   cauliformis, 39
   fistgularis, 21
   fulva, 41
   lacunose, 21
   morio, 295
Arachnanthus nocturnes, 119
Arbacia punctulata, 381
Arctides guineensis, 195
Arenicola cristata, 147
Armisa sp. 303
Ascidia sydneiensis, 403
Asterina folium, 369
   hartmeyeri, 368
Astichopus multifidus, 391
Astropecten articulatus, 363
   duplicatus, 363
Astrophyton muricatum, 377
Astropyga magnifica, 379
Aurelia aurita, 85

B

Balanus trigonus, 240
Barnacles
   Black Coral, 243
   Grooved Goose-Neck, 240
   Red Netted, 241
   Scaled Goose-Neck, 241
   Sessile, 241
   Smooth Goose-Neck, 241
Bartholomea annulata, 93
Basket Stars
   Giant, 377
   Sea Rod, 377
Beroe ovata, 133
Berthellina engeli, 295
Bispira brunnea, 149
   variegata, 151
Bivalves
   Amber Penshell, 333
   Antillean Fileclam, 327
   Atlantic Pearl-Oyster, 325
   Atlantic Thorny-Oyster, 329
   Atlantic Wing-Oyster, 329
   Bicolor Purse-Oyster, 330
   Flat Tree-Oyster, 333
   Frons Oyser, 331
   Knobby Scallop, 331
   Lister Purse-Oyster, 331
   Rough Fileclam, 327
   Spiny Filecalm, 327
   Sunrise Tellin, 333
Bornella calacarata, 323
Botrylloides sp., 413
   nigrum, 413
Botryllus sp. 413
Bracebridgia subsulcata, 249
Brachycarpus biunguiculatus, 169
Branchiomma nigromaculata, 157
Brittle Stars
   Banded-Arm, 375
   Blunt-Spined, 373
   Circle Marked, 375
   Gaudy, 375
   Red, 372
   Reticulated, 371
   Rose Lace Coral, 369
   Ruby, 373
   Short-Armed, 374
   Short-Spined, 374
   Spiny, 373
   Sponge, 371
Bryozoans
   Bleeding Teeth, 253
   Brown Fan, 247
   Peach Encrusting, 253
   Pearly Orange Encrusting, 255
   Pearly Red Encrusting, 253
   Purple Encrusting, 255
   Purple Tuft, 251
   Seaweed, 251
   Spiral-Tufted, 251
   Tan Fan, 247
   Tangled Ribbon, 249
   Tubular-Horn, 255
   White Fan, 247
   White Tangled, 249
Bugula minima, 249
   neritina, 251
   turrita, 251

Bulla striata, 287
Bunodosoma cavernatum, 98
   granulifera, 99
Bursatella leachii, 293

C

Calappa flammea, 213
   gallus, 211
   ocellata, 213
Calcareous Tube Worms
   Blushing Star Coral Fanworm, 161
   Christmas Tree Worm, 159
   Red-Spotted Horseshoe Worm, 159
   Sea Frost, 161
   Star Horseshoe Worm, 157
   Touch-Me-Not Fanworm, 159
Calcinus tebicen, 201
Calliactis tricolor, 101
Callinectes ornatus, 218
   sapidus, 218
Calliostoma javanicum, 277
Callyspongia plicifera, 25
   vaginalis, 25
Calyx podatypa, 33
Canda simplex, 247
Carpiulius corallinus, 207
Carybdea alata, 89
Cassiopea frondosa, 89
   xamachana, 89
Cassis madagascariensis, 268
   tuberosa, 269
Caulerpa racemosa, 297
Caulibugula dendrogarapta, 251
Cerberilla sp., 309
Cerantheomorphe brasiliensis, 121
Cerithium litteratum, 275
Cestum veneris, 133
Charonia variegata, 265
Chelidonura hirundinina, 289
Chicoreus brevifrons, 271
Chitons
   Florida Slender, 334
   Fuzzy, 335
   Ornate, 335
   Slender, 334
Chlamys imbricata, 331
Chloeia sp., 145
   viridis, 143
Chromodoris clenchi, 317
   grahami, 315
   kempfi, 315
   nyalya, 315
Chrysaora quinquecirrha, 87
Cinachyra alloclada, 32
   kuekenthali, 32
Cinetorhyneus manningi, 185
Clathria sp. 49
   canariensis, 59
Clavelina sp., 407
   pica, 405
   puerto-secensis, 405
Cliona aprica, 56
   delitrix, 57
   langae, 57
Clypeaster rosaceus, 387
   subdepressus, 387
Cnidoscyphus mariginatus, 73
Comb Jellies
   Flattened Helmet, 133

Red-Spot, 131
Sea Gooseberry, 131
Sea Walnut, 129
Small Venus' Girdle, 133
Spot-Winged, 131
Venus' Girdle, 133
Warty, 129
Winged, 129
Conchs, see Gastropods
Condylactis gigantea, 91
Conus cedonulli, 279
   floridanus, 279
   regius, 279
Copidaster lymani, 359
Corallimorphs
   Cup, 115
   Disc, 117
   Florida, 113
   Forked Tentacle, 115
   Fringed, 117
   Orange Ball, 119
   Parachute, 117
   Umbrella, 115
   Warty, 113
Cowries, see Gastropods
Crabs
   Antilles Sponge, 231
   Banded Clinging, 221
   Batwing Coral, 207
   Blackpoint Sculling, 217
   Blotched Swimming, 217
   Blue, 219
   Channel Clinging, 225
   Common Blue, 218
   Cryptic Teardrop, 227
   Decorator, 233
   Eroded Mud, 211
   Flame Box, 213
   Florida Stone, 207
   Furcate Spider, 229
   Gaudy Clown, 207
   Green Clinging, 219
   Hairy Clinging, 223
   Heart Urchin Pea, 215
   Neck, 225
   Nimble Spray, 219
   Nodose Clinging, 221
   Nodose Rubble, 209
   Ocellated Box, 213
   Ocellated Swimming, 215
   Paved Clinging, 221
   Plumed Hairy, 209
   Redeye Sponge, 231
   Redhair Swimming, 217
   Red-Ridged Clinging, 223
   Rough Box, 211
   Sanddollar Pea, 213
   Sargassum Swimming, 215
   Spongy decorator, 229
   Southern Teardrop, 227
   Speck-Claw decorator, 227
   Thorny Mud, 209
   Yellowline Arrow, 225
Cribrochalina vasculum, 27
Cryptodromiopsis antillensis, 231
Cyerce cristallina, 301
Cymatium labiosum, 267
   pileare, 267
Cymbovula acicularis, 285
   sp., 285
Cyphoma gibbosum, 283
   macgingtyi, 283
   signatum,285

Cypraea cervus, 281
   cinerea, 281
   spurca acicularis, 283
   zebra, 281

D

Dardanus fucosus, 196
   venosus, 197
Davidaster discoidea, 355
   rubiginosa, 355
Dendostrea frons, 331
Dendrodoris krebsii, 319
Dentitheca dendritica, 73
Desmapsamma anchorata, 34
Diadema antillarum, 379
Didemnum conchyliatum, 417
   vanderhorsti, 417
Diplastrella sp. 47
   megastellata, 47
Diplosoma glandulosum, 415
Discordoris evelinae, 319
Discosoma carlgrenia, 115
   neglecta, 115
   sanctithomae, 113
Dissodactylus mellitae, 213
   primitives, 215
Distaplia bermudensis, 415
   corolla, 415
Dolabrifera dolabrifera, 293
Doliolumn sp., 418
Dondice occidenalis, 307
Doryteuthis plei,
Doto uva, 323
Dromia erthropus, 231
Drymonema dalmatinum, 87

E

Echinaster echinophorus, 365
   sentus, 365
   spinulosus, 365
Echinometra lucunter, 381
   viridis, 379
Ecteinascidia turbinate, 407
Ectyoplasia ferox, 37
Elysia ornata, 297
   picta, 299
   subornata, 297
Encope aberrans, 389
   emarginata, 388
   michelini, 388
Enoplometopus antellensis, 191
Eostichopus arnesoni, 391
Epicystis crucifer, 95
Epitonium angulatum, 277
Epizoanthus cutressi, 107
Euapta lappa, 399
Eucidaris tribuloides, 385
Eudistoma sp., 411
   obscuratum, 411
Eunice, Long Bristle, 147
Eunice longisetis, 147
   roussaei, 147
   Euplokamis sp., 131
Eupolymnia crassicornis, 163
Eurhamphaea vexilligera, 131

F

Facelilna sp., 305

False Squilla, Ciliated, 237
Fasciolaria tulipa, 265
Favorinus auritulus, 303
Feather Dusters
   Black-Spotted, 157
   Brown Fanworm, 153
   Ghost, 151
   Magnificent, 149
   Ruffled, 153
   Shy, 155
   Social, 149
   Split-Crown, 155
   Variegated, 151
   Yellow Fanworm, 153
Feather Stars
   Beaded Crinoid, 355
   Black & White Crinoid, 357
   Golden Crinoid, 355
   Swimming Crinoid, 357
Filecalms, see Bivalves
Filograna huxleyi, 161
Fire Worms
   Bearded, 143
   Red-Tipped, 143
   Scalloped, 145
Flatworms
   Bicolored, 139
   Leopard, 137
   Lined, 137
   Netted, 137
   Splendid, 139
Folia parallela, 133
Forskalia edwardsi, 83

G

Gastropods
   American Starsnail, 274
   Angulate Wentletrap, 277
   Atlantic Deer Cowrie, 281
   Atlantic Gray Cowrie, 281
   Atlantic Hairy Triton, 267
   Atlantic Partridge Tun, 269
   Atlantic Triton's Trumpet, 265
   Atlantic Yellow Cowrie, 283
   Chocolate-Lined Topsnail, 277
   Coffee Bean Trivia, 277
   Crown Conch, 263
   Crown Cone, 279
   Emperor Helmet, 268
   Fingerprint Cyphoma, 285
   Flame Helmet, 268
   Flamingo Tongue, 283
   Florida Cone, 279
   Florida Fighting Conch, 263
   Florida Horse Conch, 265
   Florida Wormsnail, 287
   Glowing Marginella, 273
   Hawkwing Conch, 261
   King Helmet, 269
   Lettered Olive, 271
   Lip Triton, 267
   Matchless Cone, 279
   Measled Cowrie, 281
   Milk Conch, 261
   Music Volute, 269
   Netted Olive, 271
   Oblong Marginella, 273
   Orange Marginella, 275
   Queen Conch, 261
   Roostertail Conch, 263
   Scotch Bonnet, 267
   Single-Tooth Simnia, 285
   Spotted Cyphoma, 283

Stocky Cerith, 275
Striate Bubble, 287
True Tulip, 265
West Indian Fighting Conch, 262
West Indian Murex, 271
West Indian Simnia, 285
West Indian Starsnail, 275
White-Spotted Marginella, 273
Geodia neptuni, 29
Glossodoris sedna, 317
Glyptoxanthus erosus, 211
Gnathophylloides mineri, 183
Gnathophyllum americanum, 183
Gymnangium longicauda, 69
    speciosum, 69

H

Halisarca sp., 49
Halocordyle disticha, 71
Halopteris carinata, 75
Haplosyllis sp., 145
Headshield Slugs
    Leech, 289
    Miniature Melo, 287
    Mysterious, 289
    Striate Bubble, 287
Helmets, see Gastropods
Hermit Crabs
    Bareye Hermit, 196
    Blue-Eye, 199
    Giant Hermit, 196
    Orangeclaw Hermit, 201
    Polkadotted Hermit, 203
    Red Banded Hermit, 199
    Red Reef Hermit, 201
    Red-Stripe Hermit, 203
    Stareye Hermit, 197
    White Speckled Hermit, 201
Hermodice carunculata, 143
Hexabranchus morsomus, 321
Hippolyte nicholsoni, 173
Hippopodina feegeensis, 255
Hippoporina verrilli 253
Holopsamma helwigi, 35
Holothuria cubana, 397
    floridana, 397
    grisea, 395
    impatiens, 395
    mexicana, 395
    thomasi, 399
Horseshoe Crab, 243
Hydroids
    Algae, 71
    Branching, 71
    Christmas Tree, 71
    Feather, 69
    Feather Bush, 75
    Feather Plume, 69
    Seafan, 77
    Slender Feather, 69
    Solitary Gorgonian, 77
    Solitary Sponge, 77
    Stinging, 73
    Stinging Bush, 75
    Thread, 75
    Unbranched, 73
    White Stinger, 73
Hydroides spongicola, 159
Hydromedusa
    Club Hydromedusa, 79
    Jelly Hydromedusa, 79

Two-Tentacle Hydromedusa, 79
Hypselodoris acriba, 311
    bayeri, 313
    edenticulata, 311
    ruthae, 313
    sp., 311
    sp., 313
Hypsicomus sp. 153

I

Iotrochota birotulata, 43
Ircinia felix, 31
    strobilina, 31
Isognomon alatus, 333
    bicolor, 330
    radiatus, 331
Isopods, Cymothoid, 239
Isostichopus badionotus, 393

J

Jellyfishes
    Blue-Tinted, 83
    Cannonball, 85
    Mangrove Upsidedown , 89
    Marbled, 85
    Moon, 85
    Sea Nettle, 87
    Sea Thimble, 87
    Sea Wasp, 89
    Stinging Cauliflower, 87
    Upsidedown, 89
    Warty, 83
Justitia longimanus, 191

L

Learchis poica, 307
Lebrunia coralligens, 91
    danae, 97
Leodia sexiesperforata, 389
Lepas anatifera, 241
    anserifera, 240
    pectinata, 240
Leucandra aspera, 59
Leucetta barbata, 61
Leucothea multicornis, 129
Lima lima, 327
    pellucida, 327
    scabra, 327
Limulus polyphemus, 243
Linckia guildingii, 361
Linuche unguiculata, 87
Lithopoma americanum, 274
    tectum, 275
Lobiger souverbiei, 299
Lobsters
    Caribbean Spiny, 189
    Copper, 193
    Flaming Reef, 191
    Red Banded, 191
    Regal Slipper, 195
    Ridged Slipper, 195
    Sculptured slipper, 193
    Smoothtail Spiny, 190
    Spanish, 193
    Spotted Spiny, 191
Loimia medusa, 163
Loligo pealei, 339
    plei, 339
Lolliguncula brevis, 339
Lopha frons,
Lugworm, Southern, 147

Luidia alternata, 357
   clathrata, 359
   senegalensis, 359
Lychnorhiza sp., *85*
Lysiosquilla glabriuscular, 235
   scabricauda, 235
Lysmata grabhami, 171
   rathburae, 171
   wurdemanni, 171
Lytechinus variegatus, 383
   williamsi, 383

M

Macrorhynchia allmani, 73
   philippia, 73
   robusta, 75
Mantis Shrimps
   Dark, 237
   Reef, 235
   Scaly-Tailed, 235
   Swollen-Claw, 235
Marcocoeloma trispinosum, 229
Marginella carnea, 275
   gattata, 273
   oblongum, 273
   pruniosum, 273
Medusa Worm, 163
Megabalanus sp. *241*
   tintinnabulum, 240
Megalomma sp., *155*
Mellita quinquiesperforata, 389
Melongena corona, 263
Membranipora, sp. *249*
Menippe mercenaria, 207
Meoma ventricosa ventricosa, 387
Metapenaeopsis goodie, 185
Microcosmus exasperatus, 403
Micropanope urinator, 209
Micromela undata, 287
Microphrys bicormuta, 227
Mithrax cinctimanus, 221
   coryphe, 221
   forceps, 223
   pilosus, 223
   sculptus, 219
   spinosissimus, 225
   verrucocus, 221
Mithrodia sp., *267*
Mnemiopsis mccradyi, 129
Monanchora barbadensis, 47
   unguifera, 35
Munida pusilla, 197
Mycale laevis, 51
   laxissima, 27
Myrmekioderma styx, 53
Mysid Shrimp, 239
Mysidium columbiae, 238
   gracile, 238
   integrum, 238

N

Navanax aenigmaticus, 289
Nemaster grandis, 357
Neofibularia nolitangere, 37
Neogonodactylus curancaoensis, 237
   oerstedii, 235
Neopontonides chacei, 175
Niphates digitalisi, 27
   erecta, 39

Notaulax nudicollis, 153
   occidentalis, 153
Nudibranchs
   Black-Spotted, 321
   Black-Spotted Sea Goddess, 313
   Blue-Streak, 305
   Brown Doris, 317
   Brown Sea Goddess, 315
   Brown-Speckled Doris, 317
   Caribbean Spanish Dancer, 321
   Christmas Tree Hydroid, 307
   Crisscross Tritonia, 325
   Florida Regal Sea Goddess, 311
   Fringe-Back, 307
   Gold-Crowned Sea Goddess, 311
   Gold-Fringed, 309
   Gold-Line Sea Goddess, 313
   Grape-Cluster, 323
   Harlequin Blue Sea Goddess, 317
   Leather-Backed Doris, 312
   Long-Eared, 303
   Long-Horn, 305
   Lynx, 303
   Orange, 309
   Orange-Gill, 309
   Purple-Crowned Sea Goddess, 315
   Purple-Ring, 305
   Purple-Spotted Sea Goddess, 311
   Red-Line Blue Sea Goddess, 315
   Red-Tipped Sea Goddess, 317
   Sargassum, 323
   Slimy Doris, 317
   Smiling Armina, 303
   Tasseled, 323
   Tufted, 325
   White-Speckled, 307
   Yellow-Streaked, 313

O

Oceanapia bartschi, 19
Octopus briareus, 341
   burryi, 347
   defilippi, 345
   filosusi, 347
   joubini, 349
   macropus, 347
   maya, 346
   vulgaris, 343
Octopuses
   Atlantic Longarm, 345
   Atlantic Pygmy, 349
   Brownstripe, 347
   Caribbean Reef, 341
   Caribbean Two-Spot, 347
   Common, 343
   Mexican Four-Eye, 346
   Violet Blanket, 349
   White-Spotted, 347
Ocyroposis crystalline, 129
   maculata, 129
Oliva reticularis, 271
   sayana, 271
Ophidiaster guildingii, 361
Ophiocoma echinata, 373
   paucigranulata, 373
   wendti, 372
Ophioderma appressum, 375
   brevicaudum, 374
   brevispinum, 374
   cinereum, 375
   ensiferum, 375
   rubicundum, 373
Ophionereis reticulata, 371

Ophiothrix suensonii, 371
Orchistoma pileus, 79
Oreaster reticulates, 367
Oxynaspis gracilis, 243
Oxynoe antillarum,
Oysters, see Bivalves

P

Paguristes cadenati, 201
  erythrops, 199
  grayi,, 200
  punticeps, 201
  sericeus, 199
  wassi, 200
Palinurellus gundlachi, 193
Paleo jabatus, 307
Palythoa caribaeorum, 111
  grandis, 111
  mammillosa, 110
Panulirus argus, 189
  guttatus, 191
  laevicauda, 190
Paractaea rufopunctata, 209
Parazoanthus catenularis, 107
  parasiticus, 105
  puertoricense, 105
  swiftii, 105
  tunicans, 107
Parribacus antarcticus, 193
Pelagia noctiluca, 83
Pelagic Tunicates, 419
Pelia mutical, 227
  rotunda, 227
Percrion gibbesi, 219
Periclimenes antillensis, 175
  antipathophilus, 181
  crinoidalis, 179
  longicaudatus, 179
  mclellandi, 175
  meyeri, 179
  pedersoni, 177
  perryae, 183
  rathbunae, 177
  yucatanicus, 177
Petrochirus diogenes, 199
Petrolisthes armatus, 205
  galathinus, 205
  marginatus, 205
Phalium granulatum, 267
Phidiana lynceus, 303
Phimochirus holthuisi, 203
  operculatus, 203
Phorbas amaranthus, 45
Phragmatopoma caudate, 163
Phoronid, Spiral-Horn, 255
Phoronis australis, 255
Phyllidiopsis papilligera, 321
Phyllorhiza punctata, 83
Physalia physalis, 81
Pickfordiateunthis pulchella, 337
Pilumnus floridanus, 209
Pinctada radiata, 325
Pinna carnea, 333
Plagiobrissus grandis, 385
Plakortis angulospiculatus, 55
Platydoris angustipes, 321
Platypodiella spectabilis, 207
Pleurobranchus areolatus, 295

Pleuroploca gigantea, 265
Podochela sp., 225
Polyandrocapa tumida, 409
Polycarpa spongiabilis, 403
Pomatostegus stellatus, 157
Poraniella echinulata, 369
Porcelain Crabs
  Banded, 205
  Green, 205
  Red, 205
  Spotted, 203
Porcellana sayana, 203
Portunus ordwayi, 217
  sayi, 215
  sebae, 215
  spinimanus, 217
Protula sp., 159
Pseudoceratina crassa, 17
Pseudoceros bicolor, 139
  crozieri, 137
  pardalis, 137
  sp., 217
  splendidus, 139
  texarus, 137
Pseudocorynactis caribbeorum, 119
Pseudopontonides principis, 181
Pseudosquilla ciliate, 237
Pseudothyone belli, 397
Pteria colymbus, 329
Ptilocaulis gracilis, 42
  spiculifera, 42
  walpersi, 43
Pyura vittata, 402

R

Ralpharia gorgoniae, 77
Renilla muelleri, 123
  reniformis, 122
Renocila spp. 239
Reteporelliana evelinae, 247
Rhaphidophlus juniperinus, 41
  venosus, 51
Rhizophysa eysenhardti, 80
  filiformis, 80
Rhopalaea abdominalis, 403
Ribbon Worm,
  Red & White Striped, 139
Ricordea florida, 113

S

Sabellastarte magnifica, 149
Salpa sp., 419
Sand Dollars, see Urchins
Scale Worms, 145
Schizoporella sp., 255
  violacea, 255
Schizostella bifurcata, 377
Scrupocellaria sp., 247
Scyllaea pelagica, 323
Scyllarides aequinoctialis, 193
  nodifer, 195
Sea Cucumbers
  Beaded, 399
  Conical, 391
  Donkey Dung, 395
  Five-Toothed, 391
  Florida, 397
  Furry, 391
  Grub, 397

Harlequin, 395
Hidden, 397
Slender, 395
Three-Rowed, 393
Tiger Tail, 399
Sea Hares
Atlantic Black Seahare, 295
Blue-Ring, 289
Freckled, 291
Ragged, 293
Spotted,291
Warty Seacat, 293
White-Spotted, 291
Sea Pansys
Common, 122
Muller's, 123
Sea Pens, Feather, 125
Sea Spider, Caribbean, 243
Sea Slugs
Brown-Lined Elysia, 297
Harlequin Glass-Slug, 301
Lettuce, 301
Lined-Shell, 299
Ornate Elysia, 297
Painted Elysia, 299
Reticulated, 297
Striped Elysia, 299
Sea Stars
Banded, 357
Beaded, 363
Blunt-Armed, 369
Comet, 361
Common Comet, 361
Conical Spined, 365
Cushion, 367
Mottled Red, 359
Nine-Armed, 359
Orange-Ridged, 365
Red Miniature, 369
Striped, 359
Studded, 367
Thorny, 365
Tiny Blunt-Armed,
Two-Spined, 363
Sepioteuthis sepioidea, 337
Sertularella speciosa, 71
Shrimps
Arrow, 173
Banded Coral, 169
Basket Star, 183
Black Coral, 181
Bumblebee, 183
Golden Coral, 169
Gorgonian, 175
Hidden Cleaner, 171
Large-Claw Snapping, 185
Longtail Grass, 179
Nicholson's, 173
Orange Featherstar, 179
Pederson Cleaner, 177
Peppermint, 171
Red Night, 185
Red Snapping, 187
Sea Plume, 175
Scarlet-Striped Cleaning, 171
Slimy Sea Plume, 175
Squat Urchin, 183
Snapping, 187
Spotted Cleaner, 177
Squat Anemone, 175
Sun Anemone, 177
Three-Ridge Snapping, 189
Two Claw, 169
Velvet, 185

Wire Coral, 181
Sidegill Slugs
Apricot, 295
Warty, 295
Sigsbeia conifera, 369
Siphonodictyom coralliphagum, 59
Siphonophores
Floating, 81
Paired-Bell, 81
Portuguese Man-Of-War, 81
Red-Spotted, 83
Slipper Lobsters, see Lobsters
Solanderia gracilis, 77
Spaghetti Worm, 165
Spheciospongia cuspidifera, 57
vesparium, 31
Spiny Lobsters, see Lobsters
Spirastrella coccinea, 45
Spirobranchus giganteus, 159
Spondylus americanus, 329
Sponges
Antler, 57
Azure Vase, 25
Black-Ball, 31
Branching Tube, 17
Branching Vase, 25
Brown Bowl, 27
Brown Clustered Tube, 23
Brown Encrusting Octopus, 37
Brown Tube, 23
Brown Variable, 55
Convoluted Barrel, 21
Convoluted Orange, 53
Coral Encrusting, 57
Dark Volcano, 33
Elephant Ear, 53
Erect Rope, 43
Fire, 35
Giant Barrel, 29
Green Finger, 43
Lavender Rope, 39
Leathery Barrel, 29
Loggerhead, 31
Lumpy Overgrowing, 35
Netted Barrel, 29
Orange Ball, 33
Orange Icing, 51
Orange Lumpy Encrusting, 51
Orange Sieve Encrusting, 47
Orange Veined Encrusting, 51
Peach Encrusting, 48
Pink Lumpy, 35
Pink & Red Encrusting, 45
Pink Vase, 27
Pitted, 33
Red Boring, 57
Red Encrusting, 45
Red-Orange Branching, 43
Red-Orange Encrusting, 47
Red Sieve Encrusting, 45
Rough Tube, 19
Row Pore Rope, 39
Scattered Pore Rope, 41
Spiny Ball, 61
Star Encrusting, 49
Stinker, 31
Stove-Pipe, 19
Strawberry Vase, 27
Thin Rope, 41
Touch-Me-Not, 37
Variable Boring, 59
Viscous, 55
White Calcareous, 61

White Cryptic, 59
White Lumpy Encrusting, 45
Yellow Calcareous, 59
Yellow Tube, 21
Sponge Worms, 145
Squat Lobster, Common, 197
Squid
Arrow, 339
Atlantic Brief, 339
Caribbean Reef, 337
Diamond Back, egg case, 349
Gianteye, 341
Grass, 337
Longfin, 339
Starfish, see Sea Stars
Steginoporella magnilabris, 253
Stenocionops furactus, 229
Stenoplax bahamensis, 334
floridana, 334
Purpurascens, 335
Stenopus hispidus, 169
scutellatus, 169
Stenorhynchus seticornis, 225
Stichodactyla helianthus, 91
Stomolophus meleagis, 85
Stomotosa ptorophylla, 79
Strombus alatus, 263
costatus, 261
gallus, 263
gigas, 261
pugilis, 262
raninus, 261
Stylocheilus longicauda, 289
Symplegma viride, 409
Synalpheus sp., 185

T
Tedania ignis, 35
Tellina radiata, 333
Telmatactis americana, 97
The Thing, 147
Thor amboinensis, 173
Thyroscyphus ramosus, 71
Thysanoteuthis rhombus, 349
Tonicia schammi, 335
Tonna Maculosa, 269
Tozeuma carolinense, 173
Trematooecia aviculifera, 253
Tremoctopus violaceus, 349
Tridachia crispata, 301
Trididemum solidum, 417
Tripneustes ventricosus, 385
Tritonia bayeri. 325
Tritoniopsis, frydis, 325
Trivia pediculus, 277
True Jellyfishes, see Jellyfishes
Tube-Dwelling Anemones
Banded, 119
Giant, 121
Lavender, 121
Lined, 123
Transparent, 122
Wideband, 12
Tunicates
Black Condominium, 411
Black Overgrowing, 417
Blue Bell, 405
Bulb, 407
Button, 415

Encrusting Social, 409
Flat, 413
Geometric Encrusting, 413
Giant, 403
Globular Encrusting, 415
Green Tube, 403
Mangrove, 407
Mottled Encrusting, 415
Mottled Social, 409
Overgrowing, 419
Overgrowing Mat, 417
Painted, 405
Pelagic, 419-20
Reef, 403
Row Encrusting, 413
Strawberry,
White Speck, 417
White Condominium, 411

U
Ulosa hispida, 51
ruetzleri, 51
Urchins
Common Arbacia, 381
Five-Keyhole Sand Dollar, 389
Five-Notched Sand Dollar, 388
Inflated Sea Biscuit, 387
Jewel, 383
Long-Spined, 379
Long-Spined Sea Biscuit, 385
Magnificent, 379
Notched Sand Dollar, 389
Notched Key-Hole Sand Dollar, 388
Red Heart, 387
Reef, 379
Rock-Boring, 381
Sand Dollar, 387
Six-Keyhole Sand Dollar, 389
Slate-Pencil, 385
Variegated, 383
West Indian Sea Egg, 385

V
Velamen parallelum, 133
Vermicularia knorrii, 287
Vermiliopsis sp., 161
Verongula gigantean, 29
rigida, 33
Viatrix globulifera, 99
Voluta musica, 269

W
Worm Rock, 163

X
Xestospongia muta, 29

Z
Zoanthids
Brown, 109
Brown Sponge, 107
Golden, 105
Hydroid, 107
Knobby, 110
Maroon Sponge, 105
Mat, 109
Row, 108
Sponge, 105
Sun, 111
White Encrusting, 111
Yellow Sponge, 107
Zoanthus pulchellus, 109
sociatus, 108
Zyzzyzus warreni, 77

PERSONAL RECORD OF CREATURE SIGHTINGS

1. PORIFERA
Sponges

No.	Name	Page	Date	Location
	Branching Tube Sponge *Pseudocer atina crassa*	17		
	Rough Tube Sponge *Oceanapia bartschi*	19		
	Stove-pipe Sponge *Aplysina archeri*	19		
	Yellow Tube Sponge *Aplysina fistularis*	21		
	Convoluted Barrel Sponge *Aplysina lacunosa*	21		
	Brown Tube Sponge *Agelas conifera*	23		
	Brown Clustered Tube Sponge *Agelas wiedenmyeri*	23		
	Branching Vase Sponge *Callyspongia vaginalis*	25		
	Azure Vase Sponge *Callyspongia plicifera*	25		
	Strawberry Vase Sponge *Mycale laxissima*	27		
	Pink Vase Sponge *Niphates digitalis*	27		
	Brown Bowl Sponge *Cribrochalina vasculum*	27		
	Netted Barrel Sponge *Verongula gigantea*	29		
	Giant Barrel Sponge *Xestospongia muta*	29		
	Leathery Barrel Sponge *Geodia neptuni*	29		
	Loggerhead Sponge *Spheciospongia vesparium*	31		
	Black-ball Sponge *Ircinia strobilina*	31		
	Stinker Sponge *Ircinia felix*	31		
	Orange Ball Sponge *Cinachyra aLloclad*	33		
	Dark Volcano Sponge *Calyx podatypa*	33		
	Pitted Sponge *Verongula rigida*	33		
	Pink Lumpy Sponge *Monanchora unauifera*	35		
	Lumpy Overgrowing Sponge *Holopsamma helwigi*	35		
	Fire Sponge *Tedania ignis*	35		
	Touch-Me-Not Sponge *Neofibularia nolitangere*	37		
	Brown Encrusting Octopus Sponge *Ectyoplasia ferox*	37		
	Lavender Rope Sponge *Niphates erecta*	39		

No.	Name	Page	Date	Location
	Row Pore Rope Sponge *Aplysina cauliformis*	39		
	Scattered Pore Rope Sponge *Aplysina fulva*	41		
	Thin Rope Sponge *Rhaphidophlus Juniperinus*	41		
	Green Finger Sponge *Iotrochota birotulata*	43		
	Erect Rope Sponge *Amphimedon compressa*	43		
	Red-orange Branching Sponges *Ptilocaulis* sp.	43		
	White Lumpy Encrusting Sponge *Ptilocaulis* sp.	45		
	Pink & Red Encrusting Sponge *Spirastrel1a coccinea*	45		
	Red Sieve Encrusting Sponge *Phorbas amaranthus*	45		
	Orange Sieve Encrusting Sponge *Diplastre11a* sp.	47		
	Red-orange Encrusting Sponge *Diplastrella megastenata*	47		
	Red Encrusting Sponge *Monanchora barbadensis*	47		
	Peach Encrusting Sponge *Clathria* sp.	49		
	Star Encrusting Sponge *Halisarca* sp.	49		
	Orange Veined Encrusting Sponge *Rhaphudophlus venosus*	51		
	Orange Icing Sponge *Mycale laevis*	51		
	Orange Lumpy Encrusting Sponge *Ulosa ruetzleri*	51		
	Convoluted Orange Sponge *Myrmekioderma styx*	53		
	Orange Elephant Ear Sponge *Agelas clathrodes*	53		
	Viscous Sponge *Plakortis angulospiculatus*	55		
	Brown Variable Sponge *Anthosigme11a varians*	55		
	Antler Sponge *Spheciospongia cuspidifera*	57		
	Coral Encrusting Sponge *Cliona langae*	57		
	Red Boring Sponge *Cliona dentrix*	57		
	Variable Boring Sponge *Siphonodictyom coraBiphagum*	59		
	White Cryptic Sponge *Leucandra aspera*	59		
	Yellow Calcareous Sponge *Clatbrina canariensis*	59		
	White Calcareous Sponge	61		
	Spiny Ball Sponge *Leucetta barbata*	61		

2. CNIDARIA

Hydroids – Hydromedusas – Siphonophores – True Jellyfishes – Box Jellies – Sea Anemones
Zoanthids – Corallimorphs – Tube-dwelling Anemones – Sea Pens

No.	Name	Page	Date	Location
	Feather Hydroid *Gymnangium longicauda*	69		
	Slender Feather Hydroid *Gymnangium speciosum*	69		
	Feather Plume Hydroid *Aglacphenia latecarinata*	69		
	Branching Hydroid *Sertularella speciosa*	71		
	Christmas Tree Hydroid *Halocordyle disticha*	71		
	Algae Hydroid *Thyroscyphus ramosus*	71		
	Unbranched Hydroid *Cnidosoyphus marginatus*	73		
	White Stinger *Macrothynchis philippia*	73		
	Stinging Hydroid *Macrirhynchia allmani*	73		
	Stinging Bush Hydroid *Macrorhynchia robusta*	75		
	Thread Hydroid *Hakioterus carubata*	75		
	Feather Bush Hydroid *Dentitheca dendritica*	75		
	Seafan Hydroid *Solanderia gracilis*	77		
	Solitary Gorgonian Hydroid *Ralpharia gorgoniae*	77		
	Solitary Sponge Hydroid *Zyzzyzas warreni*	77		
	Club Hydromedusa *Orchistoma pileus*	77		
	Jelly Hydromedusa *Aequorea aequorea*	79		
	Two-tentacle Hydromedusa *Stomotoca pterophylla*	79		
	Portuguese Man-Of-War *Physalia physalis*	81		
	Floating Siphonophore *Rhizophysa* spp.	81		
	Paired-bell Siphonophore *Agalma okeni*	81		
	Red-spotted Siphonophore *Forskalia edwardsi*	83		
	Warty Jellyfish *Pelagia noctiluca*	83		
	Blue-tinted Jellyfish *Phyllorhiza punctata*	83		
	Moon Jelly *Aurelia aurita*	83		
	Cannonball Jelly *Stomolophus meleagris*	83		
	Marbled Jelly *Lychnorhiza. sp.*	85		

No.	Name	Page	Date	Location
	Stinging Cauliflower *Drymonema dalmatinum*	87		
	Sea Nettle *Chrysaora quinquecirrha*	87		
	Sea Thimble *Linuche unguiculata*	87		
	Upsidedown Jelly *Cassiopea frondosa*	89		
	Mangrove Upsidedown Jelly *Cassiopea xamachana*	89		
	Sea Wasp *Carybdea alata*	89		
	Giant Anemone *Condylactis gigantea*	91		
	Sun Anemone *Stichodactyla helianthus*	91		
	Elegant Anemone *Actinoporus elegans*	93		
	Corkscrew Anemone *Bartholomea annulata*	93		
	Knobby Anemone ** lucida*	93		
	Beaded Anemone *Epicystis cruciferu*	95		
	Pale Anemone *Aiptasia tagetes*	95		
	Club-tipped Anemone *Telmatactis Americana*	97		
	Hidden Anemone *Lebrunia coralligens*	97		
	Branching Anemone *Lebrunia danae*	97		
	Turtle Grass Anemone *Viatrix globulifera*	99		
	Light Blub Anemone Unidentified	99		
	Red Warty Anemone *Bunodosoma granulifera*	99		
	Hitchhiking Anemone *Calliactis tricolor*	101		
	Sunburst Anemone Unidentified	101		
	Pale Clumping Anemone *Aiptasia* sp.	101		
	Sponge Anemone Unidentified	103		
	Berried Anemone *Alicia mirabilis*	103		
	Sponge Zoanthid *Parazoanthus parasiticus*	105		
	Golden Zoanthid *Parazoanthus swiftii*	105		
	Maroon Sponge Zoanthid *Parazoanthus puertoricense*	105		
	Brown Sponge Zoanthid *Parazoanthus caternularis*	107		
	Yellow Sponge Zoanthid *Epizoanthus cutressi*	107		

No.	Name	Page	Date	Location
	Hydroid Zoanthid *Parazoanthus tunicans*	107		
	Brown Zoanthid Unidentified	109		
	Mat Zoanthid *Zoanthus pulchellus*	109		
	White Encrusting Zoanthid *Palythoa carbaeorum*	111		
	Sun Zoanthid *Palythoa grandis*	111		
	Florida Corallimorph *Ricordea florida*	113		
	Warty Corallimorph *Discosoma sanctithomae*	113		
	Forked Tentacle Corallimorph *Discosoma carlgreni*	115		
	Umbrella Corallimorph *Discosoma neglectum*	115		
	Cup Corallimorph Unidentified	115		
	Parachute Corallimorph Unidentified	117		
	Disc Corallimorph Unidentified	117		
	Fringed Corillimorph Unidentified	117		
	Orange Ball Corallimorph *Pseudocorynactis caribbeorum*	119		
	Banded Tube-dwelling Anemone *Arachnanthus nocturnus*	119		
	Giant Tube-dwelling Anemone *Ceriantheomorphe brasiliensis*	121		
	Transparent Tube-dwelling Anemone Unidentified	121		
	Lavender Tube-dwelling Anemone Unidentified	121		
	Lined Tube-dwelling Anemone Unidentified	123		
	Wideband Tube-dwelling Anemone Unidentified	123		
	Muller's Sea Pansy *Renilla muelleri*	123		
	Feather Sea Pens Unidentified	125		

3. CTENOPHORA
Comb Jellies

No.	Name	Page	Date	Location
	Sea Walnut *Mneniopsis maccadyi*	129		
	Warty Comb Jelly *Leucothea milticomis*	129		
	Winged Comb Jelly *Ocyropsis crystalline*	129		
	Spot-winged Comb Jelly *Ocyropsis maculata*	131		
	Red-spot Comb Jelly *Eurhamphaea vexilligera*	131		

No.	Name	Page	Date	Location
	Sea Gooseberry *Euplakamis* sp.	131		
	Venus' Girdle *Cestum veneris*	133		
	Small Venus' Girdle *Folia parallela*	133		
	Flattened Helmet Comb Jelly *Beroe ovata*	133		

4. PLATYHELMENTHES – RHYNCHOCOELA
Flatworms – Ribbon Worms

	Name	Page	Date	Location
	Leopard Flatworm *Pseudoceros pardalis*	137		
	Lined Flatworm *Pseudoceros crozieri*	137		
	Netted Flatworm *Pseudoceros texarus*	137		
	Bicolored Flatworm *Pseudoceros bicolor*	139		
	Splendid Flatworm *Pseudoceros splendidus*	139		
	Red & White Striped Ribbon Worm Unidentified	139		

5. ANNELIDA
Fireworms – Elongated Worms – Feather Duster Worms
Calcareous Tube Worms – Spaghetti Worms

	Name	Page	Date	Location
	Bearded Fireworm *Hermodice carunculata*	143		
	Red-tipped Fireworm *Chloeia viridis*	143		
	Scalloped Fireworm *Chloeia* sp.	145		
	Scale Worms Unidentified	145		
	Sponge Worms *Haplosyllis* sp.	145		
	Southern Lugworm *Arenicola cristata*	147		
	The Thing *Eunice roussaei*	147		
	Long Bristle Eunice *Eunice longisetis*	147		
	Magnificent Feather Duster *Sabellastarte magnifica*	149		
	Social Feather Duster *Bispira brunnea*	149		
	Variegated Feather Duster *Bispira variegata*	151		
	Ghost Feather Dusters *Anamobaea* sp.	151		
	Yellow Fanworm *Notaulax occidentalis*	153		
	Brown Fanworm *Notaulax nudicollis*	153		

No.	Name	Page	Date	Location
	Ruffled Feather Duster *Hypsicomus* sp.	153		
	Split-crown Feather Duster *Anamobaea orstedii*	155		
	Shy Feather Duster *Megalomma* sp.	155		
	Black-spotted Feather Duster *Branchiomma nigromaculata*	157		
	Star Horseshoe Worm *Pomatostegus stellatus*	157		
	Christmas Tree Worm *Spirobranchus giganteus*	159		
	Red-spotted Horseshoe Worm *Protula* sp.	159		
	Touch-Me-Not Fanworm *Hydroides spongicola*	159		
	Sea Frost *Filograna huxleyi*	161		
	Blushing Star Coral Fanworm *Vermiliopsis n.* sp.	161		
	Spaghetti Worm *Eupolymnia crassicornis*	163		
	Medusa Worm *Loimia medusa*	163		
	Worm Rock *Phragmatopoma caudate*	163		

6. ARTHOPODA

Shrimp – Lobsters – Hermit Crabs – Porcelain Crabs – True Crabs – Box Crabs
Swimming Crabs – Spider Crabs – Sponge Crabs – Mantis Shrimp – Isopods
Mysid Shrimp – Barnacles – Horseshoe Crab – Sea Spiders

No.	Name	Page	Date	Location
	Two Claw Shrimp *Brachycarpus biunguiculatus*	169		
	Banded Coral Shrimp *Stenopus hispidus*	169		
	Golden Coral Shrimp *Stenopus scutellatus*	169		
	Peppermint Shrimp *Lymata wurdemanni*	171		
	Hidden Cleaner Shrimp *Lymata rathbunae*	171		
	Scarlet-striped Cleaning Shrimp *Lymata grabhami*	171		
	Arrow Shrimp *Tozeuma carolinense*	173		
	Squat Anemone Shrimp *Thor amboinensis*	173		
	Nicholson's Shrimp *Hippolyte nicholsoni*	173		
	Sea Plume Shrimp *Neopontonides chacei*	175		
	Gorgonian Shrimp *Periclimenes antillensis*	175		
	Slimy Sea Plume Shrimp *Periclimenes mclellandi*	175		
	Pederson Cleaner Shrimp *Periclimenes pedersoni*	177		
	Spotted Cleaner Shrimp *Periclimenes yucatanicus*	177		

No.	Name	Page	Date	Location
	Sun Anemone Shrimp *Periclimenes rathbunae*	177		
	Longtail Grass Shrimp *Periclimenes longicaudatus*	179		
	Brown Featherstar Shrimp *Periclimenes meyeri*	179		
	Orange Featherstar Shrimp *Periclimenes crinoidalis*	179		
	Black Coral Shrimp *Periclimenes antipathophilus*	181		
	Wire Coral Shrimp *Pseudopontonides principis*	181		
	Basket Star Shrimp *Periclimenes perryae*	183		
	Bumblebee Shrimp *Gnathophyllum americanum*	183		
	Squat Urchin Shrimp *Gnathophylloides mineri*	183		
	Red Night Shrimp *Cinetorhynehus manningi*	185		
	Velvet Shrimp *Metapenaeopsis goodie*	185		
	Large-claw Snapping Shrimp *Synalpheus* sp.	185		
	Red Snapping Shrimp *Alpheus* spp.	187		
	Snapping Shrimp *Alpheus spp*	187		
	Three-ridge Snapping Shrimp *Alpheopsis trigonus*	189		
	Caribbean Spiny Lobster *Panulirus argus*	189		
	Spotted Spiny Lobster *Panulirus guttatus*	191		
	Flaming Reef Lobster *Enplometopus antellensis*	191		
	Red Banded Lobster *Justitia longimanus*	191		
	Copper Lobster *Palinurellus gundlachi*	193		
	Spanish Lobster *Scyllarides aequinoctialis*	193		
	Sculptured Slipper Lobster *Parrribacus antacticus*	193		
	Regal Slipper Lobster *Arctides guineensis*	195		
	Ridged Slipper Lobster *Scyllarides nodifer*	195		
	Common Squat Lobster *Munida pusilla*	197		
	Stareye Hermit *Dardanus venosus*	197		
	Giant Hermit *Petrochirus diogenes*	199		
	Red Banded Hermit *Paguristes erythrops*	199		
	Blue-eye Hermit *Paguristes sericeus*	199		

No.	Name	Page	Date	Location
	White Speckled Hermit *Paguristes punticeps*	201		
	Red Reef Hermit *Paguristes cadenati*	201		
	Orangeclaw Hermit *Calcinus tibicen*	201		
	Red-stripe Hermit *Phimochirus operculatus*	203		
	Polkadotted Hermit *Phimochirus operculatus*	203		
	Spotted Porcelain Crab *Porcellana sayana*	203		
	Green Porcelain Crab *Petrolisthes armatus*	205		
	Red Porcelain Crab *Petrolisthes marginatus*	205		
	Banded Porcelain Crab *Petrolisthes galathinus*	205		
	Batwing Coral Crab *Carpilus corallinus*	207		
	Florida Stone Crab *Menippe mercenaria*	207		
	Gaudy Clown Crab *Platypodiella spectabilis*	207		
	Plumed Hairy Crab *Pilumnus floridanus*	209		
	Thorny Mud Crab *Micropanope urinator*	209		
	Nodose Rubble Crab *Paractaea rufopunctata*	209		
	Eroded Mud Crab *Glyptoxanthus erosus*	211		
	Rough Box Crab *Calappa gallus*	211		
	Ocellated Box Crab *Calappa ocellata*	213		
	Flame Box Crab *Calappa flammea*	213		
	Sanddollar Pea Crab *Dissodactylus melitae*	213		
	Heart Urchin Pea Crab *Dissodactylus primitivus*	215		
	Ocellate Swimming Crab *Portunus sebae*	215		
	Sargassum Swimming Crab *Portunus sayi*	215		
	Blotched Swimming Crab *Portunus spinimanus*	217		
	Redhair Swimming Crab *Portunus ordwayi*	217		
	Black Point Sculling Crab *Portunus* sp.	217		
	Blue Crab *Callinectes* sp.	219		
	Nimble Spray Crab *Percnon gibbesi*	219		
	Green Clinging Crab *Mithrax sculptus*	219		

No.	Name	Page	Date	Location
	Banded Clinging Crab *Mithrax cinctimanus*	221		
	Paved Cling Crab *Mithrax verrucosus*	221		
	Nodose Clinging Crab *Mihtrax coryphe*	221		
	Red-ridged Clinging Crab *Mithrax forceps*	223		
	Hairy Clinging Crab *Mihtrax pilosus*	223		
	Channel Clinging Crab *Mithrax spinosissimus*	225		
	Yellowline Arrow Crab *Stenorhynchus seticornis*	225		
	Neck Crabs *Podochela* sp.	225		
	Cryptic Teardrop Crab *Pelia mutica*	227		
	Southern Teardrop Crab *Pelia rotunda*	227		
	Speck-claw Decorator Crab *Microphrys bicomuta*	227		
	Spongy Decorator Crab *Marcocoeloma trispinosum*	229		
	Furcate Spider Crab *Stenocionops furcatus coelata*	229		
	Antilles Sponge Crab *Cryptodromiopsis antillensis*	231		
	Redeye Sponge Crab *Dromia erythropus*	231		
	Decorator Crabs Unidentified	233		
	Scaly-tailed Mantis *Lysiosquilla scabricauda*	235		
	Reef Mantis *Lysiosquilla glabriuscula*	235		
	Swollen-claw Mantis *Neogonodactylus oerstedii*	235		
	Dark Mantis *Neogonodactylus curacaoensis*	237		
	Ciliated False Squilla *Pseudosquilla ciliate*	237		
	Cymothoid Isopods *Anilocra* spp.	239		
	Mysid Shrimp *Mysidium* spp.	239		
	Sessile Barnacles *Megabalanus tintinnabulum*	241		
	Red Netted Barnacle *Megabalanus* sp.	241		
	Smooth Goose-neck Barnacle *Lepas anatifera*	241		
	Black Coral Barnacle *Oxynaspis gracilis*	243		
	Caribbean Sea Spider *Anoplodatulus* sp.	243		
	Horseshoe Crab *Limulus polyphemus*	243		

7. ECTOPROCTERA
Bryozoans

No.	Name	Page	Date	Location
	White Fan Bryozoan *Reteporellina evelinae*	247		
	Brown Fan Bryozoan *Canda simplex*	247		
	Tan Fan Bryozoan *Scrupocellaria* sp.	247		
	Purple Reef Fan *Bugula minima*	249		
	White Tangled Bryozoan *Bracebridgia subsulcata*	249		
	Tangled Ribbon Bryozoan *Membranipora* sp.	249		
	Spiral-tufted Bryozoan *Bubula turrita*	251		
	Seaweed Bryozoan *Caulibugula dendrograpta*	251		
	Purple Tuft Bryozoan *Bugula neritina*	251		
	Bleeding Teeth Bryozoan *Trematooecia aviculifera*	253		
	Pearly Red Encrusting Bryozoan *Steginoporella magnilabris*	253		
	Peach Encrusting Bryozoan *Hippoporina verrilli*	253		
	Pearly Orange Encrusting Bryozoan *Hippopodina feegeensis*	255		
	Purple Encrusting Bryozoan *Schizoporella* sp.	255		
	Tubular-horn Bryozoan *Schizoporella violacea*	255		
	Spiral-horn Phoronid *Phoronis australis*	255		

8. MOLLUSCA
Gastropods – Conchs – Tulip Shells – – Tritons – Helmet Shells – Olive Shells – Cone Shells
Simnias – Shell-less Snails – Chitons – Bivalves – Squid – Octopuses

No.	Name	Page	Date	Location
	Queen Conch *Strombus gigas*	261		
	Milk Conch *Strombus costatus*	261		
	Hawkwing Conch *Strombus raninus*	261		
	Florida Fighting Conch *Strombus alatus*	263		
	Roostertail Conch *Strombus gallus*	263		
	Crown Conch *Melongena corona*	263		
	Florida Horse Conch *Pleuroploca gigantean*	265		
	True Tulip *Fasciolaria tulipa*	265		
	Atlantic Triton's Trumpet *Charonia variegata*	265		

No.	Name	Page	Date	Location
	Atlantic Hairy Triton *Cymatium pileare*	267		
	Lip Triton *Cymatium labiosum*	267		
	Scotch Bonnet *Phalium granulatum*	267		
	King Helmet *Cassis tuberosa*	269		
	Atlantic Partridge Tun *Tonna maculosa*	269		
	Music Volute *Voluta musica*	269		
	West Indian Murex *Chicoreus brevifrons*	271		
	Netted Olive *Oliva reticularis*	271		
	Lettered Olive *Oliva sayana*	271		
	Glowing Marginella *Marginella pruniosum*	273		
	White-spot Marginella *Marginella gattata*	273		
	Oblong Marginella *Marginella oblongum*	273		
	Orange Marginella *Marginella carnea*	275		
	West Indian Starsnail *Lithopoma tectum*	275		
	Stocky Cerith *Cerithium litteratum*	275		
	Chocolate-lined Topsnail *Calliostoma javanicum*	277		
	Angulate Wentletrap *Epitomium angulatum*	277		
	Coffee Bean Trivia *Trivia pediculus*	277		
	Florida Cone *Conus floridanus*	279		
	Matchless Cone *Conus cedonulli*	279		
	Crown Cone *Conus regius*	279		
	Atlantic Deer Cowrie *Cypraea cervus*	281		
	Measled Cowrie *Cypraea zebra*	281		
	Atlantic Gray Cowrie *Cypraea cinerea*	281		
	Atlantic Yellow Cowrie *Cyprea spura acicularis*	283		
	Spotted Cyphoma *Cyphoma macgintyi*	283		
	Flamingo Tongue *Cyphoma gibbosum*	283		
	Fingerprint Cyphoma *Cyphoma signatum*	285		
	West Indian Simnia *Cymbovula acicularis*	285		

No.	Name	Page	Date	Location
	Single-tooth Simnia *Simnia uniplicata*	285		
	Florida Wormsnail *Vermicularia knorrii*	287		
	Miniature Melo *Micromela undata*	287		
	Striate Bubble *Bulla striata*	287		
	Mysterious Headshield Slug *Navanax aenigmaticus*	289		
	Leech Headshield Slug *Chelidonura hirundinina*	289		
	Blue-ring Sea Hare *Stylocheilus longicauda*	289		
	Freckled Sea Hare *Aplysis* sp.	291		
	White-spotted Sea Hare *Aplysis parvula*	291		
	Spotted Sea Hare *Aplysis dactylomela*	291		
	Ragged Sea Hare *Bursatella leachii*	293		
	Warty Seacat *Dolabrifera dolafrifera*	293		
	Atlantic Black Seahare *Aplysia morio*	295		
	Warty Sidegill Slug *Pleurobranchus areolatus*	295		
	Apricot Sidegill Slug *Berthellina engeli*	295		
	Ornate Elysia *Elysis ornate*	297		
	Brown-lined Elysia *Elysia subomata*	297		
	Reticulated Sea Slug *Oxynoe antillarum*	297		
	Painted Elysia *Elysia picta*	299		
	Striped Elysia *Elysia* sp.	299		
	Lined-shell Sea Slug *Lobiger souverbiei*	299		
	Harlequin Glass-slug *Cyerce cristallina*	301		
	Lettuce Sea Slug *Tridachia crispate*	301		
	Smiling Armina *Armina* sp.	303		
	Long-eared Nudibranch *Phidiana lynceus*	303		
	Lynx Nudibranch *Phidiana lynceus*	303		
	Long-horn Nudibranch *Facelina* sp.	305		
	Blue-streak Nudibranch Unidentified	305		
	Purple-ring Nudibranch Unidentified	305		

No.	Name	Page	Date	Location
	Christmas Tree Hydroid Nudibranch *Learchis poica*	307		
	Fringe-back Nudibranch *Dondice occidentalis*	307		
	White-speckled Nudibranch *Paleo jubatus*	307		
	Orange Nudibranch Unidentified	309		
	Gold-fringed Nudibranch *Cerberilla* sp.	309		
	Orange-gill Doris Unidentified	309		
	Florida Regal Sea Goddess *Hypselodoris Edenticulata*	311		
	Gold-crowned Sea Goddess *Hyselodoris acriba*	311		
	Purple-spotted sea Goddess *Hyselodoris* sp.	311		
	Gold-line Sea Goddess *Hypselodoris ruthae*	313		
	Black-spotted Sea Goddess *Hyselodoris bayeri*	313		
	Yellow-streaked Sea Goddess *Hyselodoris* sp.	313		
	Purple-crown Sea Goddess *Chromodoris kempfi*	315		
	Red-line Blue Sea Goddess *Chromodoris nyalya*	315		
	Brown Sea Goddess *Chromodoris grahami*	315		
	Harlequin Blue Sea Goddess *Chromodoris clenchi*	317		
	Red-tipped Sea Goddess *Glossodoris sedna*	317		
	Brown-speckled Doris *Aphelodoris antillensis*	317		
	Slimy Doris *Dendrodoris krebsii*	319		
	Brown Doris *Discodoris evelinae*	319		
	Leather-backed Doris *Platydoris angustipes*	321		
	Black-spotted Nudibranch *Phyllidiopsis papillgera*	321		
	Caribbean Spanish Dancer *Hexabranchus morsomus*	321		
	Sargassum Nudibranch *Scyllaea pelagica*	323		
	Grape-cluster Nudibranch *Doto uva*	323		
	Tasseled Nudibranch *Bornella calcarata*	323		
	Tufted Nudibranch *Tritoniopsis frydis*	325		
	Crisscross Tritonia *Tritonia bayeri*	325		
	Atlantic Pearl-oyster *Pinctada radiata*	325		

No.	Name	Page	Date	Location
	Rough Fileclam *Lima scabra*	327		
	Spiny Fileclam *Lima lima*	327		
	Antillean Fileclam *Lima pellucida*	327		
	Atlantic Thorny-oyster *Spondylus americanus*	329		
	Atlantic Wing-oyster *Pteria colymbus*	329		
	Knobby Scallop *Chlamys imbricata*	331		
	Frond Oyster *Dendostrea frons*	331		
	Lister Purse-oyster *Isognomon radiatus*	331		
	Flat Tree-oyster *Isognomon alatus*	333		
	Amber Penshell *Pinna carnea*	333		
	Sunrise Tellin *Telina radiata*	333		
	Fuzzy Chiton *Acanthopleura granulata*	335		
	Caribbean Slender Chiton *Stenoplax purpurascens*	335		
	Ornate Chiton *Tonicia schammi*	335		
	Grass Squid *Pickfordiateunthis pulchella*	337		
	Caribbean Reef Squid *Sepioteuthis sepiodea*	337		
	Arrow Squid *Loligo plei*	339		
	Longfin Squid *Loligo pealei*	339		
	Atlantic Brief Squid *Lolliguncula brevis*	339		
	Gianteye Squid *Abralia veranyi*	341		
	Caribbean Reef Octopus *Octopus briareus*	341		
	Common Octopus *Octopus vulgaris*	341		
	Atlantic Longarm Octopus *Octopus defilippi*	345		
	Caribbean Two-spot Octopus *Octopus filosusi*	347		
	White Spotted Octopus *Octopus macropus*	347		
	Brownstripe Octopus *Octopus burryi*	347		
	Atlantic Pygmy Octopus *Octopus joubini*	349		
	Violet Blanket Octopus *Tremoctopus violaceus*	349		
	Egg Case Diamond Back Squid *Thysanoteuthis rhombus*	349		

9. ECHINODERMATA
Feather Stars – Sea Stars – Brittle Stars – Basket Stars
Sea Urchins – Heart Urchins – Sand Dollars – Sea Cucumbers

No.	Name	Page	Date	Location
	Golden Crinoid *Davidaster rubiginosa*	355		
	Beaded Crinoid *Davidaster discoidea*	355		
	Black & White Crinoid *Nemaster grandis*	357		
	Swimming Crinoid *Analcidometra armata*	357		
	Banded Sea Star *Luidia alternata*	357		
	Striped Sea Star *Ludia clathrata*	359		
	Nine-armed Sea Star *Ludia senegalensis*	359		
	Mottled Red Sea Star *Copidaster lymani*	359		
	Comet Star *Ophidiaster guildingii*	361		
	Common Comet Star *Linckia guildingii*	361		
	Beaded Sea Star *Astropecten articulatus*	363		
	Two-spined Sea Star *Astropecten duplicatus*	363		
	Orange-ridged Sea Star *Echinaster spinulosus*	365		
	Conical Spined Sea Star *Echinaster sentus*	365		
	Thorny Sea Star *Echinaster echinophorus*	365		
	Cushion Sea Star *Oreaster reticulates*	367		
	Studded Sea Star *Mithodia* sp.	367		
	Blunt-armed Sea Star *Asterina folium*	369		
	Red Miniature Sea Star *Poraniella echinulata*	369		
	Rose Lace Coral Brittle Star *Sigsbeia conifera*	369		
	Sponge Brittle Star *Ophiothrix suensonii*	371		
	Reticulated Brittle Star *Ophionereis reticulata*	371		
	Spiny Brittle Star *Ophiocoma paucigranulata*	373		
	Blunt-spined Brittle Star *Ophiocoma echinata*	373		
	Ruby Brittle Star *Ophiocoma rubicundum*	373		
	Banded-arm Brittle Star *Ophiocoma appressum*	375		
	Gaudy Brittle Star *Ophiocoma ensiferum*	375		

No.	Name	Page	Date	Location
	Circle Marked Brittle Star *Ophiocoma cinereum*	375		
	Sea Rod Basket Star *Schizostella bifurcata*	377		
	Giant Basket Star *Astrophyton muricatum*	377		
	Long-spined Urchin *Diadema antillarum*	379		
	Magnificent Urchin *Astropyga magnifica*	379		
	Reef Urchin *Echinometra viridis*	379		
	Rock-boring Urchin *Echinometra lucunter lucunter*	381		
	Common Arbacia Urchin *Arbacia punctulata*	381		
	Jewel Urchin *Lytechinus williamsi*	383		
	Variegated Urchin *Lytechinus variegates*	383		
	West Indian Sea Egg *Tripneuster ventricosus*	385		
	Slate-pencil Urchin *Eucidaris tribuloides*	385		
	Long-spined Sea Biscuit *Plagiobrissus grandis*	385		
	Red Heart Urchin *Meoma ventricosa ventricosa*	387		
	Inflated Sea Biscuit *Clypeaster rosaceus*	387		
	Sand Dollar *Clypeaster subdepressus*	387		
	Notched Sand Dollar *Encope aberrans*	389		
	Five-keyhole Sand Dollar *Mellita quinquiesperforata*	389		
	Six-keyhole Sand Dollar *Leodia sexiesperforata*	389		
	Furry Sea Cucumber *Astichopus multifidus*	391		
	Five-toothed Sea Cucumber *Actinopygia agassizii*	391		
	Conical Sea Cucumber *Eostichopus arnesoni*	391		
	Three-rowed Sea Cucumber *Isostichopus badionotus*	393		
	Donkey Dung Sea Cucumber *Holothuria mexicana*	395		
	Slender Sea Cucumber *Holothuria mexicana*	395		
	Slender Sea Cucumber *Holothuria impatiens*	395		
	Harlequin Sea Cucumber *Holothuria grisea*	395		
	Florida Sea Cucumber *Holothuria floridana*	397		
	Grub Sea Cucumber *Holothuria cubana*	397		

No.	Name	Page	Date	Location
	Hidden Sea Cucumber *Pseudothyone belli*	397		
	Beaded Sea Cucumber *Euapta lappa*	399		
	Tiger Tail Sea Cucumber *Holothuria thomasi*	399		

10. CHORDATA
Tunicates – Pelagic Tunicates

No.	Name	Page	Date	Location
	Reef Tunicate *Rhopalaea abdominalis*	403		
	Giant Tunicae *Polycarpa spongiabilis*	403		
	Green Tube Tunicate *Acidia sydneiensis*	403		
	Painted Tunicate *Clavlina puero-secensis*	405		
	Bulb Tunicates *Clavelina* sp.	407		
	Mangrove Tunicate *Ecteinascidia turbinate*	407		
	Encrusting Social Tunicate *Symplegma viride*	409		
	Mottled Social Tunicates *Polandrocarpa tumida*	409		
	Strawberry Tunicate *Eudistoma* sp.	411		
	Black Condominium Tunicate *Eudistoma obscuratum*	411		
	White Condominium Tunicate *Eudistoma* sp.	411		
	Flat Tunicate *Botrylloides nigrum*	413		
	Row Encrusting Tunicates *Botylloides* sp.	413		
	Geometric Encrusting Tunicates *Botryllus* sp.	413		
	Mottled Encrusting Tunicate *Distaplia bermudensis*	415		
	Button Tunicates *Distaplia corolla*	415		
	Globular Encrusting Tunicate *Diplosoma glandulosum*	415		
	White Speck Tunicate *Diplosoma conchyliatum*	417		
	Black Overgrowing Tunicate *Didemnum vanderhorsti*	417		
	Overgrowing Mat Tunicate *Trididemum solidum*	417		
	Overgrowing Tunicates Spp.	419		
	Pelagic Tunicates *Salpa* sp.	419		

ADDITIONAL SPECIES

No.	Name	Page	Date	Location

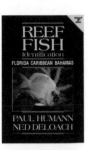
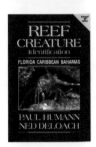
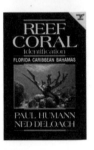